CONTENTS

~

v

PREFACE

∼

Today's professional music teachers must be skilled in content areas from music history to special education, have a minimum standard of performance proficiency on a myriad of instruments, be expert in engaging students of all ages, and write lesson plans that artfully flow with assessment strategies for state-mandated content for each grade. They typically spend their four years of college developing these skills and understandings necessary to become a practitioner.

For the most part, undergraduate music education programs are designed to help students answer the questions "What will I teach?" and "How will I teach?" *Critical Issues in Music Education: Contemporary Theory and Practice* is intended for music educators who have initial answers to the "what" and "how" questions. It is designed to serve as an introductory text for those entering the music education profession, to be used either as a culminating undergraduate text or as an introductory graduate text. This text provides an in-depth examination of critical issues for early-career music educators. It links theory to teaching practice, offering a variety of perspectives to give music teachers the comprehensive grounding they need to become leaders in the field. Rather than focusing on answers to "what to do" questions, *Critical Issues in Music Education* focuses on "why" questions through examining underpinnings for the field and encouraging teacher inquiry.

Each of the contributing authors has unique expertise and experience as a practicing music teacher and music teacher educator, yet the authors share a common background—each is either a faculty member or a graduate of Teachers College, Columbia University. Consequently, *Critical Issues in Music Education* is grounded in current educational theory and practice, informed by the authors' work in the field with both music teachers and P–12 students and linked by a commitment to progressive education. Offering contemporary perspectives on music education, *Critical Issues in Music Education* provides a foundation for understanding the complexities, challenges, and rewards of music teaching across diverse contexts.

ORGANIZATION

The text is organized into four sections. In the first section, we trace the historical, philosophical, and social underpinnings of current beliefs and practices surrounding foundational issues in an attempt to question basic assumptions about the field: What is music? How and why should it be taught? What is music education? Where and how does it occur? In the second section, we introduce the multiple ways in which learners are perceived in teaching environments. We address core issues from developmental, social, creative, and cognitive perspectives and ask readers to consider reexamining basic assumptions about music learning. How do students learn? What is the role of the teacher? How do context, culture, and content interact to facilitate or inhibit music learning?

The third section addresses considerations that music teachers face in implementing educational practice. We ask readers to make links among issues in pedagogy, curriculum, assessment, repertoire, and technology and the specific political and social contexts, inferred philosophical stances, and often conflicting expectations for music teachers and their students. The final section of the book examines the profession of music teaching by looking at common experiences and diverse paths to both becoming a music educator and maintaining a level of excellence throughout a career. We suggest reflective tools and professional development strategies that contribute to creating a lifelong support system for music teachers.

We have included discussion starters, projects ideas, and suggested readings at the end of each chapter. Our hope is that these will be a source for further inquiry and action in schools and that you find ways to identify and wrestle with your own critical issues in schools, concert halls, garages, living rooms, and virtual worlds—wherever and whenever music education happens.

ACKNOWLEDGMENTS

We want to acknowledge scholars who reviewed the manuscript and whose recommendations have contributed to this book: Lynn Brinckmeyer, Texas State University; Birch Browning, Cleveland State University; Elaine Gates, Long Island University; Al Holcomb, University of Central Florida; Estelle Jorgensen, Indiana University; Robert Lee, Miami University; Ken McGuire, University of Alabama; Jennifer Mishra, University of Houston; Nathalie Robinson, Hofstra University; Alan Spurgeon, University of Mississippi; and Betty Anne Younker, University of Michigan.

We would also like to thank our many students—past, present, and future—who continue to help shape our notions of what is critical in music education. Finally, we owe much gratitude to our spouses, Mary Hafeli and Neal Custodero, who provided much support and encouragement throughout this process.

Harold F. Abeles and Lori A. Custodero
Teachers College, Columbia University

CONTRIBUTORS

~

Harold F. Abeles is Professor of Music and Music Education at Teachers College, Columbia University, where he teaches courses in research and assessment strategies, as well as the foundations of music education. He received his bachelor's and master's degrees in music education from the University of Connecticut and his Ph.D. from the University of Maryland. His research interests include assessment and evaluation in the arts and gender associations in instrumental music and instrumental music pedagogy. Dr. Abeles has contributed numerous articles, chapters, and books to the field of music education. He is coauthor of *Foundations of Music Education* (Second Edition, Schirmer, 1994).

Lori A. Custodero is Associate Professor and Program Coordinator of Music and Music Education at Teachers College, Columbia University, where she teaches courses in early childhood and research design. She has degrees in piano performance and music theory and holds a doctorate in music education from the University of Southern California. Focusing on intersections between human development and musical development, Custodero studies challenge, engagement, and meaning making of young children and adults in classrooms and family settings. Active in international music education, she has also developed early childhood programs with local institutions including Jazz at Lincoln Center and the New York Philharmonic.

Randall Everett Allsup, Ed.D., is Assistant Professor of Music and Music Education at Teachers College, Columbia University. Allsup holds a bachelor's degree in music from Northwestern University and completed his graduate work in music education at Teachers College. He became interested in issues surrounding social justice and democracy from his work in schools in neglected neighborhoods of New York City, teaching at Cardinal Hayes High School in the South Bronx and at Our Children's Foundation in Harlem. Allsup writes about the challenges of reconceptualizing music pedagogy. His teaching and scholarship is influenced by thinkers like Maxine Greene, Paulo Freire, and John Dewey.

Cathy Benedict (Ed.D., Teachers College, Columbia University) is Assistant Professor and Coordinator of Undergraduate Studies in Music Education at New York University. Her scholarly interests lie in the reciprocity of the teacher-student relationship and the challenges in facilitating music education environments in which students take on the perspective of a justice-oriented citizen. To this end, her research agenda focuses on the processes of education and the ways in which teachers and students can interrogate taken-for-granted normative practices. She has most recently published in journals such as *Philosophy of Music Education Review, Music Education Research*, and *Research Studies in Music Education*.

Colleen Conway (BM, MM, Eastman School of Music; Ed.D., Teachers College, Columbia University) is Associate Professor of Music Education at The University of Michigan in Ann Arbor. Her primary expertise is in preservice and inservice music teacher education. She has presented her research at national and international conferences and has published over 60 articles on these topics in all of the major music education journals. Book publications include *Great Beginning for Music Teachers: A Guide to Mentoring and Induction* (MENC, 2003), *Handbook for the Beginning Music Teacher* (GIA, 2006), *Teaching Music in Higher Education* (Oxford, 2009), and *Handbook for the Music Mentor* (GIA, 2010).

James Frankel is the Managing Director of SoundTree, the Educational Division of Korg USA. Before taking the helm at SoundTree, he was the instrumental and general music teacher at the Franklin Avenue Middle School in Franklin Lakes, NJ, for 11 of his nearly 15 years in the New Jersey Public Schools. Before that he taught at the elementary level for four years. He earned his BA in Music Education from Montclair State University and his MA and Ed.D. in Music Education from Teachers College, Columbia University. Dr. Frankel is an Adjunct Assistant Professor at Teachers College, Columbia University, where he teaches courses on music technology.

Roberta Lamb (Teachers College-CU, Ed.D, 1987) is Associate Professor, School of Music, Queen's University, Canada; Adjunct Professor, Faculty of Education, University of Victoria, Canada, and Sibelius Academy, Music Education Department, Finland. Lamb's research areas include history, culture, equity, feminism, and gender in music education and Ruth Crawford Seeger, with a dash of labor relations and union organizing. She is founder of the organization Gender Research in Music Education, and her chapter in *The New Handbook of Research on Music Teaching and Learning* (R. Colwell & C. Richardson, Eds., Oxford University, 2002) was the first major exploration of feminism in music education research.

Patricia A. St. John (Ed.D. Teachers College, Columbia University) is the Founder/Executive Director of Carondelet Music Center, an independent music school (est. 1992) in Northeastern United States with 300 students from 3-months-old to 94-years-young. An adjunct Assistant Professor of Music Education at Teachers College, Columbia University, her scholarship is shaped by complementary perspectives as music practitioner, performer (pianist), and researcher. Over 30 years of teaching experience across various age groups and in diverse music settings inform her research. Using a multidimensional lens, which includes *flow* experience, Vygotskian theory, and Cultural-Historical Activity Theory, St. John focuses on early childhood music-making, the social dimensions of musical experience, and the community of learners.

CHAPTER 1

The Historical Contexts of Music Education

Harold F. Abeles

INTRODUCTION

Music education does not exist isolated in the music classroom. It is influenced by trends in general education, society, culture, and politics. What is taught in music classes today is different from what was taught 50 or 100 years ago because music education has evolved and responded to changes in our society and cultural values as reflected in education and government policies.

This chapter provides an historical context for music education within the framework of general education, and society, culture, and politics. It is designed to underscore the relationship among these factors. Music education is particularly influenced by themes, theories, and approaches to general education as well as the societal, cultural, and political milieu within which education and music exist. These relationships can be illustrated well if we look at totalitarian governments such as the Soviet Union in the 20th century. At the beginning of the Communist state, Lenin saw education to be in service of the state. During this period in the Soviet Union, education was conceived of as having three major purposes: developing literacy, developing an allegiance to socially productive labor, and undermining the values, traditions, and way of life of czarist Russia. With such a specific mission, specific curriculum was relatively easy to design. Textbooks were reviewed and selected by government officials. Soviet officials were particularly focused on preschools, as preschools were viewed not only as a convenience for workers with children but also as a place to influence children's social, moral, aesthetic, and political value formation. With such a clear agenda for education, music teachers in the Soviet Union were expected to exclude music belonging to certain periods that were politically unacceptable (Schwadron, 1967).

While the relationship between totalitarian regimes and school curriculum might be particularly strong, links between political perspectives, social trends, and cultural values and what is taught in schools exist even in democracies.

For example, during World War II, performances of the repertory of German composers, particularly those with nationalistic themes such as Wagner were limited and generally not performed in US schools. It can also be noted that more recently the ethnic diversity of the US population is increasingly reflected both in a more diverse general school curriculum and in a culturally diverse music repertory taught in US schools.

Most of recorded education history has focused on education that takes place in formal settings, that is, within organizations like schools and religious institutions. Thus, most of what is reported in this chapter describes formal educational systems—what happens between teachers and students. It is important to acknowledge that for many music traditions a considerable amount of music learning throughout history has taken place in informal settings, for instance, in families. This general process, or informal education, is the means by which people acquire skills and knowledge, such as learning to use a cell phone, which enables them to function in their society.

This chapter focuses on the links between music education and general education, society, culture, and politics beginning in the 20th century. Mark (2002), Mark and Gary (1992), and Birge (1984) are sources that provide a history of music education prior to the 20th century.

MUSIC EDUCATION IN THE FIRST HALF OF THE 20TH CENTURY

The first 50 years of the 20th century can be viewed as a time when countries in Europe, Asia, and North America were defining and redefining their political perspectives and power. Industrialization was a fact that affected developed countries' economies and societal structures. Competition for resources by groups formed by economic, geographic, or racial similarities and differences strongly influenced education and politics. Education was viewed by many as a means to change status.

Among the most influential education theorists of the 20th century was John Dewey. Dewey was familiar with Pestalozzi's reforms of the 19th century, and their ideas share some overlapping notions. Dewey's educational ideas served as the basis for the Progressive Education Movement that dominated the first half of the 20th Century (the Progressive Education Association was established in 1918 and ended in 1955). The main tenets of Progressivism are that individuals should be recognized for their own unique abilities, interests, ideas, needs, and cultural identity (child-centered) and that education should promote effective participation in the affairs of the community. Music and the other arts fit well within the tenets of Progressivism. These Progressivists' views competed with the need for state-supported schools to promote cultural uniformity, to educate loyal, not necessarily critical citizens, and to support an expanding industrial economy by preparing workers for vocational roles (Cremin, 1961). By the 1950s, conservatism and the Cold War provided reasons to repudiate ideas of Progressivism, yet many of Dewey's ideas can be found in the writings of postmodern educators of the latter part of the 20th century.

Cremin (1961) reports that the curriculum in elementary schools varied depending on the perspectives of the community or the educators in the community. During the first half of the 20th century, there were many schools adhering to basic curriculum structures (Essentialism) that included the study of reading, writing, arithmetic, history, English, and foreign languages. Instructional approaches in these schools emphasized basic skills, examinations, and discipline—not the ideas of progressivism. The few progressive schools in existence featured curricula based on children's interests and cooperative learning experiences. Progressive approaches were often project oriented—projects that included focusing on the aesthetic experience of music. Dewey's colleague at Teachers College of Columbia University, William Heard Kilpatrick, specifically advocated developing "appreciation projects," whose purposes included the enjoyment of an aesthetic experience in music (Gutek, 1995, p. 489).

In the 20th century, the high school became a central component of the American education system. Prior to this period, the high school had served primarily as preparation for college. Now, a more expanded role was seen including the development of more vocational training at high schools. By the 1930s, high school attendance rose dramatically, and the socioeconomic diversity of the high school population had widened. Comprehensive high schools, which included both college preparation and vocational training, were more of an ideal than reality. While suburban high schools focused on college preparation, urban high schools in high need areas were more likely to stress on vocational education. In smaller communities with socioeconomic diversity, high schools with comprehensive strands tended to track students into specific vocational, college preparatory, or business tracks (Cremin, 1961).

In music education, this period was one of refinement and expansion. Instrumental music programs became well established as a consequence of professional orchestras being established in more cities and the use of military bands in World Wars I and II. In addition, music appreciation was introduced into the secondary school curriculum, and class piano became an option in some schools. Because of a shortage of college-prepared music teachers, schools hired professional musicians to teach, particularly in secondary schools. As a consequence, music in secondary schools became even more performance oriented, as these professionals' teaching strategies were largely limited to rehearsing ensembles (Mark & Gary, 1992, p. 270).

It was during the first part of the 20th century that the Music Educators National Conference (MENC) was formed. Initially a place for music supervisors to share ideas and challenges, MENC grew to become an important source of support for music teachers. Through journal publications, the development of curriculum documents, and biennial conferences, the organization began to coalesce isolated music teachers into a profession.

FEDERAL EDUCATION POLICY AND
MUSIC EDUCATION: 1950 TO PRESENT

During the last half of the 20th century, actions taken by the federal government, such as establishment of the Department of Education in 1979, and rulings by the Federal courts gave increased influence to federal rather than local government agencies in the area of education. While local groups, such as community school boards, still provide primary direction for schools and curriculum within communities, and while states still maintain the primary responsibility for licensing teachers, federal funding was increasingly persuasive in providing overall direction for the nation's schools. What follows is a closer examination of events, societal changes, federal education policy, and music education in the last part of the 20th and the beginning of the 21st centuries.

National Defense Education Act

In October 1957, the Soviet Union successfully launched the first man-made satellite into an orbital path around the Earth. There was an immediate and strong reaction to the event in the United States, as not being the first into space was thought to be a sign that the United States was no longer technologically supreme. This gloomy perspective was reinforced by perspectives from leading scientists. In response to Sputnik, Dr. Elmer Hutchisson, director of the American Institute of Physics, stated, "the nation's youth must be taught to appreciate the importance of science or the United States' way of life is doomed to rapid extinction" (*New York Times*—October 8, 1957, in Schmeck). In response, President Eisenhower established the National Aeronautics and Space Administration (NASA), and, in 1958, he signed the *National Defense Education Act (NDEA)*, which was designed to reform the educational system in the United States to meet this new challenge. The *NDEA*, which primarily allocated funds for higher education and research, provided loans for students showing interest in studying science, math, or foreign languages in college.

This period of educational reform can be described as "back to basics". Curriculum areas that were not focused on math and science were considered nonessential. Americans were engaged in a fight over what should be included in the school curriculum. Several articles addressing the role of music in the curriculum appeared in *The Music Educators Journal* (e.g., Hanson, 1958; Trillingham, 1959; Harris, 1962). These music educators highlighted the important role that music plays in humanizing students, suggesting that a narrowing of the curriculum would limit the full development of scientists and mathematicians. Branscome (2005) reports that one response from music educators to this back-to-basics movement was for music textbooks to include songs about science and rockets in an effort to secure music's place in the curriculum.

Prior to this period of curriculum reform, Progressivism (see Chapter 3 and earlier in this chapter) had been gaining a foothold in American educational thinking. With the anxiety produced by Sputnik, Progressive education was repudiated. While music education fit well into a Progressivism context, it faced new challenges within the new, more conservative education milieu articulated by *NDEA*. Classroom teachers were encouraged to focus on math, sciences, and foreign language, and areas that might distract teachers from this focus, like the arts, were discouraged.

These political and societal changes required music educators to consider more carefully the role of music in education. Music's place in the curriculum was being challenged. A strong cohesive rationale was needed to articulate the place of music in schools.

What emerged from this need was a rationale for music education based on aesthetics. This perspective was articulated by several music educators during this period, notably Britton (1958), Leonard and House (1959), Schwardon (1967), and Reimer (1970). In distinguishing this new rationale for music education from the previous, more utilitarian views, these writers highlighted the role that music (as well as the other arts) uniquely serves in developing the aesthetic nature of children while other curriculum areas developed more utilitarian outcomes.

The next important federal education legislation was the *Elementary and Secondary Education Act (ESEA)*, signed by President Lyndon Johnson in 1965. As part of President Johnson's "War on Poverty," it was targeted to provide more support for education of disadvantaged children. *ESEA* had a different focus than its predecessor, the *NDEA*. President Johnson did not see as strong a prohibition against the federal government influencing education as did President Eisenhower (Gutek, 1995, p. 514). *ESEA* funds were used to provide both quality education for children from low income families and innovative educational projects including research in art and music education, including the *Manhattanville Music Curriculum Program* and the *Juilliard Repertory Project*. Mark and Gary (1992) report that this act facilitated many children's participation in music and art. When *ESEA* was revised in 1973, in a more constrained fiscal climate, it focused more on basic literacy. As a consequence, funding for music and art programs was greatly reduced.

Nation at Risk

When Ronald Reagan was elected President in 1980, he was confronted with several economic challenges including high interest rates, high unemployment, and declining industrial productivity. The new administration speculated that these challenges were related to a perceived declining US educational system. Consequently, President Reagan appointed a National Commission on Excellence in Education, which in April 1983 produced a report titled *A Nation at Risk: The Imperative for Educational Reform.*

The report presented evidence to support the statement that the nation was at risk of forfeiting its place as a world leader. The evidence cited in the report concluded that when compared to students in other industrialized countries US students performed lower on tests of student achievement, particularly in the areas of math and science. In addition, declining SAT scores and the increase of remedial courses at the secondary and college levels were identified as evidence that the educational system in the United States was declining. The report linked aspects of the educational system that were contributing to these performances by US students, such as an increase in the number of electives (e.g., culinary and driver's education) at the secondary level, a decrease in the amount of homework required by teachers, and a shortage of qualified teachers.

Nation at Risk listed several recommendations to remediate the educational challenges the report had identified. These included raising standards and academic requirements, encouraging teachers to use more stringent grading practices, lengthening the school day and year, using better and more challenging textbooks, grouping students by ability level instead of age, increasing the amount of homework, using stricter discipline and attendance policies, encouraging more parental involvement, and improving teacher quality through higher standards, financial incentives, and professional development programs. The report also identified the subjects that the report's writers considered most important to the proper development of students—English, mathematics, science, social studies, and computer science—and titled them the "five new basics."

The report paid little attention to the arts, as the Commission did not see the arts as part of the solution to the primarily economic challenges identified. The Commission did recommend, though, that at the elementary level the curriculum should include a high level of the basics along with work in the fine and performing arts and foreign languages (National Commission on Excellence in Education, 1983).

Educators responded to *Nation at Risk* in different ways. Schools, colleges, and universities began to adopt measurable and more rigorous standards and expectations. There was an increase in standardized testing and more focus on scores on tests at important transition points in education, such as the transition from high school to college. New instructional materials were developed that focused on curriculum areas identified by the *Nation at Risk Report* (NCEE, 1983). Reforms also include increases in the length of the school day and school year and the amount of homework assigned.

Responding to the report, MENC supported the efforts of the federal government to improve the quality of education. MENC recommended that school districts implement comprehensive music education programs at all levels of school based on *The School Music Program: Description and Standards* (1986). The organization also emphasized guidelines recommended by the College Board that included the arts as part of the expectations for preparation for prospective college students (College Board, 1983).

Teacher Education Reform

In response to the *Nation at Risk*, a group of 96 research universities and professional education programs formed an organization (the Holmes Group) to improve the education of teachers. The Holmes Group sought to strengthen the connections between schools of education and other parts of the university, particularly colleges of arts and sciences, and to increase collaboration with professionals, including teachers and administrators. In *Tomorrow's Teachers* (1986), the group provided its vision of the teaching profession and teacher preparation. The pillars of this vision included five goals:

1. Make teaching intellectually sound by requiring prospective teachers to have a broad liberal arts foundation.
2. Recognize differences in teachers' knowledge, skill, and commitment by providing internships for new teachers and identifying certain experienced teachers for leadership roles including mentoring their colleagues with less experience.
3. Create relevant and intellectually defensible standards of entry into teaching through the development of multiple evaluation instruments for measuring diverse kinds of competence.
4. Connect schools of education to K-12 schools.
5. Make schools better places for practicing teachers to work and learn by forming partnerships between schools and universities, where university and school faculty members can examine questions of teaching and learning together (http://www.holmespartnership.org/).

Paralleling the Holmes Group work, the Carnegie Forum on Education and the Economy established the Task Force on Teaching as a Profession "in recognition of the central role teachers play in the quality of education" (http://www.carnegiefoundation.org/index.asp). This Task Force was asked to examine teaching as a profession and present its findings and policy recommendations. In *A Nation Prepared: Teachers for the 21st Century* (1986), the Task Force recommended the creation of a National Board for Professional Teaching Standards that would establish high standards for what teachers need to know and be able to do and to certify teachers who meet those standards. The proposed National Board was conceived not to replace state certification for teachers but to identify the expertise developed by experienced teachers and to identify those who demonstrated that expertise.

In response to the Task Force's recommendation, the National Board for Professional Teaching Standards was established in 1987. While teacher certification at the state level continues to be required for most teachers as a gatekeeper for the profession, National Board certification is a voluntary certification process for experienced teachers who demonstrate a high level of expertise in both content and pedagogy.

In 1991, the National Board identified five core propositions on which all of the National Board's work was founded:

- Teachers are committed to students and their learning.
- Teachers know the subjects they teach and how to teach those subjects to students.
- Teachers are responsible for managing and monitoring student learning.

- Teachers think systematically about their practice and learn from experience.
- Teachers are members of learning communities (Harman, 2001).

In 1984, MENC appointed a Task Force on Music Teacher Education, whose purpose was to articulate both the process of developing music educators and standards to evaluate potential music educators. Their report paralleled several of the ideas put forth by the Holmes Group and the Carnegie Task Force, including closer partnerships between schools and teacher education programs. The Task Force called for a professional development plan for each beginning music teacher to enable teachers to systematically grow into experienced teachers capable of different leadership roles.

Curriculum Reform

In 1989, President George H. W. Bush called for an educational summit at which governors from across the country came together to discuss education. This meeting established the political momentum for the *AMERICA 2000* plan (USDOE, 1991), which included a National Council on Education Standards and Testing. In 1994, President Bill Clinton embraced this reform movement, identifying it as *Goals 2000: Education America Act* (1995). *Goals 2000* focused on standards-based education. It can be characterized as a curriculum reform movement that embraces an accountability model, that is, one that focuses on student achievement by developing "clear and rigorous standards for what every child should know and be able to do" and monitoring student progress through testing (USDOE, 1995, Sec. 2).

It is important to note that when *Goals 2000* was passed the national goals included the arts as a core academic subject. Previous federal policy statements, like *AMERICA* 2000, had identified the core academic subjects as English, math, science, history, and geography. It was only through extensive lobbying by arts organizations that the arts were eventually identified as a core academic subject. This designation led to Department of Education funding to establish standards in the arts, which were published by MENC in 1994.

The publication of the National Standards stimulated most states to develop writing standards in each of the disciplines identified as core academic subjects. While some states immediately formed committees to develop music standards, others took almost a decade to develop them. By 2006, almost all of the states had published state music standards, which for the most part, paralleled the *National Music Education Standards* (1994).

The "standards movement" was supported by many professional associations in education. Indeed, many discipline-based groups helped develop them. MENC was not an exception. Since the publication of the *Standards* in 1994, most of the organization's professional development activities, including both conference programs and publications, have been oriented to support them. These include both publications and activities to help elaborate and provide rationales for the music standards (e.g., *Aiming for Excellence: The Impact of the Standards Movement on Music Education*, 1996) as well as publications and activities designed to help music teachers implement the standards, such as Kvet and Williamson's *Strategies for Teaching High School Band* (1998). The description for each of the 11 books that comprise the "Strategies for" series states that they are designed to help music teachers implement the *K-12 National Music Education Standards*.

Educational Accountability

The accountability movement in education grew during the period of the 1960s and 1970s with a majority of the states having passed accountability legislation. Educational accountability is closely related to a systems approach to education tied to explicitly stating the outcomes of instruction by writing instructional objectives (see works by Tyler, such as his classic *Basic Principles of Curriculum and Instruction*, 1949). Accountability systems in education are generally characterized by two components—clear statements of outcomes (e.g., national or state standards) and an assessment component to determine if students have reached the outcomes. Assessment results are then typically used to examine other components of the "educational system," such as teachers and instructional materials.

The National Standards legislation clearly called for a strong assessment component. Initially, states were asked to assess students' progress in "core academic areas, typically English, math, science, history and geography but focusing primarily on literacy skills, math, and science at the end of the fourth-, eighth-, and twelfth grade. Eventually, assessments would be required at the end of each grade. The plan included making assessments available to the public so that parents would have an index on how their child's school was performing. For many political leaders and educators (see *Leaving No Child Behind?: Options for Kids in Failing Schools* (2004) by Frederick M. Hess, ed. & Chester E. Finn, ed.), this approach was a logical remedy for the nation's educational problems; for many other educators (e.g., see Maxine Greene, 1995, *Releasing the Imagination: Essays on Education, the Arts, and Social Change*), this emphasis on accountability was leading the country's educational system completely in the wrong direction.

Reporting on music education and the accountability movement in the 1970s, both Colwell et al. (1974) and Labuta (1974) indicate that music educators did not often fully participate in process. Many teachers viewed the accountability process as an imposition. Music teachers asserted that the outcomes of their instruction were not easily assessed. During the 1970s and in the last decade of the 20th century and the first decade of the 21st century, neither state nor federal government agencies appeared to be concerned about accountability in music. Thus, parents, who were encouraged to look at assessment results for their children's schools, were not provided with data that reflected the strengths or weaknesses of the music program at their children's school. Potentially, this may lead to parents assuming that school quality had nothing to do with the strength of the school's music programs.

No Child Left Behind (NCLB)

Public Law 107–110, the *No Child Left Behind Act of 2001* was signed by President George W. Bush in January 2002. The stated purpose of the Title I of the Law, *Improving the Academic Achievement of the Disadvantaged* is "to ensure that all children have a fair, equal, and significant opportunity to obtain a high-quality education and reach, at a minimum, proficiency on challenging State academic achievement standards and state academic assessments" (http://www.ed.gov/policy/elsec/leg/esea02/index.html).

The *NCLB Law* identified ten core academic subjects that the legislation was to impact. They were English, reading or language arts, mathematics, science, foreign languages, civics and government, economics, arts, history, and geography.

The legislation also described strategies that were designed to accomplish the stated purpose. The strategies emphasized accountability through systematic assessments of children's progress; that is, to monitor the progress of the states in meeting the goals of *NCLB*, the law required each state to develop an accountability system that assessed measurable annual objectives for all public school students. While *NCLB* identified 10 core academic areas, the law required that at a minimum, each state must assess mathematics, reading or language arts, and science. Therefore, most states designed their annual testing program to provide information on those three areas.

As stated earlier in this chapter, the US Constitution does not define a role for the federal government in public education. Education is the responsibility of state and local governments. Nevertheless, federal laws like *NCLB* have dramatic effects on education because of the large amount of federal funding available for states that comply with the Federal Law. (For fiscal year 2002, the funding for *NCLB* totaled $54.5 billion, a considerable increase in education spending over previous years.) States seeking *NCLB* funding were required to implement the strategies identified in the Law.

Laws that define educational outcomes in a particular way, such as literacy, math, and science, affect what is taught in schools. If in order to obtain significant funding school systems must demonstrate that students are improving in literacy, math, and science, curriculum at the schools is likely to emphasize those areas. While *NCLB* clearly identified the arts as a core academic subject, the arts were not one of the areas identified as an area for which states must show that their students are making progress.

Soon after the legislation was signed, it became clear that the requirements for standardized testing in literacy, math, and science led local school districts to divert resources away from other subject areas. In a 2003 article, *The New York Times* reported that junior high schools in New York City were cutting programs in art and music because of the push to have students master basic skills required by the new standardized curriculum implemented. When asked about these decisions, New York City School's Chancellor Joel Klein is quoted in the article saying, "... if I have the forced choice, I think I have to put it [funding] into math and literacy, even though I don't like that" (Herszenhorn, p. B1).

In some school districts, music educators discovered that NCLB produced challenges in the area of scheduling. To increase the amount of time students spent on areas tested by NCLB, they were scheduled out of music. School counselors advised students that to beef up their classes in English, math, and science they should drop band or choir.

As a reaction to these actions in local school districts, organizations concerned with supporting arts education made efforts to have the federal government further clarify the role of the arts in NCLB. In July 2004, Rodney Paige, Secretary of Education at the time, wrote a letter addressed to school superintendents. The letter emphasized the arts as one of the core subjects. It quoted the then President George W. Bush as saying: "the arts allow us to explore new worlds and to view life from another perspective ... they encourage individuals to sharpen their skills and abilities and to nurture their imagination and intellect" (para. 4). Paige's letter also stressed that NCLB should not be interpreted so narrowly that the arts were diminished or eliminated from the curriculum. Secretary Paige continued by highlighting states that had included the arts in their curriculum reform efforts in response to NCLB.

In addition to widely distributing Secretary Paige's letter, arts education associations like MENC developed their own position papers to assist their members at the local level in maintaining music programs. *Music Education in the Law—and What to do About it,* was distributed by MENC in 2002. It pointed out that the NCLB legislation provided more Education Department funds designated for the arts than ever before ($30 million) and that the arts were included as a core academic subject. This position paper also identified the potential for some school administrators to interpret NCLB as narrowing the curriculum. The document recommended several actions for music educators to pursue at both state and local levels. The recommendations urged music educators to contact school administrators and state and local education agencies that make decisions about spending the federal education dollars provided by the Law to remind them of music's place in the Law. The position paper also recommended that music educators urge members of the US Congress to support full funding of the "Arts in Education" section of NCLB.

As states responded to the NCLB, much of the focus was on student testing. In several states, both the tests and the criteria for demonstrating proficiency were modified, which often resulted in a larger portion of students passing the test. Subsequently, the public and government officials questioned whether the tests were being made easier and the criteria for passing lowered, so that states could demonstrate compliance with NCLB guidelines and secure more of the NCLB funding.

Laws like NCLB differentially affect school districts and tend to correlate directly with the availability of district resources for education. For school districts with adequate resources, *NCLB* simply presented scheduling challenges that may have diminished the time spend in music classes or limited the number of students who could participate in music. In districts with fewer resources (particularly if the district's students were receiving low scores on state proficiency tests), administrators reacting to a narrow interpretation of the Law may have eliminated music and other arts from the curriculum.

NCLB continues to receive mixed reviews from both politicians and educators. The law illustrates well the influence that federal legislation can have on school curriculum and the importance of music educators understanding policy issues that affect education. Music education professional associations at both the state and national levels are important resources for music educators regarding the effect of education policy on music in schools.

EQUITY ISSUES IN MUSIC EDUCATION: 1950 TO PRESENT

School Segregation

One of the most important social issues affecting schooling in the last half of the 20th century was civil rights. This was a time when considerable attention was focused on the rights of minority populations, particularly African-Americans.

Legal separation of the races was sanctioned by the Supreme Court in 1896 with its ruling in *H.A. Plessy v. J.H. Ferguson*. It held that separate but equal facilities did not violate the US Constitution's Fourteenth Amendment. In fact, school segregation was incorporated into the laws of many states. Prior to the 1950s, only 16 states had laws that prohibited segregation, while 17 states required segregation and 4 additional states permitted segregation in varying degrees (Gutek, 1995, p. 509).

In 1954, the Supreme Court ruled on a challenge to an 1879 Kansas Law that permitted racially segregated elementary schools in certain cities on the basis of population. The case, which originated in Topeka, Kansas, is known as *Brown v. Board of Education*. A legal team—which included Thurgood Marshall, who a decade later became the first African-American member of the Supreme Court—argued the case in front of the Court. The Court's decision that "separate educational facilities are inherently unequal" unraveled the legal basis for racial segregation in schools and other public facilities, refuting the *H.A. Plessy v. J. H. Feguson* decision. *Brown v. Board of Education* served as a catalyst for a comprehensive social movement for equal opportunities that extends into the 21st century (US Supreme Court, 1954).

This ruling did not immediately make dramatic changes in US society or in schools. Some changes were made in school curriculum such as the development of curriculum materials about African-Americans and the beginning of the elimination of racial and ethnic stereotyping in textbooks and other materials.

The Civil Rights Movement, which began in the 1950s, is a culmination of the building ferment and frustration of African-Americans who had yet to realize the promise of the *14th Amendment,* which was ratified in 1868. By the early 1960s isolated acts of civil disobedience in the 1950s were coalesced, by leaders such a Martin Luther King Jr, into a movement. In addition to serving as a spur for government actions, such as the *Civil Rights Act* (1964), the "movement" drew attention to African-American culture as well as to the cultures of other ethnic groups in the United States.

Paralleling this social movement, schools and universities began to respond. Course work and materials focusing on the contributions of members of different ethnic groups were developed. The first Black Studies courses appeared on college campuses in the late 1960s, and by 1975, more than 500 academic units across the country were offering courses in this area (Bobo et al., 2004). With such dramatic growth, issues of the shape and direction of this new curriculum approach were debated. Should ethnic studies be primarily for members of specific ethnic groups? Should ethnic studies displace the studies of Western European Culture in the curriculum? Should curricula be developed that balance the contributions of members of a wide or narrow range of different ethnic groups?

In 1967, MENC sponsored the *Tanglewood Symposium.* Organized as an opportunity to reflect on the role of MENC and its place in society, it addressed many of the issues that were confronting social movements and education in the 1960s. The *Symposium* brought together scientists, labor leaders, social scientists, educators, corporate and government representatives, musicians, and music educators. The goal of the meeting was to define the role of music education in a rapidly changing society. After a week of presentations and discussions, a smaller group of music educators and consultants remained to develop a statement to summarize the meeting. The statement they developed, the Tanglewood Declaration, is a pivotal document that served to influence music education for the next several decades. It called for music to be placed at the core of the curriculum because the study of music contributed to several of the major goals of education including "the art of living, the building of personal identity, and nurturing creativity." Related to the issues of societal change, the Declaration stated that educators must address "the needs of a society plagued by the consequences of changing values, alienation, hostility between generations, racial and international tensions, and the challenges of a new leisure." The Declaration listed eight points on which the writers agreed. These addressed several social issues, including the need to prepare music educators to work with the very young, with adults, with the disadvantaged, and with students with special needs. The writers agreed that the profession must seek to contribute to "the solution of urgent social problems of the 'inner city' or other areas with culturally deprived individuals." Possibly, the most influential of the eight points listed in the Declaration is the following: "Music of all periods, styles, forms, and cultures belongs in the curriculum. The musical repertory should be expanded to involve music of our time in its rich variety, including currently popular teen age music and avant-garde music, American folk music, and the music of other cultures" (Choate, 1968, p 139).

The impact of the Tanglewood Symposium can be seen in the profession quite quickly. One index that can be used to examine this influence is the topics that were being discussed at professional meetings and that were written about in professional journals. Volk (1994) reports that there was an increase in the number of articles in the *Music Educators Journal* (MEJ) about music from a variety of cultures after Tanglewood and that the 1970 MENC national conference included an Ethnic Musics Institute. The November 1971 issue of *MEJ* was devoted to African-American music, and the *MEJ* published in October 1972 focused on Music in World Cultures.

In the 1960s and 1970s, slow progress was made by K-12 schools in broadening the curriculum. Mostly slight changes were made, such as additions to traditional curriculum often consisting of token reports or units on famous people of color. By the 1980s, an increasing number of education scholars sought to make more dramatic changes by conceptualizing schools as multicultural environments in which all aspects of schooling—policies, teachers' attitudes, classroom climates—would be examined and transformed. As the 1980s progressed, more scholarship in multicultural education highlighted traditional educational systems that were based on a privileged conceptualization of education and did not provide equal educational opportunities. This oppressive educational system, which was viewed as "the norm," was now the subject of criticism by multiculturalists for the way it deprived all children of an equal education (Stern, 1992).

Multicultural education is a relatively new field. It is developing and searching for new approaches and models that provide equal educational opportunities. In the 1990s and into the 21st century, it has proceeded by deconstructing traditional models of K-12 and university level education. Multicultural education is inextricably intertwined with social and political movements of the larger society as it strives to eliminate inequities.

Since Tanglewood, music education has reflected these societal and educational movements by broadening the school music repertory. MENC has supported these efforts through sponsoring symposia such as *The 1984 Wesleyan Symposium on the Application of Social Anthropology to the Teaching and Learning of Music* and the *1990 Symposium: Multicultural Approaches to Music Education*. In 2006, MENC appointed its first MENC National Mariachi Advisory Council. During the 1980s and 1990s, the *Music Educators Journal* had continued to publish individual articles and specially focused issues on multicultural music education. By the beginning of the 21st century, the MENC publication list included an increased number of resources for assisting teachers in this area. An examination of the resources available to music teachers from commercial sources reflected the same changes. Music book series incorporated a more diverse repertory into their content, and there were an expanding number of pieces available for both instrumental and choral groups that reflected more diverse music traditions.

What impact has this support for multicultural music education had in the classroom? One survey reported that almost all music teachers believe that music from other cultures should be included in school music curriculum (Legette, 2003). In 2005, music teachers were much more likely to hear music from diverse cultures sung at a December holiday concert than they would have in 1970. In 2005, it was more likely that there was an instrumental group at an elementary, middle, or high school that specialized in playing jazz. In 2005, it was more likely that a school had a performing group that played ethnic instruments (e.g., a steel drum band or a mariachi band), particularly if the school had a substantial number of families with a particular ethnic heritage. Also in the first part of the 21st century, music educators were more likely to reflect the diverse heritage of the US population and were not as likely to feel that they must limit the music they teach to Western Art Music.

At the same time, colleges and universities have made little progress in preparing future music educators for teaching diverse musics. The survey that reported music teachers believe that diverse musics should be in schools also indicated that only 35% of music teachers had received training in multicultural music as undergraduates (p. 56). In the first part of the 21st century, Western Art Music continues to be the cornerstone of the repertory studied by music education majors.

Women's Movement

There are many parallels between the struggle for equity that ethnic minorities faced in the last half of the 20th century and the efforts of women toward achieving equity during the same period. The general movement toward equity, crystallized by the *Brown v. Board of Education* decision, created an atmosphere that supported the women's movement. Another contributing factor was the publication of the best-selling book *The Feminine Mystique* (Friedan, 1963). *The Feminine Mystique* sparked a national debate about women's roles. In it, Friedan paints a depressing status of the women she surveyed, Smith College graduates, and suggested that social, economic, and political changes were required for women to reach their full potential. Friedan was one of the founders of the *National Organization for Women* and along with other feminist leaders such as Gloria Steinem, the founding editor of *Ms. Magazine*, began to influence government policy in the late 1960s and early 1970s.

The women's movement helped influence the passage of important pieces of legislation including *Title VII of the Civil Rights Act of 1964*, which prohibited discrimination in employment based on race, color, religion, sex, or national origin, and *Title IX of the Education Amendments of 1972* and the *Women's Educational Equity Act*, which provided funding for implementing *Title IX*. *Title IX* states that "no person shall on the basis of sex be excluded from participation in, be denied the benefits of, or be subjected to discrimination under any education program or activity receiving Federal financial assistance" (Section 1681 (a)).

One effect of social changes during this period was to broaden vocational opportunities for women. For both social and economic reasons, more women entered the workforce in a wider variety of vocations. As a consequence, during the last half of the 20th century, there was a dramatic increase in the number of women in the workforce. In the 1940s, fewer than 20% of women with children worked outside the home, while by 1998 65% of women with children below the age of six worked, and 78% of women with children older than the age of six worked (US Dept. of Labor, 1999).

The impact of the women's movement on school curriculum follows a pattern similar to that of the Civil Rights Movement and multicultural education. Initially, curriculum efforts tended to focus on additions to traditional content, such as adding units on significant women in US history. During the 1970s, Women Studies programs began to appear at academic institutions. In universities, courses on women, feminism, and gender initially were housed in different academic departments. The first Women's Studies Program was formed in 1970. By the end of that decade, there were units at many universities providing structured programs of studies in the area. In the first decade of the 21st century, there were more than 600 Women's Studies programs across the country and internationally (Howe & Buhle, 2000).

Through *Title IX*, the women's movement also sought to expand the opportunities for women in educational settings. While there has been considerable publicity around the impact of *Title IX* on athletic programs in colleges and universities, *Title IX* programs also endeavored to help change attitudes, assumptions, and behavior, and consequently, our understanding about how sexual stereotypes can limit educational opportunities, increase the number of women pursuing majors in math and science, and increase opportunities for women in professions in which they were underrepresented.

As the scholarship increased, the view of how women's perspectives should be represented in the curriculum changed. What is referred to as the third wave of feminism began in the early 1990s. Expanding on the issues on which feminism focused in the 1960s and 1970s, third wave feminists were interested in an expanded definition of gender and sexuality and in broadening constructs of feminism to include nonwestern perspectives. While their predecessors pursued equality, third wave feminists examined the differences between genders, but like their predecessors, they questioned and challenged the status quo (Lamb, Dolloff, & Howe, 2002). The evolution of the impact of the women's movement is illustrated by the development of feminist pedagogy. While there is not one definition of feminist pedagogy, teachers practicing feminist pedagogy are sensitive to how classroom dynamics (the relationships among students as well as between teacher and students) are affected by gender. Feminist pedagogy has less to do with how a classroom might be physically organized than with who is or is not in the classroom, who is spoken or listened to, and what or who is spoken about.

Aspects of music education do reflect the impact of the women's movement during the past 40 years, but change has come slowly. Scholarship in the 1970s and 1980s focused on uncovering the contributions of women performers and composers. These contributions began to be reflected in the music curriculum, but primarily as additions to the traditional content presented, by including music by women composers in programs and class activities, inserting more pictures of females in music textbooks, and studying the role of women in music history.

McCarthy (1999) suggests what a feminist pedagogy in music might look like, which she described as "gendered discourse." As in general education, feminist music pedagogy must be sensitive to how gender influences students' and teacher's perceptions. A gender-sensitive approach to music teaching must be composed of an inclusive music content, a redefinition of the musical canon to include more diversity. In addition to a change in content, advocates called for a new gender-sensitive pedagogy, one less focused on product and more focused on personal authentic engagements with music—a pedagogy in which students' voices are a central part of constructing new meanings.

Another effect of the women's movement on music was reflected in the number of women pursuing professions in nontraditional areas of music, such as jazz. Because the number of women and men in cross-gendered areas of music was and continues to be small, few role models or mentors are available for students. As the number of women in positions such as high school or college band director slowly increased, vocational options in music for both boys and girls gradually expanded.

Inclusion

Brown v. Board of Education also influenced the momentum toward equal access to education for parents of children with disabilities. The 1954 ruling motivated parents of children with disabilities to advocate for equal access to education for their children. Individual parents and groups concerned with disabled children initiated court cases asking for equal educational opportunities.

In the class-action case *Pennsylvania Association for Retarded Children (PARC) v. Commonwealth of Pennsylvania* (1972), the court ruled that children with mental retardation were entitled to a free, appropriate public education (Heward, 2006). Federal legislation soon followed. *Public Law 94–142*, titled the *Education for All Handicapped Children Act*, initially was passed in 1975. It has been modified several times and is now known as the *IDEA (Individuals with Disabilities Education Act, 1997)*.

When *PL 94–142* was passed in 1975, most teachers were not well equipped to work with children with special needs. Initial pedagogical strategies called for mainstreaming children with disabilities. Mainstreaming, as practiced, typically meant selectively integrating children with disabilities into some, but not all, "regular" classes. In classes where students with disabilities were mainstreamed, they were expected to demonstrate that they could "keep up" with other students in the class. For example, all special education students might receive math instruction with a special education teacher with special training but might be integrated with the general classroom population for music, art, and physical education. However, mainstreaming was not well understood, and parents and educators had difficulty agreeing on how the concept of mainstreaming should be operationalized. In addition, mainstreaming was problematic as the legislation supporting it did not provide for sufficient funding to develop curriculum and to adequately educate staff in order to have it succeed (Heward, 2006).

By the middle 1980s, several factors contributed to a shift in policy toward educating children with disabilities. These included (1) recognizing that mainstreaming was not working well; (2) inadequate funding of the policy; and (3) an increasing number of students being identified as needing special education, thus making the cost of special education increasingly expensive. The alternative approach advocated, often identified as "inclusion," works toward fully integrating children into the general classroom for the entire day. Inclusion is based on the principle that all learners are unique, with some having strengths and others weaknesses in certain learning areas. (Inclusion might be defined as a commitment to educate each child to the maximum extent possible in the school and classroom that he or she would usually attend. It means bringing support services to the child rather than moving the child to the services.)

Thus, resources of both the classroom teachers and learning specialists should be available to all learners. Some advocates of inclusion believe that regardless of the severity of a child's disability the child should be fully integrated into the general classroom. Others view inclusion as a goal while providing additional services for those exceptional children who cannot be educated in the general classroom.

The implementation of *P.L. 94–142* presented challenges for music educators as music classrooms were often one of the first classes to be mainstreamed. Early in the 1980s, a national survey reported that 63% of music educators participated and taught in special education settings (Gilbert & Asmus, 1981). Shehan (1977) reported that music educators were insufficiently prepared to meet the individual needs of disabled students.

Administrators as well as special education teachers often made decisions to put students with disabilities in music, art, and physical education classes without consulting with the teachers in those areas. These decisions did not acknowledge the cognitive or motor skill requirements of different disciplines. In response to these actions, MENC provided guidelines for integrating children with disabilities into music classrooms (*MENC: Description and Standards*, 1986). These included recommendations that music educators be involved in the decision to place special education students, that placement in music classes be determined primarily on music achievement, and that placement decisions not result in a disproportionate number of children with disabilities in any classes (p. 18, *MENC: Description and Standards*, 1986).

An important aspect of the *IDEA* legislation is the notion of the *Individual Education Program* or *IEP*. *IEP*s are developed for each student with a disability by a team of teachers, professionals, parents, and students. Unfortunately, music teachers are often left out of this planning process. While *IEP*s should be available for each student with a disability, music teachers often must seek them out. Music educators who have written articles on music and special education (e.g., Atterbury, 1989; Gfeller & Darrow, 1988) strongly recommend that music teachers take a proactive stance in helping the students with disabilities in their classes. There is a consistent call for collaboration among all teachers in inclusive settings. Many of the authors of these articles stress that the *IEP* for each student should be examined carefully by each teacher as this is the best way to make sure that the needs of all students are met in the classroom.

As students with disabilities have become an increasingly important segment of the public schools population, more emphasis has been placed on preparing in-service and prospective teachers to work with children with a variety of needs. In the last two decades of the 20th century, this typically meant in-service workshops for teachers. Often these were of a general nature and not explicitly directed to discipline-specific issues. More recent reforms in teacher education have often included requirements that all prospective teachers receive education in strategies for students with disabilities. However, coursework to specifically address special education and inclusion is ineffective when it lacks field experience (Wilson, 1996). During their preservice preparation, music students reported that their special education experiences were largely limited to students with mild retardation and students with visual or hearing impairments. Little or no time was spent on more profound conditions. Students also reported observing few special learners during field experience (Hammel, 2001).

In 2003, MENC published a position statement titled "Inclusivity in Music Education." In it, the role of the music educator is defined as follows: "(1) to strive to ensure that all students have access to music programs that address achievement in all nine areas set forth in the National Standards; (2) to present a curriculum that encompasses a wide variety of styles and genres of music; and (3) to embrace the best instructional techniques and practices" (http://www.menc.org/about/view/inclusivity-in-music-education). The document proceeds to provide the following guidelines:

- Teachers' backgrounds and their own communities' needs should inform efforts to achieve inclusivity.
- Inclusivity comprises any and all students who want to learn music, regardless of exceptionality.
- Music educators should employ the best practices identified by professionals in the field.
- All students should have access to music programs that address achievement in all areas set forth in the National Standards.
- Students should study and be engaged by the widest practical variety of styles and genres of music that are broadly representative of America's cultural diversity.

SUMMARY

In this chapter, the relationship between music education and general education, society, culture, and politics within the framework of history was highlighted.

Of these different relationships, music education is most strongly linked with general education. Defining the position of music education within general education will be an underlying theme of several of the succeeding chapters in this book as issues such as teaching philosophy, instructional strategies, and approaches to curriculum in music education are inextricably intertwined with the same issues in general education. There are clearly historical periods in general education such as the Progressive Education Movement in the first half of the 20th century within which music education fits comfortably and can thrive. There are also historical periods in general education, such as the period immediately after the passage of the NDEA, where the position of music education within the larger education picture was threatened.

If politics is realized in modern times through legislation, then in the 20th century politics has clearly impacted music education through legislative initiatives, particularly Title I of the *Elementary and Secondary School Act,* both in the 1960s and again in the early part of the 21st century with *No Child Left Behind.* In other historical periods, such as Ancient Greece, music education also tended to reflect political themes. If a city state, like Sparta, was militaristic, it makes sense that students learned songs that would inspire them in battles.

The ways in which societies are structured, which seem to overlap both with politics and cultural values, strongly influence which educational outcomes are valued. Until the last century, the structure of society greatly impacted who was educated, for example, just aristocrats, and how much education they received. This relationship is also reflected in the 20th century as the shape of the economy in the United States continues to prioritize certain disciplines over others. In the last half of the 20th century, the emphasis on math and science in the curriculum can clearly be traced to a society that has defined its economy in particular ways.

Finally, the relationship with a culture's values and music education may be less direct, but possibly most influential. The importance and role of the arts within a culture clearly affects the need for and the shape of music in schools. It seems clear that the arts are important in the way a culture defines itself, as was the case in Athens in Ancient Greece. Thus, we see that education curriculum in Athens contained a rich music component. This relationship seems also evident in the latter part of the 20th century as the content (repertory) of music education in the United States becomes broader, reflecting the cultural changes in American society.

The implication of these relationships for the music educator is that our work does not exist in isolation, and as professionals we need to be aware of the context within which our work takes place.

Class Discussion

1. Identify a social or political issue that is having an impact on schools in your community. Discuss how the issue has affected (a) education in general and (b) music education in your community specifically.

2. For a federal policy that has emerged since 1950, such as *Title IX*, discuss how the policy has or is currently affecting music education.

3. Debate which recent social issue has had the most influence on music education.

4. Some music educators would say that the *No Child Left Behind Act* had a negative impact on the place of music in the curriculum by prioritizing certain subjects over music and other arts. Discuss strategies for developing education policies that stress a more balanced curriculum.

Projects

1. Identify an educational issue that has been discussed in the news recently. It should be a broad issue, not one that impacts music education only. In one page, briefly summarize the issue, documenting the source of the news (e.g., internet site, newspaper article—with date). Then, in two or three pages describe, suggest, or speculate how this issue might impact either the field of music education or individual music educators (e.g., competes with music for time in the curriculum). Finally, suggest what action(s) might be taken in relationship to the issue (e.g., write to local politicians to make your views known and/or provide your superintendent with an MENC position paper on the issue).

2. For an historical period prior to 1900, such as the Industrial Revolution or Colonial America, develop a diagram (or a flowchart) that depicts the relationships between historical events, political perspectives, the social milieu, the economic structure, the culture, and the role of music in society. In your depiction, illustrate how these factors relate to the structure of education and how music education existed within education or within communities.

3. For a social/political movement not reviewed in this chapter, such as the *environmental movement*, describe the issue in general. How has it been manifested in education or society? Are there government (federal, state, or local) policies or educational policies developed in reaction to the issue? What books or policies are central to understanding the issue? Then describe how the issue affects music education. Have professional associations such as MENC formally reacted to it? What do music educators write about the issue? What evidence is there that changes were made in the teaching of music as a consequence of the issue. Be sure to document the sources of your information (e.g., internet site, journal article, books, etc.). Use APA style for referencing. Your paper should be approximately 1500 words.

SUGGESTED READINGS

Cremin, L. A. (1961). *The transformation of the school: progressivism in American education 1876–1957*. New York: Knopf.

Gutek, G. L. (1995). *A history of the Western educational experience* (2nd ed.). New York: Random House.

Mark, M. L., & Gary, C. L. (1992). *A history of American music education*. New York: Toronto; New York: Schirmer Books; Maxwell Macmillan Canada; Maxwell Macmillan International.

Nash, P., Kazamias, A. M., & Perkinson, H. J. (1965). *The educated man; studies in the history of educational thought*. New York: Wiley.

CHAPTER 2

~

Music as Sociocultural Phenomenon: Interactions with Music Education

Roberta Lamb

INTRODUCTION

The social contexts for music change depending on the individuals, groups, musical genres, and all the many characteristics or factors creating and modifying each individual, each group, and each genre. All these factors interweave into dynamic, multidimensional webs. Musical genres interweave with individuals and groups; groups interweave with other groups; factors interweave across all classifications; and so forth, ad infinitum. Music education sociologist, Hildegard Froehlich, calls this vibrant complexity "webs of interaction" (Froehlich, 2007, p. 53). Although Froehlich is the first music educator to use this term, she credits anthropologist Clifford Geertz (1973) with its origination. From a sociological perspective, webs of interaction are not about whom we teach or what we teach or how we teach or why we teach; however, they are about the relationships among all these factors, and more that remain unknown. Froehlich sees ever-changing webs of interaction as significant for making sense of music education and notes that an individual's or group's or musical genre's webs of interaction do not remain static but constantly evolve. She recommends music educators always question our own practices because the movement or path of any web of interaction is not predictable, especially to a general population. Thus, the webs of interaction model does not prescribe music teacher practices but advises self-reflective, self-critical identification.

To continue, we must define provisionally what we mean by music as sociocultural phenomenon. It brings together what we can learn from sociology, anthropology, social history, social psychology, and cultural studies about our human experiences. In many universities sociology began its disciplinary life within history. Anthropology, too, links with both history and sociology. Sociology examines structures and institutions, all of the social organizations and situations. These include governments, schools, religion, and families. Anthropology examines similar artifacts but from the point of view of a culture. Culture is a problematic word, so problematic that many anthropologists would rather not use the term at all. Clifford Geertz discusses these issues thoroughly (1973, 1983). Much of what music education scholars know of anthropology comes through ethnomusicology, just as much of what we know of sociology comes through education research. Educational psychology offers pertinent studies also; and the newer field of social psychology brings these two areas together. In addition, the recent fields of popular music studies (often placed within ethnomusicology) and cultural studies (which, although beginning in Birmingham, U.K., within adult education, now focuses on research into popular culture as glocalized phenomenon [Wright & Maton, 2004]) contribute to what we generally call the sociocultural. Leading the way into these newer areas of research have been studies of, about, and by previously understudied and underrepresented groups: women, people of color, working class, lesbian-gay-bisexual-transgendered (LGBT) sexual orientations, non-European, and non-American. Such research is even more recent within music education, per se. The first *Handbook of Research on Music Teaching and Learning* (1992) did not include the section called "Social and Cultural Contexts" deemed necessary for the *New Handbook* (2002). Section editor Marie McCarthy tells us, "In fact, only three of the nine topics addressed here—sociology and music education, multicultural music education and historiography—were included in discrete chapters in the first Handbook" (McCarthy, 2002, p. 564). Yet, the chapters in the Social and Cultural Contexts section only begin the interactive research-to-practice-to-research process. Music education requires so much more research into these issues and phenomena to establish explanations or comprehend the diverse sociocultural webs of interaction. For example, even though research from and about LGBT perspectives has been significant in historical musicology and ethnomusicology since the 1990s (Brett, Wood & Thomas, 2006; Whiteley & Rycenga, 2006), it is still difficult to find published studies that focus on LGBT sexual orientations in music education.

We need to understand the frameworks explaining music as sociocultural phenomenon in order to maintain awareness, improve research quality and reduce lacunae, and increase our ability to apply such knowledge effectively. The first step after this introduction is to explore sociology in education, music, and music education. Secondly, we analyze social justice in music education and survey popular culture music technology as sociocultural phenomena forming webs of music teaching and learning interaction, briefly observing where music making takes place, where it is cultivated, and what that means for musicians, teachers, and students. Finally, we focus on the meanings we make of these frameworks of explanation and webs of interaction in music education.

SOCIOLOGY IN EDUCATION, MUSIC, AND MUSIC EDUCATION

Education sociology focuses on the social settings and contexts of education. Studies in this area focus on teachers as workers and as members of educational communities. In addition to examining teachers as workers, education sociology focuses on the students, the schools, and the communities within which the schools are located. The definitions of teachers as workers include discussions of teaching as a profession. Is teaching a profession? Is it a craft? How are the working conditions of teachers "professional" and how are these conditions like those found in a factory? What is the role of teachers' unions in defining the teaching career? What is the role of the state, for example, government regulation and funding, elected school boards? What do teachers' associations and unions contribute to defining the teaching career? How does a person become a teacher? Concerning students, education sociology asks questions such as who are the students? What social groupings do they form in classrooms? How are these groupings different on the playground? How are they different away from the school? What kinds of families do the students come from? What are the neighborhoods like where the students live? What advantages and challenges do the students attending a particular school face? How do students relate to each other? How do students and teachers interact? These are only a few examples as many other questions make up the full fabric of education sociology.

Sociology of music education is, by nature, an interdisciplinary project through which we approach music and music education using a variety of methods and perspectives to expand our ability to understand music as a social phenomenon. Thus, our perspective on music is not limited to the experiences and knowledge of professional or even amateur musicians, but focuses on cultural practices. We understand cultural practices of music by the ways individuals and groups interact with each other and with the music. We understand music education in parallel ways: how, where, and why students interact with each other and the musical practice; how, where, and why students interact with teachers about music or with music; how, where and why music is created, transmitted, and/or re-created through educational practices. This emphasis on interaction differs from the emphasis on music education as either skills or talents. By emphasizing the interaction and the meanings of these interactions to the individuals, groups, social structures, and institutions, we gain much richer and deeper knowledge that subsequently demonstrates music as a meaningful and relevant educational endeavor.

Professional associations present one type of institution important to sociology of music education. In North America, as both the MENC and the Canadian Music Educators Association (CMEA) turned increasingly to focus on advocacy and the priorities established by corporate and music industry sponsors, participation in national conferences and the organizations dropped substantially, causing CMEA to abandon its national conference in 1997. CMEA symposia replaced the national conference. There have been three symposia since the last national conference: 2001, 2003, and 2006. The Coalition for Music Education in Canada took over the advocacy function. Regional conferences sponsored by provincial music educators' associations remain strong, focusing on music skills and activities for teachers to utilize in classrooms. MENC held its last national conference in spring 2008 and now plans to replace the national conference with an annual summer "Music Education Week" for K-12 music teachers and a biennial conference focused on higher education, collegiate students and leadership. Nationalist concerns, the advocacy issues primary to the corporate sponsors and music industry, and the maintenance of the status quo in teaching and learning may no longer be music educators' primary focus.

Music educators' concerns emerge as more local and problem-based within an increasingly global context, a phenomenon named "glocalization." "The word glocalization derives from the Japanese term dochakuka, meaning 'global localization'... (Robertson, 1992: 173–4, 1995). Sociological usage of glocalization highlights the simultaneity or copresence of both universalizing and particularizing tendencies in globalization, that is, the commonly interconnected processes of homogenization and heterogenization (Robertson, 1994; Robertson and White, 2005)," as quoted in (Giulianotti & Robertson, 2007, p. 134). Glocalization provides a model for examining internal and external cultural politics affecting a group as well as the symbiotic and symbolic interactions between groups (Giulianotti & Robertson, 2007, p. 149). Glocalization is key to the webs of interaction encompassed by social justice issues and technologies.

Music Sociology Categories

The framework an education sociologist uses to lay the foundation for his/her research determines what questions are emphasized, what answers are sought, and what meaning is ascribed to the results of the research. The same is true for a music educator who wishes to understand music and music education as sociocultural phenomena. Several broad categories (or schools) of sociological thought underlay common practices of education sociology in North America; among them are formalism, critical theory, interaction theory, and social justice theory. While postmodernism, feminism, critical race theory (frequently called antiracism outside the United States [Dei, 1996]) precede social justice theory in historical development, they are explored under the social justice theory rubric. Postcolonial studies are included there, too. The parallel schools in music sociology and music education sociology are summarized in the same section. Although presented historically, all these categories pertain to today's educational contexts.

FORMALISM: FUNCTIONALIST (DURKHEIM) AND RATIONALIZED (WEBER)

Emile Durkheim (1858–1917) was a professor of education at the Sorbonne and one of the founders of sociology as a discipline. He developed ideas of education within social structures that were later identified as functionalism in sociology. The premise is that society seeks equilibrium through the cohesion of different groups, each performing a function toward that equilibrium. In other words, the actions of groups have consequences for social cohesion, and all parts of society must function together. In education, this means that rational thinking brought about through schooling in values and behaviors leads to a cohesive social order. Educational policies such as busing for racial integration, Head Start, Title IX, and No Child Left Behind all come from functionalist viewpoints.

Max Weber (1864–1920) placed music within a scientific sociology making use of his knowledge of the physics of sound as well as more commonly used sociological tools like economic theory. Weber's principle of rationalization suggests that Western societies propel themselves to an ever more efficient division of labor, material wealth, and scientific progress. Weber applied this rationalization principle to music wherein he demonstrated the pinnacle of Western thought through music, making direct connections from the social to the musical. He relied on music theory and social analytic tools to undertake this project. He never did complete it. What remains are his (translated) rough notes for a book, yet Weber's thoughts on the sociology of music have been influential. The English translation of *The Rational and Social Foundations of Music* was reviewed briefly in *Music Educators Journal* (Vol. 45, No. 1 Sep–Oct, 1958, p. 82) and in *Journal of Research in Music Education* (Vol. 7, No. 1, Music Education Materials: A Selected Bibliography, Spring, 1959, pp. 148–149). Weber believed that (Western art) music had become as rationalized as possible and that any further development would impair its expressivity. What continues to influence sociology of music is the Weberian principle that Western art music is the most highly developed, rational, and organized expression of social structure.

The strength and persistence of formalism in functionalist and rationalized principles of music contributes to the difficulty music educators have had in seeing music as a sociocultural phenomenon in education. Formalism flattens distinctions making disparity invisible. One example is that we still debate the value of including popular music and world musics in music education classes in schools as equal to Western art music. Another example is that we often focus on music education as a means to social equilibrium.

CRITICAL THEORY, THE FRANKFURT SCHOOL, AND CRITICAL PEDAGOGY

Critical theory in education sociology shares connections with critical theorists of the Frankfurt School, such as Theodor Adorno, as well as earlier theorists, such as Karl Marx and Max Weber. Both Weber and Adorno wrote extensively about music in sociology; thus, they have a particular relevance to music educators; however, Adorno was also a musician himself. He studied music composition with Alban Berg (Levin & Linn, 1994). Adorno wrote *Introduction to the Sociology of Music* in 1963. He did not think highly of popular music or jazz because of what he identified as their massification and commodification in entertainment through recordings, broadcast media, and club venues. He valued Western art music. Recently, Adorno's work is being reevaluated, as demonstrated by Tia DeNora and Alexandra Kerz-Welzel, who relate Adorno's theories to music education. DeNora's (2003) focus is on music sociology; however, she points to education through examining his work on music cognition and connecting Adorno to an action-oriented, grounded music sociology, most relevant in music education. Kerz-Welzel states Adorno's educational goal is "for students to realize and identify music's structure and aesthetic message," such that "aesthetic experience as a sensorial and an intellectual understanding of music" becomes central to performing music correctly (Kerz-Welzel, 2005, p. 8).

The MayDay Group, a music education organization, avails itself of critical theory as a central tenet. According to the group's web site:

> The MayDay Group is an international community of scholars and practitioners with a two-fold purpose:
>
> [a] to apply critical theory and critical thinking to the purposes and practices of music education, and
>
> [b] to affirm the central importance of musical participation in human life and, thus, the value of music in the general education of all people. (http://www. maydaygroup.org/index.php, accessed 23 November 2008)

Position papers (Tom Regelski) housed on the web site draw extensively from the Frankfurt School to support this two-fold purpose. Yet, Renate Mueller points out that "the thinking of [the Frankfurt School], and one of that school's scholars, Adorno, is partly responsible for the persistence of the aesthetic ideology and of the massification perspective in music sociological and music education thinking" (Mueller, 2002, p. 589).

Marxist theories of tension, power discrepancies, and economic and cultural capital also influence critical theory in education. The most productive applications of Marxist theories in education sociology come through the critical pedagogies defined by Paolo Freire, Ivan Illich, Henry Giroux, and Michael Apple, all of whom examine oppression and empowerment in cultural settings including schools. These authors react against functionalism and seek to empower students and teachers to turn education toward their own liberation. Yet, critical pedagogy theory in education has been criticized for not placing sufficient emphasis on the impact of gender and race in the lives of students and teachers. This resulted in exchanges between those who defined critical theory and feminists (e.g., David & Clegg, 2008; Ellsworth, 1989; Weiler, 1991) and antiracism scholars (e.g., Bradley, 2006; Dei, 1996; Dillard, 2006; Shahjahn, 2008).[1] Critical pedagogy has had more impact in general education than in music education.

INTERACTION THEORIES IN MUSIC EDUCATION

Interaction theories were first known as social interaction and symbolic interaction. More recent developments to interaction theories are social constructivism,

---

[1] Note that David & Clegg, Ellsworth, and Weiler identify as antiracist feminist scholars while Bradley and Dillard as feminist antiracist. These categories are not mutually exclusive.

social transmission, social transformation, and situated cognition. As constructs, they have common components of sociology, psychology, and philosophy, and the relationships, or interactions among different aspects of communication, context, and society. Consequently, current practice of sociological interaction theories, with the focus on communication, expressivity, social activity, or work, becomes interdisciplinary in these contexts.

Max Kaplan was a sociologist (music, leisure, gerontology) and an accomplished violinist, who contributed to music education in many ways. With Robert Choate, he founded the Greater Boston Youth Symphony. From 1954 through 1980, he published many articles in the *Music Educators Journal*. He participated in the original Tanglewood Symposium. He wrote *Foundations and Frontiers of Music Education* (1966), one of the first such textbooks published. According to his obituary in the *New York Times* (9 August 1998),

> He told the Music Educators National Conference in 1967 that sociologists could help music teachers by examining the process by which new audiences, especially among the poor, might be introduced to the arts and by studying the schools' music programs in relation to community needs. (Saxon, 1998)

Kaplan returned to music education in 1995 to address the first sociology of music education symposium held under the auspices of the Oklahoma Music Education Symposium at the University of Oklahoma, April 1995. There he presented a multidimensional model of the arts in society that grew from interaction theories. He called it his string quartets, naming the model after his favorite musical genre. Due to his breadth of interests, Kaplan drew psychological theories into his sociological studies of musicians, particularly in case studies. He looked at the way work and leisure can overlap, that is, interact. He examined the complex roles of the music educator, who often occupies conflicting positions or holds conflicting values that resolve according to which role predominates at a given moment, only to interact in a different mode at a different time and in a different mode. These complex roles can be visualized as interacting wheels or cogs. Kaplan's theories of interaction that brought psychology into sociology became the basis for Hildegard Froehlich's webs of interaction (Froehlich, 2007), fundamental to this exploration of music as sociocultural phenomenon.

SOCIAL JUSTICE: INTERACTIONS WITH WEBS OF DIFFERENCE

Social justice interweaves many different webs of difference. When music education scholars engage in social justice interactions in music and education as educational research that is not separate from politics and see the ethnography of music as sociocultural phenomenon as politics (Wright, 2006), then social justice provides possibilities. Although not one of the webs described can be fully separated from the other, they are separated for the purposes of explanation. Noticing similarities and differences is part of sociological study of education. Similarities within a community create social cohesion, differences present challenges that may (or may not) erupt. However, the assumption that there are no differences and all the students, all the teachers, all the families, and all the neighbors within a school community come from similar backgrounds and belief systems and support the same educational goals does not create cohesion. Philip Jackson coined the term "hidden curriculum" to describe the curriculum not explicitly outlined in the planning documents, textbooks, and procedures of teaching but implemented through practice (Jackson, 1968). The hidden curriculum shows itself in ignorance of differences and their impact on education. This ignorance underlies our greatest problems in schools because people are not recognized for who they are and what they have experienced. In contrast, focusing totally on differences and presupposing no similarities within groups or among groups presents another extreme that does not encourage community. The webs of interaction model helps us to engage with the complexities found in pursuing social justice.

Web of Postmodernism in Education

Postmodernism in education sociology draws from the postmodern theories of cultural production and reception, semiotics and the French post-structuralist literary, and psychology theorists, for example, Foucault, Derrida, Cixous. Postmodernism is the more comprehensive term because it refers to the range of cultural processes and products to include film, music, social events, style, and so forth; therefore, it is more accurate to use the term postmodernism in relation to sociology and education. Postmodernism is a philosophical approach that allows the exploration of multiple perspectives and multiple subject positions. This fluidity affords postmodernism a means for dealing with difference as influence. Consequently, many advocates for egalitarian music education adapt postmodernism to their research methods as a means of imagining what could be possible (e.g., Gould, 2008; Vaugeois, 2007). On the other hand, postmodernism can delay meaning and extrapolate the subject positions and multiple perspectives to the point where no action is possible and the postmodern becomes the site of impossibility and stasis. A related criticism of postmodernism is that it takes relativism to an extreme. However, postmodernism remains a useful tool for many equity-seeking educationists (e.g., Lather, 1992). Postcolonial theory, as a supplement to postmodernism, provides a framework for addressing racism (Subedi & Daza, 2008). Patti Lather suggests that such a proliferation becomes "a 'disjunctive affirmation' of multiple ways of going about educational research in terms of finding our way into a less comfortable social science full of stuck places and difficult philosophical issues of truth, interpretation and responsibility" (Lather, 2006).

Differences among human beings include, but are not limited to, gender, race, socioeconomic status (or class), sexuality, age, ethnicity, religion, abilities and disabilities, geographic location. Negotiating the interaction among these different multilayered characteristics, wherever they occur, impels education practices within postmodern theory. When engaging postmodernism, education scholars do not have one explanation, but rather many to consider in different ways and from different viewpoints. Presenting case study research, Australian teachers Naylor and Keddie, examining their own practice, recognize the value of postmodern analyses for education:

> For teachers to analyse their pedagogical practice as partial, interested and potentially oppressive to others is to engage in rich and generative professional work. Such analysis is central to working towards social justice goals because it requires teachers to think deeply about how their own identities, beliefs and practices might be implicated in perpetuating but also potentially transforming the inequitable social relations of schooling. (Nayler & Keddie, 2007, p. 199)

Web of Gender, Feminism, Sexualities in Music Education

The webs of feminism in music education have been spinning since Roberta Lamb completed her dissertation at Teachers College, Columbia, in 1987, more than 20 years ago. This web has the longest history of these webs of interaction, but, along with LGBT studies, the least direct influence on music education. Music educators remain more comfortable with gender than with feminism or sexualities. The general public believes that music and music education provide "safe space" for LGBT people, but this cannot be verified through published research. Elizabeth Gould writes philosophy and feminist theory that includes examination of lesbian identity in music education. She is the first to have published articles with a title that includes the word "lesbian" (Gould 2005, 2007). Guillermo Rosabal-Coto has published the only article directly focused on gay males in music (Rosabal-Coto, 2006). Gould's philosophical arguments show precision and originality. In addition to writing on sexuality, she documented experiences of women band directors.

Research with sex or gender as a variable has been part of music education research programs since the first generation of modern music education research. The most common quantitative studies seek to determine whether instrument sex-role sterotyping exists or why boys do not sing. These do not aim to change practices but only document. Now there are studies about girls and boys who break these steroptypes. During the past decade, research into boys' education has increased, particularly from educational policy makers and government agencies. Unfortunately, much of this research creates a false boy versus girl dichotomy using rigid and essentialized categories that do not provide men/boys or women/ girls with more flexibility and possibilities. Mills, Martino and Lingard observe that the Australian parliamentary inquiry into boys' education ignores racism and negative assumptions about working-class boys, silently essentializing all boys as marginalized. This silence regarding the differences among boys effectively hides the privileged, white and middle-class (2007). Yet, it is possible to connect research into boys' education with the dissolution of gendered hierarchies rather than their perpetuation where male role models and mentors are themselves free from masculinist discourse (Keddie, 2005).

Web of Critical Race Theory, Antiracism, and Postcolonialism in Education

Critical race theory is the term common to the United States, but in Australia, Britain, and Canada, the more common word is antiracism. The definition most frequently used is the following:

> Anti-racism: An action-oriented, educational and political strategy for insti-
> tutional and systemic change that addresses the issues of racism and the inter-
> locking systems of social oppression (sexism, classism, heterosexism, ableism).
> (Bradley, 2005, p. 2)

This definition demonstrates that it is not possible to separate one oppression or discriminatory practice from another. In some jurisdictions, the compounded study of these factors from a systematic antioppressive model is defined as equity studies. This kind of academic work is not a theory separated from practice but rather it is a praxis, activism (Shahjahan, 2008). Through greater attention to this complex web of interactions, educators can become aware of the unequal power relationships and expose the performative aspects of race, class, and gender to students concretely, so that social change is seen to be possible. Educators from various disciplines collaborate to make such learning rich and rewarding (North, 2007). In order to be effective, such antiracist equity initiatives need to be integrated and woven into the very fabric of the institution, so that it becomes inclusive of diverse bodies and knowledge forms (Shahjahan, 2008). Deborah Bradley writes most clearly (and kindly) to music educators about our need to improve antiracist comprehension and actions.

> Our penchant for "perfect positivity" in the classroom is, I believe, one of the
> obstacles we must overcome to address race more meaningfully in music edu-
> cation. [...] Once we stop evading race talk in music education, we will begin
> to see changes that have proven very elusive over the years. [...] Talking openly
> about race and about music education's racialization is a small but crucial step
> towards social justice through music education, and towards a more socially
> just music education. (Bradley, 2007, p. 162)

Web of Social Justice in Education

Differences among human beings include, but are not limited to, characteristics such as gender, race, socioeconomic status (or class), sexuality, age, ethnicity, religion, abilities and disabilities, geographic location. Such differences often determine the basis for the missing "others" in music sociology. We simplify the web to a point of inaccurate sociology when we neglect to recognise these "others," while focusing on the familiar.

Social justice as a guiding factor for music as sociocultural phenomenon calculates the effects of oppression and empowerment considered within critical theory and critical pedagogy. It draws legitimacy from social movements of feminism, antiracism, LGBT rights, and economic rights. The expectation is that specific practical concerns are met through improvement in the way people live. Like feminism and antiracism, social justice is praxial because it integrates theory and practice into meaningful authentic approaches to understanding social contexts of education and applying principled theory to achieve honorable, practical results.

Still, music education has been slow to engage in music as a social justice web. While individuals have been writing on these themes for decades, a sense of engagement from the profession is most recent. Music education tends to prefer the "softer" approach of social justice to the direct challenges of political movements. Within social justice, music educators can talk about racial and ethnic diversity (Butler, Lind & McCoy, 2007; Joseph & Southcott, 2007), yet antiracism, feminism, and LGBT rights are not in the music education vocabulary in the same way that they are in the general education vocabulary. Music education moves cautiously to implement new approaches of any kind. Another example is the confusion between critical theory and the methodological approach called critical thinking. This is seen on the MayDay Group web site (see above). Music educators are so involved in the practice of music that reflection on what we are doing is difficult and often contradicts our practice. Again, the MayDay Group provides an example. The MayDay Group colloquia provide one of the few places where music education scholars may present thoughtful research critical of the established North American music education paradigm, but many colloquium participants experience such discomfort with the contradiction between the liberatory MayDay Group principles and the white, male-dominated practices at the colloquia, such as aggressive debate that they do not return.

Freire's critical pedagogy frequently occupies the liberation pedagogy category because his theories were born from the need to empower citizens to solve their problems of poverty and literacy within particular communities in Brazil. Similarly, liberation pedagogy is often associated with liberation theology in Latin America. Antiracist and feminist sociologies of education each developed from the particularities of racism and sexism. As these sociologies gained standing, many educators and researchers began to consider a wider model of social justice. Some researchers in education show concern that antiracist or feminist sociologies are negative, owing to the focus on racism and sexism, or narrow, owing to a perceived emphasis on only a part of the population. A positive approach and greater inclusivity are often the rationales given for choosing social justice as the name for this school of education sociology. On the other hand, feminist and antiracist education sociologists wonder if the specifics of racism and sexism will be lost in a more generic approach of social justice. Whether liberation, feminist, antiracist, or social justice, all these approaches aim toward social transformation.

Social justice as a guiding factor for music as sociocultural phenomenon calculates the effects of oppression and empowerment considered within critical theory and critical pedagogy. Another common point of departure is that each draws legitimacy from social movements. They address specific practical concerns and seek improvement in the way people live. They are praxial because they integrate theory and practice into meaningful authentic approaches to understanding social contexts of education and applying principled theory to achieve honorable, practical results. These categories of education sociology often form the basis for generic definitions of music as sociocultural phenomenon because of this focus on honorable, practical results.

TECHNOLOGY TRANSFORMING MUSIC EDUCATION

Considering characteristics of teaching and learning situations, broadly defined, helps us understand that music education webs of interaction are not solid but flexible, perhaps fragile at some points and very strong at others, just like spider webs. We probably are most aware of the formal settings, such as the school music education class, private lessons, and church choirs; however, direct active involvement to gain prescribed knowledge and skill as a result of exact instruction from an expert musician-teacher over a long period of time is no longer a common music education. Lucy Green recommends that learners always start with music they know and like; learners copy recordings of real music by ear; learning takes place alone or in groups of friends without adult supervision; learning be holistic, idiosyncratic and haphazard; listening, performing, improvising, composing be integrated throughout learning (Green, 2008, p. 178). We may not even think of informal settings as music education because the emphasis in the informal setting is on participation rather than on teaching and testing that learning. Often we consider informal music education merely recreational, such as the drumming circle in the park, the teenage garage band, the background music at a dinner party, the rock concert spectacle, the iPod , YouTube, or MySpace. The latter should interest music educators especially because musicians started MySpace to communicate with other musicians and promote their music directly to their audience, bypassing record companies and managing their own creations. Nevertheless, we may not identify the self-directed sociocultural phenomenon as either musical or educational. "If educators fail to grasp this major cultural shift, music as a curriculum subject will become increasingly alienated from young people's lives and they will find their music education elsewhere" (Savage, 2007).

Nearly every middle-class child has a cell phone or iPod. This consumer technology is ubiquitous, to the point where schools make rules regarding the presence of these devices in classrooms and their use on school property. It appears to be essential, according to its marketing and use. Thus, the source of music for most young people is electronic, mediated, and virtual, rather than acoustic and performance-based. For decades, music has been changing from a social and productive endeavor to a commodity to be reproduced and consumed, such that this was Adorno's major concern in post-World War II Europe. Yet, today's commodified music is only a partial narrative of popular culture. While we do observe young people walking together but in apparent isolation from each other because of the ear buds and phones in their ears, we can find many situations where they are using these devices to tell stories of their lives, to actively craft their identities by engaging creatively and productively with cell phones, iPods, and other technololgies. They use these devices as tools within their everyday lives to enhance social networking and express their individuality. The technological innovation of the "shuffle" means playlists become improvisational. The form of the musical suite can be altered at will and at random. Playlists are also shared physically and intimately when two young people simultaneously use one iPod by each listening through a single ear bud from the same machine. Frequently, they engage in conversation or dance moves at the same time. Phones and iPods with photo or video capacity add another dimension to identity construction and documentation as the signifiers of social networks. Now some schools utilize Podcasts to make connections with the new technologies of youth culture (Adam & Mowers, 2007). Even so, many music educators know "little about students' ICT [information and communications technology] musical activities beyond the classroom" (Marina & Breeze, 2007, p. 53).

The source of music transforms quickly through technology. The television is as relevant now as it was in the 20th century. The profusion of "reality" shows that seduce a viewer into being a participant through identification with the subject of the show and as a judge who votes on the future direction of the show encourages a manufactured-celebrity model for aspiring musicians. Karaoke often demonstrates this pseudo-identity where one has moments of impersonating favorite musicians. MuchMusic and MTV create opportunities for glocal identity creation (Pegley, 2008). The entry point to a band is more likely karaoke, "Guitar Hero" or "GarageBand" than an actual guitar. Students then want to study music on the basis of their experience with the virtual band software found on their computers. It is not necessary to play by ear or read music to succeed in composing and arranging in this genre. This computer-based introduction encourages students to learn more about music and, thus, enroll in theory courses in college or university. An extreme and disconnected juxtaposition frequently leaves students disappointed by what they encounter. Yet, some do grow past the internal identity and extend and develop their musicianship in ways traditional music educators might have thought impossible, in ways that actually were impossible a decade earlier. Supportive music educators in all levels of education recognize, value, and promote this self-directed learning. At the same time, music educators need to be aware of social justice problems that appear as music technology develops, especially when considering gender, "race," and social class. Victoria Armstrong warns us that while technology "can be enormously useful to those children who may previously have felt excluded from music due to lack of 'traditional' music skills [...] a technological focus may actually encourage a particular style of working that does not always allow for diversity and may favour males" (2001, p. 42). Armstrong further suggests, "we must be mindful of technologically determinist discourses currently prevalent in music education that reinforce existing gender–technology relations that blind us to gender bias and difference" (2008, p. 384).

SUMMARY

Most music education texts identify four divisions within the field: choral, band, orchestra, and general music, but this division presents false dichotomies, relevant primarily in the United States, revealing a hidden curriculum operating in much of officially sanctioned music education. For many, the meaning of "band" is rock band, jazz band, ambling band, or brass band. Adolescent pupils identify concert bands and large choirs with school music, not their own, "real" music. The music education cultural location of local school boards, state departments of education, university music departments, and national standards in the United States operates as hegemony in differentiated cultures around the world. These officially sanctioned cultural locations remain problematic in the United States as well because the separation of music into these four divisions suggest a hierarchy and does not provide the opportunity to focus on musics not endemic to these divisions. Many ensembles are not choirs, orchestras, or concert bands. Many musical activities and ways of being musical do not fit into these three ensembles or the term "general music." In fact, the term "general music" presents confusion in Ontario, Canada, where, contextually, general is understood by student music educators as a level or stream of education that is of a mediocre level meant for pupils who lack academic ability. They do come to understand that general music has a different meaning in these textbooks from the United States; they may begin to use the term; however, music educators in Canadian provinces often think about teaching music, rather than teaching band or choir or orchestra or general music. The performance aspect of learning music most likely is an extracurricular activity similar to a sports team, while the academic component following ministry of education curriculum includes more music theory, music history, and other aspects of music study. Even so, within this Canadian model, music education remains prescriptive.

   Much of what is central to music as a sociocultural phenomenon is missing from the choir, band, orchestra, and general music education model. By reviewing the sociological explanations of music, the frameworks of explanations we started with in this chapter, we focus on the social settings and cultural contexts. We interpret and explain music transmission. We can consider technology authentically within music education. We come to realize that little of the music learning experience is controlled by music educators in schools, colleges, or universities Throughout this chapter, we explored some meanings attached to music and make from music as musicians, teachers, and students. We examined how these meanings change in different social settings and different cultural contexts, calling up social justice issues. Both students and teachers bring their own identities to the collective music-making experience in the studio, classroom, rehearsal hall, or stage. Knowing ourselves and our students in terms of musical experiences, ethnic and religious backgrounds, social class, and family circumstances informs pedagogical decisions, either implicitly or explicitly. Our goal, as mindful music educators, is to increase our awareness so that explicit pedagogical decisions have greater influence in our work than the implicit ones.

Becoming aware of self-directed and informal community contexts of music education opens up possibilities for participation. Imagine what would happen if "hanging out" with iPods, chatting through online communities and drumming in the park were all claimed as music education. We might find that ensembles need not be static groups but that their existence can ebb and flow with student interest. This is a challenge to our current regulatory practices in music education, no doubt. We might find more collaboration and interaction among different communities. We might see less authority invested in directors and conductors and teachers as we develop a collaborative, equitable music education. In this way, we might come to see music education as a sociocultural phenomena of infinite possibilities.

Class Discussion

1. Suspend your disbelief. Brainstorm ways that a traditional performing group (e.g. choir, concert band, orchestra) could be organized to increase student participation through self-direction and decision-making; decrease reliance upon a conductor as the authority; allow for more flexible membership; and, perform more diverse musics. What are the issues arising from these possibilities, and how do you propose to resolve them?

2. Technology changes so quickly. Extend the discussion of technology to include more up-to-date devices and networks. Develop the idea of technological webs of interaction. What other aspects of music as sociocultural phenomenon need to be examined? Why? How? What does it mean?

3. Human beings frequently are uncomfortable talking about the tough issues such as racism, sexism, homophobia, and other discriminatory practices. Begin a discussion of one of these issues, starting from the basis of this chapter. What will you do to ensure that antidiscriminatory practices become central to your vision and engagement with music as a sociocultural phenomenon?

Project

1. Design a framework of explanation or a web of interaction to represent the sociocultural context(s) of music(s) within your community. Compare your framework or web with others in your class. Collaborate with a partner or a small group to observe and document community music activities that fit within your framework of explanation or web of interaction. Revise your framework or web based on what you observe. What did you learn from your comparison and collaboration that you can apply to teaching and learning music as a sociocultural phenomenon?

2. This would be a good project for a class to do. Choose two or more journals with a theme issue of "Social Justice and Music Education." Two available issues are *Action Criticism and Theory for Music Education (ACT)* v6, n4, December 2007 Theorizing Social Justice in Music Education http://act.maydaygroup.org/php/archives_v6.php#6_4 and *Music Education Research*, Volume 9, Issue 2, 2007 Music Education, Equity and Social Justice. Compare the content of the two issues. How is social justice defined? What topics are included within the social justice rubric? What topics are excluded? Whose voices are heard, and whose are absent? What webs of interaction are apparent? What webs are more difficult to find and understand? If you were the editor of such a theme issue, what changes would you encourage your authors to make?

3. Keep a log for one week of all the newer technologies you experience. Consider their sociocultural contexts of transmission, teaching, and learning. Describe the technologies, the sociocultural contexts, and your experiences in as much detail as possible. How do these technologies involve music or sound? How do they involve communication with others and expressive modes of being? How do these technologies facilitate or hinder creativity? How do you learn or teach with these technologies? What would be different about your answers to these questions if your parents were the ones keeping this log? Your grandparents? Your younger siblings or children?

SUGGESTED READINGS

Green, L. (2002). *How popular musicians learn: A way ahead for music education.* Aldershot, Hants & Burlington, VT: Ashgate.

Hahn, T. (2007). *Sensational knowledge: Embodying culture through Japanese dance.* Middletown, CT: Wesleyan University.

McCarthy, M. (section editor) (2002). Part V. Social and Cultural Contexts. In Richard Colwell & Carol Richardson (Editors-in-Chief), *The new handbook of research on music teaching and learning: A project of the Music Educators National Conference.* Oxford & New York: Oxford University Press.

Pegley, K. (2008). *Coming to wherever you are: MuchMusic, MTV and youth identities.* Middletown, CT: Wesleyan University Press.

CHAPTER 3

Philosophical Perspectives of Music Education

Randall Everett Allsup

INTRODUCTION

This chapter concerns the study and practice of philosophy and music education; it rests on the belief that asking questions and thinking reflectively about the teaching and learning of music can better prepare music educators for the contingencies of contemporary life. Philosophy, in spite of its perception as an isolated endeavor, is a natural fit for educators. Constructing classroom challenges, posing questions, and thinking deeply echo the Latin term for education, to "bring forth" or "bring up." This idea that teachers bring about or bring forth learning is self-evident. With regard to the job of education, a philosophical perspective presupposes a curious and flexible mind, a disposition on the part of the teacher to unpack and reassemble everyday problems or assumptions.

Most music educators, busy with the multiple requirements of their programs, may be forgiven if they too often confuse the activities of school with what it means to teach. When music teachers step back and critically examine their world, they soon discover a host of philosophical problems to contend with. The challenge that philosophy poses is to engage actively in meaningful problem-solving, to construct what may only amount to temporary responses in ever-changing contexts. Take as example the following commonplace assertions:

Popular music is simple and not complex enough to teach.
The boys in my choir are too shy to sing.
The music of Vaughn Williams is beautiful.

Each of these statements begs philosophical scrutiny. The educator who practices philosophy might wish to investigate these claims, uncover the assumptions that lie hidden therein, and try, if possible, a solution or response. *Can or should we teach popular music? Why don't the boys in my school join chorus in the same number as girls? How can I get my students to love what I love?* The teacher-philosopher will look around and ask: Are these statements true, possibly inaccurate, or biased? What have others to say about these concerns? How do I determine the correct way forward?

This fundamental notion of contingency and self-agency is what brings to mind the lover or seeker of wisdom [Greek: *philos*, "loving" + *sophos*, "wisdom."] Socrates knew this, as we will see. "The greatest good that can befall [us] is to daily argue about virtue ... examining both myself and others. The unexamined life," he warned, "is not worth living" (Plato, p. 39). To live and teach, otherwise, would be to surrender that which gives education its very meaning: *inquiry*. Inquiry is the very heart of education—indeed life itself. For educators, it is not enough to "call forth" or bring about learning as mentioned earlier; the teacher-philosopher must also *"go forth."* He/she must stake a claim no matter how difficult the problems encountered and proceed forward doing his/her ethical best (see Allsup, Chapter 10).

This chapter is designed to be read as a model for inquiry, an open text that is an introduction to various philosophic perspectives in music education, and not as summation. Its first section will advance the ancient notion that philosophy is a way of being in the world as much as it is the study of a particular text or discourse (Hadot, 2002). The middle sections will focus on influential philosophic trends, ideas, and thinkers that have influenced how we understand music and why we teach it. The conclusion will look at new challenges in the 21st century—new voices and new questions.

PHILOSOPHY AND EDUCATION

Surely philosophy has been around a long time, in many places and among many people. The human need to wonder, to decide among choices, and live a good life means that no singular culture or historical discourse has a monopoly on its practice (Shih, 1963). A survey of education and philosophy that begins as this one does in ancient Greece must need preface to this fact. It is for three reasons we begin here. First, the Greek gift of "speculation" has provided Western culture with so many of its formative concepts and approaches to education. Secondly, the earliest records of inquiry as to the meaning of music and a musical education were recorded in ancient Greece. And finally, because philosophy is a field of study that is built upon critiques that occur between and among texts, recovering its earliest beginning places the teacher-philosopher within an ongoing and ever-evolving dialogue.

Socrates and the Pre-Socratics

The earliest recorded philosophers were the so-called pre-Socratics of ancient Greece. They were "universalists" philosophers who looked for evidence of order and predictability [*harmonia*], and were especially drawn to the fields of music, mathematics, and science. The discovery by Pythagoras (c. 571–496 B.C.E.) of musical harmonics became a unique example of natural law [*logos*] at its best. The overtone series, the pure ratios between octaves and perfect fifths was compelling evidence that there was a sense of order to the universe [*kosmos*]. Pythagoras's contemporaries postulated that because universal properties like musical and mathematical concepts exist independently of what we can touch or observe, their study and contemplation enables one to escape the messy confines of the natural world. The Pythagorean notion that music puts the listener in contact with a realm of pure forms and pure ideas went on to influence centuries of philosophers, artists, and clergy from Plato, Kant, and Schopenhauer to Beethoven and Samuel Beckett.

However, by the time Athens reached its golden age, its citizens began to wonder what exactly philosophy was good for, especially when its study contradicted traditional teachings. New technologies, war, cultural conflict, relativism, nostalgia for the good-old-days: fourth century Greece was overwhelmed by change. Enter Socrates [469–399 B.C.E.] who argued that it is the job of the philosopher-educator to use the cultural and contextual problems of one's time as starting points for wisdom, especially as these problems are neither naturally occurring nor metaphysical but deal foremost with ethics and human conduct. Using dialogue or "dialectic" as a philosophical method [Greek: *dialektike* = debate, dialogue], Socrates conflated the term philosopher with educator: one was both or neither. This had the profound effect of turning universalist philosophy on its head. Here, knowledge comes foremost from within, and nothing handed-down is sacrosanct. Rather, the philosopher-educator was a *gadfly* whose job it was to sting others to think for themselves. Athenian society, in spite of its rapid sociological change, was like "a great and noble horse that is somewhat sluggish on account of his size and needs the fly to wake him up" (Plato).

The Art of Dialogue

The Socratic method is a process of deduction where ideas or beliefs are challenged through dialogue. The term Socratic irony is often referred to because the teacher acts as "devil's advocate," playing both sides of an argument or feigning ignorance to elicit debate. Although he refused the title of teacher (another example of irony), Socrates was very much a learner-centered educator, one who focused his attention on the opinions or beliefs of his debate partner. The "student" in this scenario might be someone who is a bit too confident in his knowledge; a soldier might be asked about courage or a politician might argue the meaning of justice.

In the Socratic tradition, a philosophic debate would begin at the intersection of perplexity and doubt. Before a question can be properly investigated, the learner or interlocutor must recognize his ignorance and become induced into a state of "*aporia*" [a state of confusion or paradox]. If a group of Athenian music teachers were to investigate the question *why should children have an education in music?* all parties would be required to set aside their long-held beliefs and begin debate with a skeptical frame of mind. After *aporia*, a kind of cross-examination would follow called *elenchus* [refutation]. This is where old definitions are tested and new ones tried. If an Athenian suggested, for example, that an education in music is good simply because it promotes self-discipline, the claim would be refuted with any number of counter claims. Do not gymnastics and military exercises also promote discipline? What makes music special in this regard? The process of *elenchus* [point and counterpoint] uncovers inconsistencies and weak arguments. The role of the discussion leader is to guide the debate in such a way that greater clarity results.

"Old Education" vs. "New Education"

The foremost advantage of the Socratic method is the development of a critical habit of mind. Virtue is knowledge, Socrates would say, when and only when the citizen-student learns to think for himself. In the case of music education, there would be no "virtue" to a given performance, even a well-executed one, if the student were merely following directions or playing by rote. No action, skill, or thought can be considered "good" if it is performed reflexively, whether this "goodness" deals with the phrasing of a melodic line or the reasons we give to include music in the schools. Recall the metaphor of the slumbering horse: education that fosters critical thinking aims to awaken or enliven the student. If the unexamined life is not worth living, then the unexamined subject is not worth learning.

It should come as little surprise that the teachings of Socrates interrupted long-held views on the method and purpose of education. The very earliest educational records reveal that the children of Ancient Greece were expected to learn sports and music with a mind toward obedience and tradition. Music was not quite the self-expressive or creative art we know it today; rather it was enjoyed as a form of story-telling, a way to pass on traditions and learn history. "The style of the songs was plain and unaffected. Most commonly, they were in praise of the men who had died for their country," wrote Plutarch (Boyd & King, 1995/1921). Even reading was not considered terribly important; students were expected to memorize the great works of Homer, not critically debate their meaning.

Of course the world changes, even in ancient times, and the past tends to look better than the present. With the arrival of Socrates, the nostalgic term "Old Education" came to represent a semifictional time when Greek children actually obeyed their elders, memorized their music, and longed to join the army (Nussbaum, 1997). It used to be, the elders complained, that discipline, tradition, and moral clarity were taught without apology in school. "Very well, I will tell you what was the Old Education," wrote Aristophanes in *The Clouds*, it was a time when justice was taught and modesty was held in veneration. It was required of a child that he should not utter a word. ....In the street, when they went to the music school, they marched lightly and in good order.... They had to stand with their legs apart and sing "*Pallas the Terrible, Who Overturneth Cities*" (Aristophanes, p. 579). Written to lampoon the tenets of "New Education," Aristophanes's comedy portrayed Socrates as a cunning relativist, a teacher who helped a student use philosophy to argue that it is good and right to beat his father!

Critique

What is the lesson of this and what has it to do with music education? The most obvious point is that the conflict between rote learning (Old Education) and child-centered learning (New Education) is as old as school itself. These examples also suggest that exaggerated and polarizing claims by those who speak on behalf of the education community are not limited to recent history. Today, for example, debates continue concerning the degree to which music educators should emphasize product and process, the role of dialogue in the classroom, and the place of expert-directed vs. student-centered learning. Yet, a reasoned critique need not fall prey to false alternatives. Dualisms tend to simplify arguments, and false alternatives prevent the ability to imagine different possibilities. The Socratic method, for example, can be very time-consuming and potentially cumbersome in a large group setting. If a band director were to run his/her wind ensemble like a Greek symposium, very little music would be ready for a scheduled performance. Yet, a false argument suggests that no discussion can or should occur, say, in a rehearsal setting and that all decisions about music must be made by the conductor. Surely, different alternatives are possible. These, of course, are philosophical questions.

AESTHETIC PHILOSOPHY

What distinguishes sound from music? What qualities separate an ordinary object from an "art" object? What is this something, this *extra*-ordinary feeling that we experience through music and the arts? As educators and musicians, we understand deeply and intuitively the value of what we do, but there is no universal agreement as to how we define or explain our craft, let alone justify its study. This section is about the various ways people have thought about music and the arts. The branch of philosophy that deals with the arts—with imagination, perception, and sensation—is commonly referred to as aesthetics [Greek: *aesthesis* = perception].

The study of sense perception alone, however, is not aesthetic philosophy until its inquiry concerns the *problems* of art—questions of human-made beauty, feelings, purpose, and taste, and also particular problems related to form, expression, rhythm, tone, dynamics, and more. How do musical domains work? Or more puzzlingly, why does music have a powerful effect on us? Why is it practiced in every culture? What does music tell us about ourselves and our world? To attempt a quick answer to any of these questions is to provoke no small amount of frustration. Think how difficult it is to agree on a movie recommendation without having to tackle the very reason we see movies in the first place!

Recall from the previous section that one of the major goals of philosophy is to help us know our world. It is likely that the more we think about our world, the more we will experience a sense of wonder about it, about our place in it, and how we should or shouldn't act. The more we wonder, the more curious we become and the more questions there are to ask.[1] The process is circular. Let's agree that this same circular process holds true for the study of art. An important goal of aesthetic philosophy would be to help us get to know our *artistic* world better— not necessarily to explain it, but to consider it or ponder its meaning. Rather than experiencing frustration at its contradictions and complexities, such deep thinking would produce a sense of variegated wonder, which would lead us to consider still more questions. As facts give way to interpretation and personal truths, a peculiar kind of clarifying process is revealed, one that is deeply analytical but terribly unsure.

The Origins of Aesthetics

If a survey of philosophy and education required starting with the Ancient world, then the study of modern aesthetics would locate its beginnings in early 18th century Europe. At this time, autonomous categories were drawn around what came to be known as *les beaux arts*: painting, sculpture, poetry, architecture, and music (Kristeller, 1951). Out of this "modern system of the arts" grew specialized fields of musical performance, national conservatories for their study, codified forms like the symphony and sonata, and, of course, exacting methods of instruction. It is important to emphasize that until the Age of the Enlightenment, the fine arts were not particularly elevated or "enlightened." Early opera, for example, served as popular entertainment and little more, and motets were reserved for worship and certainly not sung in salons and concert halls. Before the arrival of this new way of thinking, an opera aria or church motet would not expect to enjoy what later aesthetic philosophers called disinterested contemplation, nor were these musical forms free-standing units of philosophical study set apart from the context from which they evolved and developed.

Once the fine arts were categorized, the quest for a defining characteristic began in earnest. A new project for philosophers, this effort lead to many subcategories of aesthetic analysis, broad labels we will examine, like representationalism, expressionism, and formalism. Convinced that all the arts communicated something in common—something *peculiar*—aesthetic thinkers staked out new philosophical positions as discrete and clearly marked as the forms they were studying. Just as dance split from music and hard lines were drawn between sculpture and painting, new categories of thinking produced rival camps of philosophical inquiry, each with their attendant drama, controversy, and passion. The debates that ensued make a particularly strong claim on contemporary scholarship and are worthy of review.

The Problems of Representation

The idea that the meaning of art lies in its ability to represent or depict the natural world is a common one and goes back thousands of years. Poems, for example, are good at telling stories of love, and sculpture is an excellent medium for

---

[1] A negative formulation is equally true. Philosophy can be viewed as a pedagogy of limits, where its study reveals how little one knows. A poor instrument for knowing the world, some say that the best one can do is to know one's self.

depicting courage and valor. But how and when is music representational? How well does this theory work in an art form based on sound? One can argue that music is representational only to the extent that it has lyrics and that these lyrics must be understandable and clearly communicated. But, surely, words are not the only musical considerations a composer or listener pays attention to. Take, for example, a polyphonic setting of an *Alleluia*. Should the worshiper attend only to the word "alleluia" and little else? What happens when compositional innovations, like those of Guillaume Dufay give emphasis to musical considerations like form, texture, melody, and rhythm? Long before instrumental music secured an independent position among composers and the public, a crisis was brewing concerning vocal music and its ability to "represent" its text. For centuries, the church deliberated about whether to abolish polyphonic vocal music in order to foreground the vanishing or increasingly hidden meaning of their sacred texts.

The growing popularity of symphonic forms presented a thorny philosophical problem. How does pure sound mean anything? According to Peter Kivy, instrumental music caused a veritable artistic revolution; it became "the avant-garde of the age of Enlightenment" and subsequently required a complete rethinking of mimetic art (Kivy, 1997, p. 6). Music's problem with literal representation inspired some philosophers like Kant, Schopenhauer, and Schiller to consider that all the arts, particularly music, spoke of a "peculiar" kind of otherworldly knowledge, one that represented the Sublime (Kant), the Will (Schopenhauer), or moral value (Schiller). In their own way, they argued that there must be knowledge that goes beyond "pure" reason; this reaction against rationalism uncovered in art (especially absolute music) a sort of "secular divinity."

The problem of representation continues to exacerbate today's music educators and their advocates. How do we justify our band and orchestra programs when we cannot accurately depict the meaning of the activity under consideration? Song forms may have it the easiest. At a very minimum, musical theater productions and concert choruses can be said to "represent" the substance of the songs that are programmed, and their texts can be seen to have teachable content beyond tones and rhythms. In contrast, how exactly does a band director say what Nelhybel's *Festivo* really means? How is the subject matter of "absolute music" communicated? To answer this question, two sometimes contradictory, sometimes overlapping impulses will now be explored. Broadly conceived, one philosophical domain saw art as the reflection of the life and feelings of the composer. Another broad domain saw art, particularly instrumental music, as a self-contained activity, a realm of purity that refers only to its own beauty. As the following sections examine the problems of "feeling" and "form" that came to fruition in the 19th century, the reader is likely to recognize some contemporary overlap, or even a personal kinship with certain viewpoints.

The Problems of Feeling

Famous actors, writers, and musicians will talk about their work very singularly in terms of feelings and emotions. Trained musicians understand that to perform expressively means to play with great feeling or to produce an appropriate emotional impact upon the audience. When asked, most music teachers will say that one of the great values of music education lies in its ability to help children express themselves emotionally; they may even relate that the most challenging students behave best in music class, that music has an emancipatory effect on their children[Although the connection between music and feelings is universal to all cultures, it was not until the Romantic period that this perspective enjoyed widespread philosophical study and debate.]

The idea that all art works speak to us through the "language of feelings" found its most articulate voice in Leo Tolstoy [1828–1910].[2] "Whereas by words a man transmits his thoughts to another, by means of art he transmits his feelings," he wrote (Tolstoy, 1960, p. 44). The associated term *expressionism* "is based on the fact that a man, receiving through his sense of hearing or sight another man's expression of feeling, is capable of experiencing the emotion which moved the man who expressed it" (p. 44). For the Romantic artist, however, the aesthetic route is never direct. If, for example, a friend laughs and another smiles, this is not art. The go-between, of course, is the art work—an *object* that communicates through the various languages of paint, pitch, rhythm, form, and so forth. The criteria for expressionistic art are not based on abstract or metaphysical principles like beauty or perfection but on the degree to which (to use Tolstoy's words) the artist successfully "infects" the receiver[Although odd-sounding, this so-called infection makes some degree of sense. We don't listen to slow music at the gym, and we don't play loud music at a funeral. Nor, if a piece of music is well-composed, do we need a formal education to enjoy its affects.)

This theory, presented in a simplified form, begs several questions. To what extent is the receiver required to hear music the way the originator intended the piece to be heard? There is no guarantee furthermore that a minor key will elicit sadness and little else. And, can't what we call self-expression really be the representation of many kinds of feelings or the formulation of an inner life that resembles feelings? This was to be Susanne Langer's (1895–1985) point a half-century later. People mistake feelings for music because they are so much alike (Langer, 1957) Music, according to Langer, is *analogous* to the inner life of feelings, but not identical. How can real sadness be the same as musical sadness? Certainly we don't enjoy *being* sad, but we may be quite fond of sad movies, minor keys, and slow *adagio* movements.)

To be considered seriously, any theory of expression must hinge on the indirect communication of feelings. While language is nothing without an explicit message, art in this context seeks the expressive *exploration* of a message, a suggestion without a name. Thus, the Romantic ideal was often celebrated as illogical. Although it sought the communication of an idea or feeling, it did not seek to communicate through the head, preferring instead the heart. The purpose of expressionism in the musical arts is the transformation of feelings from composer

---

[2] Composer Richard Wagner was likewise a proponent of this view. However, it is generally agreed that Wagner's philosophical writings do not share Tolstoy's rhetorical clarity and rigor.

to listener through the artistically rendered object, not the accuracy of its correspondence or the directness of its relay. Instead of seeing the artist as someone who releases an emotion and causes an identical effect in the listener or receiver, both parties are involved in some form of aesthetic reconstruction. If a photographer constructs a work that is open and metaphorical, say an image that allows for a multitude of meanings (meanings that are inseparable from feelings), then the receiver enjoys the option of multiple emotional responses. If a photographer constructs something closed and literal, say a piece of photojournalism or a simple snapshot, the photographer is not communicating through artistic language and thus is not producing art. According to this interpretation, if there is only one intended response for the receiver (emotional or otherwise), transformation or exploration cannot take place. Expressionism can be said to be educational to the extent we debate and analyze the "unclear" message we are enjoying.

The Problems of Form

The 19th century witnessed new experiments in chromatic harmonies, extreme ranges of dynamics, wider tonal palettes, increasingly prolonged approaches to cadences, Wagnerian leitmotifs, and programmatic suggestions. All these compositional techniques were meant to "represent" something outside the structural properties of music itself [the principles of heteronomy]. Let's imagine what goes on in the mind of a listener who is attending to a programmatic work, taking as example Felix Mendelssohn's tone poem *The Hebrides*, also known as "Fingal's Cave." *A dark, repeated cello passage seems to announce a cold wet wind. A steady crescendo in the brass section builds anticipation and woodwind flourishes mystify the ear. One imagines the parting mist, which reveals the shelter of a lonely cave. The music presents a place of great mystery, and who or what lurks inside? Man or beast?* A story is being told without words.... Or is it? And how long should the story last? Will the visual keep going after eight minutes of music? And what if it does not? What if one's story changes from "Fingal's Cave" to "Last Summer's Family Vacation in Florida?" Is something missing if that happens?

By contrast, the principles of aesthetic autonomy hold that music is powerless to refer to anything at all, not feelings, ideas, moods, myths, or family vacations. Rather, music is a realm of pure autonomous sound, and its meaning resides in its formal properties alone [formalism]. Is Mendelssohn's *The Hebrides* enjoyable because of the story it tells or really because the music is structurally beautiful? "The course hitherto pursued in musical aesthetics," begins Eduard Hanslick in the seminal treatise on aesthetic formalism, *The Beautiful in Music*, (1857) "has nearly always been hampered by the false assumption that the object was not so much to inquire into what is beautiful in music as to describe the feelings which music awakens" (p. 7). By refocusing music on form, Hanslick sought to rectify the excesses of Romantic thinkers like Wagner, Mendelssohn, and Tolstoy whose "languages of feelings" and programmatic suggestions appeared self-aggrandizing and philosophically off target. According to Hanslick, the beautiful aims at nothing, with no aim beyond itself (1957, p. 9). If art inspires passion, so be it; beauty will always exist independent of the receiver.

Of course, music and the fine arts serve to excite or stir us but not with stories or feelings but with our "organ of pure contemplation"—that is, through our mind and through our imagination (Hanslick, 1957, p. 11). This is a disinterested stance—disembodied, receptive, singular, and attentive—where an engagement with music resembles a mental inspection, or what formalists call "contemplation with intelligence." According to this theory, the essence of music is sound in motion. "It is through the unhampered play of its functions, then, that a work [of art] is revealed and justified," wrote Igor Stravinsky (Stravinsky, 2003, p. 49) . If it is only through form that music can be studied and composed, then it is only through its contemplation as "pure sound" that it can be appreciated. A work like *The Hebrides* is beautiful because it is beautifully written and for no other reason. In this sense, we enjoy program music *in spite* of its extramusical allusions; equally, the famous "Tristan chord" in Wagner's *Prelude to Tristan and Isolde* is beautiful because of its harmonic function and not for the unfulfilled passion it is claimed to express.

This theory creates new problems for understanding vocal music. Because of vocal music's historical relationship to representationalism and expressionism, it is hardly surprising that Hanslick and his followers were strongly prejudicial in favor of instrumental music, which they called "pure." Indeed, evidence can be cited that Hanslick did not think much of vocal music at all, especially opera (especially Wagner's operas!). The formalist would assert that when music and words are united, it is always music that wins: "Whenever music steps forth in its true character it leaves language far behind" (Hanslick, 1957, p. 30). Hanslick continues, "Even the most wretched poem when set to beautiful music can scarcely lessen the enjoyment to be derived from the latter, whereas the most exquisite poetry fails to compensate for dullness in the musical part" (p. 30). To test this theory, consider the following piece of poetry:

> Yesterday.
> Love was such an easy game to play.
> Now I need a place to hide away.
> Oh I believe in yesterday. (Lennon & McCartney, 1965)

Do we recognize this verse because it is a brilliant piece of poetry, or because it is attached to one of the most recognizable melodies ever written? Who would disagree that the musical beauty of "Yesterday" far overshadows the banality (what Hanslick might call the wretchedness) of its lyrics? Wouldn't almost any set of words arranged to this particular tune sound just as right, just as beautiful?

Critique

For the purposes of learning more about a topic of interest, philosophy requires distance, some kind of temporary removal from experience. The danger in this exercise is that the philosopher (or aesthetic theorist) may neglect to return to the very experience that initiated the investigation. This is the charge that many critics will level against the contemporary followers of aesthetic philosophy. When art becomes an object of detached contemplation or subject to specifiable extrinsic stipulations, "the continuity of esthetic experience with normal processes of living" becomes increasingly difficult to recover (Dewey, 1938, p. 10). To think of music as a musical work, or art as an artwork, or dance as a dancework, is to leave unexplored a considerable field of *lived* experience.

PHILOSOPHICAL RATIONALES FOR MUSIC IN THE SCHOOLS

The philosophical study of music education as it is understood today is a fairly recent accomplishment. Its growth followed the free school movement of the 19th century and music's widespread adoption in the North American public education system. It is important to underscore that this evolving discipline would grow almost entirely out of a need to rationalize the inclusion of music in public schools. During this time, the older notion of the "fine arts" and its philosophical fascination with the sublime would move steadily down to earth, from esoteric issues that concern the composer's will to practical matters about classrooms, teachers, students, and what to teach.

Emerging Rationales

While Wagner was arguing with Hanslick about feelings and form, and Nietzsche debated Wagner on the value of music and life, and Count Tolstoy pretended to be a peasant (as part of a vision for socialist life and art), schools in New England were quietly debating the role of publicly funded music education. It shouldn't be surprising that very little of early music schooling concerned itself with aesthetic theory; instead its advocates staked out claims that were mostly related to student health and societal welfare. These claims were a hodgepodge of familiar rationales (and a few that strike one as bizarre today). In pressing for the inclusion of music in the Boston city schools, Lowell Mason [1792–1872] proposed as foundational the belief that music helps us to read, speak well, and learn foreign languages; music cultivates religious devotion; singing prevents disease, especially tuberculosis; it elevates the mind and soul, and makes one a virtuous citizen; music nurtures a love of one's parents, extending even to teachers and dumb animals (Mason, 1824).

It is important to emphasize that while the debates around aesthetic philosophy were entering their second century in Europe, very little of this talk made its way into the growing discussions about why music should be taught in public schools. Music education historian Michael Mark writes that the "developmental process" of music education philosophy "was not evolutionary because the philosophy remained essentially the same from Plato's time to mid 20th century" (Mark, 1982, p. 20). Generally speaking, music education philosophy (as opposed to the philosophical study of music) has historically based its arguments on the rationale that the "musical development of the individual influenced behavior in such a way that a better citizen (in terms of cultural, civic, religious, or other values) was expected to be developed" (Mark, 1982, p. 15).

Meanwhile, school music programs were chugging along with their increasingly sophisticated performing ensembles, mostly without the help of philosophers. During the early 20th century, large groups like glee clubs, bands, and orchestras were growing at an astonishing rate. By 1929, there were nationwide an average of 20,000 band programs and approximately 30,000 school orchestras (Hansen, 2005, pp. 65–66). Who needs a philosophy for what the band does? With entertainment provided at football games, national contests (the first in 1923), and outdoor concerts in the park, the utilitarian functions of bands were framed—like their populist predecessor, the 18th and 19th century singing school—in terms of outreach, discipline, and local pride (Hansen, 2005, p. 66).

At risk of stating the obvious, music teaching and learning in these large ensembles was and remains primarily experienced through performance. Curricular choices address the right level of challenge for a particular group (and attention to audience needs), and assessment comes in the form of a well-played concert or high festival rating. This is a simplified description of a highly complex learning environment. However, the educational logic of bands, orchestras, and choirs has never needed a rationale beyond its apparent functionalism. It is a remarkable testament to their utilitarian appeal that these expensive forms of teaching have survived a century of budget swings.

In many ways, the 20th century saw the invention of music education; the effects of these early efforts continue to shape how today's children are taught and how teachers are trained. The following section will look at what took place in the latter half of the 20th century when a rupture occurred with how our profession came to view itself and the degree to which a larger societal break informed new philosophical projects. The backdrop for this change was the great "modernist project," begun in the Age of Enlightenment and reaching its zenith in the mid 20th century. What came after is popularly called *post*-modernism, a break with the past that gave rise to neglected voices and a flood of new perspectives.

The Modernist Backdrop

The roots of the modernist project can be said to reach back to the Age of Enlightenment when "mankind" claimed the right to objective science and universal ethics. The term to which "modernism" is often referred is the "high" period energized by the Industrial Revolution, reaching its artistic apotheosis in the 1960s with such advances as the hyper-serialism of Elliott Carter, the new jazz language of Ornette Coleman, the modern dance movement of Martha Graham, and the literary theater-projects of Samuel Beckett. The central tenet of modernism was linear progress and invention. Every great accomplishment would be a grand step forward in time, building with ever-increasing complexity, rationality, and difficulty toward a newer, better way of looking at the world.

Modernist composers were energized by conflict; they eagerly tore down the traditions that came before them, putting their musical world in crisis (and always competing for the last word). Many like Arnold Schoenberg, Igor Stravinsky, Paul Hindemith, Aaron Copland, and Milton Babbitt shaped university programs and advanced a self-proclaimed elitist music education philosophy through their positions of authority. Unlike the early advocates for music education that preceded them, these composers responded favorably to the aesthetic philosophy. Utterly disdainful of utilitarian rationales for music, they proclaimed (unsurprisingly) that the composer was the very exemplar of the modern age, a lofty genius whose inspiration "must always remain hidden from human comprehension" (Hindemith, 1942, p. 11). They were composer-writers, teachers, and tastemakers, as in Copland's *What to Listen For in Music*. Most were deeply suspicious, like Stravinsky, of performers' ability to "translate" their genius (Copland, 1939; Stravinsky, 1942). And each complained bitterly about the poor quality of American music education, which nominally disqualified the public from any right to say whether their music was enjoyable or good (Schoenberg, 1950). Of course, the music itself was not to blame. In these intellectually impoverished circumstances, the best a composer could do, wrote Babbitt in an essay entitled "Who Cares if You Listen?," is to remove himself from public life and delve further into the cloistered safety of the university's tenure system (Babbitt, 1958).

If the prevailing theme of modernism was progress, then its principal form of disclosure was the *manifesto*—self-conscious proclamations of a particular ideology with a primary impulse to convince rather than question. During the 1960s and 1970s, music education witnessed a stretch of manifestos. Declarations, proclamations, reports, and studies were issued from the Tanglewood Symposium, the Manhattanville Music Curriculum Project, the Yale Seminar, and the Contemporary Music Project, all in an attempt to address the problems of a public that was poorly educated in music. Yet cracks in the modernist veneer were showing, and many of the manifestos of the 1960s and 1970s were newly critical of the "high art" rationales that faculty composers were advocating and especially critical of the tired utilitarian justifications that had served large ensembles for so long. Reviewing these documents, one gets a palpable sense of a deep desire for new voices and new experiences. But before postmodern theories make an appearance the music education profession coalesced around an older philosophic rationale: aesthetics.

Bennett Reimer

In 1970, Bennett Reimer's highly influential *A Philosophy of Music Education* would go on to establish aesthetic philosophy as the principal rationale for music education in North America for several decades. The success of Reimer's aesthetic philosophy was due to a unique confluence of historical and philosophical scholarship, professional necessity, and good timing. Calling his philosophy a "continuing refinement" rather than a new voice or a new theory,

Reimer cited as influences the philosophical writings of Dewey, Langer, and Leonard B. Meyer; music education advocates like Charles Leonard and Robert W. House; historical analyses of the 18th and 19th century aesthetic philosophers; and the calls for action that were issued from the Tanglewood and Yale symposia, MENC, and others (Reimer, 2003, p. 8). The term aesthetics would be applied "in the broadest possible sense, encompassing all past and present philosophical discourse on the entire range of issues related to aesthetics and philosophy of art" (p. 7).

Reimer begins with the assumption that "music and the arts are basic ways that humans know themselves and their world; *they are basic modes of cognition.*" [emphasis added] (Reimer, 2003, p. 5). While there are many ways to think and be intelligent, the activities and disciplines associated with "conceptual thinking" and their concomitant symbol system—(say) the languages of math, science, English, and French—are understood by the public as more important than ways of thinking that address the "nonconceptual" domains of art, the domains of music, dance, theater, and painting, whose symbol systems operate quite differently from the former. For Reimer, this is a primary concern. If we can discern the advantages and disadvantages of conceptual thinking and nonconceptual thinking, then the music education profession can embark upon an articulated defense for music in the schools.

Concepts require three essential characteristics that differ from art in their intent. First, a concept must exist as a phenomenon with a range of common qualities or identifiable characteristics. Second, a particular phenomenon must be attached to a corresponding sign or marker. Finally, there must be a regular and stable relationship between the phenomenon and its conventional marker (Reimer, 1989, p. 81). An apple, for example, is not a concept. "However, if you notice something about [the apple] that it has in common with other things ("fruit" "round" "edible" etc.)" and you apply this knowledge to new arrangements, you are learning conceptually (p. 81). Concepts help us to sort out and classify the events of daily life; they are structures of thinking that yield what Reimer calls "knowledge about" (p. 83).

Music, however, yields "knowledge of" rather than knowledge about. Because our cognitive relationship to music is dynamic, and because every musical experience is never the same twice, and because one's understandings and values about music vary immensely from person to person, music's cognitive function is necessarily nonconceptual. According to this perspective, the arts seek to clarify one's inner life, the world of affect, and the life of feelings. While both conceptual and nonconceptual ways of knowing involve symbol systems, the process of conceptualization is basically informational, "while the nature of an expressive form [music or a musical act] is such that a single agreed-upon meaning acceptable to everyone is neither possible or desirable" (Reimer, 1989, p. 57). This sets the stage for both a rebuttal of past aesthetic writers and a new justification for school music that goes well beyond everyday utilitarianism.

An Education in Feeling

According to Reimer, music's strength lies in its ability to engage in the dynamic qualities of experience, particularly the experience of feeling or sentience. Music should not be considered a language because as a phenomenon its meaning can be neither agreed upon nor can a particular feeling or emotion be assigned to any given piece. Neither is music a failed language, in spite of its nonconceptual nature. "The fact is, the arts are not vague or indefinite at all. They are exquisitely precise in doing what they do, which is to capture and display the dynamics of feelings in meticulous, specific, exacting detail" (Reimer, 1989, p. 43). This position is a nuanced rebuttal to the three general concerns of 18th and 19th century aesthetics: the problems of form, representation, and feeling. Recall that formalists denied any connection between an art object and one's emotions. In Reimer's philosophy, the study of form and the specific information it reveals teaches us not only more about the artwork itself but more about *us*, more about the dynamic quality of our "felt life."

Reimer uses the metaphor of the ocean to describe how music resembles the inner world of one's feelings. The vast realm of human subjectivity is like the sea, a deep chasm of ever-changing currents and ever-modulating feelings. Our "feelings themselves—experienced subjectivities—are incapable of being named," and the best we can do is assign a simple emotion to the complexity of what we are feeling (Reimer, 1989, p. 47). Love, for example, is an emotion so full of compound feelings that it acts as a signpost only, a buoy marking a general place atop the oceanic waters of experience, "reminding us that underneath it lies a vast realm of possible ways to feel" (Reimer, 1989). Writes Reimer, "the difference between an emotion and a feeling is a real one—it is the difference between words [love = word = a concept] and experiences [the feeling of love = experience = the nonconceptual], the one being only a symbol (or sign) of certain possibilities in the other" (Reimer, 1989). The "arts are the means by which humans can actively explore and experience [this] unbound richness of human subjective possibilities" (Reimer, 1989, p. 59). Because music and feelings are analogous in quality and purpose, humankind has always used one to understand the other. Thus, an education in music can be understood as an education in feeling, "a unique way of extending (refining, enhancing, deepening, etc.) our emotional lives" (Reimer, 2003, p. 89).

What does aesthetic philosophy look like in the classroom? The practical objective of Reimer's philosophy sees music as one piece of a multifaceted and interconnected school-wide endeavor. The study of K-12 music would be "rebalanced" so that the majority of educational resources go to the development of so-called *aficionados*, what the music education community might call nonmusicians or nonmajors, with a smaller number of elite activities that prepare students for lives as professionals (Reimer, 2003, p. 255). According to this view, students do not need to be performers to understand music. Later philosophers will critique this position, suggesting that it is only through active participation—*through performance*—that students can understand the nature of music and how it operates.

Postmodernism

Today, it is common to hear the word postmodern used to describe just about anything new, from a fancy restaurant menu to a newly renovated post office. But confusion around the term has less to do with a general naiveté among the pubic than its broad application both inside and outside of academia. Before exploring what this umbrella term indicates, it is best to keep in mind that the "isms" that represent ideas and people are useful only to the extent that they help us to frame good questions—"isms" should characterize more than classify. With that caveat in mind, scholars have described much but not all of the philosophical activity of the end of the 20th century as a response to the modernist project, a break with the past that is distinctly *post*-modern.

Postmodern concerns share a deep suspicion of universal truths, attention to the nature of power and its inequitable distribution, and a fascination with identity, culture, and "otherness." We are multiple, ever-evolving selves, nested in overlapping human-made systems, some of control, reward, punishment, and pleasure, but each with their own gravitation pull. All ideas, actions, and cultural undertakings are conscripted by one's place within a given arena. Determinations of good and bad or high and low are necessarily suspect. What counts as high art or good music, for example, has nothing to do with a work's "inherent" quality, and more to do with status, cultural expectations, and access to power.

For postmodern music education philosopher Thomas Regelski, musical value should only be determined by its "use-function," by how well it satisfies the role a particular culture has created it for (Regelski, 1998). This means that the rules that govern quality in popular music are not the same—should not and cannot be the same—as the rules that govern, say, classical music, jazz, or folk. Harmonic complexity in Western art music, for example, is highly valued, but rhythmic complexity (generally) is not. In contrast, Western popular music favors complex rhythms and (generally) straightforward harmonies. What rationale do we use when we choose to teach one form of music rather than another? The historical values that have shaped Western classical art music? How would we justify such an apparent bias? Regelski would ask us to consider how *all* curricular choices are implicated in issues of power, access, and history.

From the postmodern perspective, nothing human-made is politically neutral or culturally innocent. Art is best understood as "artifact," philosophy as "discourse," and analysis as "archeology." One might hear a postmodernist describe an interpretation of a musical work as a "reading of a text." Music is not a thing or an art object in which self-contained meanings reside, but a subjective form of cultural discourse whose value is determined by its sponsors. This notion would have been a terrible affront to 20th century composers like Stravinsky, Babbitt, and others: interpretation was an anathema to them (which may be one reason why so many modernist composers fell in love with the analogue synthesizer and the tape recorder).

Yet, it is reasonable to ask what counts as valid when an author no longer controls his medium and all contributing perspectives are legitimate? Responding to this concern will continue to be the great postmodernist project, one that will outlast the writing of this chapter. Nonetheless, the problem of relativism is frequently dealt with through self-disclosure on the part of the author as well as the reader. If the manifesto was the guiding light of modernity, then the personal narrative may be the best a postmodernist can do. Philosophers after modernity, like Maxine Greene in particular, often use the small form of the essay to tackle big societal issues, integrating the substance of their lived world with the questions they are asking. Such disclosures often include the perspectives of one's gender, race, class, sexual identity, or politics.

It is important to note that the "isms" that mark particular perspectives in intellectual history never end just as a new period gets under way. There is plenty of evidence that we live in an age that is both modern and postmodern. This is especially apparent in the field of music education research where traditional science-based inquiry now shares journal space with qualitative examinations of gender, ethics, multiculturalism, and so forth. David Elliott's *Music Matters: A New Philosophy of Music Education* (1995) is a good case in point. This seminal text is modernist in scope asking big questions about the very meaning of music and what music is good for, but postmodern in intent using the notion of culturally specific musical practice as its philosophical unit of analysis.

After Aesthetics: Praxis and Performance

By the end of the 20th century, a floodgate of philosophical research on music and music education poured forth, altering the educational terrain in profound ways. Some of this new scholarship was a sharp response to the dominant position that aesthetic philosophy enjoyed for decades; but much of it was the result of what one might call a professional incubation period out of which scholars claimed new theoretical territory and made the field of music education philosophy worldwide an exciting place to do research (McCarthy, M. & Goble, S., 2005). In 1990, Estelle Jorgensen founded the Special Research Interest Group (SRIG) in music education philosophy that was officially recognized by the research establishment of MENC that year. By 1993, Jorgensen launched the scholarly journal *Philosophy of Music Education Review*. This same year also saw the creation of the MayDay group, an independent philosophical organization founded by J. Terry Gates and Thomas Regelski for the dissemination of research on music education and critical theory. Meanwhile, several important books captured the excitement of this time: Elliott's *Music Matters* (1995), Jorgensen's *In Search of Music Education* (1997), and Christopher Small's *Musicking: The Meaning of Performing and Listening* (1998).

Some of these voices associated themselves with the term "praxis" which came to represent an action-based response to the widely held perception that mid-century aesthetic music education too closely resembled the passivity and high-art elitism of classic aesthetic theory (Alperson, 1991; Sparshott, 1987). *Praxis*, from the Greek word for practice, signifies the intersection of deliberate thinking and deliberate doing. One doesn't just think about music in its abstract,

contends Elliott; nor does one focus exclusively on music's structural properties independent of their social and cultural function. Rather, we understand,
enjoy, and participate in music for what it reveals about the very particular web of
relationships that constitute our lived world. "Music's primary meanings are not
individual at all," writes Christopher Small, "but social" (Small, 1998, p. 8). For
Small, there is no such thing as music, per se; rather, it exists as an action better
understood as a verb, not a noun. The act of "musicking [sic] establishes in the
place where it is happening a set of relationships, and it is in those relationships
that the meaning of the act lies" (1998, p. 13). Music may be universal, but it is
made manifest through culturally specifiable and culturally learnable practices.

This idea turns 19th century aesthetic philosophy on its head. Praxialism
has little room for a metaphorical world of feelings or ineffable insights into the
mysteries of humankind. Music is *not* nonconceptual, but to use Elliott's phrasing, music is the "em-body-ment" of replicable, understandable, and teachable
practices (Elliott, 1995, p. 58).[3] Instruction that is praxial would concern itself
with two related processes. First, the development of procedural know-how or
the skills and craft of a given tradition; and secondly, the development of musicianship: musical thinking that can match the demands of a given tradition with
the know-how to execute said tradition. "Developing musicianship is essentially
a matter of induction; students must enter and become part of the musical practices (or music cultures) they intend to learn. This is so because musicianship is
context-dependent" (Elliott, 1995, p. 67). From this perspective, there can be no
such thing as a course or class called "general" music. Any kind of general or liberal education in music must always be a *specialized* music education.

Elliott defines musicianship neatly: musical understanding is musicianship
and musicianship is musical understanding. In this light, it is useful to contrast *understanding something* from *knowing about something*. Understanding
requires, foremost, the "practice" of information or knowledge. Musicianship,
thus, is necessarily procedural; it is undergone, something done rather than
thought about. This does not mean, of course, that as musicians we don't think
about what we do or that we don't talk about and analyze isolated aspects of musical information. But for these analytical processes to make any sense at all, they
must be applied in a musical setting—in the performance or production of music.
Regarding questions of curriculum and the role praxialism would play in shaping
school-based music education, Elliott's philosophy recommends that all classes
in music become classes in the practice or performance of music.

New Voices and New Questions

Philosophy can be a maddening process for people who want complete answers.
Elliott offers a partial solution to the problem of aesthetics: that we know music
best through the actual work of doing of music and that schools should therefore become laboratories for the study and performance of music. But the praxial

---

[3] In this sense—contra Reimer—music is very much a learnable language.

emphases on technical skills and knowledge, and its umbrella term for procedural understanding, leave relatively unexplored the question of why schools should bother with music in the first place, nor are important ethical questions about *whose* music should be included in increasingly diverse public schools adequately addressed by praxialism. If real musical learning resembles a cultural internship, then the music teacher in a given classroom may be "culturally licensed" to teach only the musical style she grew up in. Students in such a scenario will experience only what the music teacher knows, likes, and is good at—and in all likelihood, this hypothetical music teacher was probably apprenticed in a Western classical style, less probably in the idioms of jazz, folk, or rock. The question remains, how do we approach the study of multicultural music? What about popular music? For Estelle Jorgensen, questions about shifting cultural landscapes, rapid technological change, social upheaval, commercial influences on education, and the inequitable distribution of resources demand that the music education profession consider a host of new seemingly unanswerable questions. She argues that we have come to an historical point where our teaching field must embark upon a new search for a philosophy that can speak to these conditions (Jorgensen, 1997).

Important to Jorgensen is the lifetime of choices a music educator must decide between (Jorgensen, 2003). Does such a teacher pass on or transmit what has gone on before him/her, or does he/she work as a meditating agent, adjusting to change and thereby acting to transform the culture he/she is teaching in? For those who wish to engage in transformative music teaching, a useful theoretical tool for framing one's curricula is the practice of "dialectical thinking." Recall that in ancient Greece, the term dialectic referred to the back and forth of an engaging conversation, where an interlocutor might take an opposing side just to see where an argument might lead. Likewise, in modern terms, the idea of dialectic is the simultaneity of opposing ideas, a this-with-that view, writes Jorgensen, "where various elements and perspectives are in tension with each other, one or another coming to the fore at a particular time and place as actors might move about on the stage" (Jorgensen, 2003, p. 56).

In Jorgensen's philosophy, disparate or opposing values do not seek to resolve or reconcile their inherent contradictions; each retains its identity without compromise. Take, for example, the conflict that surrounds the aesthetic and praxial debates. A dialectical stance asks educators to consider the merits of both perspectives and how they might be incorporated together. "Things in dialectic do not always mesh tidily, simply, or easily" (Jorgensen, 1997, p. 69). The tension that results is seen as a good thing; it refers to both the frustration and joy that music educators encounter when they refuse handed-down methods or philosophies that speak for them. The dialectical perspective, however, is not a mix and match approach where teacher choices occur willy-nilly. Rather, the educator in this context must act according to conscience, determining what is good for her students and what she can provide (see Chapter 10).

Recall that this chapter began with the Ancient Greek perspective that philosophy is a way of life and much more than the study of a text, or a required course in college. Unfortunately, the European tradition that survived ancient philosophy tended to drain experience from the study of philosophy (Hadot, 2002). As ideas took the place of experience, the history of philosophy moved away from the process dimensions of life, toward "isms," great books, and explanatory manifestos. Today's reengagement with the lived dimension of music is due, in large part, to the field of postmodern theory generally and feminist scholarship specifically, with scholars like Wayne Bowman, Lori Dolloff, Elizabeth Gould, Estelle Jorgensen, Julia Koza, Roberta Lamb, and others making important contributions to our profession. The feminist project, as such, seeks to expand what counts as meaningful, legitimate, and valuable in all spheres of life. Thanks to the work of feminist thinkers, artists, and activists, we see the world differently today, more varied than even a generation or two ago.

Maxine Greene is one of the first feminist writers in the field of arts education. She recalls how as a young woman philosopher she felt tempted to abandon the voice in which she wished to write in favor of the standard, masculine voice of objective authority. "I wanted so much to be accepted in the great world of wood-paneled libraries, authoritative intellectuals, sophisticated urban cafés. My response to the criticisms I received early on was to turn away from the local and particular in my life, to strive for an incarnation of values that promised to transcend gender and class and race" (Greene, 1995, p. 114). But being a woman, this was not an option. At Greene's interview for the position of professor of philosophy at Teachers College, Columbia University, she was made to wait in the ladies' restroom because women were not allowed into the all-male faculty room. Suddenly words like objective, normal, tradition, acceptance, authority, and intelligence become unstable and highly problematic. This wait room anecdote will ring true to anyone who has felt excluded from (or even uncomfortable in) a powerful community due to one's race, gender, sexual orientation, dis/ability, or class.

Greene, like many women writers, is concerned with questions of mutuality and the discovery of spaces where new ways of thinking and being might be uncovered and explored in common. There is a qualitative value to the experience of art that is at once extraordinary and personal. "I think that what we want to make possible is the living of lyrical moments, moments at which human beings (freed to feel, to know, and to imagine) suddenly understand their own lives in relation to all that surrounds" (Greene, 2001, p. 7). Encounters with the arts entangle us in relationships, and we are likely to experience a wonder about the world. At the same time, "technical culture tends to focus on abstract explanations; stress is laid upon objectivity and neutrality, on impersonal ways of looking at the world" (Greene, 2001, p. 30). Too often, schools ask us to "accede to the world," to accept the "plain sense of things" (Greene, 2001, p. 30). The arts are a way of undertaking the world lyrical spaces to test one's freedom and question "plain sense." Greene takes to task the anesthetic nature of schools, leadership that sees children as human resources, and a political preoccupation with economic competitiveness and standards. The arts are a counterweight to rationalist discourses: interrogative, incomplete and "useless in the sense they can't cure toothaches" (Greene, 2001, p. 158). The experience of art—performing, inter-preting, and attending to art—"is an act of confidence in the freedom of human beings," writes Greene, affording students "the freedom to interpret, to reflect, and (now and then) change our lives" (84).

Critique

The 1990s saw the emergence of music education philosophy as a diverse and challenging discipline. These days, most graduate students and many under-graduates are required to take courses in the philosophy of music education. Unfortunately, while the field of philosophy has helped to inform the practice of teacher education writ large, an articulated philosophical rationale for large performing groups that goes beyond the profession's utilitarian functionalism is missing from the music education community. Bands, choirs, and orchestras continue to rely on their "apparent-ness." Even with the leadership of perfor-mance educators like David Elliott and others, too little philosophical research is emanating from our conductors and performers. This is especially problematic because large ensembles represent the vast majority of our profession's resources and are often the most visible aspect of public music education.

CONCLUSION

Iris Murdoch once wrote: "philosophy has in a sense to keep trying to return to the beginning." It can be said that philosophy's failure is its lack of progress that no matter how hard we try, we will never really find answers to the ques-tions most worth asking. This chapter tells a story of music education philosophy, although it is certainly not the story of music education philosophy. It is intended to engage readers in a love of questions rather than an armchair stroll through a chronology of perspectives. But what this chapter's story reveals—this story of music, education, and philosophical history—is that the questions never end. It is reassuring to know that future generations will carry forth this task, and return-ing to their own beginnings, they will write their own story of music, education, and philosophy.

Class Discussion

1. What is philosophy good for? Why should music teachers concern them-selves with philosophy? How can philosophy help (or impair) the preservice and in-service educator?

2. What does Socrates mean when he asserts that one is both a teacher and a philosopher or neither? Do you agree with this statement? Cite an example of a teacher in your life who excelled in both roles. What pedagogical lessons can you draw from him or her?

3. For Socrates, the philosopher is like a "gadfly" whose job it is to sting oth-ers to think for themselves. What are the problems associated with this approach? How can a teaching perspective that is associated with pain be justified?

4. What are the problems with perceiving music as an "art object"? Is music a thing? A process? An experience? A function? What does Christopher Small mean when he asserts that music is a verb, not a noun? What are the implications of the following quote: "the act of musicking establishes in the place where it is happening a set of relationships, and it is in those relationships that the meaning of the act lies" (Small, 1998).

Projects

1. Write a brief paper that compares and contrasts the ideas associated with representationalism, expressionism, and formalism. Cite contemporary examples of each. How and where are each of these "isms" played out in the contemporary music classroom?

2. Write a dialogue between two philosophers representing contrasting views of the value of music education in the school curriculum.

3. Develop a rationale for music in your communities' schools. Your rationale should be appropriate for presentation to the Board of Education. Your statement should be brief, about two or three pages. It should be persuasive and in language appropriate for presentation to an informed lay audience.

SUGGESTED READINGS

Elliott, D. (Ed.). (2005). *Praxial music education: Reflections and dialogues*, New York: Oxford University Press.

Jaspers, K. (1954). *Way to wisdom: an introduction to philosophy.* New Haven, CT: Yale University Press.

Jorgensen, Estelle (2006). On philosophical method. In R. Colwell (ed.), *MENC Handbook of Research Methodologies* (pp. 176–198). Oxford: Oxford University Press.

Reimer, B. (2003). *A philosophy of music education: Advancing the vision* (5th ed.). Upper Saddle River, NJ: Prentice Hall.

CHAPTER 4

Meaning and Experience:
The Musical Learner

Lori A. Custodero

INTRODUCTION

An inquiry into music learning must start with how and why music is meaningful to students and teachers. Relevance connects us to subject matter and to people; it calls us to attend, participate, incorporate, and transmit. Lilla Belle Pitts, president of the Music Educators National Association from 1942 to 1944, wrote: "We are beginning to find that learning and teaching are not synonymous, that courses of study and courses of learning are not identical, and that the true curriculum for any learner, regardless of age, is everything [s]he 'goes through' or 'undertakes' in the course of living and experiencing" (1943, p. 21). The significance of experience is at the heart of understanding what is valued and what is possible for an education in music. Like each pitch of a song or symphony, we are shaped by the interactions of immediate context, in part defined by what has come before and the anticipation of what is to come: We make sense of our experiences through negotiations between what we are, what we do, and what we are becoming—through our identity, actions, and potential.

The meanings we make of music are constructed with others and are influenced by our social and material environments. We construct meaning *through* music, as it functions in our daily lives, providing a soundtrack to our physical, emotional, cognitive, and spiritual strivings. We also construct meanings *in* music, attending to images and interpretations of musical content as performers and audience members, and *with* music, in creative interactions with musical materials and ideas. This chapter addresses the making of musical meaning through the interconnected sensory, cognitive, and expressive modes of experience from a variety of disciplinary perspectives. The first question to address is "How is musical experience meaningful?" I begin this multifaceted inquiry through the most direct mode of interaction—embodiment, which is grounded in feelings and action. Embodied musical meaning is made through sensory engagement with sounds and provides a means of demonstrating implicit knowledge. Next,

I examine meaning as manifest in cognitive processing of musical experience. Here, external sources in contact with the internal interpretations make meaning through the structures and processes of organizing, labeling, and associating; it is deductive and explicitly shared, usually through language. The meaning made from creative experiences, through the thoughtful and purposeful expression of ideas, messages, and feelings may be the culminating act of conceptual knowing—to work with materials and understand them through their relationship to ourselves and our world(s).

Once "how" meaning is made has been explored, the experience of the music learner is considered in terms of contemporary music educational contexts and the difficult questions with which teachers must grapple. A view of learning through experience requires teachers to challenge some of our own assumptions (as Pitts suggests) in order to more fully understand the complexities of musical meaning in educative environments.

MUSICAL MEANING AND EMBODIMENT

Hold out your hands to feel the luxury of the sunbeams. ... Pile note on note the infinite music that flows increasingly to your soul from the tactual sonorities of a thousand branches and tumbling waters. ... if a fairy bade me choose between the sense of sight and that of touch, I would not part with the warm, endearing contact of human hands or the wealth of form, the mobility and fullness that press into my palms. (Keller, 1957, p. 25)

Musical experiences are corporeal; they are located in the body. This means that we experience the movement and associative aspects of music in correspondence with our physical being. Such musical knowing is intimate and renders us vulnerable to both welcomed and uninvited interaction, open to insight and exposed to irritation or invasiveness. When looking at a painting, we can make a choice to turn away or shut our eyes: however, we cannot shut our ears to unwanted sonic images. For music educators, this speaks to the depths at which our subject is connected to our common humanity and our differences; the directness of the musical "signal" suggests that we need to be aware of the meanings conveyed by our pedagogical choices.

The importance of embodied meaning in music education has been acknowledged across a spectrum of musical activity—from the use of Dalcroze Eurhythmics in general music classes, to marching bands whose members move and play simultaneously as a collective, to the incorporation of Alexander technique, an approach to body awareness often used as a coaching tool for advanced performers (Chin, 2006). In these examples, using our bodies to move with music provides insight into what music means—such as the discovery of a gesture whose intensity matches the sound. Reciprocally, the music brings new understandings of our physical selves as movement and sound are synchronized. Collective movement with others often engenders collective understanding.

Next, the characteristics of embodied meaning making are discussed in terms of technical and expressive skill, self regulation, and the sensory parallels between modalities.

Bodies of/as Knowledge

> In childhood the cognitive process is essentially poetic, because it is lyrical, rhythmic, and formative, in its generative sense: it is sensory integration of self and environment, awaiting verbal expression. The child knows or "re-cognizes" that he makes his own world, and that his body is a unique instrument, where the powers of nature and human nature met. (Cobb, 1977, p. 89)

If a 3-year-old child is asked to draw a picture of a fast car, she will most likely run the crayon around the paper as fast as she can (Gardner, 1982). Her representation actively portrays the concept by becoming it—this is similar for music as well. After a preschool group took a musical walk around the classroom, following the gradually accelerating tempo cues of Grieg's "Hall of the Mountain King" they were asked which picture looked like the end of the piece:

They chose the picture on the right, "because it looks like when we were almost running into each other at the end!" Such a representation demonstrates Cobb's claim: With the body as instrument, a visual representation is recognized as the child's experience.

Conducting calls upon the visual senses to represent movement as well. It is a gestural art, and one of its greatest exemplars was Leonard Bernstein, known as "Leaping Lenny" to some because of his exaggerated movements reflecting the score; he was often hailed as one of the most effective educators to work from the podium. In his Young People's Concerts, he spoke of meaning in music as "the way it makes you feel when you hear it … if it makes us change inside, then we are understanding it" (2005, pp. 27–28). He would have also appreciated the response above to the physical engagement with concepts: "It's all in the way music moves. We must never forget that music is movement, always going somewhere, shifting and changing and flowing from one note to another. That movement can tell us more about the way we feel than a million words can" (p. 28).

We use specific gestures to aid in pitch perception and production and to support musical skill development, making musical meaning of concepts through engaging the body. Conjure an image of a wind player reaching for a high note—are the eyebrows raised? Perhaps the most common example is the use of Curwen hand signs with solfege syllables, intended to augment singing accuracy. Research on language shows children's gestures are linked to learning, helping with cognitive skills like memory and referencing The intuitive wisdom that adding motions to songs helps children learn that material more effectively is born out in research: Gestures provide not only a way that learners can help advance their own skills through engaging multiple sensory modalities, but they also provide a way for teachers to instinctively know what the child needs to learn (Goldin-Meadow & Singer, 2003).

Gestures are also commonly used to facilitate technique in the applied studio, as when vocalists use their arms in sweeping gestures to mimic the opening up of their throat and to better project sound. Instrumental teachers demonstrate appropriate ways to hold the arms, fingers, and embouchure—students need to know what it feels like to apply the right amount of pressure as they bow a string or blow a horn. We learn through attending to what the instrument and the sound feels like, often preceded by attending to what it looks like when someone else plays. This type of knowing in the body relies on mimesis—actively imitating a given model (Tolbert, 2001). The mimetic function in music learning works both aesthetically, as we perceive how music takes on the properties of the natural world around us, and socially, as we take on the valued movement/ physical properties of specific people. In the former, we may sense the mimicking of "human correspondences," that is, how characteristics of music such as resolution, unison, and counterpoint, for example, have roots in human interaction. Focusing on people in order to partake in the musical process, music learners might mimic their favorite rock star, a peer with perceived expertise, or even their music teacher!

Because of interactions with other development traits (as discussed in Chapter 6), embodiment and mimesis takes on different guises across the lifespan. Its beginnings in early infancy in the mother-child interactive context provided the model of mimesis, which Trevarthen (1999) writes of as motive sharing, leading ultimately to the understanding of intention in another. In early childhood, what others have called "sympathetic kinaethesia" (see Davidson & Malloch, 2009) begins to flower—that is the movement response such as swaying or bouncing to music as heard in the environment. In middle childhood, learners become increasingly able to internalize their movement responses, learning to inhibit the urge to move in deference to their social awareness, and to use their words to describe sound phenomena. In adolescence, the internalized abstractions often call to be externalized in ways both in imitation of and in resistance to conventional thought-in-action. The role of social construction is clearly evident during this period, when identity is defined by the ways in which knowing in the body is demonstrated through physical responses to music as well as physical appearance. Such visual codes serve to conjoin groups and cohere the musical identity of various subcultures of youth, thereby providing a context for meaning making.

Embodied knowledge presents to others our direct relatedness to music, and re-presents recognizable and interpretable cues leading to learning and teaching. These characteristics of purposeful gesture and spontaneous movement response are linked to brain studies on "mirror neurons," which indicate that this nonverbal relating is the way we become social beings, understanding intentionality on the part of others (Molinar-Szakacs & Overy, 2006).

Embodied Structures: Modality, Regulation, and Plasticity

The subject matter of music education is experienced through multiple senses—we can *hear* sound; we can *feel* vibrations, instrument keys, and the resonance in our head when singing. We can *see* a score and/or a conductor or other representation of the music, including audience members and musicians moving to the rhythms and contours of our playing. *Proprioceptive* responses also contribute to how meaning is made; these are the physiological reactions to qualities of sound, like changes in heart beat rates or tears or "chills" (Panksepp, 1995). These multisensory experiences offer multiple entry points and contribute to the complexity and possibility of how musical meaning is constructed.

Neuroscientists' understanding of how the brain is wired for music has taken giant strides in the last decades due in part to new technology involving functional magnetic resonance imaging (*f*MRI), which has provided more detailed evidence of activation centers in the brain. The knowledge about the brain's structure has expanded from the conveniently simplistic dual hemispheric model of left brain/right brain to a modular model of brain regions where skill areas are more differentiated. This seems especially important for musical activity, which registers in both hemispheres, unlike language, which is localized to the left hemisphere (Turner & Ioanniddes, 2009). The multi-sensory nature of musical activity is seemingly mirrored in the brain's multiple locations for musical characteristics.

Most research on sensory interactions in musical experience deal with the visual and auditory modalities. An example of how they might work was offered earlier in the "Mountain King" episode described above. The motor area of the brain is activated even in listening to music; though we are able to inhibit unsanctioned movement with conscious effort, our minds are still dancing. And it seems like practicing matters: For performers, listening to pieces they had rehearsed resulted in more excitability in the motor cortex than did pieces which were novel (D'Ausilio, A., Altenmuller, E., Belardinelli, M.O., & Lotze, M., 2006).

Just as music provides many possibilities for engagement and links visual and aural modalities of experience, it also provides a resource for monitoring and adapting physical and psychic states when we need to regulate our activity (DeNora, 2000). We use music to structure our everyday lives and activity and to "make special" (Dissanayake, 1992) the every day and mundane. The structures of music—beat, meter, tonality—are used in therapeutic settings to offer patients means to help structure their experience. In neo-natal intensive care units, rocking and singing to premature infants often soothes them by helping them to regulate breathing and sucking, important in their ability to thrive (e.g., Standley, 2002). De Nora refers to music as a "prosthetic technology" (2000, p. 103), a device whose use expands human capabilities.

Adjusting one's physical state to match the salient characteristic of the music as heard—the swing of a waltz, the syncopated pattern of the bass line of a funk tune, the ethereal floating of Buddhist monks chanting—is called entrainment.

It is a uniting with sound, the process by which a baby is calmed through rocking and singing lullabies. It is also what the drummers of an infantry group generate as they control the moving of hundreds of troops through miles of desolate territory and what hearing Aretha Franklin sing "R E S P E C T!" does to invigorate an aerobics class. Entrainment engenders synchronous activity, which can be meaningful in both socially positive and negative ways.

Linking Body and Mind: Musical Meaning, Feelings, and Emotions

Throughout this discussion of embodied meaning, the work of neuroscientists has been purposefully woven into the fabric alongside educator and anthropologist views. Damasio's (2003) focus on the 17th century philosopher, Spinoza, and his claim that "the mind is the idea of the human body" (p. 12) sets the stage for an examination of how emotions lead to feelings and their role in music educational settings. The direct and unfiltered quality of musical experience and its expressive nature may be at the heart of why scholars have been considering the body as an untrustworthy source and have chosen to dichotomize mind and body in both philosophical and empirical approaches to research. The roots of this thinking are historically deep—in ancient Greece, there were Dionysian and Apollonian musical practices, the first representing the physical, spontaneous, and intuitive side of music, and the second, the rational and measured.

Feelings and emotions are what create meaning from experiences, serving to integrate doing and thinking. Damasio (2003) writes "Mental processes are grounded in the brain's mapping of the body, collections of neural patterns that portray responses to events that cause emotions and feelings" (p. 12). So, for the neuronal circuitry to engage, we must experience the active emotion in the body, which is represented in a mental image as feeling. This integration is central to development and learning, and is influenced by interpersonal relationships in the educational context (Siegel, 1999). Music connects us to our selves through feelings; this meaning-making process is strengthened by its occurrence in positive social contexts.

Ultimately, meaning is made through connections, and embodiment may be the most intimate connection we make to music, leaving us vulnerable to the consequences of unexpected memories or general mood states being evoked through associations with specific music. Hubbard (2007) refers to this as a "lending of self" in her discussions on adolescents' interpretations of visual art. The ease in which music can be associated with strong feelings has implications for music learners, suggesting both much potential for personal growth and also a need to approach musical choices with caution and sensitivity.

When we ask students to listen to music, we are asking that they attend to the sound. Focused and engaged, they process their immediate musical experience through the filters of past experiences, current awareness, and hypothesized future. When we think in music, we are making connections to memories, resources in the environment and expectations. The connections made through embodiment lead to implicit understandings inasmuch as they are demonstrated in behavior, and come from integrated sensory experience. "Being with" the moment precludes more distanced reflection that makes musical meaning more explicit. However, in the context of doing, we may connect so strongly to an "outside" relative experience that we are temporarily taken away from the immediate musical context in order to comprehend the larger implications of what it offers. Often dismissed as "off-task" behavior, we might reconsider some of the messages students are providing when they appear to disengage. Creating time for reflecting on musical experience is key to making meaning, yet how often do teachers include such opportunities in a lesson or rehearsal plan?

Reflection on experience results in meaning making, articulating understanding through relevant connections to past and present and possibilities for the future. In the following section, supportive structures and processes that facilitate and build upon these connections are discussed.

PROCESSING EXPERIENCE: COGNITIVE STRUCTURES AND CONNECTIONS

Our processes of acquiring musical understandings are guided by structures: Configurations in the music, in our physicality, and in our neurology, which both define and enable redefinition in adapting to new situations. Structures of music such as tonality, meter, and formal motivic and thematic organization are culturally recognized frameworks that provide a foundation for our making meaning of familiar and novel information. Serafine (1988) realized this in her generative study entitled *Music as Cognition,* in which she claimed existing theories of music had no meaning because they could not simultaneously refer to both the processes and products of music making. She addressed the role of musical structures in generating thinking-in-music, and characterized them as either temporal (simultaneous or successive) or non-temporal (closure, transformation, abstraction, hierarchic levels).

The structures of our bodies provide a framework for making meaning of elemental and extended characteristics of sound. A pulsing heartbeat, whose tempo is responsive to dramatic events, is an example of a foundational structure, which, like the "Mountain King" example, has variability. Our bipedal body structure dictates a duple mobility, as we walk left, right, left, right, we reinforce a basic form from which to map our experience of metric divisions. We can interpret the differences between the precision of a march and the lilt of a waltz, because they exaggerate or resist patterns defining our physical reality.

Our neurological structures are gloriously multifaceted and complex; and our understandings of how they operate are based on a rapidly growing field of inquiry. Given this situation, the necessary caveat that it is beyond the scope of this chapter to address this topic in detail is offered and readers are referred to the bibliography (e.g., Levitin, 2006; Patel, 2008). One of the more common misconceptions we have about how the brain is structured concerns the location of musical processing—it is not, as was a popular belief in past decades, limited to the right hemisphere, considered to be the "creative" side. We now know much more about the functions of specific regions of the brain, and know that musical activity is represented in almost every region of the brain. This wide distribution of specialized processors means that musical activity requires the integration of parts to make sense of information. See Figure 4.1 for a view of the brain regions associated with specific musical activity.

Information processing is probably the most widespread model used to describe the way we process data that is represented as sensory memory, long-term memory, and working memory. Sensory memory is the retention of large amounts of information for a short term—the structural limitations here are with time of accessibility. Long-term memory is stored as three types of representations: (1) specific events or episodes (perhaps your first performance on your major instrument); (2) stable qualities or "facts," such as the concept of a triad and what it looks like in conventional notation; and (3) procedural, or how to do something, like singing a song learned in childhood. We can retrieve whole memories or components of these events, facts, or procedures stored in long-term memory. Automatization is a process where the sensory memory is converted into long-term memory, when experience with a required skill, say transferring certain notational conventions from the score to our fingers, embouchures, and vocal mechanisms becomes automatic and requires less cognitive engagement than sight-reading a passage which contains non-conventional patterns. When portions of a task can be relegated to occur automatically, attention is freed to focus on the less familiar aspects of the task.

Working memory is associated with active thinking and finding solutions to immediate problems, drawing from sensory memory and long-term memory as needed. This system reads information in workable units or "chunks." It is estimated that the maximum number that can be processed at any one time ranges from 3 to 7. The size of each unit depends on how related they are—each unit must be a *meaningful* whole, so our ability to process information is a result of our understanding of the particular content area with which we are engaged. This may have ramifications for the adage, "the more you know, the more you know you need to know," since bigger chunks (relating more pieces to one another) allow a greater realm of possibilities to be considered. Retaining information in working memory is enhanced with practice and improves with age.

Musicians perceive sound differently than nonmusicians because experience breeds familiarity, and concept formation is aided when one can identify or encode what she hears. Encoding involves attention to a recognizable context. An early study showed learners who had started to play an instrument early were more likely to have absolute pitch (Sargeant, 1969); what we know now is that it could be linked to the categorical context for pitch that playing an instrument provides. We encode pitch according to corresponding contexts such as scale and key. People who have spent years singing and/or teaching in either fixed or movable systems often have trouble when asked to switch systems. They have

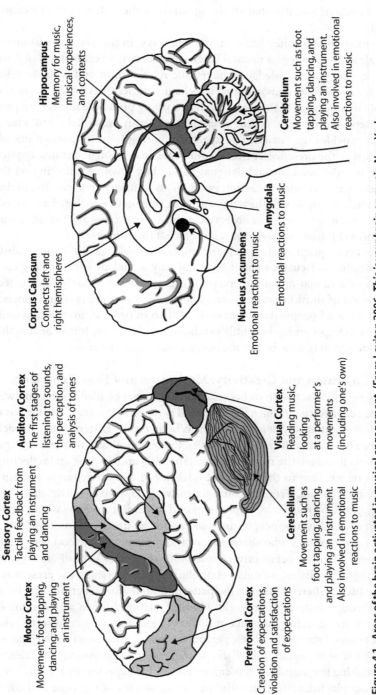

Figure 4.1. Areas of the brain activated in musical engagement. (From Levitan 2006. *This is your brain on music.* **New York: Plume, 270–271.)**

Sensory Cortex
Tactile feedback from playing an instrument and dancing

Auditory Cortex
The first stages of listening to sounds, the perception, and analysis of tones

Motor Cortex
Movement, foot tapping, dancing, and playing an instrument

Visual Cortex
Reading music, looking at a performer's movements (including one's own)

Cerebellum
Movement such as foot tapping, dancing, and playing an instrument. Also involved in emotional reactions to music

Prefrontal Cortex
Creation of expectations, violation and satisfaction of expectations

Hippocampus
Memory for music, musical experiences, and contexts

Cerebellum
Movement such as foot tapping, dancing, and playing an instrument. Also involved in emotional reactions to music

Corpus Callosum
Connects left and right hemispheres

Nucleus Accumbens
Emotional reactions to music

Amygdala
Emotional reactions to music

established contexts for pitch that are disrupted when the system of identification is changed.

Learners show what they know in different ways. In the example just given, singing scale tones in solfege, a musical language of sorts, is an explicit way of demonstrating conceptual knowledge of intervallic relationships and scale. Implicit cognition is experiential, demonstrated in behavior rather than words. An example of implicit knowledge of the scale would be a young preschool learner jumping down the steps singing a descending scalar patter. It is an embodied way of knowing, and so provides the "insider" perspective, coming from immersing oneself in *doing* music—the preschooler became the scale descending the stairs. Explicit knowledge is articulated through language and often involves reflecting on the experience, afterward. Such reflection provides an "outsider" perspective, giving distance a chance to hold still the temporal event so it may be revisited and considered. Implicit knowledge can be observed in children as young as 12 months; and by age 5, most children can verbalize some of what they understand.

Awareness of qualities of explicit and implicit knowledge acquisition should keep us mindful and curious about how and why a student is expressing connections to or articulating an understanding about music. Broadly interpreted, these two ways of thinking can be complementary, and there is some evidence that highly focused people dance between the two in order to understand their subject matter deeply and to be highly productive and creative. It may be that this reflection-in-action is what brings meaning to our musical pursuits.

Between Cognition and Creativity: Motivation and Flow Experience

Music may be so attractive to us because it has inherent challenges that are well suited to our capabilities. From a physiological perspective, *music challenges us to be completely attentive with mind and body*. Whether we are listening to a musical performance or making the music ourselves, the temporal nature of music experience calls us to stay in the moment, simultaneously anticipating and reflecting, our bodies responding to the corporeal qualities of tempo, dynamic intensity, and harmonic tension. From a communicative perspective, *music challenges us to express and be responsive to personal and cultural meanings*. We associate music with specific events, people, and places—music transports us, bonding us together in communities who share understanding that goes beyond verbal language. From a cognitive perspective, *music challenges us perceptually, to organize sound in time*. As we listen, we must retain the past to understand the present and predict the future, thereby discovering patterns and formal structures that bring meaning through ordering our world. Finding relationships in sound reminds us that there are unifying elements in the world and that we may also be resonant with others. From an aesthetic perspective, *music challenges us to elaborate the everyday, and to "make special" the sounds we create* (Dissanayake, 2000b). Through making the mundane musical, we elevate life experiences, transforming activities into playful, artful, beautiful moments, worthy of our time and effort. Making music adds value to time spent in active engagement.

When challenge can be interpreted as something positive, it can create sustained involvement through meaningful experience. Challenging activity is welcomed if it occurs in a enjoyable activity: Consider the following dialogue from an interview with two 12-year-old girls (Custodero, 2003). G1 is in a community chorus:

R: It sounds like what both of you are saying is that if something is really challenging it's not a fun thing. Is that true, do you think?

G1: No, it's not always. Well, sometimes it could be, but sometimes it could be really fun. Like mountain climbing, some people say it's really challenging, but some people really enjoy it, and-

G2: Like math homework. It's really challenging but you don't want to do it.

G1: Yeah. So there's different things. It depends on whether you like it or you don't like it.

R: So what about some of this music stuff?

G1: I like it so it's fun for me.

R: So if that was really challenging it would be a positive thing for you?

G1: Yeah

This linking of challenge and fun has significant implications for music learning. Csikszentmihalyi (e.g., 1975, 1997) studied artists and surgeons, and yes, G1, he also studied rock climbers (!) to see how and why people engaged in focused and complex activity. Many of the participants indicated that their ideas "flowed" without effort, giving neuroscientists reasons to study the role of implicit cognitive strategies in this psychological state of "flow" (Dietrich, 2004). Below is a list of flow experience characteristics adapted from Csikszentmihalyi (1997) with annotations linking to musical meaning:

Perception of high skills match perception of high levels of challenge. What is often missed here is whose perception determines the experience, that is, the individual or student, rather than the observer or the teacher. This makes it incumbent upon music educators to look to the student to know whether they are bring appropriately challenged. When skills are more developed than the challenge requires—boredom ensues. When skills are less developed, then anxiety is the usual outcome.

Goals are clear. There are cues common to each musical culture that provide predictability as to the direction of the sounds. For example, in western music we can expect the piece to end with a certain chord based on the scale established at the beginning (culturally encoded).

Feedback is immediate. We can hear music, we can see other people moving to music and sometimes see musical notation as we perform, and we can feel music in our bodies as we perform it and listen to it. All these sensory possibilities for immediate feedback coalesce in musical experience, compelling our complete attention and fueling our ability to adjust our actions.

Action and awareness merge. Because of the features mentioned above, doing and thinking are fused together and we can be fully present in the moment of musical creation and/or interpretation, hence the forging implicit understandings.

Concentration is deep. Since music offers so many venues of attention, we can devote our entire selves to the musical experience. Many people speak of losing their sense of time and being transported by music—such complete involvement may also help develop dispositions that transfer to other areas.

Control is possible. The sense of agency that the arts provide individuals means that in an artistic endeavor what we do matters. This sense of consequential action provides evidence necessary for experiencing self-efficacy.

Self-consciousness disappears. Related to the involvement cited above, music motivates us by virtue of its temporal nature, inviting us as audience to join the performers on the path of expressive rendering or inviting us as composers and improvisers to create the path.

In the context of this chapter, flow experience might be described as the state in which meaning is sought through active engagement with challenging and enjoyable musical activity.

THE "CREATING" MIND: CONSTRUCTING AND INTERPRETING MUSIC

When presented with a perceived opportunity, learners' intuition and knowledge merge in efforts to interpret or create meaning. Such reliance on existing personal resources makes expressive renderings interesting and valid sources of information about learners and learning. Feldman (1994) makes a case for creativity as a developmental strategy, as children re-create for themselves the process of working with materials in service to problem solving or problem finding tasks. Creativity, in this view, is a way of learning rather than an individual trait, which is currently the most conventional view. In addition to viewing creativity as located in the learner, investigations into the role of culture and context are generating new theories as to how and why we may be creative.

These differences in perspectives on creativity should not be new to most musicians enculturated in the Western European tradition, who have been exposed to the stories comparing Mozart and Beethoven. The first was notorious for having compositions so clearly conceived before writing them down, that he rarely did revisions; the second was equally infamous for his reconsiderations of notated decisions, scribbled notes in the margins of musical scores, reflecting the evident labor. Mozart's style might best be described in today's vernacular as "crystallized" or gestalt experience, meaning form and content merged in a single image; Beethoven's style may be compared to a characteristic referred to as "discovery orientation" (Getzels & Csikszentmihalyi, 1976), a willingness on the part of the artist to change their original intent as a result of allowing the artistic materials to "speak" to them about the next "right" note or brush stroke. Tchaikovsky wrote a letter in June of 1878 in which he was describing such a process. He talked about transcribing his work from the original sketches and how it "is something more than copying, it is actually a critical examination, leading to correction, occasional additions, and frequent curtailments" (excerpted in Barron, Montuori, & Barron, 1997, p. 183).

These dispositional differences between creative people suggest there may be multiple definitions of the creative process. As might be expected, scholars also vary in their approaches—research has usually focused on either testing for creativity as a trait in the general population or case studies of individuals who have demonstrated remarkable creative productivity. Aspects of intention, value, structures, and the interaction between core content and cultural interpretation are all evident in the research over the past century.

A Chronology Creative of Scholarship

Guilford (1950, 1957) was interested in how intellectual aptitudes, in general, were related to creativity. His model of the intellect is a system of bifurcation, beginning with division into memory and thinking, He further divides thinking by what he terms "actions"—that is *cognition* (what he terms "awareness"), a responsive *production*, and an *evaluation* of that product. The act of producing is further broken down into convergent and divergent categories; and it is the latter that he calls creativity.

Three characteristics of creativity were especially salient to Guilford: fluency, flexibility, and originality. Fluency refers to a collection of traits measured by idea- and word-associations, and favors the quantity of responses generated; fluency also includes expressivity.[1] Flexibility refers to variation in the ways items can be conceptualized; one might say flexibility represents a proclivity for possibilities. Guilford identifies verbal and nonverbal types of flexibility, and considers the ability to adapt as a type flexibility used in problem solving. Originality was a different skill revealed in testing through unconventional responses.

Torrance (1984a) carried on this tradition of inquiry testing and measurement of creativity, especially notable in his longitudinal work with high school- and elementary-aged students. He was interested in the construction of tasks with measurement tools with more varied and relevant tasks. Below is a list of skills that are tested in the figural (or non-verbal) part of the Torrance Test for Creative Thinking.

1. Fluency, number of responses.
2. Flexibility, number of ways circles or lines were used.
3. Originality, unusualness, or rarity of the response.
4. Elaboration, number of details that contribute to the "story" told by the response.
5. Abstractness of the title, level of abstraction of the response.

---

[1] Swanwick (1999) has used the term fluency in descriptions of music learning, drawing parallels to language learning in the way we might play and sing music before score reading, in the same say we learn to speak before we read words.

6. Resistance to closure on the incomplete figures or the ability to "keep open."
7. Emotional expressiveness of the response.
8. Articulateness of storytelling, putting the response in context, giving it an environment.
9. Movement or action shown in the response.
10. Expressiveness of the titles, ability to transform from the figural to the verbal and give expression.
11. Synthesis or combination, joining together two or more figures and making it into a coherent response.
12. Unusual visualization, seeing and putting the figure in a visual perspective different from the usual.
13. Internal visualization, seeing objects from the inside.
14. Extending or breaking the boundaries, getting outside the expected.
15. Humor, juxtaposition of two or more incongruities.
16. Richness of imagery, showing variety, vividness, liveliness, and intensity.
17. Colorfulness of imagery, exciting, appeal to the senses, flavorful, earthy, emotionally appealing.
18. Fantasy, unreal figures, magic, fanciful fairy tale characters, science fiction characters.

Abilities tested on the figural forms of the TTCT (Torrance, 1988).

Peter Webster (1990) modeled his approach on the concept of creative thinking in music as linked to divergent thinking skills. In the 1980s, he was developing tests to measure creativity, following in the path of Torrance. They involve such things as using a sponge ball to roll across the piano and playing questions and answer games with temple blocks, and imaginations are engaged with images of rain, elevators, frogs, and robots. Traits like originality, extensiveness, and flexibility, as well as musical syntax were assessed. Built on a comprehensive theory of creative thinking in music, this work provides an important contribution to our attempts to understand children's creativity. These clinical tasks showed children's responses to be random before the age of 6, whereas ecological studies have found discernible structures in the creative renditions of very young children.

Expanding the traits of divergent and convergent thinking, Csikszentmihlyi (1996) describes the personality of creative individuals as dynamic and complex, operating within the dialectic tensions of paired qualities. They are (1) energetic and at rest; (2) smart and naïve; (3) playful and disciplined; (4) imaginative and rooted in reality; (5) extroverted and introverted; (6) humble and proud; (7) masculine and feminine; (8) traditional/conservative and rebellious/iconoclastic; (9) passionate and objective; (10) sensitive to both pain and joy. These traits also help explain the diversity within and between creative individuals and the types of products they invent and construct. This complexity also may help us understand students' seemingly inconsistent behaviors and attitudes, calling upon teachers to be inquirers and to ask why unexpected actions occur, using our own creativity to suggest possibilities.

Universal or Domain Specific

Like general IQ and the concept of multiple intelligences, creativity research has also been studied from both the universal and the specific. Milgram (1990) presents an interesting case related to the concept of flow experience discussed above. She categorizes creativity as either general or domain (or talent-) specific. Feldman had to wrestle with his own seemingly incongruent points of departure—his studies of child prodigies and his developmental theory of transformation (1982)—the first being a demonstration of particular creativity and the second being, a generalized version. He came up with a continuum that linked the two as extreme cases:

Universal   Cultural   Discipline-based   Idiosyncratic   Unique

If we are to apply the notion of creativity as being domain specific in music education, we have models in practice. From 1966 to 1972, the Manhattanville Music Curricula Project was funded by the U.S. Department of Education to explore ways to improve the quality of music education in elementary and secondary schools. The result was a curricular approach based in authentically musical activity—that is, domain-specific modes of creative expression, such as performing, composing and improvising. Activities were posed as problems to be solved, and this process involved teachers as learners as well. Lenore Pogonowski, a key figure in this project, writes "The creative classroom functions optimally when the teacher, as well as each student, is involved in creative discovery, forming a community of musical inquirers" (2001, p. 26).

Domain specific ideas about creative people must emanate from more select groups than the general population. Therefore, the types of research often done to support this field are case studies—in depth research on the lives of individuals who are generally thought to be creative. Perhaps the most important work in that field was done by Howard Gruber (1993) in his monumental work on the life of Charles Darwin. From this type of focused research, scholars have developed theories regarding influences on creativity—enabling conditions and systems that support the individual's ability to contribute.

Conditions that Support and Inhibit Creativity

Motivation is a key factor in creativity and speaks to the meaning of particular activities—we are generally motivated to do things that are intrinsically meaningful to us. Hennesey and Amabile (1993) write of the importance of "task motivation" (p. 15) and the two components that define its trajectory: the individual's attitude toward the task, and the presence or absence of cues in the environment. People seem to be most creative when they are intrinsically motivated; creativity is inhibited when external factors such as the evaluation, surveillance, or competition are employed. Restricted choice and reward also have been shown to have negative effects on creativity. It seems that rewards take away from the intrinsic desire to work on a task, as reported in experimental studies involving people who reported having high enjoyment for a particular activity (Deci, 1995). They were rewarded each time they engaged in that activity; and then the rewards were withheld. When the rewards were stopped, the interest in the activity had been replaced by the interest in the reward, and the activity stopped as well. By providing extrinsic rewards for engaging in music activity, it may be that teachers are robbing students of developing an intrinsic and potentially lifelong practice orientation in music.

Steps, Stages, and Systems of Creativity

Most theorists agree that the general steps in the creative process are closely tied to Wallas' (1926) proposition, which included preparation, incubation, illumination and revision. These steps have been expanded by various contemporary scholars such as Hennesey and Amabile (1993), who list problem presentation, preparation, idea generation, and validation as the key steps in what they perceive to a universal process. Csikszentmihalyi (1996) discusses the importance of identifying problems, or problem finding, as a significant step in the process.

Taylor (1959) looked over time to suggest developmental stages of creativity. Beginning with children's play behaviors which he referred to as Spontaneous, these continued with Expressive, Productive, Inventive, Innovative, and finally, Emergenative, which he felt was rare and culminated in the creation of a new disciplinary domain. In music, Kratus (1995) has theorized about a similar series of steps in improvisation ranging from Exploration (Level 1) to Personal Improvisation (Level 7).

The ideas of individual traits and domain specificity are acknowledged in Csikszentmihalyi's theory of creativity. He interprets the production of creative work in a systems approach that situates the individual in a certain historical time within a domain of expertise. These factors give rise to a focused perception of opportunity and lead the individual to moments of illumination, as described above. The value of the creative work is determined by a field of experts or stakeholders in the domain. Considering the interactions of these facets explain why some musicians may have considered themselves "ahead of their time," when their music writing or playing was not readily embraced by the field. For Donald Pond, a composer involved in an 8-year study observing the musical play of young children in the 1930s to 1940s, the field was music educators and he had to wait over 30 years until the findings from the study were acknowledged within the community at a Music Educators National Conference (MENC) regional conference (Pond, 1979).

Yet Pond might have been gladdened to find that good things come to those who wait. The National Standards, although perhaps not all encompassing, have included improvisation and composition as content areas—a bold and risky move with the possibility of transforming music educational practice or at least challenging it a bit.

In considering how learners might make meaning, we looked at how meaning is experienced through our sensory, cognitive, and creative capacities. As a way to apply these ideas directly to music education contexts, three key issues for music learners and their teachers are addressed, around agency and power, musical content and difference, and value and inclusion. The first of these challenges considers who controls the making of musical meaning, and addresses how we position ourselves in regards to learners. Second, given differing backgrounds that learners bring to educational settings, the universality of musical meanings is questioned in terms of what is core and what is cultural. Finally, as a way to interrogate how our profession names what we do and how that activity is placed in domains, relative to others, the notion of what is valued is interrogated. Such comparisons provide opportunities to consider meaning making across music disciplines and provide direction for future efforts to keep our work contextually relevant and musically authentic.

KEY ISSUES IN MUSIC LEARNING

Positioning Action and Intention: A Tale of Two Theories

Of the many theoretical perspectives that have come in and out of favor in the past century, it is Behaviorism and Constructivism that perhaps best inform our understanding of the differences in attitudes toward learning that permeate not only trends in pedagogy and curriculum but also the research in music education. Behaviorism carries with it a positivistic attitude about control and the existence of a single truth (Howe & Berv, 2000): for teaching this might be expressed in the belief that learning is predictable and dependent upon the controlled delivery of instruction. Constructivism, whose pedagogical roots are in the work of Piaget and Vygotsky (See Chapters 5 and 6 in this volume), is expressed in the belief that learning is variable and dependent on the learner's immediate and past experiences with the material content of instruction. At the risk of oversimplification, it may be broadly stated that behaviorist teaching is the purposeful delivery of information under strictly limited conditions, intended to elicit a predicted response. Constructivist teaching is the purposeful design of contexts that allow for student discovery and multiple possibilities for response.

Behaviorism came out of a need in the early 20th century to "make scientific" the study of actions by looking at others rather than within ourselves (Howe & Berv, 2000). This felt need was in direct opposition to philosophical traditions that had informed education for so long as well as to the parallel psychoanalytic movement based on introspective reflection. Propelled by earlier Darwinian discoveries supporting our biological relationship to animals and the concomitant research on animal behavior, inquiry about human behavior began to become more systematized.

Evidence of learning was demonstrated by a predicted behavioral response to a controlled situation, guided by a belief that people are conditioned to respond by either positive or negative associations with the task. Learners are then operating not out of volition but from manipulations of the setting to cause a predicted result; they are motivated by rewards and fear of punishment. This stance assumes that behavioral response to the presentation of a stimulus is universal, that it can be predicted and, therefore, be controlled. For behaviorists, the locus of learning is the teacher, who controls student motivation through systems of rewards.

In comparison, in constructivist teaching the locus of control for learning is clearly in the student, who is viewed as responsible for the inquiry and ultimate meaning making. Two schools of thought have arisen around the issues raised by general constructivist theorizing: Von Glaserfield's (1995) radical constructivism and Gergen's (1994) social constructionism. In the first, focus is on the individual construction of knowledge; in the second, it is the culture into which a learner is born and the social settings in which she constructs meaning that are the salient factors in the learning process.

Although music educators have found constructivist perspectives helpful in providing insight into studio and classroom teaching, there remain traditions within the field that resist a constructivist approach. Expert-apprentice relationships in applied teaching and learning contexts, and director-follower models for large ensembles seem permanently ensconced in the system of education, at least in the United States. The development of programs with smaller ensembles and an emphasis on creating in "garage band" formats are constructivist strategies that have provided options to serve learners in new ways (e.g., Allsup, 2003).

Even with these strides, questions remain unaddressed concerning the locus of meaning making in music educational settings. If what we teach is not what is learned, then what IS learned? Perhaps we can take from Behaviorism the idea that what learners do tells us something about what they are learning, expanding the theory to include the ideas of implicit demonstrations of knowledge. However, instead of controlling the behavior, we might stop and ask "What are your actions telling me about what is meaningful to you?"

Interpreting "Core" and Cultural Meanings

Phillip Phenix was an educational philosopher active in the mid-20th century. He writes that "general education is the process of engendering essential meanings" (1964, p. 5). Following Phenix, we might say that music education involves engendering essential *musical* meanings. Essential meanings infer the existence of universal experiences that are inherent and fundamental, and that may serve to articulate cross-disciplinary connections. For example, the field of ethnomusicology arose from a need to know about culturally varied musical practices; it continues to flourish because, as Merriam (1964) noted at the beginning stages of the discipline, we are ultimately interested in our sense of humanity, manifest in the common capacity for making and enjoying music. Contemporary scholars attribute meaning making to a sense of narrative—stories and systems drawn from the complexities of their experience (Bruner, 1990; Dissanayake, 2000b). These perspectives allude to intention and directionality, and to some type of disruption or tension. Two examples of personal encounters with music serve to demonstrate the relevance of these views of meaning making.

Symphonic Simplicity

It was one of the first meetings I had with a small group of about eight members of the New York Philharmonic who had self-selected to be part of a new venture, a series of concerts designed especially for children between the ages of 3–5 years and their parents. Memories are still clear around how committed they each were to doing this well, which meant understanding not only the music they were performing but how best to convey meaning to this new audience. This particular meeting focused on sharing the idea of matching sound to iconic image and what it meant to see representation that looked like what was simultaneously heard. I played a recording of Saint-Saen's "Kangaroos" from the *Carnival of the Animals*, holding up a small listening map with colored dots and blocks representing the rhythmic durations, texture, contour, and form of the piece. As the 1:18 went by, my hands danced across the "score," embodying the qualities of perceived sound. At the end of this simple, very familiar work, the room was filled with the sounds of delight—joyful applause and awestruck laughter. It seemed that somehow, the sensory integration of sight and sound had elicited a similar response in these expert musicians as it has consistently evoked in young children.

Using MRI technology, neurological research has investigated aural and visual pattern recognition suggesting the possibility that a relationship between what is seen and what is heard may be essential to how we make meaning from music (Norton et al., 2005). This cross-modal indication is not limited to notated representation but has also been extended to visual properties of observed performances (e.g., Chapidos & Levitin, 2008), which seem to influence the emotional experiences of listeners.

Misreading Mambo

In the spring of 2002, I attended a children's community event at a park in the eastern United States; there were craft projects to make, games to play, food to buy, and an Afro-Cuban band playing in the background. I was enjoying the music, moving to the undulating rhythms, when a friend came up to explain to me they were singing about the events occuring on September 11, a few months before. Suddenly aware of conflicting interpretations, I quickly stopped moving and proceeded to listen with due reverence to the composer's intention.

Such a clash indicates the danger of assumptions around cultural mediation—although the symbol system of rhythms and harmonies were shared, the language was not. Bruner (1990) describes meaning as "a culturally mediated phenomenon that depends upon the prior existence of a shared symbol system" (p. 69). Bruner's definition suggests meaning is determined by the social context in which it is experienced and the extent to which those in that environment share a common understanding of what music represents. Cultural sensitivity is directly linked to the creation of meaning, and it is especially important to maintain a diligent watch on our interpretations, especially in musical cultures with which we have had little direct experience. In music teaching and learning, how do the spaces of interaction support common or "core" elements of meaning making and honor difference? How do the moments of experience, when we are "inside," interact with reflection, when we step "outside"? How do we read the universal and particular? Musical meaning gleaned from the core understanding can be both resilient and responsive to difference, calling for sensitivity to local-ized cultural meanings that may be consonant or dissonant with the outsider view.

Naming and Claiming: The Meaning of Music in Music Education

Meaning making is influenced by what and how we name things, and in the conceptualizing of musical meaning in education we must seriously consider what is meant by music. Howard Gardner created a great stir when he included music as one of seven "intelligences" in his Multiple Intelligence (MI) theory (1983): Musical, Logical-mathematical, Linguistic, Bodily-kinesthetic, Spatial, Intrapersonal, and Interpersonal. After many years of trying to find a place for the specialized skills exhibited by Darwin, he added an eighth intelligence, Naturalist. His definition of an intelligence was "The ability to solve a prob-lem or fashion a product that is valued in at least one culture or community" (1997, p. 3). These intelligences were not related to general IQ and met the fol-lowing criteria: they were observable in individuals with brain damage as well as in specially gifted populations like prodigies and savants; and they reflected an existing set of operations and symbol system. When asked what was special about musical intelligence, he evoked the then new research on spatial-temporal reasoning and replied that it may have a "privileged role in the organizing of cognition" (p.10).

When music is conceptualized as intelligence, then the development of musical skill is determined by a diverse array of aptitudes inasmuch as MI theory invites a variety of possible music making roles such as composer, per-former, or critic. Gardner describes the first of those as the most closely linked to musical intelligence, while the second may have strengths in kinesthetic and interpersonal intelligences and the third, additional proclivities in the area of linguistic intelligence. It is possible that the ability to observe and notice details about our surroundings, described as naturalist intelligence, may be linked to teaching.

In defining music as cognition or as intelligence, meanings are inferred around who is making it, the practices surrounding it, and where and when it is experienced. Blacking (1990) was interested in the differences between musical thought and musical intelligence. He wrote that the latter was a cross-cultural attribute, reflected in the "cognitive and affective equipment of the brain" (p. 72), that it was an abstract system of ordering related to other skills, and that it represented the belief that all human beings are musically competent. Musical thought is the keeper of diversity, manifested in culturally-specific practices including listening, performing, composing, and talking about music: it is dependent upon social context.

The social component of music supports the conception of music as language, and it is the argument of musical thought that resists the notion of a universal language. The scholarly relationship between music and language has been complex—we have drawn it close by using language-based research to substantiate the acquisition of musical skills and kept it at bay when making a case for music as a unique intelligence, separate from linguistic intelligence.

Music and language have been inextricably linked through the medium of song. From the lullaby to the requiem, from folk song to aria, when combined, music intensifies language's meaning. Yet music teachers often find it necessary to break those links in order to help children focus on tone by comparing "singing voice" and "speaking voice" or by offering wordless patterns to be imitated in order to draw attention to pitch accuracy.

The issue speaks to how we run our classrooms—how much music verses language is heard, seen, and practiced? What types of values come along with specific meanings we give music? Linguistic information has a shared semantic; music, however, communicates through the shared pulse, the synchronicity of "two hearts beating as one." This temporal nature of music—the shared sense of how time is experienced—is at the root of communicative musicality (Malloch & Trevarathan, 2008). If musical meaning is conceptualized as language, then the communicative meaning is valued, and pedagogy would support students' ability to listen and respond. It is expected that all members of a community learn a shared language, suggesting a range of values for music education, depending on whether music is given native language status or is interpreted as a "second language," and in that case, of secondary importance.

As a final way to address the relationship between conceptions of music education and music, a comparison of disciplines and recent historical perspectives is offered. The intent is to demonstrate certain universals across fields of music study while also revealing a provocative relationship between what is named and what is left unnamed.

Table 4.1 is a comparative table that begins with the familiar taxonomies of *learning*. These are juxtaposed with references to specific works representing three fields of study that might be regarded as possible taxonomies of *musical* meaning, chosen for their historical and disciplinary characteristics. The 1960s were a dynamic period of our history, and two disciplines, educational psychology and ethnomusicology, were breakthrough influences at that time. Bloom and colleagues were classifying domains of behavior in the forms of cognitive (Bloom, 1956); affective (Krathwohl, Bloom, & Massia, 1964); and psychomotor (Simpson, 1966) taxonomies. In a merger of psychological research with educational practice, these domains were viewed as conceptually comprehensive at the time.

Table 4.1 Comparison of Musical Meaning across Domains

Psychology	Ethnomusicology	Cultural Anthropology	Neuroscience	Music Education
Bloom et al. (1956, 1964, 1967)*	Merriam (1964)	Dissanayake (2000)	Levitin (2008)	MENC (1994)
Taxonomies of Educational Objectives	*The Anthropology of Music*	*Art and Intimacy*	*The World in Six Songs*	*National Standards*
Cognitive *Remember, understand, apply, analyze, evaluate, create*	Symbolic representation	Meaning making	Knowledge	*Improvising melodies, variations, and accompaniments*
				Composing and arranging music within specified guidelines Reading and notating music
				Listening to, analyzing, and describing music Evaluating music and music performances
Affective *Receive, respond, value, organize, characterize*	Social protest Conflict-solution Release Aesthetic enjoyment Entertainment Communication	Mutuality	Love	*Singing and performing on instruments, alone and **with others**, a varied repertoire of music*
			Joy	
		Belonging	Friendship	

Singing, alone and with others, a varied repertoire of music

Performing on instruments, alone and with others, a varied repertoire of music

Understanding music in relation to history and culture

Understanding relationships between music, the other arts, and disciplines outside the arts

Comfort

Religion

Hands on competence

Elaboration

Physical responses

Validation of social institutions and religious rituals

Contribution to the continuity and stability of culture

Contribution to the integration of society

Psychomotor
Perceive, prepare, imitate, perform, adapt

[Culture]

*Note: Based on Bloom (1956); Krathwohl, Bloom, & Masia (1964); Krathwohl (2002); Simpson (1966).

The second domain is ethnomusicology, the study of musical meaning as it relates to the cultural beliefs and practices of a group. Merriam (1964), writing around the same time as Bloom and colleagues, defines musical function as being situated in culturally specific activity, and names nine different functions of music. When one compares the two disciplines, it is interesting to note similarities in the attention to affect; and the discipline-specific sociocultural function of ethnomusicology and the cognitive realm of educational psychology.

The next two columns represent 21st century views of musical meaning. Mirroring the different perspective-taking of the first comparison, they are from the disciplines of cultural anthropology and neuroscience. Both respond to Pinker's (1999) comment that music was evolutionary cheesecake. Dissanayake's (2000) five psychobiological needs as described in *Art and Intimacy: How the Arts Began* are indeed very similar to what Levitin (2008), a neuroscientist and former rock musician, wrote about in *The World in Six Songs*.

The U.S. K-12 National Standards for Music Education (MENC, 1994) are in the last column and represent content areas in music teaching. Because of the phrase "with others," the singing and playing instruments standards are listed twice—once alongside the psychomotor, given their performance-based activity, and also in the row aligned with the social aspects of other disciplinary views. There is a clear alignment with the cognitive domain, a possible residual from the Woods Hole and Tanglewood meetings concurrent with Bloom (see Chapter 1). Looking more deeply at the longer list of achievement standards accompanying each content standard, the word "expressively" appears under the performance standards—a subtle nod to the emotional component of musical meaning. However, the obvious exclusion in this discipline is in the realm of the affective. This omission can be interpreted from many perspectives. One possibility is that the affective component is so important to the experience that it is integrated into the essential understanding of music as a construct. An alternative interpretation is that the affective domain is not addressed as fully because it is so difficult to assess. The former suggests a hidden curriculum whose exposure may benefit the profession, given the literature linking cognition and affect.

Affective experience may be why we do what we do. Our field acknowledges this for non-specialists in music by calling school- required musical exposure "music appreciation." That term would not be applied to music courses required for professionally prepared musicians. Are implicit understandings to remain hidden? How is music "domain-ed" in your practice?

MEANINGFUL ENGAGEMENT IN MUSIC TEACHING AND LEARNING

The material presented in this chapter addressed how learners make meaning; embodiment, which integrates feeling and action; conceptualization, which connects the novel to the familiar; and creativity, which seeks to interpret in order to make meaningful. Questions of power regarding who controls musical-meaning making, of culture difference and essential musical qualities, and about what is valued in music are omnipresent as we shape and are shaped by our experiences in music education. At the beginning of the chapter, meaning was described in three ways: meaning in music, meaning with music and meaning through music. In closing, I revisit them from a new perspective, adapted from a study on music making in families who drew upon multiple resources in musical activity (Custodero, 2008).

Meaning in: Engagement [with]in Self

Before we can lead others to discover meaning in music, we must look inward, asking ourselves questions about our own journey as learners and as teachers. Through our own embodied learning we can integrate who we are with what we do; through reflection, we can integrate who we were with what we can become.

Meaning with: Engagement with Others

Musical meaning is made through interaction with others, and to genuinely engage with music, we must be genuinely engaged with musicians. The processes of a meaningful music education are musical—reflection about classroom culture and our roles as teacher-musician require thoughtful consideration.

Meaning through: Engagement through Imagination

Musical meaning is not fixed; it is fluid, open to the changes in awareness and in conditions that might provide engagement in, with, and through new possibilities. It is our own resistance that contains our experience in the world of the known. To move through, or to understand more deeply, we raise questions around key areas of possible discomfort, to be considered for both ourselves and the people we teach.

In summary, I turn to improvisation as an archetype for constructing meaning in music education. It is "in the moment" music making that calls upon all our knowledge accrued from past experiences, while requiring attention to the immediate environment. It is the sensing of possibilities and acting upon them. It is responsive and open to new directions that collaborators may want to try. It is a give and take, a willingness to listen and an invitation to play. It is music teaching on a very good day.

Class Discussion

1. Describe one teaching moment that you remember as being especially satisfying. What were you doing? What were the students doing? What was the musical content? Why do you think you remember it? What was meaningful?

2. When are teaching and learning not synonymous? What might change in order for them to become synonymous?

3. What would a National Standard that directly addressed the Affective domain look like?

Projects

1. Learner Interview

   Interview a person of your choice who is currently involved as a student in some music education experience. Write your report of the interview as a story of their experience, briefly describing the person (age, gender, brief family background if available, how you know this learner). Include information about where they are studying and what they like most and least. Avoid questions which are answerable with a simple "yes" or "no." It is often helpful and inviting to use the phrase "tell me more about that"—it also yields important information. Your final question should be "Is there anything else you want to tell me about your music class (or lessons)?" How does this learner make meaning from his or her experiences?

2. Music as...

   Choose repertoire for a music lesson for a familiar group of students. How would you teach the lesson if you were conceptualizing music as...

   a. Intelligence, thinking about multiple entry points?
   b. Cognition, thinking about reflection?
   c. Language, thinking about communication?

3. Listen to a favorite piece of music.

   Trace your interest—what attracted you to this piece? Consider your response to it in terms of embodiment—what feelings does it bring to the foreground? What is the movement quality of the piece and how does that relate to human physicality and your physical response to the music?

SUGGESTED READINGS

Cobb, E. (1977). *The ecology of imagination in childhood.* New York: Columbia University Press.

Deci, E. L. (1995). *Why we do what we do: Understanding self-motivation.* New York: Penguin.

Dissanayake, E. (2000). *Art and intimacy.* Seattle, WA: University of Washington Press.

Feldman, D. H., Csikszentmihalyi, M., & Gardner, H. (1994). *Changing the world: A framework for the study of creativity.* Westport, CT: Praeger.

Patel, A. (2008). *Music, language, and the brain.* New York: Oxford University Press.

~

CHAPTER 5

The Learner in Community
Patricia A. St. John

INTRODUCTION

Consider the various communities of music learning of which you have been a part in your musical life. Perhaps you had a special studio teacher who also served as a confidante. Possibly, you remember extraordinary synchronicity with your jazz ensemble, grooving together and lost in the music. Maybe you recall magical moments in your garage, jamming with friends or times in chorus when you were overcome with the sheer sonorous beauty of collective singing. Undoubtedly, these communities of learning impacted your musical development and influenced your musicianship. The extraordinary power of music to cross boundaries, intersect cultures, and connect people is intuitively shared among musicians who have experienced its socializing force. To better understand the relevance of the social dimension of music making, this chapter explores environmental factors, learning strategies, and psychological theories related to the rich social context of the community of learners. Three headings serve to organize the discussion: the Community of Learners, Learning Strategies in Community, and Communities of Music Learning.

THE COMMUNITY OF LEARNERS

Historical Overview
The social aspects of learning—the role of context and the influence of community—have shaped commentary in educational debate since the 1800s when schools became tax-supported. Ideological dissent between educators and the public has focused on such issues as authority in classrooms, teacher-directed or student-centered learning, and interest centers versus state-mandated curricula, to name a few. For more than 30 years, the social aspects of the classroom culture have included such topics as Open Classrooms, Cooperative Learning,

Mutual Learning Cultures, and Communities of Learning. These more recent social structures are briefly discussed below.

The open classroom, originating in Britain, burst onto the American educational scene in the late 1960s. The ideology grounding this paradigm mirrored the social, political, and cultural changes of the 1960s and early 1970s; its concept resonated with a chorus of critics reacting to the culture of conformity that defined the 1950s. In the context of a rising youth-oriented counterculture amidst profound political and social challenges, such as the Civil Rights Movement, anti-war protests, and feminist and environmental activism, to name a few, schools across America literally saw the classroom structure crumble. Replacing walls with interest centers and substituting desks with learning circles, open classrooms offered students a hands-on educational experience. Within a teacher-prepared environment, individuals progressed at personal pace, and small group interactions facilitated mutual growth. This approach to teaching and learning promoted student-directed and student-initiated learning through a variety of media. Active engagement in educational endeavors went beyond paper and pencil *and* the spoken word to include a wide array of cultural artifacts and experiences, tools and expressions.

Pedagogical models in Music Education also reflected this philosophy. Educators sought to design curricula shaped by cooperative, collaborative music making experiences. The Manhattanville Music Curriculum Project (MMCP: 1965–1970), for example, was sponsored by the United States Office of Education (Arts and Humanities Division) and conducted by Manhattanville College in New York. MMCP sought to address students' dwindling interest in formal school music and their expanded involvement with music informally outside of academic settings. This student-centered curriculum presented music as an emergent, evolving phenomenon, contrasting sharply to the static view of Western music. I benefited from this approach, participating in group projects and collective music making generated in learning circles involving peer collaborators. Each of us found ways to express individual ideas musically. With a carefully framed teacher-posed "problem," we sought solutions in small groups, collaborated on compositions, and performed, recorded, and critiqued them from a process perspective and an aural orientation. The connections between this innovative curriculum and the open classroom philosophy are apparent. Our teacher functioned as facilitator, not evaluator. She participated in the process providing feedback and offering direction when consulted. The energy and creativity generated by collective student-driven activities resulted in experiences beyond what anyone could have imagined alone, but that everyone could own together. (see Walker, R. (1984). Innovation in the music classroom: II The Manhattanville music curriculum project. *Psychology of Music, 12*(1), 25–33).

Another area of music instruction mirroring sociocultural changes may be found in the philosophy and pedagogy of Dr. Robert Pace, Professor of Music and Music Education at Teachers College, Columbia University from 1951 until his retirement in 1995. While at Teachers College, Dr. Pace was influenced by the educational theories of Abraham Maslow, John Gardner, and Jerome Bruner. Reflecting on these theories and how children learn, he observed that his piano students seemed more interested in the next student's lesson than their own. Desiring to harness this curiosity, he developed the Robert Pace Piano Method. In this group approach to piano instruction, students engage in creative and collaborative music making, benefiting from each other's contributions as they find ways to express themselves musically. Like MMCP, Pace's methodology is one of comprehensive musicianship. Learning this way, my lessons were filled with a sense of personal accomplishment while participating in group improvisation, composition, performance, and critique. I found connections in the diverse repertoire of group members and identified with them as peer musicians. As relationships evolved and competence developed, a musical community emerged.

As the sociopolitical climate shifted in the mid-to-late 70s, educational reform was central. Amidst the turmoil of a deeply divided nation, critics of the open classroom called for a return to basics: schools rebuilt classroom walls, and states constructed minimum high-school competencies for graduation.

The essence of the open classroom concept, searching for relevant and authentic educational experiences, cannot be reduced to a fad or footnote. Its core principle is one of perspective: teacher-directed or student-centered, information disseminated or knowledge discovered. Different forms of teacher-centered instruction have dominated US classrooms for the past century. The first decade of the 21st century in America favors the teacher-directed approach with standard-driven curricula and test-based accountability. Nevertheless, the principles of open education—active student involvement, interdisciplinary projects, and cross-disciplinary engagement among small groups—are still embraced by challenging and creative educators witnessing the power of collaborative efforts in cooperative learning environments. This is reflected in such endeavors as the Manhattanville Curriculum Project and Group Piano instruction discussed above and in colleges and universities integrating theoretical, historical, and compositional curricula through Comprehensive Musicianship structuring.

As a teaching strategy, Cooperative Learning reflects the values inherent in collaborative work; success depends largely upon individual contributions to the collective experience. Every student is involved in the task or project swapping ideas and alternating roles as facilitator, reporter, or recorder. The benefits of such collaborative work are commonly acknowledged: students learn faster and more efficiently; they retain more of what is learned; their learning experience is more positive, meaningful, and authentic.

The basic tenets of cooperative learning are reflected in what Bruner (1996) calls "mutual learning cultures," characterized by reciprocal contributed efforts. In this model, the teacher takes on the additional function of encouraging others to share classroom "authority." The invitation to learn comes from multiple perspectives as participants encourage and empower each other to contribute from an entry point of strength, highlighting capabilities, not underscoring deficiencies.

Such an environment fosters the development of good judgment, self-efficacy and self-reliance; it promotes working together. Bruner (1996) writes:

> ... [the mutual learning community structure] models ways of doing or know-ing, provides opportunity for emulation, offers running commentary, provides "scaffolding" for novices, and even provides a good context for teaching delib-erately. (p. 21)

Consideration of social influences in the classroom, the impact of the learn-ing environment on cognition, and the role of others in the learning process con-verge in the concept of the community of learners (see Rogoff, 1990, 1994). This notion finds its origins in and draws inspiration from the works of John Dewey (1916) and Lev Vygotsky (1978). Dewey (1938) distinguished the teacher's role in the classroom community as one of "cooperative enterprise" shared through "contributions from the experience of all engaged in the learning process" (p. 85). Through the dynamic interplay of reciprocal contributions, learning becomes bidirectional. The interactions transform learner **and** community. Vygotsky's general law of cultural development emphasizes the crucial role that others play as we make sense of the world. As we build on prior experience, draw from past and present interactions, and participate in cultural norms, we grow cognitively.

Two examples of such cooperative activity include the role of apprenticeship in learning—where learners seek out more capable peers or experienced adults to facilitate and enhance their learning and the formation of communities of practice—where members join in shared partnership toward common interests and mutual goals to problem-solve and problem-find.

As we consider this emergent model of the community of learners, what is the music educator's role as a member of the learning community? How might teach-ers design musical experiences that invite student contributions and encourage mutual inquiry?

Building the Music Community

Music's social dimension, its inherent nature to engage people and to engen-der community, has been documented from a number of rich and diverse per-spectives. From infant-mother musical exchanges, Dissanayake (2000a) and Trevarthen (1999) research the primary bond that music facilitates. Musical play inquiry (Littleton, 1998; Marsh, 2008; Moorhead & Pond, 1978; Tarnowski, 1994; Young, 1999, 2003) considers the impact of the social environment and peer/adult involvement. Ethnographers (e.g., Blacking, 1995/1967; Addo, 1997) exam-ine how cultural and communal practices assist children's music learning.

Music as Personal Expression

Cultural anthropologist, Ellen Dissanayake (2000a), traces the socializing power of music as a vehicle for shared meaning-making to the intimate infant-mother lyrical exchanges. Departing from speculation about the biological origins of music arising from male competition or adult courtship, she writes: "... human

music originated in perceptual, behavioral, cognitive, and emotional competencies and sensitivities that developed from primate precursors in survival enhancing affiliative interactions ... between mothers and infants under six months
of age" (p. 389). Music's specific power to coordinate and conjoin individuals
evolved out of the primate's innate need for relationship or emotional commu-
nion, not simply sociability. These exchanges—ritualized sequences of vocal,
facial, and kinesis behaviors—evolved to enhance and ensure it. Characteristics
include rhythmic and temporally patterned communicative interactions or lyrical vocal play that varies in intensity and spatial/temporal patterning. Analyses
show mother and baby engage in mutually improvised interactions, responding
sensitively to the emotional content of the other's behavior.

Colwyn Trevarthen (2002), a psychobiologist, contends that we have a
uniquely human inborn musicality that is evidenced in infants' earliest expressions of communication. The parameters of musicality are intrinsically determined in the brain where images of moving and feeling generate and guide
behavior in time (Trevarthen, 1999). He argues that the "rhythmic impulse of
living," the primary beat that permeates all movement and communication, is
essentially musical (p. 157). His *theory of the motives of musicality*—Intrinsic
Motive Pulse—explains the fundamental features of human movement; therein
is the genesis of musical expression and artistic creation. He describes the perceptual and cognitive appreciation of musical patterns in infant responses to
familiar persons, ritual events, and preferred songs: flagging arms as if conducting, kicking legs in rhythmic synchrony or whole-body bouncing to the beat.
Trevarthen (2002) writes:

> Taken with the infant's clear preference for particular companions, this music
> 'showing off' looks like the beginnings of his or her social identity as a mem-
> ber of a group—a group with known habits, celebratory experiences and
> acting skills that are valued for the bonds that they represent and reinforce.
> Cultivation of intrinsic musicality is a way of declaring allegiance with a friend
> or a social band. A newborn knows its mother by the tone and inflection of her
> voice. When a 6-month-old smiles with the recognition of a favourite song, and
> bounces with the beat, it is like knowing his or her name, displaying a social
> 'me' within the family's affectionate pleasure of sharing. (p. 22)

These musical interactions expand and find expression across various contexts and among diverse age groups. In early childhood music, researchers (e.g.,
Custodero, 2002; St. John, 2004) have examined how child-adult/child-child interactions scaffold experience and facilitate enjoyment in music-making endeavors.
Feldman (1994) refers to the supportive community as a "cultural organism,"

> ...a cooperative structure that is formed and reformed in order to enhance the
> possibilities for discovery, development, and (occasionally) optimal expression
> of human talents in various domains. (p. 169)

I visited the Celia Cruz High School for Music in New York City (Spring
2007) and interviewed (unpublished raw data) a representative group of students,

freshmen to seniors. The young musicians discussed a sense of belonging, strong bonds among peer-musicians, pride in shared efforts, and how perceived "best players" modeled excellence and challenged cohorts. "[Omar's] like the best (*other students concur*); if I could be like him when I am a senior (*she pauses and reflects*)...that's my goal ... I would be awesome!" exclaimed Elaine of her wood-wind section leader. Jamie reflected, "... [T]his is my family. Here everybody gets it; they understand you. We all work together so we can be our best."

Bailey's (1992) interviews with jazz musicians are replete with phrases that speak to evolving musical styles developed in communal settings: "We grew through playing with each other, listening to all kinds of music and creating a personal approach towards our instrument" (p. 75). The American saxophonist Steve Lacy reflects on his development as an improviser: "...it all had a lot to do with the musical environment. You have to get some kindred spirits" (Bailey, 1992, p. 56).

Consider these musical interactions in light of Bronfenbrenner's "nested realities," discussed in the next chapter. Think of these as *musical* nested realities, moving from the intimate infant-mother exchanges to the sensitive "groove" (see Keil & Feld, 2005; Monson, 1996) jazz musicians create jamming together. The next consideration is the *macrosystem*, incorporating cultural context.

Music as Cultural Expression
Making music collectively is an expressive cultural tool. John Blacking (1995/1967), curious about the nature of music in the socialization and encul-turation of the Venda people, spent 22 months in Vendaland, located in Thohoyandou, Northern Province, South Africa. In addition to professional anthropologic undertakings, he actively participated in community-oriented musical experiences immersing himself in sociocultural practices. He learned about the musical culture of the Venda by studying the musical processes and songs of their children. Examining children's songs—their function, transmission, and acquisition—he gained an understanding of adult music. The elitist view of Western music sharply contrasts that of the Venda, where music perme-ates every aspect of life: rites, rituals, and social occasions. Blacking's research poignantly reveals the inherent human need to share music socially and to cre-ate music collectively.

Addo (1997) found a supportive and collaborative model of learning, central to Ghanaian cultural knowledge, transferred to music performance and practice situations as each player defines and complements the other. "Whole-making is accomplished through participatory music-making" (p. 22). She observed three ways of knowing embedded in the singing games of Ghanaian children which resonate across cultures of similar backgrounds: (1) Knowledge is uninhibited shared constructions; (2) Knowledge grows when everyone is involved; and (3) Knowledge is like "mid-wifery," that is, encouraging words are used to rouse par-ticipants, urging them on during singing games.

Addo concludes that particular skills are needed to make knowing possible. She contends that the particular learning abilities revealed by Ghanaian children during singing games are driven by their consciously-held knowledge, skills, and ways of thinking. This implicit knowledge is related to children's lived cultural context; the idiomatic expressions found in their singing games reflect the traditions of the culture within which they occur.

Building the music community, we are challenged to consider established traditional genres of musical expression—symphony orchestras, marching bands, and professional choirs,—*and* emergent models that may be viewed as less legitimate in contemporary Western culture. Jones (2005) identifies these more organic, diverse, and participatory idioms—such as jazz combos, garage bands, and drumming circles—as "street-level" cultural life.

Allsup (2003) investigated the value of one such idiom. He found that high school band students who chose to use an alternative genre, garage band, enjoyed the collective musical experience more than their counterparts who chose traditional orchestral instruments. Allsup observed an emphasis on interpersonal relationships, peer-learning, and peer-critique in this group's process as the self-directed musicians delighted in new-found autonomy and previously undiscovered musical skill.

Jorgensen (1995, 2003) challenges us to open up the curriculum, to dramatically revolutionize not only our understanding of the world of music but the means by which people come to know it. How do we nurture such musical communities inclusive and respectful across and between diverse venues? How do we model a spirit of musical inquiry that moves us beyond our comfort zone in order to discover something new?

The Environment

The unique community culture emerges in the learning environment. This environment may be formal, comprising informal engagement with learning brought into the formal context, as Green (2008) proposes, or informal settings such as those discussed above. Creating contexts for learning, defining the situation, finding one's place within that space, and drawing upon available resources all contribute to finding and making meaning. Vygotskian theory purports that all learning finds its impetus socially through interaction with persons, material, and cultural resources.

At the heart of teaching and learning is the importance of relationships and the quality of interactions. Developing relationships is fundamental to building community. Through mutual trust and respect, students give and take invitations, and offer and receive contributions. Interacting with others and playing with content, relationships form; students discover environmental resources, enabling them to actively participate in the learning process. They find what and who is most needed next to assist them. How does the music educator cultivate this mutually supportive environment?

Consideration of sociocultural influences reveals how shared partnership facilitates knowledge acquisition from individual transmission to social transaction. Materials for learning include cultural artifacts—such as computers, books, markers, and symbol systems—**and** the dynamics of discourse, opportunities for collaborative problem-solving/finding and reciprocal scaffolding strategies. The richness of the classroom culture is also influenced by nonverbal exchanges among the members: aural cues, glances, gestures. This ecological approach to learning (Gibson, 1988) depends upon the student's perception of possibility inherent in the environment. Defined as "affordances," these found resources are explored, manipulated, and negotiated as potential is discovered.

Consider, for example, instrument exploration in a preschool music setting. As children examine multiple shapes, textures, and materials or explore various timbres, sound production, and tonal qualities, they discover not only "what can this instrument do," but "what can I do with it?" Potential may move beyond individual exploration to interpersonal negotiation as peers manipulate the material differently. The instruments offer possibilities with aural and textural qualities; observation of and interaction with others provides opportunities for action and re-action.

Perhaps, you have observed young children enthusiastically dancing to a spirited selection from a Virginia Rodriguez CD, for example. Already fully engaged embodying the pulse and style of the music, one participant notices a peer moving differently and copies him. This initial imitation then gives way to an expanded gesture that personalizes and intensifies the experience.

With a keen perception of what is needed and who is available in the environment, the learner finds *where* to be and with *whom* to be as she/he negotiates the learning process and moves to the next step. Choral teachers, for example, may strategically place perceived "strong voices" or designated "section leaders" next to less-experienced singers. Alternately, students may situate themselves next to a singer whom they perceive as potentially assisting them.

Instrumental instructors, for example, may draw upon individual strengths when grouping students for instruction in between ensemble rehearsals or by seating musicians differently during practice. Kim-Cassie (2008), using the flow paradigm as a framework for teaching and learning, is experimenting with alternative seating arrangements in Beginner Orchestra Classes. Preliminary results suggest that *how* students are seated influences motivation and skill development. Each of Kim-Cassie's four self-designed arrangements draws upon the social context: where and how students are situated. Working collaboratively and listening carefully to each other in progressive predetermined group configurations, orchestra members monitor their own skill development and negotiate increased levels of challenge. The experience, Kim-Cassie observes, culminates in a flow-producing learning environment as students find meaning and joy through interactions and in mutual engagement.

"Situated-ness" (Lave & Wenger, 1991) becomes an important strategy as students use the environment as a learning tool to construct knowledge. For some, peripheral participation is a necessary first step, an initiation into the community that enables them to clarify what is being asked and how to become involved. In band rehearsals, for example, directors may observe and hear tentative or weak performances from inexperienced players or those perceived as less talented. Desiring to be in the band, these students may still be searching for what is required to make a contribution and how to belong to the community. Perhaps you have seen them select or switch an instrument based on a friend's choice. Self-taught music students who have picked up progressions or riffs from informal settings like basement or garage jam sessions, tabs from the internet, or aurally from their iPods, for example, use these environmental and cultural resources as a way to find their place in more formal instructional settings (see Green, 2002, 2008). Our challenge as music educators is clear: to foster and nurture inclusive environments that draw upon both formal and informal music learning practices, recognizing and rewarding the development of musical skills and knowledge from multiple sources.

These examples demonstrate how proximity and periphery relative to the active learning space become legitimate means of participation. The use of space is one way to access environmental resources; finding the person with whom to be is another. How might we use situated-ness to inform teaching strategies? Why is situated-ness an important consideration for music educators?

LEARNING STRATEGIES IN COMMUNITY

The Role of Others

Within the same historical framework of emerging alternative educational structures, psychological theories addressing the impact of social context on learning were also developing. This intersection is compelling and begs the question, Was theory and practice evolving simultaneously? How is learning manifested in the rich, social context of the music learning community? This section considers learning strategies in conjunction with theory. The discussion moves from imitation to collaboration, much like the student's path as she/he finds and makes meaning in the community of learners.

Imitation

While Vygotsky was a contemporary of Piaget, his sociocultural theory was not available in English until 1978. Vygotsky's (1978) theoretical framework suggests meaning is socially constructed: social and individual processes co-construct knowledge interdependently. Imitation is a form of social expansion linked to Vygotsky's Genetic Law where the activity that occurs builds and expands on what the individual knows initially, and moves to a whole new level of function. The task may first be imitated before it is fully internalized. This social expansion involves influences of social experience **and** internal transformations of the child's intellectual operations.

Similar to Vygotskian Theory, Social Learning Theory (Bandura, 1977) examines bidirectional influences of personal and environmental factors to understand the complexity of human behavior. Particular situations and unique dispositions jointly portray the breadth and intricacy of human response.

Individual behavior, personal temperament, and environmental factors operate as interlocking determinants of each other. They *create* each other through multifaceted interplay. The influence exerted by any single aspect changes in various settings and for different behaviors. Bandura sought to identify the intervening mechanisms responsible for these changes.

In the past, some theorists thought such interior motivational forces as needs, drives, and impulses determined human behavior. Developments in behavior theory shifted, moving from internal determinants to external influences: by manipulating external influences, response patterns can change. Determinants of behavior were now thought to reside in environmental forces, not within the person.

Social learning perspective views individuals neither driven by inner forces nor directed by environmental stimuli. The continuous reciprocal interaction of personal and environmental determinants informs psychological functioning. Bandura identifies three uniquely human cognitive processes pertinent to social learning theory: vicariousness, representation, and self-regulation. In the first process, vicariousness, all learning which results from direct experience occurs explicitly: we observe other people's behavior and what it might mean consequentially for us. Consider, for example, the social influences available to the learner in a general music classroom. A student may observe a peer during a free-movement activity. Not sure how to respond to the music, the student imitates the peer's movement to engage and become involved. Conversely, the music learner may imitate a peer to intensify the experience, perceiving her/his response more challenging or compelling.

The second process, representation, enables us to preserve experiences for future behavior using symbols. The use of symbol systems is a centerpiece of Vygotskian theory. Vygotsky (1978) believed sign- or symbol-use revealed a "culturally-elaborated organization" of human behavior, going beyond limited psychological functions endowed by nature (p. 39). Signs, internally oriented psychological functions, mediate mental activity. Concrete manifestations of sign-using activities include drawing pictures, writing, reading, and using number systems. Children's symbol-use in music incorporates iconic images for sound and dot-dash marks or thin-thick vertical lines for rhythmic organization. Aural cues may also function as signs, mediating the transfer of one musical skill to another. A child singing a simple *sol-mi-la* song may later transfer the melodic pattern to an instrument. The aural preparation serves as an intermediary step to the visual/kinesthetic skill.

Signs create a new relationship between the stimulus-response. They assist learning, particularly as students attempt to represent musical ideas. For example, elementary music students collaborate in small groups to create a composition. Exchanging ideas, they find ways to generate a score and then perform their composition. Studies on children's invented notation, the manipulation of signs in music making, provide insight into developing cognitive processes (Davidson & Scripp, 1988; Barrett, 1999; Gromko, 1994).

Self-regulation, the third feature, gives students a sense of control. Self-regulation is directly related to the learner's interpretation of the teacher-presented task, adjusting challenge to perceived skill. Zimmerman (2002) suggests that because students' use of self-regulatory processes—goal-setting, use of strategies, and self-monitoring—requires time and effort, motivation is a key factor (p. 85). Self-efficacy is related to motivation. Determining who/what is needed to facilitate learning and making self-determined changes necessary to achieve the goal, engagement is possible.

Collective musical experiences provide a relational context from which to draw to realize competence: a student may self-correct his/her tempo simply by observing a peer's bodily response or by matching a partner's aural cue. This personal adjustment is facilitated by the presence and contribution of others; personal agency communicates control as the learner finds what is needed.

These theoretical considerations prompt reflection on social context and musical interactions. Recall the communities of music learning described in the opening paragraph. Each of us has had the experience of imitating a colleague's riff, learning to finger a musical passage through modeling, or adjusting intonation or embouchure based on immediate feedback. If you were part of a garage band, perhaps your skill improved simply by playing together with other musicians, working out progressions and transitions.

Acquiring patterns of behavior and monitoring their expression through the interplay of self-generated *and* external sources of influence are central to sociocultural theory. The opportunity to explore or to participate in problem-solving leads thought as the learner moves beyond imitation. Vygotsky (1978) notes that a child imitating his/her elders in "culturally patterned activities" generates opportunity for intellectual development that ultimately leads to an elementary mastery of abstract thought. Through imitation, the learner develops "an entire repository of skills" (p. 84). Skill development leads to mastery of a domain, which is necessary for creativity (Csikszentmihalyi, 1996).

Changing how things are done or changing a way of thinking requires mastery of the old ways of doing and thinking. Mozart could not have changed the music world as he did without first having mastered the domain of musical composition and then produce convincingly, culturally recognized musical compositions. This period of apprenticeship, grappling with and imitating established form and style, seems necessary not only to craft an original contribution but in terms of development in general. Beethoven, too, had an imitative period, reflecting influences of Haydn and Mozart; he found his own voice in the Third Symphony.

Peer imitation in music making enables the learner to rely on a more competent "other," heightening the experience until she/he can control the activity's content. Imitation enables engagement; it provides an entry point. As the learner finds a way to participate in the activity, she/he grows in confidence and competence, finding personal expression. What is needed to facilitate internalization of the music material? What is the music educator's role as model and how does she/he respond to the student's efforts to become involved?

The period of apprenticeship for Stravinsky (with Rimsky-Korsakov) and Shostakovich (with Mussorgsky) enabled them to master the psychological tools of music, transforming the experience into original work.

> This mode of appropriation illustrates a dual process, that of strengthening the novice's knowledge of orchestration while also finding the young composer's own voice. This view of internalization is an active process of co-construction that can lead to creative contributions. (Lee & Smagorinsky, 2000, pp. 16–17)

Imitation may empower a learner with musical fluency that leads to mastery. With appropriate, carefully crafted guidance, this new-found competence leads to freedom of expression. This nonlinear progression is a dynamic, multidimensional interplay of internal and external processes that are coordinated and integrated as in Vygotsky's *functional systems approach* to cognitive development.

> Functional systems provide an important alternative to dichotomous ways of representing diversity in human cognitive processes and allow us to explore beyond linear representations of learning and development (John-Steiner, Meehan, & Mahn, 1998, p. 127).

For Vygotsky, children's imitation is more than a mechanical, automatic process; children can profit from instruction. The music educator's role, then, must be carefully considered, reflecting the right moment of intervention and just enough assistance to encourage self-realized musical expression. With careful guidance and an awareness of shared discovery, the teacher empowers the child as co-constructor of knowledge. The learner discovers self-efficacy as she/he finds multiple ways of interpreting the teacher-presented task. Self-initiated exploration and guided assistance facilitate personal accomplishment.

Children are capable of intellectual, insightful imitation. Vygotsky (1978) discovered that children could imitate a variety of actions that go beyond predictable potential, especially in collective activity (p. 88). Imitation provides a repository of skills that may be appropriated later.

Zajonc (1965, 1980, 1984), researching the cognitive/affect interface, suggests that motor responses are held in our memory. This is relevant to music making given the multisensory nature of musical experience. Physical responses serve as representational functions without cognitive mediation (Zajonc and Markus, 1984). The implication for music is that we learn about music by making it.

> ...Learning awakens a variety of internal developmental processes that are able to operate only when the child is interacting with people in his environment and in cooperation with his peers. Once these processes are internalized, they become part of the child's independent developmental achievement. (Vygotsky, 1978, p. 90)

Imitation, a form of scaffolding, enables the learner to move toward mastery and potentially, initiation and invention. In the music community, students draw from and contribute to the collective experience. Giving and receiving ideas, they scaffold learning.

Scaffolding

Scaffolding, the process of building on prior experience to move beyond imitation and modeling to task competency or even task transformation, finds its origins in Vygotsky's Genetic Law. The *term* itself, not original to Vygotsky, was introduced as a component of tutoring (Wood, Bruner, & Ross, 1976). Adult-guidance or collaboration with more capable peers enables the learner to problem-solve, to actively engage in knowledge-construction, to scaffold learning.

Vygotsky believed that individuals realize concept development in social context. This external process is spatially evaluated in a dynamic learning space called the *zone of proximal development (ZPD)*. The movement from what the child is able to do now (A), to what the child might be able to do with the help of an adult or a more capable peer (B), occurs incrementally across time. Once the child has internalized the concept and is able to express it externally, a new zone is created along the continuum.

The stimulating interplay of these internal and external processes results in a dynamic course that enables the learner to move from imitation to mastery. The vibrant interconnection between "nested realities" and how they impact the forces affecting psychological growth reflects Vygotsky's functional systems approach mentioned above.

As students invite and honor contributions, the classroom culture intensifies; a learning community emerges. The ZPD becomes a dynamic transformative space as participants find imitative models or scaffold experience by expanding contributions.

In one setting, for example, four- and five-year-olds loved the embodiment of *The Magical Dancing Clocks*. Adjusting their movements to the recorded themes of the big-*slow* and little-*fast* clocks, the children repeatedly reinvented the experience. They found new ways to express their understanding of meter and tempo, playing off each other's contributions and scaffolding the experience collectively. They made the teacher-presented activity more complex by increasing the challenge. "I have an idea! Let's add IN-stru-ments: sticks can play the big clock music and bells can be for the little clocks." Instrument-play transformed the experience. On another occasion, Jeffrey suggested "...this time you have to stay in place during the little clock music; you cannot move your legs. You can only move for the big clocks!" The additional constraint made the familiar material more challenging.

Coordinated efforts and reciprocal support enhance the collective activity. Collective music making expands the experience beyond what we could imagine or create alone.

Scaffolding through the ZPD requires sensitive guidance: careful knowledge construction, adequate assistance, and patience until the learner internalizes the experience as his/her own. What are implications for music instruction? As reflective practitioners, how might we carefully design lessons, crafting mean-ingful musical experiences for and with participants? The music educator must provide clearly presented concepts that invite and engage, specific feedback that facilitates critical thinking, and encouragement that fosters curiosity and inquiry. Students can then devise and renegotiate the teacher's guiding foun-dation. Transforming the presented material independently or with assistance, students find and make meaning in their music learning and discover musical competence. *Who* provides the assistance, and *how* it is provided frames success-ful scaffolding techniques.

Kennel (1992) provides a detailed examination of scaffolding practice rel-evant to applied music instruction. His Teacher Scaffolding Model calls for instruction that accommodates the complexities and richness of social inter-actions within the applied lesson between novice and expert, going beyond teacher-talk and teacher-modeling. To this end, he turned to Vygotsky and the *ZPD*, and what the Russian psychologist identified as *joint problem-solving*. Inspired by Vygotsky, Wood, Bruner and Ross (1976) developed six teacher-strategies observed in joint problem-solving contexts: recruitment ("Do you remember how much you enjoyed that Bach Minuet? This piece is also a dance by Bach"), reduction in degrees of freedom ("Let's clap the rhythm of the first line"), direction maintenance ("Only work on the *A section* this week"), mark-ing critical features ("These two phrases look alike with one exception. What is different?"), frustration control ("This may be too much for one week; go as far as you can"), and demonstration ("Would you like me to play that for you?"). Kennell's pilot study revealed that teachers employed scaffolding inter-ventions—marking critical features, reducing degrees of freedom, and demon-stration—85% of the time. The remaining strategies—recruitment, direction maintenance, and reducing frustration—are instructional strategies related to teacher-student interactions.

Kennell suggests that the choice of scaffolding strategy be determined by the teacher's *assessment* **and** *attribution* of the student's performance. That is, determining *why* the student's performance was successful may be more impor-tant than why it is getting better or worse. The applied teacher observes the student's current performance and anticipates what she/he might be able to do given achievement history. Thus, a comparison of the student's actual perfor-mance with teacher expectations may inform scaffolding strategies. This type of scaffolding reveals the teacher's keen awareness of what the student *can* do, and builds on strengths. In Kennell's model, the applied lesson represents joint problem-solving while simultaneously calling forth independent problem-solv-ing skills, empowering the learner to monitor daily practice in between lessons.

Well-executed scaffolding is initiated first by guiding the student into actions that lead to recognizable solutions with clear, attainable goals. In sec-tional rehearsals, for example, difficult passages for individual players may be targeted so that collectively, the ensemble can successfully accomplish its goal. Once this initial step is achieved, feedback is necessary to interpret discrepancies for the learner. When the nature of the task is secure, the tutor provides feedback and serves a confirmatory role.

Nonverbal and aural cues enable music learners to self-scaffold as well. In early childhood music settings, for example, instrument free-play offers a plethora of options as children interact in the learning environment and engage in musical play. I arranged a variety of rhythm instruments in the center of the carpeted room. Emily picked up a triangle and immediately looked for its striker. Max noticed the shiny, silver shape and found another one. Manipulating the dangling red wooden handle, he looked perplexed, wondering how it was related to sound production. Hearing the resonant ring of the triangle behind him, Max turned and saw that Emily had something else. He went back to the instruments and found a striker, thereby scaffolding his own learning through aural cue and observation.

Stone (1993) suggests that scaffolding is a very fluid interpersonal process, "… a subtle phenomenon that involves a complex set of social and semiotic dynamics" (p. 180). Such aspects as quality of adult support, impact of interpersonal relationships, construction of meaning vis-à-vis environmental resources, and value attached to context, content, and task require further investigation to fully appreciate the dynamic relationship between sociocultural contexts and learning strategies.

Guided Participation

Sociocultural theorists have expanded the scope of the *ZPD*, reflecting the salient role of others in the learning process. Terms such as *distributed, interactive, contextual*, and the result of the *learners' participation in a community of practice* imply rich, collaborative, and "divergent environments" (Brown, Ash, Rutherford, Nakagawa, & Campione, 1993, p. 191). The community of learners scaffolds the emergent understanding of all the participants. The multifaceted sociocultural contexts of participants converge in the classroom, providing an array of multilayered resources. Through creative collaboration, the learning community explores and discovers these resources; members manipulate and develop them as understanding and meaning emerge.

Rogoff (1990) further explored Vygotsky's Genetic Law, expanding the concept of the *ZPD* to one of *guided participation*. With *guided participation*, unlike social influence perspective, students actively join with others, playing a central role in learning and even extending *how* their community functions. Communication and coordination in shared endeavors are key aspects of how people develop (Rogoff, 2003). Participants make implicitly shared adjustments as they work together, varying, complementing, and negotiating roles. Actively engaged in communal activities, participants co-construct knowledge, stretching their common understanding to fit new perspectives.

Rogoff offers two features of guided participation: *mutual bridging of meanings* and *mutual structuring of participation*. In this first aspect, participants seek a common perspective or language through which to communicate ideas to coordinate efforts. For example, during instrument free-play, preschoolers used egg shakers and a stir xylophone to organize an emergent cooking theme: making soup. As the activity unfolded, participants created a division of labor, negotiating roles of restaurant management: cook, waiter, *maitre d'*, and patron. Their imaginative play and complementary actions revealed an understanding of social knowledge while simultaneously demonstrated musical skills through invented songs, instrumental accompaniments, and complex rhythmic patterns. My role as equal partner was defined: I was recipient, given service *and* prompts as patron; it was implicitly clear that the children knew how the action would progress. Building on prior collective experiences, individuals grow developmentally through a series of shared social understandings.

The second aspect of guided participation, *mutual structuring of participation*, reflects how children, caregivers, and companions structure situations involving children. Structuring occurs with choices, determining which activities children observe and engage in. Rogoff's cross-cultural studies document various forms of child-participation and the unlimited opportunities children have to carefully observe and actively experience the skilled activities of their culture through routine arrangements and daily interactions. Supported routine and challenging situations provide children with the repetition and variety needed to become skilled practitioners in the specific cognitive activities of their communities (Rogoff, 1991, p. 351).

The manner of support and guidance is important, as is the degree to which children are granted access, enabling ownership of the task and a sense of control in determining the direction learning will take. In the classroom, this may require a loosely-held-together framework that includes established routines as well as space to manipulate material and share multiple interpretations of the teacher-presented task. Providing time for student exploration, alternative solutions, problem-solving, and even problem-finding shifts instructional focus from the teacher-intended path to student-driven needs.

Such a learning environment is exciting: it fosters shared responsibility for what is taught and learned; it invites best efforts from all participants and nurtures creativity. This model actively seeks to encourage participants' ownership in what is learned and the best way to achieve it. Through guided participation, students arrive at mutually shared understandings and determine where their learning will take them through complementary work. As a socially shared phenomenon, music seems to be an ideal vehicle to foster such communal endeavors, the music environment an ideal place for learners to thrive creatively.

Collaboration

A sense of belonging is fundamental to competence; belonging empowers students with agency as they find ways to be part of the experience through imitation, sensitive scaffolding, and/or guided participation. As imitation yields to newfound expression or observing a music-stand-partner finger a passage results in self-scaffolded skill, the student-musician grows with competence and confidence and becomes a capable collaborator. Everyone receives this gift when we foster relationships, build community, and create a welcoming environment that invites participation. Given musical time and free time to work together, find solutions, discover possibilities, and engage in problem-solving and critical thinking, students realize self-efficacy and discover the inherent joy of collective music making.

The unique subset of possibilities each member contributes to the community provides a fundamental energy which complements creative endeavors. John-Steiner (2000) writes: "...[T]he construction of a new mode of thought relies on and thrives with collaboration" (p. 7). She addresses musical collaboration with respect to the Guarneri String Quartet. The interactive energy of ensemble playing generates what one member called a "zone of magic." The relationship between the supportive community and each person's development is "... a manifestation of the interdependence of the social and the individual, of their shared growth" (p. 191).

Research on peer interaction and problem-solving (Azmitia, 1988) and reciprocal teaching (Palinscar & Brown, 1984) point to the value of collaboration among peers. In these studies, collaboration was more conducive to learning than independent work; children were able to generalize their skills. The conclusions were qualified by several factors, including imitation and the quality of verbal discussion, which mediated learning. Radziszewska & Rogoff (1988), studying adult-peer collaborators, found adult guidance more effective than peer collaboration in children's acquisition of planning skills. The adult-child pairs explored the visual cue (a map), planned longer sequences of moves, and verbalized more planning strategies. The peer dyads (9-year-olds) made decisions step-by-step, involving only single destinations. Results indicate adult guidance is more effective with complicated tasks.

> ...[It] does not suggest that peer interaction plays no role in children's cognitive development but simply concludes that, on a complex errand planning task, there are benefits from working with an adult, who is more skilled. (p. 847)

The researchers acknowledged the difficulty of the task for the child-participants and propose studying peer-adult influence using a task where children have expertise.

In partnered activity and collaborative efforts, individuals are lifted into the collective experience; the communal experience intensifies. Each of us has experienced this euphoria in ensembles; the united effort, deeply moving, astounds us. These collective experiences generate collaborative endeavors as participants share creative efforts.

In collective musical experiences, students play off each other's contributions, much like jazz musicians imitating an ensemble member's riff or motif, playing with it and taking it to a new place, and carefully weaving it into the collaborative effort. We experience this kind of collaboration in comprehensive musicianship projects, where we rely on each other's contributions, negotiate ideas, and work together to realize a common goal, or in beginner Group Piano Classes, where participants find sounds to accompany original stories, add dramatic narrative, and "perform" the group story, each adding his/her contribution. The curriculum becomes observably more effective and intensified through shared ideas and transformed material.

COMMUNITIES OF MUSIC LEARNING

We essentially make music with and for other people (Feld, 1974). We know this as musicians. As music educators, we witness it repeatedly in various settings and on multiple levels. For example, the early childhood music specialist walks down the corridor to greet her toddler music class; with a full-body-bounce, Jack declares: "Here she comes, Mommy! It's my teacher!" Before the end of the session, Clare finds her way to the teacher's lap or extends her arms as an invitation to dance. On another day, Seamus skips down the hallway to his piano lesson; eager to demonstrate his skill, he exclaims: "I'm really good at this; I can't wait to play it for you!" In a general music classroom, students work in small groups creating original compositions. Collaborating, they weave together intricate counterpoint, negotiating individual contributions and testing instrumental timbres. The students, engaged with each other and absorbed in their musical creation, are oblivious of your presence. High school students congregate in your band room, a favorite spot during free periods: sometimes they want extra practice time, other times they simply want to be with you and others. Friends meet to master sectional difficulties or gather in garages to "song get" through collective playing and listening. Whether it be early childhood music classes or community orchestras, children's choirs or collegiate choruses, people come together to make music for and with each other. Why is shared music making so compelling?

Studio Music

The strategies and theories discussed above address the important role of relationships in facilitating musical growth and development. Following the intimate bond of infant-mother, perhaps the most influential partnership in musical learning occurs between teacher-student in studio music. This special relationship, which demands enormous trust, steadily deepens as rapport develops and skill evolves. The importance of rapport in music settings has been addressed from multiple perspectives: in studio lessons (Clemmons, 2007), in the classroom (Strouse, 2003), in clinical environments (Darrow, Johnson, & Ghetti, 2001), in Elderhostel programs (McCullough-Brabson, 1995), and in research design (Roberts, 1994). The environment that the music teacher creates calls forth the aspiring musician's best efforts through acknowledgement, encouragement, challenge, and care. The unique apprenticeship is further supported through parental partnership. The bidirectional influences of and interactions between knowledge of the student, relationship with the family, interest in school issues, and attention to social concerns all aid the studio teacher in developing rapport with the student.

John-Steiner (1997) examined the influence of parents and teachers, especially in the early years, on creativity. Positive feedback and communication that expressed care and encouragement stimulated motivation and involvement. The attention stirred their interest and strengthened their dedication. Csikszentmihalyi (1996) addresses the importance of teacher-interest in their students' process of creative development, suggesting bonds of expert-apprentice.

From a musical perspective, both Howe and Sloboda (1991) and Sosniak (1985) report the powerful role that parents and teachers play in shaping young musicians' experiences. More recent studies (Davidson, Sloboda, & Howe, 1995) confirm earlier findings that the persistent music learner does not achieve competency in isolation, and that support by both parent and teacher motivates initial music making. Over time, this motivation becomes increasingly intrinsic and self-sustaining.

Brian, a graduate student enrolled in my early childhood music methods course, applied the central course objective—to design musical experiences that build on student strengths and promote self-efficacy—to his elementary level string instruction. Weekly in-class observations of our preschool guests engaged in free-play with instruments informed his teaching practice: at the beginning of each studio string lesson, he gave students exploratory time to experiment on their instrument, play with sound, and improvise around melodies. Brian commented: "Nothing was instructed or prepared, and I was more of a guide, making sure the room felt safe. They were naturally creative and experimental. They...took out their instruments and wanted to play" (personal communication, 2008). This free-play set the tone for a mutual learning environment and communicated value for collaborative efforts as the string students' discoveries were incorporated in the lesson. "Having...time to use their instruments freely gave them courage when they played in pairs or in a large group. They were ... more comfortable because they were not as intimidated by the instrument" (personal communication, 2008). As students discovered each other's music, a sense of community emerged, empowering participants to respond creatively and to work together. Free from fear of mistakes, they were guided by the confidence that belonging generates.

Clemmons (2007), focusing on the applied voice studio, explores the value of this kind of reciprocity and rapport. Finding that strong interpersonal teacher-student rapport is vital to musical success, Clemmons identified four essential aspects for a productive relationship: a competent and confident instructor creates the foundation for rapport; a safe and mutually respectful environment fosters security and trust; distinct relational boundaries with clear expectations and high standards enable successful work; and an enthusiastic and affirming teaching style generates passion and self-confidence. Student perceptions of the benefits from this sense of rapport included: care, safety, empowerment, motivation, and value.

Exploring studio teaching from the perspective of motivation, Kennell and Marks (1992) offer important relational considerations that may influence teacher-student rapport. They suggest that inquiry concerning a student's performance in the applied music lesson must include teacher participation and contributions. True artistry involves extensive knowledge of the music **and** the student. Using the Vygotskian concept, joint problem-solving, the researchers outline exemplar studio teaching practice: knowledge of the repertoire to facilitate multiple options of musical tasks with similar goals; multiple methods for teaching any one concept; a variety of repertoire to address individual student needs; accessible analogies to demonstrate technical issues; deep knowledge of students to individualize instruction and develop new teaching ideas; engaging vocabulary to capture student attention and effective pedagogical choices to facilitate performance transformation; student empowerment to define best individual learning strategies; and multiple interpretations of what an "ideal student" is (Kennell & Marks, 1992, p. 29).

Kennell (2002) further explores the relational aspects of the expert-novice apprenticeship, investigating research on studio instruction. A conception of such instruction must include "... the elements of teacher knowledge and the rise of expertise, student characteristics and development, and the interactive strategies that ensure faithful replication of these desired capabilities from one generation to the next" (p. 244). Kennell suggests that human interaction is perhaps the most compelling aspect of music instruction, attracting the attention of music researchers. Multiple layers of interaction shape this dynamic interplay, including such musical components as literature and instruments and such cultural artifacts as language and evolving instructional processes.

As compelling as human interaction is for music instruction, physical proximity may no longer be a requirement. Walden and Veblen (2008) examined teaching and learning in a virtual online community. The authors acknowledge that the term "community" is contingent upon definition, but that all communities are bound by ways of social learning specific to its members. Examining interactions within a "community of practice" provides valuable insight into how learning is facilitated within that social entity.

The researchers explore various internet platforms used by the virtual Irish traditional music community (IrTrad) to define itself: bulletin boards, chat sites, YouTube videos, and web sites devoted to live sessions and club events worldwide within which participants can actively engage. Once geographically bound and imbued with cultural significance, traditional Irish music was transmitted individually and informally, one tune at a time, in kitchens, at family gatherings, at social events, and in dances at the crossroads. Now termed, Celtic Music, it is a phenomenon enjoyed by a global community. Individual master players offer interactive lessons on YouTube, formally and informally, to aspiring Irish tin whistle players worldwide. The various mediums are fluid, and platforms are overlapping with discussions focused on issues relevant to authenticity, performance practice, and repertoire. Through interactive sites, students can submit samples of their playing to "master teachers" for feedback, learn a number of personalized interpretations that evolved regionally in Ireland, and join other players to work out fingerings and refine style.

Music Ensembles

Whether we are discussing the Guarneri String Quartet, the high school jazz ensemble, a garage band, or even the virtual Celtic Music ensembles discussed above, the joy of making music together is undeniably affirmed as players connect intuitively. Catching a nuanced intonation, imitating a riff, or complementing a rhythmic motif, musicians are astutely aware of others' contributions in collective music making. Interactions create in-the-moment musical experiences. The music comes alive through vibrant exchanges, generating energy in complementary and reciprocal play. Sawyer (2003) refers to this group creativity as *interactional synchrony*; others call it *groove* (Berliner, 1994; Monson, 1996) or define it as *a zone of magic* (John-Steiner, 2000).

Perhaps you have felt your own engagement intensify in the give-and-take between conductor and ensemble. When participants are attuned with each other, the group scaffolds the experience collaboratively, feeling the power of collective musical engagement. In my interviews with students from The Celia Cruz High School for Music, classmates talked about musical connections, commitment to one another, and dedication to hard work. They count on each other. "But, you know, you might not be 100% everyday; you know, everybody has a bad day. But that's okay," exclaimed Omar, "because we know how good everybody can be and we lift each other up on the off days." Their deep care for one another and respect for each other's efforts impressed me. The mutually shared result far exceeds expectation. Consider, for example, the choir member who comments, "You [as director] have made all the difference in our sound." You perceive it differently, recognizing the power of collaborative efforts and collective interplay, of participants inviting and integrating best efforts. It is the reciprocity of shared contributions that creates this dynamic connection, resulting in the joy of musical expression and delight in aesthetic experience.

Making music together fosters mutuality and respect; participants find a sense of belonging (Dissanayake, 2000b). Ricardo, an oboist at The Celia Cruz High School for Music, reflected, "If I wasn't here, I'd be lost; I probably would have dropped out of school." Through collective hard work, dedication to the music, and commitment to the process, students realize musical competence as confidence grows and relationships develop. The communal experience of music ensembles communicates the value of cooperative endeavors and the power of collaborative efforts.

Adderley, Kennedy and Berz (2003) conducted 60 structured interviews with high school band, chorus, and orchestra students. Four focus areas organized analysis: motivation for joining ensembles and remaining in them; perception of performance groups by participating members and the school community at large; meaning and value the ensembles engendered for participants; and the music classroom's social climate. The social aspect emerged as a pervasive element. Student references to the social domain were interspersed throughout the data and embedded within all four themes. Students noted the importance of relationships for personal well-being **and** for musical growth. The researchers conclude:

> The social climate of these ensembles is important to each member, and provides many with an outlet that they might not have had to meet others from within the larger school setting, or to form relationships away from the home environment that assist them in negotiating the often turbulent high school years. (p. 204)

How does one foster such cooperation and collaboration among student ensembles that are largely teacher/conductor directed? Jones (2005) suggests that the teacher-as-conductor model may, in fact, work against students achieving musical competencies set forth by state and national music education organizations. How is the high level of internal competition and the focus on technical mastery characteristic of performance groups reconciled within a cooperative learning paradigm where everyone makes an effort and all contributions are valued? How do we resist exclusivity and elitism, honoring each student's desire to play in an ensemble, albeit acknowledge various skill levels and abilities?

Cope and Smith (1997) argue that the culture of instrument teaching restricts competency to a select few. Yet, Sloboda and Davidson (1996) found that performance expertise is the result of practice, not innate talent. The cultural framework within which instrument teaching occurs is irrelevant to the learner, suggest Cope and Smith. They propose more germane cultural contexts would result in competent players whose facility with an instrument would be appropriate to their social context. Campbell (1995), studying garage bands, challenges music educators to draw from students' experience in this genre, to build on the skills that students repeatedly employ in their "song-getting" process, and to include personally relevant material to support musical development. Green (2008), too, argues that such informal music learning contexts inform classroom music pedagogy.

Several initiatives explore creative alternatives that balance the demand for technical excellence with student needs, enabling and empowering them to share ideas and express views. Although still grounded in a hierarchical model, these include faculty-student orchestras at the university level (Leung, 2006); student performers play side-by-side faculty mentors. Playing with more expert musicians, students have opportunities to exchange opinions and discuss interpretive decisions. In my community, one high school music director teams up with the regional orchestra. Symphony members mentor student musicians playing alongside them. The process will lead to a collaborative concert affectionately called "Stand Sharing."

Andrews (1996) adapted a cooperative learning-teaching strategy, *Student Team Learning*, in a high school instrumental music setting. Students are empowered to accept responsibility and make decisions as they work collaboratively in small groups. The teacher monitors the students' activities from the periphery. As facilitator, she/he scaffolds musical expertise through peer-adult interactions. Cooperative learning affords students peer partnerships; participants become "teachers," assisting with musical problem-solving and musical interpretations.

Also focusing on the secondary level, Allsup (2003) examined mutual learning communities as a possible framework for instrumental music education. Nine high school students, forming two distinct ensembles, were asked to create music that was meaningful and self-expressive. Group 2, choosing traditional concert band instruments, found their efforts nonproductive and lacking in community building. Conversely, Group 1, choosing a jazz/popular compositional genre and instruments typically associated with rock groups, experienced enjoyment, self-direction, and personal meaning. Allsup observed an emphasis on interpersonal relationships, peer-learning and peer-critique in the first group's process: they cared about one other and were concerned about each other's feelings. Through mutuality and reciprocity, members discovered unrealized aptitude and previously unrecognized talent. Peer-learning focused on the process of discovery, not the transmission of skills. Allsup writes: "Given a chance—given space—band students may break out of roles that are defined *for* them, and create opportunities to do more than just 'tap away'" (p. 34).

General Music Classrooms

Music's inherent nature to engage and challenge us, its value as an expressive personal and cultural artifact, and its significant role in cognitive functions renders the music classroom an opportune setting for the learner in community to thrive.

> The communal nature of classroom settings has particular relevance for the contribution of challenge to music learning: The authenticity of specific challenges is defined partially by other people's acknowledgement of them. (Custodero, 2002, p. 6)

In a safe environment, where belonging fosters trust and confidence, the child discovers freedom to explore and create. Dissanayake (2000b) suggests that belonging is fundamentally connected to our ability to find meaning, develop competence, and realize elaboration. Drawing on the collective gifts of the learning community, children creatively collaborate to construct meaning, to elaborate on it, and to transform it. Observing interactions in the music classroom community provides a unique lens through which to view children as agents of their own learning.

Dyadic partnerships take on a dynamic character in general music classrooms as peers find not only where to be (situated-ness) but also with whom to be. Studies of peer-peer dyads (e.g., St. John, 2003, 2005, 2006b) have shown the powerful role that children play in facilitating each other's music learning. Relationships provide an enabling foundation for students to find a way to engage with the music material. With a keen awareness of where others are and what others are doing, children employ deliberate social strategies to scaffold experience.

Children use peers and adults differently in the learning community (Custodero 1998, 2002, 2005). Custodero's research identifies the complexity of the social dimension in music learning environments and on flow experience. Children in flow used social interactions differently than those not in flow; social interplay facilitated their enjoyment. This provocative social dimension is consistently reported in Custodero's research and finds resonance in other studies (e.g., St. John, 2004). Children looked to adults to monitor their challenge level, give feedback and offer encouragement. Peers served as imitative models, providing a way to become involved in the music activity when the challenge was perceived as inappropriate or, to intensify their experience when already engaged.

The community of learners is a powerful influence on children's music learning experience. There are moments when simply being together, engaged in the collective activity of music making, creates the foundation from which the joy of learning emerges. Collective experiences generate collaborative endeavors and foster shared creativity among the learning community (St. John, 2006a). These dynamic interactions create a rich texture of experience. Much like jazz musicians improvising together, ideas travel around the room as children play off each other's contributions and weave together an intricate counterpoint. The curriculum becomes observably more effective as participants share ideas, expanding and transforming the teacher-delivered content. By finding and making their own meaning, participants develop the thrill of musical competence and discover the joy of musical expression as they make music together.

Such curricular approaches as the MMCP, mentioned at the beginning of this chapter, support the learner in community; they invite collective activity and encourage collaborative efforts among general music students. Learning Activity Packets (LAP) designed around a particular genre, compositional project, or musical style, foster critical thinking as students work together to problem-solve and problem-find, negotiate ideas, and incorporate contributions. These collective activities call forth each student's capabilities, celebrating creativity and collaboration in the community.

Each of these settings holds potential for community building and possibility for creative collaboration. Making music together offers promise in a divided world, uniting people from diverse backgrounds and distinct cultures. It compels us to find common ground as we explore and incorporate varied musical styles, genres, and expressions. Our challenge is to cultivate inclusive teaching/learning contexts that invite discovery, encourage mutuality, acknowledge difference, and celebrate interdependence.

SUMMARY

This chapter began with a brief historical overview of cooperative learning environments to consider the social dimension of learning. Such musical examples as the Manhattanville Music Curriculum Project and Robert Pace's Group Piano Method situate music experiences in the broader social context of general education.

Music as personal expression and music as cultural expression served as intersecting aspects of Music, Community, and Learning. Trevarthen suggests that the human capacity to communicate musically is inborn, finding expression in infant-mother lyrical exchanges, in what he calls *intrinsic motive response.* Ethnomusicologists examine music's permeating presence in cultural practices and highlight how socialization occurs through active music making in rites and rituals. As we make music together, we discover a sense of belonging, find musical partners, and realize musical synchrony with kindred spirits.

Learning strategies with salient social aspects include imitation, scaffolding, guided participation, and collaboration. These ways of knowing illustrate the primary role of others and the deliberate strategies that students employ to facilitate musical learning. Using environmental resources, the learner in community finds what and who is available to meet shifting needs as confidence deepens and competence develops.

Learning strategies complemented by supportive theories contextualized various dimensions of social influence in knowledge acquisition. Examples underscored how the learner might apply these in the music community. Bandura's *social learning theory* addresses the bidirectional influences of personal and environmental determinants to aid cognitive functions. Three uniquely human features are central to social learning theory: vicariousness, representation, and self-regulation. For Vygotsky, concept development is first realized socially. Significant to Vygotskian theory is the human capacity to use signs to mediate mental activity. Mediating tools may include aural cues, gesture, and other nonverbal forms of communication. Vygotsky argued that the *zone of proximal development,* a dynamic learning space, enables the learner to move to a new place yet unrealized developmentally. Building on prior experience, learning takes place incrementally across time. Examples of scaffolding strategies include imitation, exploration, and manipulation of materials, and guided participation.

Formal and informal collective music making generates relationships. Musical communities emerge as students draw upon available resources, personal and material, found in the intersection and interaction of multiple systems as suggested by Bandura, Vygotsky, Rogoff, and John-Steiner. Through shared efforts, students find what is most needed to scaffold learning and sustain enjoyment. No matter where we find ourselves—a concert hall, a preschool class, a marching band, a garage gig—people essentially make music for and with others.

Collective music making offers a unique opportunity to foster collaborative endeavors rather than competitive elitism. Making music together, participants create community, inviting best efforts and calling forth possibility. An interdependent learning environment characterized by collaboration invites, encourages, fosters, and includes each person's expression of innate musicality. Here, a spirit of inquiry and a sense of wonder shape musical experience as each learner in the community delights in the thrill of self-efficacy and realizes the joy of making music together.

Class Discussion

1. What considerations must be taken into account when designing collective music experiences?

2. What is needed when crafting collaborative assignments, and what is your role as educator in monitoring the group's coordinated efforts?

3. In what ways might you integrate multiple and diverse forms of musical expression in your current or future educational contexts?

Projects

1. Attend a concert featuring an ensemble. Write up a review of that concert specifically addressing the ensemble as a community of practice. Discuss the collaboration between ensemble members, noting any observations of scaffolding or attention to affordances or other learning interactions described in the chapter. How is the audience brought into the community? Join with several classmates who observed different types of ensembles and present your "findings" in a symposium format, where each person gives a short introduction followed by a panel discussion.

2. Playing his cello, virtuoso Yo-Yo Ma has developed relationships in a variety of musical communities, exploring a plethora of musical styles, and challenging personal technique to access the musical expression of the world community. In small groups, explore Ma's life and work by considering his collaborative projects. Create a visual representation. Reflect on the collage of multiple genres and styles displayed. What compelling message about community and learning do you find as music educator? How might you adapt this experience for your general music class? What musical skills and concepts are embedded in such an activity?

SUGGESTED READINGS

John-Steiner, V. (2000). *Creative collaboration*. New York: Oxford.

Malloch, S. & Trevarthen, C. (Eds.) (2009). *Communicative musicality: Exploring the basis of human companionship*. New York: Oxford University Press.

Moll, L. (1990). *Vygotsky and education: Instructional applications of sociohistorical psychology*. New York: Cambridge University Press.

Rogoff, B. (2003). *The cultural nature of human development*. New York: Oxford University Press.

Sawyer, K. (2007). *Group genius: The creative power of collaboration*. Pennsylvania: Basic Books.

CHAPTER 6

∿

Music Learning and Musical Development

Lori A. Custodero

INTRODUCTION

As music teachers, we are called upon to respond to *moments* of musical potential. We interpret learners' activity and determine their needs, offering the appropriate expert assistance to scaffold musical skills and understandings. Such responsive teaching requires dual perspectives—seeing learners as both "being" and "becoming," acknowledging both who they are and what they can be. Our ability to act in these moments is informed by an understanding of developmental trends—a knowledge base of general timelines for maturation that suggest certain teaching strategies and sequenced content coincident with students' age-related strengths.

Development is an interdisciplinary topic used to connote some type of change that is expected and understood to be progressive. From a psychological perspective, development has been theorized to reveal defined patterns of human maturation responsive to individual difference and experience, and where cognitive, social-emotional, and physical changes are viewed as playing a major role in learner readiness. The connections between general and musical development provide insight to best teaching practices, informing the design of curriculum, the approach to instruction, and the assessment of musical skill and conceptual understanding.

Because of the strong relationship between musical, cognitive, social, and physical factors, this chapter weaves the threads of general developmental views and those which are musically specific, noting their mutual influences. An overview of key issues surrounding the concept of development presents a context for situating the discussion as a whole. Next, specific theories in general development and their influences on the understanding of musical growth and learning are examined, followed by a review of musical skills and their trajectories for development. An age-related synthesis of music developmental trends relates the previous materials to pedagogical settings, considering implications for creating environments for growth. The chapter concludes with a summary and reconsideration of developmental views, including consideration of the usefulness and potential for misuse in music teaching and learning.

KEY ISSUES IN MUSICAL DEVELOPMENT

Developmental Change and Musical Growth

What is the nature of innate musical capacities? What can we do to optimize our potential for musical enjoyment and expertise? How can we measure various musical skills and their stability or variation over time? To answer these questions, important to music educators, we need to look to the intersections of general and musical development across the lifespan, where we can see how the developmental function of music supports human growth. For example, our earliest interactions with others are sources for social-emotional learning. Melodies and rhythms are the first vehicles for social communication and personal expression: infants respond to cues in caregivers' voices with their own lyrical coos and playful babble. Singing, moving, and playing with objects-as-instruments are activities that define the preschool years as children engage in spontaneous creation, and later focus on mastering the musical models of their culture. Such performance expertise during early school-age years becomes even more pronounced in adolescence. At this age, learners are experiencing biological transformations that change their identity from child to adult. In this period of transition, people often find constancy in associations with specific musical styles or roles.

Perspectives on musical development are guided by questions about specific musical characteristics that change over time. In the descriptions above, it was noted that the types of music children produce changes, incorporating language, patterns, more controlled use of objects, becoming less spontaneous and more methodical over time. Musical perception also changes over time—there are certain musical qualities that we can perceive as infants, such as scale organization and formal phrase structure (Trehub & Schellenberg, 1995; Trehub, Unyk, & Trainor, 1993) and certain characteristics of musical sound that become differentiated in later childhood, like harmonic progressions. Our preferences are developmental as well and are defined in large part by the company we keep: In our early years we enjoy the music making of and with family members, the lullaby sung by a mother or the dancing music played on a favorite CD of our parents. In middle childhood, we are linked and find new enjoyable experiences with teachers and peers; the latter becomes even more pronounced as we pull away from our childhood and move into adolescence, resisting our elders' preferred music as a way to establish an identity of our own.

These musical changes we see over the course of time are propelled by an array of factors, coinciding with general social, physical, and cognitive changes that occur throughout our lifespan. For example, as we develop fine motor skills, we are better able to perform on musical instruments, and as we learn to label qualities we are better able to hear those qualities. In addition to maturation, which, as will be discussed later, is dependent upon more than just chronological age, we also need to consider the availability of resources and quality of early experiences in students' lives, inasmuch as they seem to be especially influential in the development of musical skills.

Nature and Nurture: Musical Inheritance and Enculturation

Perhaps one of the most influential issues that has guided research and theories about development involves the roles of biology and experience—what we are born with and what we gain as a result of being exposed to certain conditions of our environment. Was it that Johan Sebastian and Anna Magdalena [and first wife, Maria Barbara] Bach passed on their genetic codes for great musicianship, or did all those family music-making sessions account for their children becoming musically successful? And what about Branford, Wynton, Delfeayo, and Jason Marsalis? Was it musical DNA or sharing his passion for music accompanied by a strong work ethic that led Ellis, music educator-father, to raise four world-class jazz musicians? It is clear that both factors contribute, but it seems that family inheritance will only take us so far. Although musical ability is manifested in multiple family generations, studies involving twins (e.g., Coon & Carey, 1989) found that shared environmental conditions were more influential than shared genes. For the Bach and Marsalis families, having access to quality and valued experiences with specific musical instruments, and sharing those experiences with family members who had expertise and interest created situations for musical growth to flourish.

Our familial musical legacies are perpetuated very early in life, with parents and siblings as first teachers, providing musical experiences both directly and indirectly by supporting children's efforts to study and create music. Such nurturing starts in infancy, when babies' responses to parents encourage their musical speech and song and has long-term consequences for subsequent generations: Parents who have memories of their own parents singing to them are much more likely to sing to their children (Custodero & Johnson-Green, 2003). In studies that look at successful musicians and family backgrounds (e.g., Bloom 1985; Moore, Burland, & Davidson, 2003), there are many common experiences that involved parents and siblings who supported efforts to learn music and imparted beliefs that music was a valuable activity.

When it was time to learn an instrument, successful musicians had first music teachers who tended to be child-sensitive and positive; later experiences involved a different style of teacher, usually one whose focus was on technical prowess. This relationship between teaching style and learner's changing needs is an important issue to consider in the development of both educators and students.

The nurturing of musical development by both families and teachers is a cultural phenomenon. Musical styles and functions vary throughout the world, and musical development is highly influenced by these cultural practices. Venda children in South Africa are enculturated into rich musical traditions at an early age through their active participation in the abundant community singing and drumming that accompanies work and ritual (Blacking, 1995). Musical traditions of daily life of children in New York City may involve exposure to a myriad of musical styles heard in the subways and streets, resulting in an ability to recognize and articulate a broad array of musical characteristics. These musical strengths may differ from those of children nurtured in a Navaho community in New Mexico, where natural sounds like bird calls and the wind blowing across a field are readily available for listening and are valued in a rich oral literary heritage. For these children, musical development may be manifest in sensitivity to subtleties of musical sound and in the ease with which they can conjure images and narratives around musical cues.

Although musical practices differ greatly across cultures, and inasmuch, produce a variety of musically valued skills, we seem to all begin our musical education by listening to the voice of our mother and other significant caregivers. In addition to the messages sent in the rhythms and melodic contours of infant-directed speech, there are common features of lullabies from around the world: narrow pitch range, simple repeated melodic patterns, a swaying or rocking feel to the rhythm, and the use of repetitive syllables (such as "la la"). These early experiences are guided by an innate urge on the part of the parent to nurture his/her infant, one that manifests itself powerfully in musical ways. This commonality suggests that music may have a special place in human development: A universal disposition toward music making by parents that spans cultural boundaries suggests that what musical interactions teach is core to our humanity and provides a strong rationale for music as integral to a complete education.

Developmental Trends and Individual Differences

Another consideration when looking at developmental change is the notion of what may be generalized and what may be uniquely individual. When considering both common trends and individual pathways, it becomes clear that general development and musical development are mutually influential. Within the framework of general trends, the path of development is unique to each student because they are influenced by a unique set of circumstances, both experiential and biological. Even in families, differences are important—Teacher-parent Ellis Marsalis noted that he taught each of his musician children differently because *they* were different (Ellison, 2001). Considering developmental trends helps music educators make meaningful curricular choices for students; awareness of difference within the student community provides clues to how to adapt teaching to meet individual needs. Trends in the development of musical behaviors, that is, the interpretation and creation of musical forms through singing, responsive movement, and playing instruments, tend to follow a general sequence beginning with exploratory behaviors and moving to exemplars closer to culturally valued descriptions of music making. In order to more critically examine patterns of typical development addressed throughout the remainder of the chapter, we review ways in which the profession has identified differing developmental paths, and how perspectives on the timing of specific musical experiences and musical "talent" might inform the content of music instruction.

Receptivity to musical nurturing has been identified as having a window of development—in other words, our potential to learn music later in life can be increased with early musical experiences. This perspective is based in the work of Gordon (1998) and colleagues (Valerio, Reynolds, Bolton, Taggert, & Gordon, 1998), who define musicality by the ability to internalize and differentiate tonal and rhythmic patterns. Using a standardized test called the Primary Measures of Music Audiation (PMMA) and its related versions for young children and adolescents, these researchers found that such aptitude, which includes potential for later learning, is stabilized by age 9.

The curriculum developed from this theory offers carefully sequenced, composed patterns of rhythms and melodies in both common and uncommon modes and meters delivered by an adult to a child, usually on a neutral syllable so as to avoid any interference by spoken language. This perspective has its roots in language research, where children's ability to recognize phonemes is greatest at birth and begins to deteriorate when these sounds are not reinforced in the spoken language of a culture.[1] This is due to the natural pruning process, a necessary "choosing" of neural pathways that are used most, while those not needed for operating in a particular culture tend to die off. Gordon's music learning theory supports the idea of maintaining as many musical pathways as possible, even if they are not part of the musical culture of the child (e.g., patterns in the Locrian mode), in order to optimize later potential for hearing and producing a wide array of musical sounds. With recommendations to begin as early in a child's life as possible, proponents of this educational intervention aim to alter "natural" developmental pathways in favor of increased musical skills, specifically audiation, the ability to internally represent music without any aural model present.

The study of distinctively individual pathways in musical development has been a source of interest for psychologists who have studied the lives and development of creative processes of exceptional musicians, from child prodigies (e.g., Feldman, 2000; Pruitt, 1990) to composers such as Robert Schumann (Ostwald, 1985) or Stravinsky (Gardner, 1994). Psychoanalytic studies of professional musicians (Kemp, 1995) as well as studies of the daily lives of adolescent musicians (Csikszentmihalyi, Rathunde, & Whalen, 1993) indicate that musicians considered "gifted" are more introverted, or at the least, are comfortable being alone, enabling them to work in a solitary environment to practice the skills needed for success. It could be that by nurturing musical initiative and autonomy on the part of learners, we might support musical development over a lifetime.

While development is a valuable concept, because it clarifies general trends of change throughout our lives, it is important that educators attend to the individual pathways of their students, which are created through interactions

---

[1] See Chapter 4 for a comparative discussion of music and language learning.

between acquired experiences and inherited traits and interpreted through cultural beliefs and values. In addition to these factors which happen to us, and over which we have little control, music calls forth our abilities to change—to transform the ambiance of a quieted concert hall through tapping out the clave of a Tito Puente classic or change the chaotic environment of a 5:00 subway ride to a personal oasis by humming a private tune. Music invites us to participate: Through its rhythmic drive, emotional expressivity, and anticipated patterns of continuity, we are drawn to action and can hear and feel consequences as a result of musical choices.

Based on this engaging quality of musical sound, it is not always clear whether general development leads musical development, or whether participation in musical activity leads physical development through the call to move or social development through the call to vocally communicate, or cognitive development through the call to find patterns in sound. Before being able to discuss those possibilities, we must first understand general theories of development and their relationship to research in musical development.

GENERAL THEORIES OF DEVELOPMENT AND MUSICAL APPLICATIONS

In this section, general theories of development are introduced as explanations of how change happens over time, with a focus on four major forces that have shaped the direction of research and related practices: Psychoanalytic Theory, Cognitive-Stage Theory, Sociocultural Theory, and Ecological Theory.

Psychoanalytic Theories

General theories of development strive to explain from a particular perspective how we change over time and to what we might attribute that change. Sigmund Freud's psychoanalytic theory, popular in the early 20th century, provides two relevant contributions to our current understanding. First, his interest in childhood experience as informing adult dispositions is still accepted today. Through his interviews with composers such as Arnold Schoenberg, and artists such as Egon Schiele, he concluded that artistic behavior was cathartic and a means for resolving personal tensions. The idea that musical activity functions in service to the self is also a concept still being explored today by writers like Anthony Storr (1992) and by Anthony Kemp (1995), whose work has focused on personalities of musicians.

Freud's stages of psychosexual development focused on sensory experiences (e.g., the oral stage in infancy) and were derived from adult recollections of childhood. These were adapted to psychosocial stages by Erik Erikson (1968) in a framework that was more contextual and immediate, where tensions or conflicts between who and how we are with others drives development. For infants, the conflict involves trust and mistrust. The adult-child bond is the context in which trust is developed, learned in part, through the musical cues of reciprocal vocal interactions. School-age children are dealing with the tension between industry and initiation; their identities associated with their actions, their "I am what I do" thinking has implications for the ways we provide feedback to our students. It also speaks to the practice of labeling students as musical and nonmusical at this age (from 6 to approximately 12 years): Messages received at this juncture about not being able to sing could create permanent self-images that put at risk the future development of musical promise. In adolescence, developmental attachments to music-associated peer groups figure prominently as youth seek to establish new identities (Erikson, 1968). Erikson's conception of the psychosocial ramifications of individual maturation and societal implications speak to the personal and collective contexts for musical meaning making discussed in Chapter 4. Musically speaking, psychoanalytic theory is about attention to dissonance as it provokes development.

Cognitive Stage Theory

The Swiss biologist, Jean Piaget, contributed the most widely known theoretical framework for understanding human development, although there are several elements of his work that are controversial. This cognitive-developmental stage model focuses on children's interactions with objects, rather than with people, and is an outcome of Piaget's observations of his own children. It offers several important contributions to our understanding of the developing learner. First, Piaget's work provides evidence that children at different ages construct [their understandings of] the world differently than adults do (Piaget, 1962). This is very important to us as teachers inasmuch as we need to consciously consider how our students might perceive a lesson idea rather than rely on our own response and understanding as the standard. Secondly, Piaget provided evidence that children inherently seek stimulation; they are, in a sense, programmed to learn. Thirdly, his analyses interpreted "mistakes" as indications of ways of thinking, rather than just being wrong. Consider the differences between a teaching approach which treats unexpected answers as opportunities to probe complexities of both the concept and the child's thinking, as opposed to shutting down opportunities by interpreting the answer as simply "incorrect."

Perhaps, the most well-known (and controversial) aspect of Piaget's theory is the division of development into cognitive stages, each of which is marked by a distinctive motivational drive to resolve cognitive tensions through self-initiated activity he refers to as "play." The dissonances between what is known and what the individual wants to know are eventually harmonized, and a resultant list of conceptual understandings called schema becomes internalized. In the sensorimotor stage, which roughly covers the first 2 years of life, we are motivated by the pleasure at being the cause; such joy in the doing of something and noting a direct consequence leads to the repetition necessary for learning basic survival skills, a process psychologists call "Mastery motivation" (e.g., McCall, 1995). Piaget also described this self-initiated activity throughout childhood as ways children *play*; in the sensorimotor period, we learn through this functional, practice play.

One of the most noticeable schema that children formulate in the sensori-motor stage is object permanence—learning that objects can disappear tempo-rarily and reappear. This is related to a gradual differentiation of the self from the environment: the child learns that "I exist separate from my mother" and "my mother can leave me and return to me." Parents instinctively play peek-a-boo with infants as a way to support learning, hiding their face with their hands and then revealing the hidden with an expression of surprise. Likewise, as music teachers, we can support learning by introducing games which incorporate the schema of developmental interest to our students. Adding a musical tune to a peek-a-boo activity with scarves with infants might extend into early childhood with "aural peek-a-boo," playing music with instructions to stop or "freeze" when the music stops. For these older children, the less tangible aural cue and addresses schema involving imagination and the symbolic embodiment of sound, which come later and are discussed below.

The preoperational stage covers a span from approximately age 2 to 7 and is defined by a process called adaptation, in which children assimilate information into their understanding of the world and change or accommodate their worlds to take in new information. It is this constant adjustment of thinking that requires imitation, the practicing of newly observed skill to insure its fit into preexist-ing models of the world, and imagination, the clever ways children assimilate the new information to conform to their existing frameworks of understand-ing. These processes are not mutually exclusive, as demonstrated in 4-year-old Chuckie's musical epiphany. He was sitting at his keyboard playing patterns on a group of three black keys, when suddenly, a rush of discovery overtook him and he came running to the teacher saying "My piano is singing to me! It sang 'I step up!' Come, listen!" This recognition of a familiar [teacher-led] ear training activity from his keyboard class was experienced in a new context, resulting in the accommodation of melodic contour into his own performance, imaginatively anthropomorphized.

In the preoperational stage, young children engage in symbolic play, where one can clearly see the imagination take flight. Pretend play with objects replaces functional play, and the question changes from "What can this object do" to "What can I do with this object?" and the hypothesis testing that ensues is an extension of pleasure at being the cause. The importance of the action is replaced by the conceptual information represented by the action. In a music education setting, when teachers ask young children to move to music, they may observe some responding to the exploratory question "What can my body do?" seemingly responding to the kinesthetic pleasure of the movement itself. Other children may be responding to the application of knowledge they have about how their bodies move: "What can I do with my body that will match what I hear?" In this last scenario, they "become" the symbolic representation of the sound. Symbolic play with musical instruments and props often leads to pretend play: Children serve meals of shaker eggs on a hand drum platter and use scarves as capes or baby blankets, providing opportunity to conceptualize adult roles as superhero and parent. These ways of interacting with the world have strong implications for how teachers design curricula.

As children approach middle childhood, they begin to internalize their actions and use them to perform what Piaget called "concrete operations"— including reversal, seriation, and conservation. These operations are often represented in the music curriculum and may provide guidance around students' developmental strengths. For example, when playing a bordun on the xylophone, a 7-year-old will play C – G – C^1 – G (going up and down) with little effort, whereas a 4-year-old who hasn't yet mastered reversal may do better playing C and G simultaneously, as a bordun. A musical task involving seriation might entail putting the tone bars in order from lowest (biggest) to highest (smallest); conservation would require recognizing a melody as the same, even if the tempo or style or key changed. Marilyn Zimmerman (1964, 1967; Zimmerman & Sechrest, 1968) did a series of conservation studies in which she tested the developmental differences between 5-, 7-, 9-, and 13-year-olds in conserving thematic identity, metric groupings, augmentation and diminution, transposition, and inversion. She found in general that performance improved with age, supporting the interaction between general development and musical development.

In the concrete operational period (ages), children's play takes the form of games with rules. These behaviors differ from those in the preoperational stage, in that the play becomes ordered through an implicitly agreed symbol system— one that is culturally salient. Circle dances that have requisite moves and performing specific rhythmic and melodic patterns are activities better suited to this age group than to younger children, whose movement and performances tend to be more eidetic (based in imagery) and improvisational.

Finally, adolescents and adults in Piaget's formal operations stage have developed abstract thinking skills; that is, they are able to hypothesize possibilities not yet imagined and take multiple perspectives. According to Piaget, they have internalized the concrete operations and are able to combine them in systematic ways to make considered decisions. Musically speaking, this might manifest in score study, where collective symbols for sound are understood as conventional notation and musical operations are recognizable, for example, the permutations of the cantus firmus in a Renaissance mass. It might be carried further by examining possible social and political ramifications of such a work and comparing findings to contemporary music.

Although these stages provide general guidelines about what to expect from children at various ages, there is a danger in oversimplification, in that teachers may begin paying more attention to theories than to the knowledge children may be immediately demonstrating. Additionally, there is a noted lack of evidence that these stages are clearly delineated and that learning is as linear as is implied. The focus on logical-mathematical intelligence and the cognitive domain also leaves questions about the relationship to overall development, including interactions with the social and emotional changes as we mature. David Feldman (1988) has addressed this last point as a result of his work with prodigies and outlines a domain-specific model for looking at development, pointing out that some domains, such as music, develop earlier than others.

In addition to Zimmerman's conservation studies, further applications of Piaget's model have been applied in music research. Perhaps, the most comprehensive is found in the spiral model conceived by June Boyce-Tillman [2] (Swanwick & Tillman, 1986) in which 745 compositions of children 3–9 years of age were analyzed. This model was also based on stages involving a process of change: Children ages 0–4 are in the mastery stage which leads to more exploratory interaction with materials; from ages 4–9 children use imitation to move from personal expression to the ability to musically "converse" in the vernacular; young adolescents between 10–15 years were thought to move from imaginative play to creative interpretation, all of which culminates in musical metacognition, the ability to reflect on one's own musical processes.

Piaget is often cited in terms of a constructivist paradigm for education. This stems from the child's intentional pursuit of learning—the interaction with what is offered in the environment, what Gibson (1977), a perceptual psychologist, termed "affordances," and the selective interpretation of those interactions based on past experiences. This is especially important in comparison to Freudian theories and the stimulus-response behaviorist model which infers that the learner passively waits for development to happen. This role of the child as an agent in her own learning suggests we attend to our teaching approach and ensure that, like Piaget, we are observing carefully, not only to assess where the students next need to go, but also to make those decisions in acknowledgement of what is expressively *present*.

Although Piaget's views on development were based on observation, he did not overtly recognize this social piece of his method and his own role in the interpretation of his children. As a biologist, he came to the subject with a focus on the individual's interactions with the environment and considered the responses as biological, rather than sociological, and therefore insinuated that the responses would be more universal than culturally-specific. In Piaget's theoretical construct, development drives learning. In the sociocultural theory of Vygotsky and his followers, we might say that learning drives development, as the *processes* children use to construct understanding about the world was of primary interest, rather than when they emerged.

Sociocultural Theory

Findings from musical studies corroborate research in general development concerning the power of adult interactions, which can either facilitate or inhibit children's "natural optimism and enjoyment of learning" (Shonkoff & Phillips, 2000, p. 159). Literature in both disciplines suggest that adults honor children's contributions to their own development through parenting and teaching

---

[2] Recent modifications have been made by Boyce-Tillman to involve the spiritual element of music making. For more information, see her chapter in Bresler's *International Handbook of Research in the Arts*.

behaviors such as promoting choices and autonomy in activities, avoiding pressures to perform, and encouraging collaboration.

Counterpoint is defined by the relationship between voices—a soprano line may lead with a melody, followed by other voices layered in imitation, each one finishing the replication by spinning into its own related part. Such playfulness continues, with the thematic material being tossed from voice to voice, each part influencing our perception of the last, repetitions converging into spontaneous harmonic coincidence. In much the same way, Vygotsky's theory of development is based on how the presence of other voices provides models for imitation and creates contexts necessary for intellectual growth.

Vygotsky's perspective on development as the process of change resonates with music making: "To encompass in research the process of a given thing's development in all its phases and changes—from birth to death—fundamentally means to discover its nature, its essence, for it is only in movement that a body shows what it is" (1978, p. 65). Rather than investigating linear change, with several stage-related, hierarchical goals, social-cultural theorists are interested in changes in the child's understanding as they relate to specific activity in a specific context, therefore making the process of development unique to each individual. St. John (this volume) has addressed the social-cultural paradigm quite thoroughly, so this chapter will limit discussion to two mechanisms for conceptual development that are particularly relevant to music education and worthy of revisiting: teacher's scaffolding the zone of proximal development, and the relationship between external articulation and internal processing of information.

A primary component of this theory is mediation, the acknowledgement that development is affected by the immediate and historical "situatedness" of the individual. Vygotsky believed that instruction led development, and although some of the influential conditions in learning environments cannot be controlled, pedagogical practices are the purview of the teacher. When determining the zone of proximal development and how best to scaffold the student's path to that potential, teachers are called to consider the specificity of context, task, and individual. Too often, it seems, the scaffolding is used to define a singular "teacher path," which is not always the most efficacious route for the learner. This counters Vygotsky's vision of development, which is individualized and based on functional systems rather than discrete stages, rendering the potential for development unlimited. Rigging the environment with accessible and meaningful affordances (Gibson, 1977) and designing tasks which allow for multiple entry points may provide students (and teachers) the means by which they can scaffold their own and assist in other's learning without limits.

According to sociocultural theory, children's conceptualizing is social inasmuch as it involves language. Beginning with ascribing words provided by someone to represent affective connotations ("Mama"), supreme curiosity about the nature of linguistic representation (What's this?") leads to what Vygotsky (1978)

calls intellectual thought, in which the child understands the concept of signifiers, and speech and thought intersect; this happens at about 2 years of age. At
around 3 years, children begin using speech to monitor their activity, and eventually, that speech becomes internalized at around 7 years. Vygotsky uses the
internalization process to explain the proliferation of imagination in adolescence
as "play without action" (1978, p. 129).

As maturation continues, so does this contrapuntal process, generated and
sustained using the psychological and technical tools at hand. Making music with
others can be interpreted, in a Vygotskian sense, as opportunity for learning, since
scaffolding is available from many sources, like fellow singers/instrumentalists
in close proximity, a score, a conducting gesture. The emergent nature of understanding, construed within the context of interactions with others, has strong
implications for music education, inasmuch as instruction leads development.

Ecological Theory

Whereas sociocultural theory deals with personal interactions, ecological theory
addresses the myriad environmental contexts that influence human development.
It is a "big picture" theory that considers how recurring forms of human interaction are shaped by characteristics of the individual, the activity being considered,
and both the immediate context (classroom) and the more distant power wield-
ing contexts (school district, state government agencies) in which related experiences may take place. For music educators, this means considering the inherent
complexities of teaching music, where instructional settings are comprised of
students who each bring a unique background that is defined by degrees of accessibility to varying types of musical experiences. Interactions between systems
of support for music education—families, neighborhoods, schools, state, and
national government organizations may be compared to the concept of swing in
a jazz combo, where the harmonic direction provided by the bass, the rhythmic
momentum in the drums, and the warp and woof of textures created in the piano
accompaniment coalesce into a whole, syncopated with the idiosyncratic variety
of individual interpretations.

Ecological theorists such as Lewin (1946) and Bronfenbrenner (1979) sought
an alternative to development research in which humans were studied in laboratories, separate from the myriad influences that actually shape people's behavior.
They were responding to a detached view of human development, where findings
were generated in a laboratory unrelated to every day life. They were especially
interested in primary systems involving family, the workplace and peer groups.
Ecologies of learning are thus understood as concentric circles, each of which represents a positioning of the individual in a system of environmental interactions.
The closest levels are microsystems, which circumscribe the most immediate
face-to-face experiences with others. Musically, these might include both environments students seek out on their own, such as garage bands and playgrounds,
and those which are provided for them in schools and community-based institutions, such as beginning orchestra class or studio trombone lessons, as well as

places of everyday life like homes and neighborhoods. Mesosystems are those which consider the connections between two of these microsystems—like home and school; these might provide important ways of thinking about practicing, for example. Exosystems consider two or more settings with at least one of those being an indirect influence, such as race or class—these interactions may reveal important information about equity and social justice in teaching.

Ecological theory focuses on individuals in activity as they exist within a variety of contexts, thus supporting the ideas of transfer in educative ways. When one views music as a human activity through this lens, relationships between general and musical development are revealed. For example, Bronfenbrenner (1979) describes the importance of an ecological approach in looking at transitions, and musical activity provides a clear model of transitional objects for people over the lifespan. Young children can transgress the boundaries of location and bring a familiar song "Twinkle, Twinkle" to a new school or classroom, maintaining the familiar in a new setting, Teachers can use popular culture as an entry point for understanding musical concepts in music from earlier historical periods or cultures—inviting interactions between points in time or global arenas. Following ecological theory, these examples demonstrate that activity is viewed as both a means and an end—it is both what develops and how it develops.

Each of these theories of human development reflects an attitude about change, and what it is that drives us to change. Psychoanalytic theory focuses on conflicts individuals face in negotiating their survival in the world. For cognitive stage theorists, it is our interactions with the tools in our environment, for sociocultural theorists, it is our interactions with others. Finally, ecological theory acknowledges the multiple contexts in which people find themselves, noting that they may support change in a variety of ways.

In considering musical development, we look at the interactions between these changes and the subject matter, so in order to best address music learning, we need to define what it is that develops—what does it mean to be musical? In the following section, musical skills and conceptual understanding are explored, with reports on research that addresses their change over time, inviting thinking as to the timing of our educational efforts.

PATHWAYS AND PATTERNS OF MUSICAL DEVELOPMENT

Musical Skills and Musical Development

Development and learning are closely related concepts; both focus on change: the first is more "standardized" in that it speaks to general principles of growth, and the second, more content-specific. Given these close relationships, teachers may view musical development differently. To a middle school band director, it might be interpreted as the learner's growing capability to play a concert Bb scale in tune; to a college-level piano teacher, it may involve performing a passage with balanced touch and nuanced dynamic expression. A choral director might focus on teaching the production of clear vowels to get a well-blended group sound, and a general music teacher might ask 3rd grade students to identify salient rhythmic patterns in a recording and invent movements to match what they hear. All are valid; all involve listening and performing or re-presenting sound. In formal assessments and "in the moment" interaction, it is important to acknowledge what we are teaching and our expectations for student acquisition of musical skill. Knowledge of development can provide a framework for understanding this pedagogical challenge.

Each of these music teachers is creating environments for specific musical skills to develop, to expand upon student potential and capabilities. In music education literature, we have referred to such potential and capability as "aptitude," "giftedness," or "talent." These words reflect a variety of perspectives on the nature/nurture issue discussed earlier and reveal beliefs about what it means to be musical. Although somewhat useful in helping to identify certain strengths or deficits in select learners, these characteristics tend to reflect a singular, simplistic, and static view of musical promise. Considering the general developmental models as catalysts for thinking about music, this section addresses the interactive and dynamic nature of musical development. Musical skills are viewed as human understandings-in-action, defined by cultural conceptions of tone and rhythm, and malleable through experience.

Perception, Culture, Listening

Listening is at the heart of musical skill development, evidenced even before birth in both anecdotal reports and experiments in which the fetus moves in response to musical stimuli (Lecanuet, 1996). Listening is present in each of the scenarios described above—playing scales in tune, varying dynamic levels for expressive purposes, blending voices with others, and identifying formal structures—all require careful listening to music. Listening involves readiness to receive the messages, or feedback music has to offer; the function of that feedback links to specific musical skills and cultural understandings of sound. In performing others' music and in creating our own, we listen and make judgments and commensurate adjustments based on what we hear and what we imagine the sound should be; when we read and write music, we must listen and match sound to symbol, whether we are listening internally (audiating) or listening to sound actually present in our environment. We also listen with cultural heritage, suggesting that we acquire meaningful associations with music through listening to it with others, and by repeated listening, we develop conceptual understanding that can be transferred to other artistic experiences and interpreted as it relates to our everyday life.

Listening, then, is meaningful perception, and is developed as a consequence of our cultural existence. Developmental change is mostly a matter of shaping that perception through enculturation. We are born with acute perceptual capabilities; this well-developed infant musicality provides evidence that humans are predisposed to musical understanding (Trehub, 2001). Below, the timing, characteristics, and extent to which this inherent musical promise manifests in perceptual, performance, and conceptualizing skills is considered in terms exposure of to culturally defined musical idioms; interactions with general development; and the physiological impact of hands-on activity.

Developmental Pathways

Experience mediates development, and Aslin's (1981) model of perceptual outcomes provides a clear picture of possible trajectories that have implications for musical development.

Viewed through the lens of perceptual development, the skill level available at the onset of experience interacts with the frequency and character of those experiences in order to determine outcomes over time. With few exceptions, the ability to make some type of meaning from sound and to respond to patterns in music is well developed at birth; parents and children are able to communicate through a common understanding of tone and rhythm. Therefore, the trajectory for musical perception might be placed somewhere near the top arch in Figure 6.1.

Studies of language indicate the strong role of experience in the perception of sound: Certain phonemes that do not exist in the infant's native language(s)—in the case of English, an example might be the nine variants of a single tone in

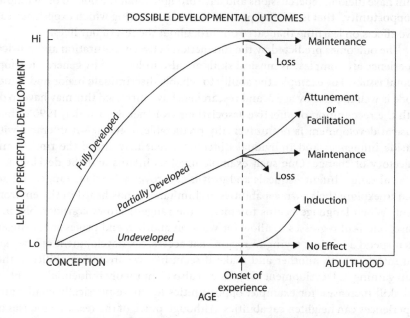

Figure 6.1. **Possible Developmental Outcomes Given Different Levels of Perceptual Development before the Onset of Experience and Different Experiences Afterward.** (From Aslin 1981. Copyright © Academic Press. Reprinted with permission.)

Cantonese—are only discernable in clinical experiments until about the sixth month of life. After that, the neural pathways not being reinforced in day-to-day living begin to die off to make way for the strengthening of those more directly functional. Musically speaking, this sensitivity to sound might manifest in a clear understanding of diatonic melody, as it is used in modern day popular music. Since we retain this perceptual skill to the extent that was experienced, sounds encountered as foreign to our musical culture will not be easily discriminated later. For example, the quarter tones of Indian raga music will be more difficult to differentiate at age 20 if we were not regularly exposed to them early on.

Thus, aural perception becomes interpretable as musical skill when viewed as the ability to differentiate culturally relevant categories—knowing how to adjust the mouthpiece to play in tune with each pitch of that concert Bb scale, for example. Seemingly limitless at birth, the ability to categorize pitch is been honed by direct experience with the instrument; early experience playing a musical instrument is associated with absolute pitch, for example. In other words, when the notion of pitch has relevance in active experience—the playing of an instrument—the listening skill has meaning and is reinforced. It is interesting to note that this change in skill development is accompanied by physiological change: Brain scan studies show differences in the size of the region responsible for auditory processing in violinists with absolute pitch who started training before age 7 (Schlaug, Jancke, Huang, & Steinmetz, 1995). These changes in the brain have lifelong repercussions and have brought about the notion of "windows of opportunity," that is, limited periods in our lives during which experience can have effects on learning that carry on throughout the rest of our lives.

The outcomes predicted by the interaction between maturation and musical experience are complex, as musical skills are also influenced by general developmental issues. For example, the ability to reliably discriminate major and minor mode is well in place by age 3, and researchers have surmised this may have to do with the recognition of affective associations (Kastner & Crowder, 1990). Thus, musical development is not universally predictable or linear—it interacts with outside influences and individual differences that may shape the timing and trajectory of change. One such example involves infants and the development of vocal range. Infants' squeals and growls can cover a 2-octave range, and are used to explore their own capabilities and imitate sounds heard in the environment. When language begins to emerge, the range narrows considerably, in a sense, one skill regresses to allow for work on another, and professional singers often spend a lifetime trying to regain that access. So, development of one skill can interfere with another and make it seem like we are losing ability, rather than gaining it. Development of skills can also be mutually influential—as physical skill increases, for example, opportunities for more physically challenging experiences can heighten capabilities. Although much of the research focuses on early childhood, perceptual understanding and musical understanding continue to develop in older children and adults. James Trybendis (2007) is a high school band director who saw the following development in his own teaching. He wrote this as part of a class assignment for which he reviewed literature on harmonic perception:

> I was working with a group of students who had been playing together for three years. Before their winter concert we were rehearsing a familiar tune. The period was almost over so I decided to end the piece with a fermata on a half cadence. As we sustained the dominant seventh chord I knew I would be unable to end the period without resolution. I cut off the chord and asked students (without looking at the music) to play the note that sounds like it would come next. The students stared at me blankly. Considering the possibility they could not find the note on their instrument, I asked them to sing the note instead. Again, the students looked at me as if I were discussing quantum physics. The half cadence was a satisfactory ending for those students. The piece could have ended there and it would have made no difference to them. What was I doing wrong? Why couldn't these students hear that this chord desperately wanted to resolve to the tonic? Now I teach my high school band students to develop the ability to hear the function of musical pitches... They acquire conceptual skills resulting in the identification of key relationships, learn to listen to and identify the chords tones being played, and to hear their own errors and make self-corrections. This is at the heart of it! My third year of teaching I decided to try the dominant seventh test that I had tried in my first year. I held out the dominant seventh fermata for an extended length, stopped the piece and asked the students to take out something new. The room was filled with cries of anguish and desire for resolution. Most students played or hummed the tonic pitch before taking out the next piece. These students had learned to listen to tonality.

Patterns of Musical Development: Typical and Extraordinary

Two broadly studied topics are introduced as examples of how musical skills develop building upon ideas presented on interactions between experience and timing. First, singing, whose development moves toward increasing complexity and internalization of processes during early and middle childhood is discussed, followed by an overview on instrument playing, where a variety of trajectories result from interactions between experiences, maturity, and dispositions. While early and middle childhood are formative years for this skill development, it is the patterns that emerge in the "tween"- and teen-age years that reveal influential factors allowing complexity to flourish in the context of abstract thought, self-knowledge, and identity construction—both in traditional and informal settings.

Singing Songs: Developing from Early Advantage

Singing competency develops from the global to the particular, from a sense of the wholeness of a song to filling in the details of melodic contour, rhythmic accuracy, and words. It has been studied widely, especially in the early years (ages 1–7), and as such, coexists with the development of language. The issue of language development as a competing goal for musical development in terms of singing range was raised earlier and brings up the important influence of models. Adults are the primary models in the first years and the lyrical, wide-ranging vocalizing adults do with infants changes quickly when they notice their conversation partners' attempts to mimic words—their focus then becomes enunciation of consonants and providing feedback about articulation and grammar of speech rather than the lyrical sound of the voice (Bergeson & Trehub, 1999). The role of modeling in music education contexts has been an important area of study throughout the lifespan, and has raised issues such as men using their head voice in order to match register when teaching young children.

Moog's (1976) historic study of close to 500 children between the ages of 3 months and 7 years in Germany in the early 1960s focused on the development of vocal and movement responses to musical stimuli. He observed children in the context of their own homes, and administered several "tests" that included (a) singing folk songs believed to be familiar and novel to listeners, (b) playing rhythmic patterns on Orff instruments, and (c) recorded performances for string quartet as well as excerpts from a Bruckner symphony and a German popular piece. He noted infants' babbling in response to the music played was rare before 6 months, but fully operating by age 2. These babble songs varied melodically, but tended to be consistent regarding the rhythmic length of tones. (This suggests a regulatory function of music for children this age.)

Starting at age 2, the spontaneous songs researchers heard were incorporating more words and took on a sense of narrative that was different than the prevailing adult culture in its organization, reflecting a proto-structure of sorts. This learning of words played a role in the learning of songs—there seemed to be subgroups of children who focused on either words or pitch, with the rhythm attuned to either the song lyrics or musical rhythm. Children demonstrated their knowledge of learned songs through their conception of formal resemblances, joining in isolated fragments at the appropriate time. They took these fragments into their spontaneous music making, and combined them with invented song, creating what Moog (1976) called potpourri pieces. From ages 3 to 4 children's singing of spontaneous songs continue; many had a repertoire of 5 to 10 songs, but by age 5, such spontaneity is becoming replaced by the more consistency of learned song, which is incorporated into imaginary play—harkening to the assimilation and accommodation principles of Piaget.

At the Ann Arbor Symposium over a decade later, Harvard Project Zero researchers Davidson, McKernon and Gardner (1981) confirmed some of Moog's findings, and referred to the proto-structural process as "topological mapping" and studied its evolution over the period of a year with the acquisition of one song. They found the developmental progression of skill next involved increased accuracy in the rhythmic surface, followed by pitch contour and finally, to the stability of tonality or key. Davidson (1994) expands this developmental process through a comparison to Piaget's model. The first general contours are considered figurative, that is, aligned with sensorimotor thinking; the larger phrase structures show concrete operations, and the understanding of tonality in terms of scale degrees constitutes operational thinking, which requires internalization of the model. This may be linked to the teacher story above where older band students responded so well to the teaching around tonality—could it be there are multiple windows for musical development? In a related study, Rutkowski and Miller (2003) found that children's pitch accuracy while singing songs improved more after first grade—that it was more malleable to training at that point.

Many early childhood scholars have been interested in a universal schema children use during their spontaneous music making during play, considering it the first interval that can be sung in tune: the falling minor 3rd (sol-mi). Although it may be common in certain parts of Europe and North America, there is not enough evidence that it is indeed universal. Researchers have found that children's spontaneous singing is influenced by sounds in their environment (see, for example, Marsh, 2008). The folk songs of Hungary might be characterized by this interval, leading Kodaly to treat it as an "ur song" in his conception of a sequenced music education repertoire. This does not mean that the Kodaly method does not "work" in other settings; however, those teaching in other regions of the world might do well to look at the indigenous music of their own area and take teaching cues from local repertoire. (See Randall Allsup's chapter on Repertoire in this volume.)

A strategy used by children and adult singers that leads to skill development involves gesture. Using the hands in a purposeful way that reflects sound qualities can increase pitch accuracy, as with Curwen hand signs, or encourage physiological adjustment that aids in the development of skill, such as the use of "floating" arm gestures to open up the vocal mechanism during choral warm-ups. Developmental studies by Goldin-Meadow (e.g., 2000) indicate that children use gesture to help themselves with language learning, and that gesture helps reinforce task memory. Such evidence indicates gesture's role in spatial orientation as well (Erlich, Levine, & Goldin-Meadow, 2006), providing an interesting connection to the research on cognitive effects of music listening (e.g., Rauscher & Shaw, 1998). It also suggests certain common themes of development across arts forms, such as the addition of details to stick-figured people in children's drawings occurring around the same age as does their increased pitch accuracy in song singing.

Development of the singing voice continues throughout the lifespan, with specific challenges for music education at each stage. Adolescence holds perhaps one of the greatest challenges in the transformation of the vocal mechanism from child to adult involving the cartilage, musculature of the larnx, and growth of the vocal tract as well as other dramatic physiological changes. One study of vocal fold length in males found an increase of 63% from prepuberty to puberty (Kahane, 1978). The vocal transition fuels adolescent self-perceptions and identity formation, which in turn, create multiple possibilities for developmental outcomes that are dependent on the types, frequency, and intensity of experiences one has with singing.

Cultivating Performance: Development of Musical Skill and Passion

Perspectives on talent vary greatly amongst scholars and teachers: Perhaps one of the most influential music pedagogues of the last 100 years, Shinichi Suzuki defined talent as the potential in every child to play an instrument. Using the natural learning of language as a model, he developed a curriculum to address what he considered were universal ways children respond to musical training in the context of family and peers. Although others might argue for the existence of a wide range of talent potential in children, there may be much to learn about teaching every student from the research on the development of what McPherson (1997) refers to as "superior performance in a specific field of human activity" (p. 74). In this section, we look at case studies and larger scaled interview studies for information on patterns involving the trajectories of performance skill.

According to Gardner (1983), musical intelligence is the first to develop—perhaps most notably in the instrument playing domain, remarkable to us because of the physical coordination required that is not usually available until later into middle childhood. In his analysis of Mozart's extreme talent, Feldman (2000) cites three particular factors that have contributed to the likelihood of an individual's potential for success in a domain such as music to be realized. Those include the traits of the child, both socially and intellectually, similar to those described above; the ability of the parents to support the child's efforts, a commitment often accompanied by personal sacrifice; and the availability of resources needed for the strengthening of musical skills and expertise, along with the value and need for the skill in society. In charting the life of arguably the most famous child musical prodigy of all time, Feldman revealed lessons relevant to those who might have influence on the development of similar gifts today. His admonitions center on early awareness and acknowledgement of giftedness and providing what we can in terms of resources and parent education.

Sosniak's (1985) study of 23 pianists showed similar patterns of instruction over time. First teachers tended to be playful and engaging, cultivating a love of the instrument. By middle childhood, there was usually a move to a second teacher, who focused on technique.

Coming from the field of social psychology, Csikszentmihalyi's (e.g., 1979, 1990; Csikszentmihalyi & Csikszentmihalyi, 1988) framework is different, believing that talent is an individual trait that responds to developmental factors, exists in a variety of domains, and must be supported by a field of people who value the particular human activity represented. In a large scale study, researchers studied 280 high school students who had been identified as talented by their teachers—of these, 79 were music students (33 males and 46 females); the others had talent in athletics, mathematics, or visual arts. There were certain personal characteristics that these youth had in common, best described as a balance between openness and concentration—they were also more comfortable being alone than were other people their age, which provided a context to practice skills. Teachers who provided the best environments for talent to thrive offered both support and stimulation, and had the "cultivation of passionate interest" (Csiskzentmihalyi, Rahtunde, and Whalen, 1993, p. 190) as their prime educational goal.

Like singing, learning to play an instrument draws upon several subsets of musical skill and general development needed to excel. It is clear that experience is needed to continue developing, so perhaps the most important question for music educators is, "What can I do to facilitate the musical development of my students?" In the next section, general development and musical developmental pathways, theories of change, and consideration for the ways in which skills are malleable to experience are used to identify age-related characteristics of music learners, presenting a broad view of how the function of music making changes for individuals over time.

DEVELOPMENTAL CHARACTERISTICS OF MUSIC LEARNERS

Music educators are often labeled as "specialists," people with focused expertise in a single subject rather than the broad knowledge base which distinguishes their classroom colleagues. Even within the spectrum of music teachers, there are those who have specialized interests and expertise such as general music, choral, band, orchestra, or group piano. In addition, the content specialty is further compartmentalized into an age-based specialty: "I teach middle school chorus." Thus, considering the interactions between music characteristics and age-related development, this section addresses learners at various stages throughout the lifespan, beginning with infancy, and continuing through early and middle childhood, adolescence, and adulthood. Starting with key developmental issues and related musical strengths, the mechanisms with which people at different life stages respond are considered and applied to implications for teaching (see Table 6.1). The chronological years provided are meant to be interpreted loosely, and the caveat to combine this information with careful and continuous observation and reflection cannot be overstated.

Infant and Toddler Music Learners (Ages 1–2)

Inasmuch as hearing is fully developed at 5 months' gestation, infants come to this world with musical experiences—hearing the rhythm of their mother's heartbeat, the melody and timbre of her voice, and even the muted musical sounds in her environment. This means that newborns respond to these sounds as familiar and also respond to adults' musical "infant-directed" speech, which is higher pitched and more melodic than speech directed toward older children. Through these early experiences involving musical speech, rhythmic rocking, and singing infant songs (which may or may not be traditional lullabies, but often popular songs delivered in a lullaby style), infants learn how to trust people. These are intimate experiences between adult and child, and music interventions which "teach" how to do music with babies need to keep in mind the child-caregiver bond as a primary developmental condition.

Infant proclivity for discriminating and reproducing sound is both a strength and an opportunity of this particular age group resulting from the plasticity of the brain. In the first year, the pruning process corrects for an overabundance of neural possibilities with which we are born. Experience with certain sounds

Table 6.1 Developmental Characteristics

Life Stage	Developmental Issues	Musical Strengths	Response Mechanisms	Teaching Implications
Infants (first year) Toddlers (2nd year)	Belonging/attachment Sensory awareness Mastery play Independence	Pitch Matching Perception Embodiment	Vocalizing Affective (Facial/ Body) Anticipatory Movement Rhythmic Bounce	Parent/child as unit Exaggerate musical cues Provide spaces during activities Repetition Freedom
Early childhood (ages 3–6)	Belonging/group Attuned to environment Dramatic play Constructive play Symbol use	Song Improvisation Expressivity Narrative forms Timbre Patterns Iconic representation	Contextual association Attends to sensory cues Embodiment Imagination Discovery/repetition Spontaneous Song Create/ interpret Problem solving Integrates visual/aural	Guided peer groups Flexibility Repertoire intensity Free movement Stories Teacher awareness Sound exploration Basic choreographed movement Sound-symbol matching

Stage				
Middle childhood (ages 7–12)	Belonging/Culture Games with rules Peer groups Concrete operations Explicit thinking Sense of Self	Performance Ensemble activity Reading Critical listening Practicing	Emulation Discerns right-wrong Friendships Mental representation Denotative language Competence	Social relevance Clear expectations Small group work Conventional notation Dialogue Instrumental lessons
Adolescence (ages 13–18)	Belonging / Select Group Identity Formal operations Introspection World View	Commitment genre Innovation & style Technical facility Expressivity	Interpretation Role experimentation Hypothesizing Abstraction Expertise Moral Sense	Diverse opportunities Authenticity Composition/solos Analysis and critique Performance Social justice
Adulthood (ages 19 and beyond)	Belonging / Coherence Experience Parenthood	Expertise Interpretation Communication	Vocation/avocation Expectations Reflection Transmission	Individualized Coaching Parenting

establishes neural pathways of perception that protect and foster further potential for growth. The "use it or lose it" principle is applicable here and speaks to implications for teaching these youngest of students in terms of quality musical models and opportunities to respond.

Very young children engage in mastery play, that is, the repetition of simple tasks in order to learn them. This learning process is evident in the vocalizing discussed above and also in the anticipatory movement they initiate to convey expectation. A common game played with infants involves holding them on the lap and bouncing with the knees. When the bouncing stops, babies will often move in some way to signal the continuation. Because these responses are mediated by the physical development and disposition of the infant, it is crucial to provide spaces within and between activities for infants to show what they know. Intersecting general development, attempts at musical mastery, such as making a sound with an object, often support the mastery of motor competencies and social environments. A child's curiosity about a maraca might incite his desire to reach, crawl, or walk to retrieve it; once retrieved he may choose to share or imitate another's performance. Children with special needs are often responsive to musical settings, because of the motivational properties and immediate feedback musical experiences can provide.

The transition to toddlerhood is marked by increased mobility and language use, providing means to exert independence. With these changes in maturation come changes in our teaching practice, such as providing more space for movement and repertoire that has short repeatable fragments, for example, "E I EI O," to provide places to join in. Preceding the more locomotor movement that appears around age 2, young toddlers engage in a rhythmic bounce, with feet planted on the ground for balance, they respond to music that is strongly rhythmic by moving up and down with knees bent. Their sensitivity to changes of style is evident in the different movement response to more melodic music, when they tend to sway laterally, from side to side.

Studies of music making in families show that there is a transition from music-focus to language-focus in song singing with children at this age (Bergeson & Trehub, 1999), as parents respond to familiar and valued skills their children exhibit (Custodero & Johnson-Green, 2008). While the intimacy of infant-parent musical communication could suggest a less active role for music educators, the transition to toddlerhood may support opportunity for educational interventions, where music's role may support additional developmental needs, such as the sense of independence.

Early Childhood Music Learners (Ages 3–6)

In a continuation from toddlerhood, children from 3 to6 years are using music as a way to develop independence—how to take care of themselves by monitoring their own psychological states. Ethnographic studies (e.g., Campbell, 1998) reveal young children often use music to regulate their own emotional and behavioral states. Keen observers can hear children singing familiar and invented songs to calm, comfort, and entertain themselves when adults are not available. On a recent airline flight, a child established a ritual of sorts by singing through several complete sequences of Barney's "I Love You," "The Itsy Bitsy Spider," and "Twinkle, Twinkle" during both take off and landing, and only at these times. Music's regulatory function for her can only be hypothesized; it might have served as emotional comfort, as a way to order a world that seemed temporally chaotic, or as aid in transitioning between different environments. The use of music as a "transitional object" to bring the comfort of familiar songs into unfamiliar settings speaks to the primacy of context in young children's association with song. As children begin spending much more time in formalized environments like preschool, they extend their sense of belonging beyond the family and into peer groups; sharing songs is a way they connect and identify with this new setting.

While the play of very young infants is functioning to help them master myriad survival skills, play in the early childhood years involves the cultivation of wonder (Cobb, 1977) through imaginative constructions that incorporate formal principles as well as improvisatory responses. Studies of children's musical free play (Littleton, 1998; Moorhead & Pond, 1978) and in music teaching settings (Custodero, 1998, 2000) show that musical instruments and musical activities are very compelling: when children are provided appropriately challenging environments and are allowed to initiate activity on their own, they are attentive and creative, often persisting for longer periods of time than may be expected. The fascination with musical activity may be related to its multisensory nature. As children engage with music, they may be hearing, moving, touching, and vocalizing—all these ways of relating to the world provide many opportunities for exploration.

Through their dramatic play, young children come to know narrative form, which makes the use of "story," a compelling way to design a lesson sequence for this age group. This imaginative sense is very strong, and children at this age become so engaged in the imagined scene that they sense it as reality. This requires sensitivity when choosing literature for listening—generally, one might exert caution when dealing with examples having intensely expressive qualities, such as orchestral works from the late from 19th century.

Attuned to their surroundings, young children pick up on visual, aural, and kinesthetic cues in their environment. Like the infant who imitated the tennis fan, children 3–6 use the affordances at their disposal, including objects and people (see St. John, this issue). To make the best of this response mechanism, lesson designs can consider learners' everyday lives and how music concepts might exist, and therefore be reinforced, outside the classroom. Teachers of this age also need to be flexible with lesson designs, inasmuch as new affordances in the classroom are often compelling and require attention, resulting in a spontaneous rethinking of the lesson.

At this age, imitation is a way of "trying on"—a knowing through the body often referred to as mimesis. Corresponding with physical development, this embodiment of musical experience is integrative, and speaks to the necessity of physical and metaphorical space children need to "become" the music. Research on movement in early childhood seems to indicate that peers are important for modeling that following the child's tempo results in better beat matching responses.

Middle Childhood Music Learners (Ages 7–12)

Children in this age group tend to be more aware of cultural definitions of music and music making—their values shift from figuring out for themselves how musical sounds can be varied to trying to emulate models who represent what they believe to be their own culture.[3] These models motivate through creating a sense of belonging to the world children know in ways they recognize: Playing the piano like Aunt Stephanie or singing in the choir with friends, this is an age when children understand rules and are willing to follow them in order to play "Für Elise" or sing the latest pop tune. This happens in both formal settings, such as lessons or school ensembles or general music classes and on playgrounds. Marsh (2008) writes of the global phenomenon of hand clapping and other stylized rhythmic games played on playgrounds over three continents. The play of middle childhood looks different than in early childhood; here there are rules that are consistent, student-invented and monitored, and meant to service the art form as a transmittable tradition.

With meaning and value now situated in shared culture, conventional notation is a relevant mode of communication. Prepared by understanding of sound to symbol relationships in creative iconic reading in early childhood, reading notation opens doors for this group to collaborate with each other and in broader settings. This is also the age of internalized thinking (Vygotsky, 1978), when the ability to use language to express what is partially conceived internally reinforces knowledge through clarification. In music settings, middle childhood learners can communicate and respond more explicitly through language to describe musical qualities and conceptualize critical understandings verbally. School experiences at this age are crucial to the formation of the musician identity. By age 7, children have fully developed social comparative skills and are aware of, even vulnerable to suggestion or evidence of their lack of skill.

Adolescent Music Learners (Ages 12–17)

In adolescence, cultural belonging, established through a shared set of beliefs and practices, becomes more clearly delineated. Musical preferences often figure prominently in those specific cultural identities, given the strong influences of emotions and feelings and the need for self-identified affiliation that differentiates youth from their past dependencies on family, and often school-based supports. These sound groups can range from neighborhood garage bands to the high school madrigal singers; from marching bands to jazz combos to mariachi ensembles. Adolescents become explorer-specialists, searching deeply within a

---

[3] For a discussion on children as consumers, see Christopher Small (1996). *Music Education, Society.*

particular genre, committed to authenticity, even in the clothes they wear; they are also searching amongst the special musical roles available for a goodness-of-fit for their skills and dispositions.

The high school student takes her identity as a musician very seriously and needs to have resources to assist in the development of technical skill, conceptual understanding, and personal voice. In the quest for musical identity, students need to have access to a variety of musical roles, which provide opportunity to express themselves as solo performer, ensemble performer, composer, arranger, conductor, critic, musical collaborator, music therapist, music educator, and musicologist.

With the development of formal operations and abstract reasoning involving hypotheses-testing, older adolescents enter what Piaget called "the world of ideas" (1962). This world encompasses the external through the ability to consider others' viewpoints and to dialogue; it encompasses the internal through the ability to internalize thought, to "play without action"—Vygotsky's explanation of the imagination. When these developmental possibilities join with the sensibility of justice and care (Gilligan, 1993) that are hallmarks of this age group, there are implications for new roles music education is beginning to entertain in areas like social justice.

Adult Music Learners (Age 19 and beyond)

Musical associations with places and people from earlier stages in life are accessed in adulthood, providing a sense of coherence. These affiliations that played significant roles in earlier parts of the lifespan: family, peers, performance cohorts become affordances, providing ways to bring close those musical experiences which served to comfort or excite or delight us in the past. More than any other period of the lifespan, adulthood covers a large range of possible transitions influencing our music learning. Three life changes with significant musical possibilities are parenthood, the development of vocational and avocational roles of music, and retirement/end of life issues.

Parenthood seems to bring with it a new repertoire of both musical material and musical practice. Some research has suggested that adults are intuitively musical with their infants, engaging in responsive vocalizing described elsewhere in this chapter (Papousek, 1996; Trehub, 2002). Parents also sing known and invented songs to babies and are more influenced to sing or play music for their own children if they have memories (or beliefs) of being sung to as infants themselves as opposed to whether or not they had musical experiences such as singing in a choir or playing an instrument (Custodero & Johnson Green, 2003). Anecdotal reports of very early song memories being rekindled upon the birth of a child are common and support this view of parenthood as particularly a musical period. There are possibilities that this exists past infancy: in an ethnographic study of ten 3-year-olds and their parents, we found that the spontaneous songs described so consistently in studies of young children were demonstrated in the parenting strategies in many of the families (Custodero, 2006).

Because so much of adulthood is determined by the work we do, musical identity becomes mediated through categories of vocation versus avocation. Being a music "professional" has its own set of developmental possibilities, many of which include periods of self-doubt, and often temporary or even permanent abandonment of the career (Conway, 2008). Also, professional growth may take the form of career changes within the music domain (see Chapter 14 in this volume). As an avocation, musical involvement provides support for development and future wellbeing through its social, cognitive, emotional, communicative, and aesthetic modes of participation. One example of how musicianship continues developing throughout the lifespan is the New Horizon program begun in 1991 by Roy Ernst. New Horizons is an international community music performance organization that supports the creation of performing groups in a variety of communities for people over 50 years of age. It started in Rochester, New York, with one group; there are around 300 bands, orchestras, and choirs registered at the New Horizons web site as of 2008. Comments from their membership are reminders of the lifelong possibilities of musical growth. Catherine Patience from Colorado offered "After not playing my clarinet for 39 years, I will never forget the feeling I had at my first band rehearsal—I felt like a part of me that had been dead came alive again."

SUMMARY: ON BEING AND BECOMING MUSICAL

This chapter has addressed the idea of music learning and developmental change, looking at the intersections of musical and general development as well as the interactions between maturation and experience in the formation of musical skills. Rather than presenting the trajectories of all musical skills, the intent was to provide ways of thinking about (a) how learners develop musically, (b) applications and critique concerning research on musical development, and (c) approaches to curriculum based on developmental issues and musical strengths of specific age groups. These ways of thinking serve to frame our work in terms of both what we know and what we need to know—the "being and becoming" of our profession:

Musical development is dependent upon cultural definitions of "music." Our perception of musical development is reflective of what we value as musical in a culture. In this increasingly globalized world, we need to be aware of our expectations for those raised in traditions that may be different than our own. Additionally, we might keep this in mind when planning to teach repertoire from other traditions, asking "how does this music reflect a theory of development?"

Musical development is complex because it interacts with experience. The ways in which we develop musically are malleable according to interactions with conditions, events, and people in our environment. Although certain trajectories are suggested by research, the opportunities for students to "show what they know" in familiar and resource-rich settings are far too few. Keeping a sense of inquiry about both what we read about learning and what we see in students' responses means we can stay open to what the Nobel prize winning poet Rabindranath Tagore (1926) called "surprise achievements" (p. 257). It also opens up possibilities for interpretation of learner responses beyond the immediate situation of a single musical activity and simplified conception of learners being right or wrong. Teachers who ask *why* a student may be performing in a certain way will be developing tools for their own understanding of what it means to musically educate.

Musical development may lead or be led by general development. Although causal relationships are difficult to determine because of the complexity described above, throughout our lifespan there are indications that musical development may influence general development. From the musical communication between adult and infant, which creates a context for social cognition, to the possible protective factors for aging experienced by those in the New Horizon program, to the use of music therapy to motivate a variety of skills, music provides contexts for growth. Similarly, readiness for musical skill development is oftentimes linked to physical maturation, socialization, and sensory integration.

Musical development is most vulnerable to experience in the early years. Because of the plasticity of the brain in the first years of life, we know that early experiences with sounds matter. One such example is the categorization of pitches acquired through learning to play an instrument early in life, which results in relative pitch discrimination abilities not typically present in the general population. Dispositions are also set early in life; attitudes toward music and the perception of oneself as musical can be determined early and put into action trajectories for later life that may be difficult to interrupt.

Musical development flourishes with opportunities for self-initiated discovery and interaction with others. The development of performance skills follows a path from spontaneity to replication of a cultural model, with a return to the initial sense of freedom or personal interpretation as the ultimate goal. Beginning exploration with musical materials leads to the discovery of both the familiar and the delightfully surprising, motivating mastery through practice. Competencies are then developed with practice and scaffolding; they become contextualized in historical precedents in both the individual's past and the expectations inherent in the idiomatic musical content. The return then, to the freedom of exploration is relative to both established personal and musical styles. These processes are closely tied to their social contexts and the qualities of interactions with people, especially teachers.

Knowledge of development provides guidelines to interpreting behavior and designing music educational activities and environments. In the opening, I suggested that an awareness of ideas born of the immediate context joins expectations based on developmental knowledge to create a responsive learning environment. With improvisatory skill, the music teacher is open to possibilities, while building on developmental strengths. This challenging process of negotiating the multiple influences on each of many students, a process that is revisited each year with a new group, holds promise for our own development as musicians and musical educators.

Class Discussion

1. Consider one of your most memorable experiences as a learner in music education. Using the general theories of development, discuss how your experience supports (or refutes) the key issues of your age group at that time.

2. Discuss the ecology of your own learning, using Bronfenbrenner's model.

3. Choose a song and trace how it could be used to teach three differently-aged student groups.

Start by assessing the developmental strengths of each age group. What would you do differently to introduce the song? How would performance media differ? How might the choice of conceptual focus represented in the song activity differ across age groups?

Projects

1. Collect lullabies from friends and classmates. How are they the same and how are they different?

2. Become a musical anthropologist. Whenever you find yourselves in the presence of young children, listen. Observe. You will most likely hear singing, chanting (rhythmic speech), and use of objects as instruments. You will also see focused movement to sounds the children are making, external sounds, or maybe even to the "songs in their heads." For each episode you observe, record information, such as date, day, and time, location, estimated age of child, and any people accompanying the child. Record with as much detail as you can what you heard and saw—be as detailed as possible.

3. Find several video clips of differently aged people making music on YouTube. What are the developmental issues demonstrated? Do an analysis of what the clip means in terms of musical skills, musical culture, and musical values.

4. Trace the developmental path of a favorite performer or composer. How did their early experiences influence the trajectory of their careers?

SUGGESTED READINGS

Campbell, P. S. (1998). *Songs in their heads: Music and its meaning in children's lives.* New York: Oxford University Press.

Deliege, I., & Sloboda, J. (Eds.). (1996). *Musical beginnings: Origins and development of musical competence.* New York: Oxford University Press.

McPherson, G. (Ed.). (2006). *The child as musician: A handbook of musical development.* New York: Oxford University Press.

Miller, P. H. (2001). *Theories of Developmental Psychology* (4th ed.). New York: Worth.

CHAPTER 7

~

Curriculum

Cathy Benedict

The conception of education as a social process and function
has no definite meaning until we define the kind of society we
have in mind.

(DEWEY, 1916/1944, P. 97)

Curriculum represents the introduction to a particular form
of life; it serves in part to prepare students for dominant or
subordinate positions in the existing society. The curriculum
favors certain forms of knowledge over others and affirms the
dreams, desires, and values of select groups of students over
other groups, often discriminatorily on the basis of race, class,
and gender.

(McLAREN, 1989, P. 183)

INTRODUCTION

Whether we realize it or not, all of us have been curriculum makers. As we sat
in our elementary music classes, our engagements with the music teacher shaped
how the lessons and curriculum would flow. As we sat in our ensembles, not only
did the repertoire shape the curriculum, but the perceived skill level of our classmates did as well. In the same way, the needs and desires of the local community
often shape what a music program will be; our own discipline often dictates for
us the norms and expectations of what a quality music program is, and thus what
quality curriculum will be.

The history of curriculum is the history of us. It is the history of our strength
and our fallibility. In ways more than one, the history of curriculum has been
similar and parallel to the history of education. Certainly, and on many occasions, the history of curriculum and the history of education have been mistaken
for the other. Unfortunately, this has established and helped to reproduce a curricular history of misconstruction and conceptualization. This in turn, has, in
many cases, led us to think of curriculum as something that happens outside of
a concern with fluidity and outside the necessity and constancy of engagement

and re-engagement with both, not as disparate elements, but as a whole. In other words, what are the challenges we face now as we move into directing and shaping our own programs that either prevent or enable us to consider those ways the norms and expectations of curriculum development can either "affirm the dreams, desires, and values of select groups of students," or as Dewey said, define the kind of society we have in mind?

What kinds of questions are these to ask when most, if not all of us, are certain of the curricular and pedagogical path we wish to take. If it worked for us in the past, why not replicate what we know to have been successful? Why not, indeed. Because, for one reason, this world does not stand still and to desire stability is to desire a stasis that cannot exist. And because, perhaps most importantly, "success" as we have come to know it may not represent success for all. It's not an issue of throwing out curriculum models that have engaged us—orchestra, concert choirs, jazz ensembles, indeed football bands, all curriculum models in their own ways, have for hundreds of years brought to many, not just musical joy, but social joy as well. It is, however, an issue of continually pursuing and questioning concepts and ideals such as "success" and "preparedness."

What then is curriculum? How simple to answer with perhaps what might be the immediate and obvious. But, as we have seen throughout this book, the immediate and obvious are never what they may seem, nor does the immediate or obvious encourage interrogation of issues and reengagements with what has come before and what becomes as we engage. Has curriculum become a slogan of sorts, an ambiguous term that has "establish[ed] a mood or a form with which people can feel comfortable and affiliate with particular pedagogical practices" (Popkewitz, Autumn, 1980, p. 304)? Is curriculum a course to be run, a course or set of experiences that shape us? Are there fundamentals, basics, or essentials that each of us should "know?" Is curriculum a way in which to address social justice? Is there a difference between the stated and operationalized curriculum? What does teaching have to do with curriculum? Who does and doesn't get to "write" curriculum? And finally, yet hardly finally, who is curriculum for and who has been left out?

As educators, we need to be mindful of curriculum theory, philosophy, modes of rationality, and the ways in which these have influenced curriculum making. As music educators, we also need to be particularly mindful of the ways in which these models have influenced, and influence, our pedagogy. We need to consider the ways in which methodologies of teaching (i.e. Orff, Kodaly, Dalcroze) and teaching "to" something (for instance teaching "to" the standards), as well as rehearsal techniques that minimize student input in order to maximize performance goals, dictates very particular curriculum models. We also need to consider that these ways of teaching and their resultant curriculum are influenced by modes of rationality that have potent, formidable historical roots. To not consider what these historical influences are, or the ways in which the parameters of these historical curriculum models have prevented us from engaging in seeing broader possibilities of what music education is and can be, is to continue to reproduce systems of education that are dictated by, and quite possibly serve, not necessarily our needs but the needs of others.

The Function of Schooling

As the opening quotes suggest, the function of curriculum has often been to shape the ways in which students could and should be prepared to enter the world. Curriculum has often been seen as a way in which to reconcile, control, and even solve the embedded tensions between the individual and society. That said, forms of social control have been, at times, more obvious, more of a "given" and perceived as more "welcome," than at others. Goals such as homogeneity, acquiescing to models of authority, social reform, transmission of culture, class structure, and nationalism are only a few objectives that have at times been explicitly stated as end points. Indeed, the beginnings of public schooling in the United States were regarded as a socialization process that would bridge the gap between what was seen as a breakdown of home/community.

Echoing those goals of homogeneity, transmission of culture, nationalism, and so forth, curriculum in music education has been no different. Based on the singing schools of the 19th century, in which the purpose was to "improve singing in the church service" (Birge, 1928, p. 88), the inception of public music education in 1838 had as its purpose goals that were based on the intellectual, moral, and physical contributions music would make in the lives of students. Music was seen to be "good for" memory, comparison, and attention; it was believed that "in music, the "very image of virtue and vice is perceived" and that music could even "defend...from diseases" (as cited in Mark, 1992, pp. 142–143). How these goals have changed or not, and the ways in which control has become hidden is that with which we must contend; for the ways in which the world has shaped and been shaped by the implications and complexity of these inherent contradictions, as well as who has been in a position to interpret and thus shape the world, has defined and framed the parameters of curricular considerations.

The Purpose of the Chapter

All of us have habits of whose import we are quite unaware, since they were formed without knowing what we were about. Consequently [habits] possess us, rather than we them. They move us; they control us. Unless we become aware of what they accomplish, and pass judgment upon the worth of the result, we do not control them. (Dewey, 1916/1944, p. 29)

This chapter seeks to address these issues and habits while at the same time presenting a way to look back and reflect; not just simply as a revisitation, but as a process of problematizing. As such, rather than framing this chapter under headings, such as traditional and nontraditional, or even modern and postmodern, this chapter uses the concept of rationality (and ideology) as a lens and as a mode of analysis. Giroux (1981) describes rationality as both a "set of assumptions and practices" and "interests" that guides, "defines and qualifies," shapes, constitutes, how we are in the world, and how we "reflect" on the world (p. 8). Thus, as we look back and consider curriculum models, we consider those ways in which models have developed and been developed by a construction of knowledge bound by something outside of practices and situations, or models in which human agency, and a critical view of the process of schooling have been denied and ignored. In this process, as we interrogate the rationality that has dictated what questions can be asked, we are then better able to pose and frame those questions that have not been asked.

The first half of this chapter focuses on curriculum that has been shaped by a technical mode of rationality that can be traced to the Enlightenment. It will be suggested that this rationality—as one in which faith in science and reasoning and that which can be observed and measured is favored over all other modes of engagement—framed and continues to frame much of curriculum development in music education. The second half of this chapter focuses on what might be considered an interrogation and reconceptualization of these models.

The space constraints of this chapter prohibit an exhaustive examination of all curriculum models; consequently, there is a need to narrow down the litera-ture. Granted, this is a subjective process. Therefore, it is hoped that this chap-ter affords spaces for mindful consideration and action that come from making and bringing continual sense to readings and engagements. We need to remind ourselves that these curricular models and theories were and will continue to be attempts and constructions of environments for possible learning. Schmidt (September, 2007) reminds us of this when stating:

> We tend to forget in education, as in history, that our beginnings are often arbi-trary, and thus that the certainty we assign to interpretations, theories and prac-tices are, while seemingly inescapable, in fact, substantively chosen. (p. 23)

In all our engagements, we choose. In this chapter, I choose to address partic-ular areas of curriculum through a framework that is not arbitrary; it is a framing that is deliberate and one through which I hope will provide the processes neces-sary for interrogating certainty.

Early Curricular Influences

Both Rousseau (1712–1778) and Pestalozzi (1746–1827) are often cited as major influences in the development of music education curriculum and methods. A closer examination of the basic tenets of these men provides a foundation upon which to consider the authority that has been afforded their work.

Rousseau believed the purpose of education was to engage in processes so that students would be able to relate to others in a natural way that would allow respect for ourselves and others. He was critical of an educative system that encouraged students to base self-worth and superiority through comparisons. Rousseau wasn't interested in parameters set by "book-learning" or methods of instruction; he was interested in the development of character so that one would enter an imperfect world and engage in virtuous acts that would lead toward social unity. He viewed anything that challenged the common allegiance of man, such as rivalries and antisocial behavior, as disruptive. Toward that end, Rousseau believed that rather than building an educative process on a foundation of symbols/signs and representations one needed to encourage and scaffold experiences based on sensory impressions and intuitive ideas.

Among other things, Rousseau was trained as a music copyist and music teacher. He laid out this vision of the teaching learning process as it applied to music:

> First give your young musician practice in very regular, well-cadenced phrases; then let him connect these phrases with the very simplest modulations; then show him their relation one to another by correct accent, which can be done by a fit choice of cadences and rests. On no account give him anything unusual, or anything that requires pathos or expression. A simple, tuneful melody, always based on the common chords of the key, with its bass so clearly indicated that it is easily felt and accompanied; for to train his voice and ear he should always sing with the harpsichord. (1956, p. 500)

This notion, further explored in Chapter 8 of this book, that music had to be introduced in manageable pieces resonates with many other curriculum makers outside and inside the domain of music education. Indeed, Pestalozzi (1894), whose own writings were influenced by those of Rousseau, articulated the "laws of teaching" and even referred to this as "Art" (p. 199). Among those stated laws was the imperative to arrange objects together through their similarities and in ways that would allow one to take them in through different senses (p. 202). Directly related to curriculum development in music education are the laws in which Pestalozzi instructs us to:

> Arrange graduated steps of knowledge, in which every new idea shall be only a small, almost imperceptible addition to that earlier knowledge which has been deeply impressed and made unforgettable.

> Learn to make the simple perfect before going on to the complex. (p. 202)

In 1834, the work of Pestalozzi influenced and framed the work of music educator Lowell Mason as he formulated the *Manual of Instruction*. The principles he devised included directives to teach one thing at a time (i.e. rhythm, melody, expression), teach sounds before signs, master each step before moving on, introduce principles and theory after practice, to "analyze and practice the elements of articulate sound in order to apply them to music," and to teach note names that corresponded to the notes of instrumental music (Birge, 1928, pp. 38–39). To this day, one can see how these laws and principles have influenced the ways music educators conceive of teaching and curriculum construction: a passing familiarity with any instrumental or music series; Orff, Kodály, Gordon, Suzuki, Dalcroze, and so forth bear witness to this.

As we have seen, both Rousseau and Pestalozzi believed students needed to first experience what was to be learned prior to the process of naming and labeling, and both believed that the distillation of the learning process into discrete manageable steps would be the most effective and efficient way to frame the teaching/learning process and thus curriculum development. In the following sections, Bobbitt and Tyler redefine, reinforce, and essentially perfect this process.

SCIENTIFIC AND TECHNICAL RATIONALITY

> Curriculum deals with the selection of desired educational outcomes and learning experiences to achieve these outcomes. Curriculum building in music education includes the formulation of objectives for the music-education program, the organization of classes and activities in which to achieve the objectives, and the selection of experiences that are appropriate to the classes and activities and will contribute to pupil growth toward the objectives. The task of selecting experiences also implies concern with the selection of teaching materials. (Leonhard & House, 1959, p. 22)

The above quote of Leonhard and House from their book *Foundations and Principles* clearly articulates goals and objectives that appear current and on-point as to what it means to write and operationalize curriculum. Yet, one cannot but realize the date of the book, and the over 50 years that separates that time from this, and wonder how it is these words and values continue to pervade and construct our understandings and engagements with the why and how of curriculum making and implementation. Thus, a closer examination of that which influenced their thinking, and much of our thinking today, is integral to our consideration of the curriculum process.

Bobbitt (1876–1952)

Looking back as to what we might consider as curricular mileposts, Kliebard (1977) cites Bobbitt's *The Curriculum* (1918) as a reflection of what came before and what was to come. While this book did not designate curriculum as a field, scholars believed that this book was, however, indicative of the "assumptions and predispositions that were to dominate the thinking of those who were identified with the curriculum field for at least half a century and extending to the present" (Kliebard, 1977, p. 257). Indeed, in a fifty-year retrospective of Bobbitt's work, Jackson (1975) writes of Bobbitt's work and suggests that he has "hacked out the path along which many of us in American education are still traveling" (p. 121).

Bobbitt speaks to the historical purpose of schools and the educative goal as one of teaching students so that they will contribute to social progress. While the definition and engagement with what "social progress" means has been of concern to many philosophers over the centuries, and of neglect to many others, Bobbitt considered social progress as one that views the importance of the advancement of civilization and humanity through a lens of action, activity, and ability. For Bobbitt, this meant not so much what it means to know but rather what one can do. Bobbitt speaks to this process as one that is as simple and as straightforward as finding the problem and fixing it; a process in which performance of low character is not desirable and can be eliminated through training.

Bobbitt felt that curriculum had been framed and defined by the "prepared subject-matter" that was found in textbooks, but also by a purposeful denial of the varying nature and needs of children. This denial of the process and child allowed one to simply choose the "appropriate" texts (in our case one could read "repertoire") and fill the "empty reservoir," in essence, making curriculum planning (and teaching) "simple and easy" (p. 46). Indeed, Bobbitt spoke of this body of abstract knowledge in textbooks as "often almost or entirely without life, embalmed, ready for the pseudo-educational process of storing their content in the memory-vaults" (1924, p. 46).

Bobbitt was particularly frustrated by the "cloudlike" language of "glorious vagueness" that spoke of objectives as "radiant" (1921, p. 607), a perhaps not-so-subtle reference to Dewey and others of the time. Searching for a systematic procedure that would move curriculum from the language of "cloudlike" to definite objectives, Bobbitt believed that the school should provide experiences and activities that were needed for advancement, stability, and consistency in life. These activities (much like the factory assembly line upon which his work was based and the scientific management movement) could be broken down from the complex into discrete subskills. In order to define and select those activities, one needed to both consult a specialist/vocationalist and go out into the world and observe the skills, abilities, and habits of men. Once these habits were identified, one could then divide these down into subsets and units so that they may be taught and learned. As a consequence of his interest in differing and varying abilities (often predicated on issues of social class), it is interesting to note that Bobbitt's concern paved the way for ability groupings in schools.

Bobbitt's writings were criticized by both progressivist educators, as not being child centered enough, and essentialists, as ignoring the contributions of subject matter. However, Bobbitt's legacy and his metaphor of filling the "empty reservoirs" of students' minds remains with us today manifesting as curriculum-as-repertoire, curriculum-as-activities, curriculum-as-fundamentals, and even as curriculum as "hear and fix" rehearsal techniques.

Tyler (1902–1994)

The curriculum work of Tyler can be anchored to his belief that the educational ends-means aims of schools were "inadequate" (1948, p. 205). For Tyler, to consider the ends-means issue was to recognize, through an either/or binary construction, that educability took on two forms, could be identified in two ways, and could provide two paths of carefully selected alternatives. One path was to identify the measurable characteristics of students that correlated with the current stated aims of the schools. This would entail identifying characteristics of students who currently flourished under a system of memorization of textbook content and did well with limited skills, such as computation and basic reading. The other, after identifying what the characteristic would be that would lead to an "enlightened citizenship," required redesigning the ends-means aims of public schooling so that students might not only analyze and think through clearly but would also "cherish significant and desirable social and personal values" (p. 205).

In 1949, Tyler proposed such a system and rationale for "viewing, analyzing and interpreting the curriculum and instructional program" (p. 1). This Tylerian logic of working back from the goal and objectives of a program or discipline permeates all aspects of music education. The rationale presents a model that speaks well to the ease, simplicity, clarity, and seemingly obvious and sensible goals of the traditional music education program; those which we can find so clearly articulated in the words of Leonhard and House. However, while it may appear obvious how this rationale, and Bobbitt's framing of the purpose of education, has influenced music education, it is important that we consider the inception of the rationale so that we may critique, interrogate, and consider curriculum design in our own areas.

The Rationale

Tyler (1949) proposed four questions that he felt would guide the curriculum development process. In the following section, these questions are outlined as well as some of the applications, issues, and critiques that have been raised.

1. What educational purposes should the school seek to attain?
2. What educational experiences can be provided that are likely to attain these purposes?
3. How can learning experiences be organized for effective instruction?
4. How can we determine whether these purposes are being attained?

In order to address the question of educational purposes, one needed to consider the learners themselves, contemporary life outside of school, the subject specialist, the use of philosophy and psychology in selecting objectives. Consequent to this, one could identify the learning experience; in behaviorist terms, that afforded control and management, or in Tyler's words, the "interaction between the learner and the external conditions in the environment to which he can react" (1949, p. 63). After such consideration and identifcation, the teacher then chooses learning experiences based on the goals and purposes that were defined in the first step. For instance, if the teacher (or subject specialist) decides that being a musician means the ability to note, read, and write, then the student must have the opportunity and experiences that will allow her to practice this in ways that are satisfying to her and within her ability. Or, if the teacher decides students are to play or sing the descending minor third in-tune, the teacher needs to present a repertoire in which the interval is prevalent. These objectives needed to be stated in a particular form, for instance:

—At the completion of this rehearsal, the trumpet section will be able to play the allegro section at letter B clearly and succinctly.

—At the completion of this class, students will be able to play the descending minor third in-tune.

—At the completion of this unit, students will able to identify the instruments of the orchestra.

Tyler believed that organization was key and influenced the efficiency of instruction and educational changes in students (p. 83); hence, the organization of the learning experiences needed to be ordered so that in their sequencing they reinforce each other. The criteria for building an "effectively organized group of learning experiences" (p. 84) was continuity; or the recurring practice of skills; sequence, having skills build upon each other; and integration, seeing how skills can be utilized in other areas.

Learning experiences in music education have often been framed by effectiveness and efficiency and are often considered the hallmarks of many classes and rehearsals; indeed, the sequential layering of experiences permeates much of the musical curriculum, whether it be music history, music theory, general music, general music methods, or a band or choral rehearsal. Continuity in the organization of this sequencing can be found embedded in the k-12 program; general music classes prepare students to read and write music; in turn, middle school programs prepare students for the sophisticated music making of high school. Both skills and the practice of skills are sequenced and layered, often dictated by teacher and a repertoire that progresses in difficulty and "sophistication."

Determining whether purposes had been attained means assessing whether the desired results are being produced and to what extent they are being realized. This evaluative process begins by returning to the goals and objectives and then deciding what evidence will addresses these goals. In this process, there is continual movement through all of the steps before one can determine evaluation. Cyclical in nature, evaluation informs and thus drives the process; can the student do the teacher's stated objective, did the final performance run smoothly, can the students read simple pattern rhythmic structures so that others may be introduced?

Critique of the Rationale

There have been several critiques of Tyler's rationale and its accompanying process. Addressing these critiques serves to both engage with Tyler mindfully and to see those ways in which the critiques were integral to the subsequent reconceptualization of curriculum theory and curriculum development. Among many of the critiques is the question as to whether objectives and outcomes can be determined prior to the process of learning, as well as the criteria that is applied in the selection of the goals and objectives. Both Bobbitt and Tyler, rather than relying solely on the knowledge of the teacher, placed their faith in the expertise of the subject specialist. However, deciding and defining who a subject specialist is and relying on their interpretation of what it means to know and do (distilled down into discrete, sequential subskills) further separates teaching from curriculum.

The ways in which the educational objectives are worded have also been critiqued. Eisner (1985) has written that "when objectives are stated behaviorally, it is possible to have specific empirical referents to observe; thus, one is in a position to know without ambiguity whether the behavior objective has been reached" (p. 110). This very particular wording, whether it be educational objectives, instructional objectives, or performance objectives, and the subsequent behaviors that are expected of the student, frames and defines and controls in measurable terms what and how the student will know and be able to do. Nor does it necessarily take into account the pedagogical and learning processes that intertwine with each other.

One of the ways Tyler framed the "needs" of students was to consider the ways in which he believed the human organism must find balance and equilibrium, so that in meeting those needs, socially acceptable behavior would result. This not only speaks clearly to the use of a particular framing of societal needs to determine the goals and objectives but also to a system of power and control through consensus rather than conflict. This rationale, as well as Bobbitt's framing of the curriculum process, operates as a deficit model, one in which stability and consistency, as well as "proficiency in citizenship" are determined by what citizens cannot do, and need to do in order to design a "directed training of systemized education" (Bobbitt, 1918, p. 3).

The Spiral Curriculum

> Grasping the structure of a subject is to understand it in a way that permits
> many other things to be related to it meaningfully. To learn structure, in short,
> is to learn how things are related. (Bruner, 1960, p. 7)

As a cognitive psychologist, Bruner was interested in the ways internal mental processes underlie behaviors, and consequently, the ways in which structure in learning, and thus, structure of the disciplines, plays a central role in how educators might go about considering teaching/learning process and curriculum development. Learning is geared towards a general understanding of the structure of a subject matter, not just the skills, but that "use" is more important than formal naming of "operations" (p. 8). Bruner uses learning a language as an example of intuiting structures without formal naming. It is in the use and the immersion in language that we unconsciously learn the ways (and even uses) in which language can be used to communicate, rather than focusing on the "mastery of facts and techniques" (Bruner, 1960, p. 12). It is in the engagement in the process of doing in which the structure becomes internalized. Bruner calls for a "continual deepening of ones' understanding" that comes from moving into "progressively more complex forms" (p. 13). It is not in exercises that isolate skills and techniques, nor is it accomplished by treating curriculum as sequential, bit-by-bit steps, but rather by creating an environment and context in which teaching/learning and curriculum development is embedded in the engagement with (for instance) the process of musicing. In order to accomplish this, Bruner speaks of the spiral curriculum, one in which "the foundations of any subject may be taught to anybody at any age in some form" (p. 12).

Bruner believes that learning should bring pleasure and serve us in the future. So, while he sees this idea of transfer as "skill transfer" (i.e. using particular musical skills in more than one context), he also sees this as limited. Another way to engage with transfer of learning is to consider it as nonspecific, or the "transfer of principles and attitudes" (p. 17). As opposed to curriculum that focuses on the introduction and subsequent proving of an assertion, this type of curriculum leads through a discovery process in which connections and relations can be made between ideas and concepts so that learning is continually broadened and deepened. While he speaks of this phenomena as playing out in the sciences, a parallel could be made in music curriculum and pedagogy. For instance, repertoire is often introduced noncontextually and uncontested in interpretation and expression, as a work of art, unconditional, and void of human engagement.

Manhattanville Music Curriculum Project

In the late 60s, the work of Bruner provided the framework for the Manhattanville Music Curriculum Project (MMCP). Musicians and educators came together in Purchase, New York, to develop a comprehensive music curriculum that would span prekindergarten through high school. Led by Ronald Thomas, the program evolved out of new musical movements, general curricular movements of the time (including the reform movements in the wake of Sputnik), and a desire to challenge the status quo. Echoing Rousseau, Pestalozzi and Bruner, Thomas (1991) articulated knowings and doings that had not been traditionally honored by music teachers. Thomas referred to those knowing skills as "music fluency skills," or skills that lead toward language facility and the sounds of music rather than symbol and notational skills (p. 28).

The project was developed based on the idea that rather than focusing solely on technical and skill development, "personal meaning through critical thinking and problem solving should be at the heart of the music making experience" (Pogonowski, July, 2001, p. 25). Thomas, not only believed that "all music written must be performed if it is to have any significance in the learning process of the student" (February–March 1964, p. 106) but that students, if given the chance, could be musically conversant in the 20th century musical idiom. The underlying notion was that improvisation as the "medium of the language for thinking in musical sound" (Thomas, 1991, p. 28) permeated the project as a way to engage with the concept of the spiral curriculum. Pogonowski (July 2001) outlined musical processes that were to underlie the ways in which students and teachers were to engage with the music-making experience, extending the list to include not only composition, improvisation, but also interpretation, performing, analyzing, conducting and listening "with critical awareness" (p. 25).

While the roots of this project stem from the 60s, Pogonowski believes "its initiatives are consistent with current curriculum theory" (p. 27). Indeed,

MMCP curricula are still to be found in projects, such as the Comprehensive Musicianship Project in Iowa and Wisconsin.

National Standards in Music

In 1994, the National Standards in Arts Education were published by Music Educators National Conference (MENC). This process did not spring up overnight nor was it without precedent. When the original proposal for the *National Education Goals* (July, 1990) was articulated, the arts were not included. Through a series of advocacy movements, including Michael Greene appearing on the Grammy show and admonishing the administration and the Secretary of Education Lamar Alexander for not including the arts in the *National Education Goals*—federal funding was received enabling voluntary music standards and assessments to be created. The Music Standards make a clear stance for not prescribing any specific methodology; they are about the content of the music. They are focused "on what students should know and be able to do, on content and not methodology or educational theories" (Hope, 1994, p. 36). Reminiscent of both Bobbitt and Tyler, the Standards are concerned with which *results* are characteristic of a basic education.

While not considered curriculum, the National Standards project has influenced and shaped the goals and purposes of curriculum. The standards were based on frameworks and wording that can be traced back in many ways to a resolution passed in 1892 by the United States Music Teachers National Association Department of School Music (Birge, 1928, pp. 234–235). In 1992, when Dorothy Straub (then president of MENC) answered the query: How could a document of such magnitude and significance have been created so quickly? She replied:

> Setting standards is not new for MENC. *The School Music Program: Description and Standards*, revised in 1986,[1] is a thoughtfully written, comprehensive document, widely read by the education and music education communities...it has served as the foundation for developing the new music standards. (p. 4)

In the content and wording of the current document, a modern and behaviorist rationality frames the standards. The nine music standards are presented as behavioral objectives, which consequently adhere more literally to what students must "know and be able to do to demonstrate that [they] are proficient in the skills and knowledge framed by content standards" (Goals 2000, p. 4). A closer examination of the Music Standards illustrates these points:

> Students (will) sing; perform on instruments; improvise melodies; compose and arrange music; read and notate music; listen to, analyze and describe music; evaluate music and music performances; understand relationships between music, the other arts, and disciplines outside the arts; and understand music in relation to history and culture. (MENC, 1994)

---

[1] *The School Music Program: Description and Standards* were originally written in 1974.

Viewed through this scientific and technical rationality, the music stan-dards appear to provide precise steps, teacher accountability, and evidence to the fact that learning music is measurable and, as a result, a necessary basic. "Since modern-day proponents of behavioral objectives insist that such objectives be quantifiably assessed as terminal products, the curriculum becomes necessar-ily narrow and mechanical" (Tanner & Tanner, 1980, p. 26). Consequently, even though these are presented as standards and not prescribed curriculum, the stan-dards virtually provide a curricular framework necessitating a method of teach-ing divorced from a social and ethical context.

In the ensuing years, conferences and publications have been devoted to the National Music Standards. Most states in the United States have adopted some version of the National Standards which has subsequently influenced the crafting and adoption of city and community standards. Accordingly, consensus, rather than conflict born of mindful interrogation, has been the professionally man-dated response to the standards. As a result, critiques of the standards often per-tain to whether the Music Standards are being met and implemented, and which specific standards are being taught. Some of the critiques suggest the standards seem relevant only to the discipline of music and do not take into account the process of learning, developmental issues, or philosophical views represented by leaders in American education (Ross, 1994). Other critiques, employ a phil-osophical lens (Stevenson, 2007) and a lens of critical theory (Kassell Benedict, 2004; Benedict, 2006) to challenge and interrogate the vision and purpose of the standards.

As will be seen in the following section, curriculum development has con-tinued to evolve and remain a topic of discussion, and often contestation and debate, in the general education community. Such discussion and even conflict have served to keep conversations of curriculum vital, fundamental, and even imperative to those who seek to engage meaningfully in the educative process.

CURRICULUM RECONCEPTUALIZED

Curriculum, from the learner's standpoint, ordinarily represents little more than an arrangement of subjects, a structure of socially prescribed knowledge, or a complex system of meanings which may or may not fall within his grasp. Rarely does it signify possibility for him as an existing person, mainly con-cerned with making sense of his own life-world. (Greene, 1978, p. 299)

These words of Maxine Greene set the stage for us to consider the shift in the field of curriculum toward something broader than content and discipline arrangement. In 1969, setting off what was to be a flurry of debate and re-engagement, Joseph Schwab famously pronounced the field of curriculum "mor-ibund" (p. 1). Desiring a renaissance in the field of curriculum, Schwab called for a return to the practical away from the theoretical. The lines that were drawn, the sides that were taken, the debates that followed, and the subsequent curricular conversations that evolved have been referred to as the reconceptualization of curriculum.

As articulated by Pinar (1978), reconceptualism was intended to be interpreted as a term to "indicate a fundamental reconceiving of the field," as a "fundamental shift —paradigm shift—in the orders of research . . . the common bond which was opposition to the traditional field" (1980, p. 200). Pinar believed that it was necessary for those in the curriculum field to step out of the "enslaving preoccupation with the classroom" so as to create intellectual distance. He was concerned that the "absorption with the application of "knowhow" (1978, p. 8) served to keep the field static. While not desiring to abandon the work of serving the practitioner, Pinar believed that "curricular possibilities" depended on generating theory that would not necessarily be used as a "prescription" or as, what Macdonald described an "empirically testable set of principles" (In Pinar, 1978, p. 7). Pinar was concerned with the practical and those ways one could conceive of "right" and "just" rather than the control technical and traditional curriculum held over teacher and student. Through the lens of Habermas, Pinar called for an emancipatory intention to guide curriculum development through reflection rather than technical manipulation. As such, Pinar believed that through curriculum research the researcher must be emancipated so that the work would be meaningful to others. He posited that if we were to continue to produce and engage in research that was mired in a static state, one characterized by an accumulation of a body of knowledge, then the curriculum field was indeed in a state of arrest.[2]

The work of the reconceptualists was hugely contested. The main areas of contention resided in the interpretation that they were calling for the separation of theory and practice and the abandonment of the practitioner. Tanner and Tanner (1979) reacted angrily[3] to (among other issues) Pinar's reference of Tyler as a traditionalist. They also dismissed Pinar's belief that there was a relationship between school and society as one that functioned to "deliberately cover repressive measures" as "rhetoric rather than rigorous analysis" (p. 9). Jackson (1980), employing a charismatic discourse, joined the debate and declared that the idea of such a thing as a curriculum field made him "uneasy" (1980, p. 163) and that this body of work, concseptualized as a field, was something that existed "only in [our] heads" (p. 164). Jackson also challenged the incorporation of a framework and lens represented by the intellectual tradition of such scholars as Marx, Heidegger, Husserl, Merleau-Ponty, Gramsci, and Habermas (among others) as sources from which to examine curriculum.

---

[2] Interestingly, Pinar warned that critical theory and phenomenology were not where curriculum theorists ought to reside; this was best done by movements in philosophy.

[3] While it may seem that anger is an interesting choice of words, Pinar (1980), in a response to these responses, used the words ill-tempered, anger, and shouting to contextualize the response of his critiques. Indeed, a close read of these articles suggests these emotional reactions.

...they are more helpful in thinking about and understanding the richness and complexity of educational phenomena than are the intellectual frameworks that have till now dominated educational thought. (Jackson, 1980, p. 168)

Such a challenge seems foreign as we tend now to take for granted a disciplinary process that engages with intellectual traditions outside one specific domain. Yet, at the time when curriculum hung between a modernist tradition and a postmodernist tradition and the paradigm shift was seen as a threat, educators engaged with taking sides in silence and anger. However, heeding Pinar's (1980) response to these criticisms seems apropos to the discipline and field of music education. Rather than engaging in "self-crippling" behaviors, and in order to "sustain disciplinary conversations" (p. 204) that would lead toward further conversations, Pinar called for dialogue rather than cathartic reactions of "ill-temper[ment]" (p. 199). This dialogue would not be one in which an appeal for consensus and agreement would be forefront. Rather, the hallmark of this dialogue would be an articulation of issues such as power, control, identity, and resistance, and the ways in which each intertwine and essentially "need" each other. Reconceptualization was a vision that was a move away from the modern paradigm toward the postmodern, a vision of content and process, not as a false dichotomy, not even as a model (Doll, 1993), but as a way of ensuring that "becomingness of process is maintained (p. 15).

In the following section some ways in which music educators have responded to this shift will be addressed.

Special Focus

In March 2005, Music Educators Journal (MEJ) published an issue entitled: Reconceptualizing Curriculum. Throughout the issue, varying views on the ways in which the traditional, linear model of music curriculum could be broadened were addressed. Hanley and Montgomery (2005) examine this curricular shift through a lens of postmodernism and suggest that educators might consider constructivism as a way to conceptualize learning and teaching. Barrett (2005) presents a model in which planning is "open-ended and responsive rather than closed and predictive." For Barrett, the lived experience of students rather than predetermine endpoints (p. 23) should become the focal point of curriculum development. She presents a situation in which a high school instrumental teacher re-engages with the traditional rehearsal schedule by providing space for individual and small group interactions. This "garage band" model is one that has been explored in detail by such authors as Allsup (Spring 2003), and in this same MEJ issue, Green (March 2005). Concerned with the disconnect between school music and music that is made outside of the formal process of schooling, Allsup (2004) considers the issue of democracy as "community in the making" (p. 24) and undertakes a project where students break into small groups in which they are asked to compose music of their own choosing. Green (March 2005), interested in similar issues, focuses on issues such as self-teaching and peer-directed learning (p. 28).

Each of these music educators is concerned with the normative practices that permeate the profession. Each challenges and interrogates the traditional, technical rationality model that is pervasive in music education. Each also speaks to the difficulty of embracing such change, citing reluctance of peers, parents, administrators, and even students to embrace new conceptions of what an education in music might mean.

The Voice of the Critical Theorist

Related, parallel, and interwoven with the reconceptualist discussion was the work of critical theorists focusing on the concept of hidden curriculum. Vallance (1973–1974), Rolland Martin (1976), and Apple and King (1977) were calling attention to issues of control and power that had once been an explicit part of the educational discourse, but had shifted and been subsumed. Hidden curriculum, or the "unintended outcomes of the schooling process" (McLaren, 2003), refers to those ways in which behaviors are shaped outside of the overt agendas of schooling. Issues, for instance, such as whose music is heard, whose music is programmed, whose voice is respected, what forms of knowledge and discourse are valued and validated, what pedagogical engagements are enacted are functions of hidden curriculum that serve to send messages of control, compliance, and obedience.

The discussion of hidden curriculum and the maintenance of dominant interests was part of a broader examination of those ways in which societal control impacted the function of schooling. The emergence of critical theory was embraced by scholars throughout music education. Influenced by the work of the Frankfurt School, Gates and Regelski established MayDay (1993), an international think-tank as a platform and community, to examine "the status of practice in music education" and

—apply critical theory and critical thinking to the purposes and practices of music education, and
—to affirm the central importance of musical participation in human life and, thus, the value of music in the general education of all people. (http://www.maydaygroup.org)

Mindful of those ways in which normative practices permeate the field of music education, Regelski speaks of engaging with critical theory as a way of challenging the blind acceptance of traditional theory and as a call for recognizing those ways in which we abdicate and deny responsibility for our actions. Regelski has written of music educators' propensity for accepting methods as curriculum models (2005, p. 13) and engagements with them as "coming close to the worship of religious idols," and as such refers to this practice as "methodolatry" (p. 13). This theme of being silenced by a particular discourse of power (often made manifest in the normative practices in music education) resonates throughout the work of many music educators. Repertoire as curriculum, and methods as common-sense practices, is challenged and interrogated by Bradley (2007) who examines, though the lens of Adorno, the ways in which repertoire as curriculum can become "fascistic." While not specifically speaking to curriculum, O'Toole (January, 2005) interrogates the choir rehearsal as a site of power; embedded and made manifest in the privileged and patriarchal positioning of the conductor and repertoire. She addresses the self-regulation established in rehearsals that serves to constitute docile bodies through self-regulation, thus producing a choir member that is "more efficient and productive" (p. 10) and ensuring the subsequent reproduction of repertoire as curriculum.

Gould (September, 2005) asks us to address those ways in which class, gender, and race influence curriculum making. As such, she asks what it might mean for us to "disrupt power relations [of] heteronormativity" (p. 12). Lamb (1996), in speaking of the problematics and difficulties in reengaging with music as ideology and the conflicting discourses that permeate pedagogical and curricular concerns, eloquently and painfully addresses the inherent difficulties in embracing this process.

> Not only do I find myself in conflicts with students about what the music education process is and what it means, I find myself trying to live up to expectations I cannot fulfill—and do not want to—but feel some responsibility to meet because this is a prepfrofessional program in music and music education. (p. 129)

The challenges of perceiving curriculum as always in flux, as rhizomatic—interconnected, moving laterally and outwardly (Gould, 2009, p. 49)—as a contest to power structures and the status quo, and as a process in which ends can't be defined in "simple and clear terms" (Bobbitt, 1934) can also be found in the historical grappling with curriculum as "multiculturalism."

"MULTICULTURAL" CURRICULUM

> If multiculturalism is to be linked to a renewed interest in expanding the principles of democracy to wider spheres of application, it must be defined in pedagogical and political terms that embrace it as a referent and practice for civic courage, critical citizenship and democratic struggle. (Giroux, December 1992, p. 7)

Issues of hidden curriculum, power, and control have framed the multicultural movement as well. As a modern conception, multicultural music and multicultural curriculum have been interpreted as a way to (among many others) differentiate traditions, to reflect diverse populations, as a tool for unifying diverse populations, for "fostering of world understanding" (Volk, 1998, p. 49), as a method and as material, and often as a code word for race and ethnicity (Morton, Spring, 2001). Elliott (1995), who views music as a diverse human and multicultural practice, believes that "music education is multicultural." Rather than an adjective or a noun, multicultural for Elliott "connotes a social ideal; a policy of support for exchange among different social groups to enrich all which respecting and preserving the integrity of each" (p. 207). To this end, he views the practices of musical cultures and developing the students' musicianship within these cultures as a way to "deepen and broaden" musicianship and as a way to "link" music education to "humanistic education" (p. 209).

In some ways, and to an unfortunate extent, the words multicultural and multiculturalism have entered our vocabulary and discipline psyche so that we often forget that these terms have been, and can be, wielded in ways that reproduce systems of oppression, rather than as critical engagements (musical and nonmusical) that challenge the status quo. Used as an adjective, these terms situate curriculum and pedagogy as something done for the "culturally different," or "culturally deprived" children. Used as a slogan, it calls our attention to the fervent possibilities about the purpose of music, yet does very little to call attention to the complexities and contradictions.

Salvation themes of unification have historically meant favoring privileged positionings of culture that often reflect those of the dominant class. Delpit (1995) warns that to engage in the educative process from this positioning is to "ensure that power, the culture of power, remains in the hands of those who already have it" (p. 28). Rather than using music to reflect diverse musics or peoples, Morton (Spring 2001) calls for us to attend to the "ethical tensions and sociopolitical contradictions manifest in cultural perspectives and hierarchies" (p. 33). Calling for a critical vision of multiculturalism, Morton does not deny that varied musics should be embedded in our curriculum, or that we shouldn't be considering multiple ways of engaging in/with these musics. Critical multiculturalism would entail recognizing curriculum development as one that is not neutral, one that cannot be depoliticized, one that is not color- or difference-blind, one that requires praxis, not rhetoric. In essence, multicultural curriculum is a process that embraces the contradictions inherent in the struggle with equity; not framed by the contingencies of private lessons or access to instruments, but as a struggle to address within the curriculum "misrepresentation, as well as authenticity, exclusion as well as inclusion" (p. 40).

Social Justice, Democratic Practices

Issues of democratic practice provide a way of reengaging with curriculum/pedagogy. In recent years, scholarship and thinking in music education have returned to the issue of democracy, particularly in philosophical terms rethinking and reconstructing Dewian ideals through politics and context of today's society.

In her search to break free of a modernist framing of curriculum and pedagogy, DeLorenzo (November, 2003) seeks to move from a curriculum model that is concept driven toward one in which music can contribute to the needs of society (p. 35). Looking at issues such as the processes of decision making within the classroom and representation of disenfranchised groups, she presents differing scenarios from those of her own practice as well as those of her graduate students.

Woodford (2005), while not addressing curriculum in a specific sense, situates a political life at the center of the educative process. He calls for liberal education, but also for a rethinking of liberalism, as "thoughtful evaluation" (p. 99). As such, he calls for those who are connected to education to take on the role of public intellectuals. Allsup (MEJ, May 2007) addresses democratic teaching and learning (and thus curriculum) that revolves around skillfulness, rather than skills, living music rather than preparing music. He asks us to conceive of the educative process as one in which "tradition as a critical conversation" (p. 54) takes precedence over mindless reproduction of what has conventionally been deemed traditional repertoire and traditional teaching. By asking ourselves the question, why a specific tradition for these specific students (p. 54), we take on a moral commitment of engaging with the teaching/curriculum process as one in which there can be "no freedom from responsibility" (p. 55).

Music educators have also begun to concern themselves with curriculum and pedagogy that reflect and respond to issues of social justice. In October 2006, the first International Symposium on Music Education, Equity, and Social Justice Conference was held at Teachers College, Columbia University. The conference brought together international educators to discuss issues of educational equity and social justice. Subsequently, the *Philosophy of Music Education Review* (2007) devoted an issue to the conference, exploring issues of curriculum development, theorizing curriculum development and pedagogical concerns. Extending this discussion, *Action, Criticism, and Theory for Music Education* developed an issue focused on "Theorizing Social Justice and Equity in Music Education" (2007). The editor's concern that music educators often embrace current issues only to drop them when the next one comes along, is one echoed by others throughout the history of music education. As such, issues that connect education and life, such as social justice, will hopefully be able to bridge and reconnect the role of education in the empowerment of a political life.

Complex Ideas in a Real World

These pages have presented complex and even complicated challenges to practices each of us has come to know and love. Once again, the point is not to throw the baby out with the bath water, but rather to consider our actions as they have come to be, and our actions as they might come to be. What of the new teacher and even experienced teacher who wants to engage differently, who wants to incorporate curricular changes into curriculum that seems to have been written in stone? What can one do when asked to sit in on curriculum committees so that these ideas and thoughts may be present in discussions? What does one do when confronted with curriculum whose parameters seems driven simply by concerts and competitions? What does one do when told either explicitly or implicitly that one's job depends on holding steadfast to a curriculum model that "favors," as the beginning quote pointed out, "select groups of students over other groups" (McLaren, 1989, p. 183)?

While our immediate reaction may be to rush right in and challenge standing traditions tested by what seems millennia, we need to consider that this reaction is quite similar to the one McLaren points out. The issue is never to favor one idea or group over another, but to engage in dialogue, conversations, relationships that begin slowly, yet thoughtfully. It may indeed be that curricular and pedagogical engagements move slowly; perhaps without discernable transformation. Yet, change not only takes time, but is constant and steadfast, whether we choose to engage or not.

What follows are examples from new teachers who chose to engage differently from their first year of teaching. They are teachers who teach in different situations and varying localities who have grappled with these same ethical issues and have taught in multiple levels in different venues, in varying communities. Their situations and backgrounds differ, but each has one thing in common: the desire to continually challenge and interrogate their own teaching. As such, each of the following examples emanates from situations in which each teacher intentionally examined his or her own practice. A few of the examples are deliberate and articulated teacher-as-researcher projects, others are simply examples of the ways in which these new teachers recognized moments in which they could speak and be heard. But all are examples of teachers who have implemented "successful" music programs in the eyes of their principals and parents, as well as examples of how they challenged normative practices.

Cara, who teaches in a large New York public high school in Queens, was asked, in her first year of teaching, to lead a professional development meeting for a group of music teachers. Previously, she had connected with the organizer of these presentations and had presented herself as willing to speak to and consider curricular issues seriously. She had not been afraid of articulating those ways the musical parameters she had inhereited might not speak to the long-term goals she had for herself and her students. As such, Cara put together a presentation in which she asked her colleagues to articulate broader understandings they hoped for their students that weren't just bound by musical engagements. She then asked them to realize these as musical goals, musical projects. She has since been asked to lead several city wide professional development meetings with larger groups of music teachers.

Cara also implemented a project with her women's choir in which she and her students raised issues of identity formation and what "multiculturalism" might mean to them. Cara kept a journal and often shared with the students her own thinking processes as she moved through curricular decisions with them.

> I have noticed quite a change in the women's choir as a result of this open dialogue between us. There is a greater sense of trust with me, with themselves, and with each other. They are not afraid to question themselves and others, and to think through things, something they were hesitant to do before for fear of being 'wrong' or being judged by their peers. I also believe that through the process of engaging in this dialogue that they have become more aware of their identity—as a female, as a singer, as part of something that is larger to them, as

part of many groups. Whereas previously, I noticed they were only identifying themselves through their culture—that is, through national affiliation, something I have consciously begun to dismantle with them. (CB 1/08)

Christine, a middle school teacher in Brooklyn, New York chose to implement a social justice research project with her students. After brainstorming definitions of social justice, the class chose to focus on those ways music has shaped and changed the world as we know it. Each student crafted interview questions and designed final projects that consisted of an interview with a family or community member, personal reflections on social justice and music, and an analysis connecting the interview results with personal views.

> This project focused on what the students learned from the people, and what they learned as researchers. Students were asked to compare their interviews to their own thoughts in order to make connections and draw conclusions about the impact of music and social justice on one's life. They made connections to themes that we explored in our initial discussions and what the students learned in their interviews. This process allowed students to link social justice issues from the past with the present concerns of family and community members. (CP 1/08)

Allison, an urban educator in New Jersey, followed her interest in language and musical development to a research project in an Arizona school district. There, she discovered that even though the community was primarily a Spanish speaking community, music teachers were asked not to teach songs in any language other than English. While the population was over 85% Latino, Proposition 213, in fact, created a situation in which no Spanish songs were allowed in the classroom. Allison then, realizing that she could no longer think through her teaching and curriculum development as she had, began rethinking this particular situation, education, and music education through a political lens.

Dion, another urban educator and a native of Barbados, spent time researching the musical communities in Barbados, assuming that locals would be listening to music of their culture. She found that in the four years she had been away, access to media and mass communication had changed the listening habits of local inhabitants. Instead of the music and listening habits she had expected to study, she found they were listening to the current musics of rap and hip-hop, and so forth. Even though Dion is herself a cultural bearer, she found herself disconnected from the speed and development of her own culture. Dion returned to New Jersey rethinking what it means to be a cultural bearer and the impact this has on one's life and one's pedagogy and curriculum development.

Each of these teachers have been impacted by the politics, policies, and practices of curriculum and curriculum development in their local school communities. And while each of the above examples differs in its origination, intent, locality, population, each has much in common. Each worked within the confines and parameters of the set curriculum in their situations, but was able to broaden the objectives and meanings found within them. Each not only reflected on their own practice but those ways they may have not heard or seen students previous to these projects. Integral to that, each dialogued and shared with their students their thinking on curriculum and pedagogy. Each shared with parents, teachers and administrators the objectives of their projects in ways that are nonconfrontational and nonthreatening. And what's more, each understood the power of first impressions and believed, that even as new teachers, they would be taken seriously if they presented their thinking in a serious manner. Unfortunately, each has also been called naïve and simple, a new teacher who will "learn" eventually. And each has recognized that not everyone will accept or even come to hear how and why they have chosen to engage outside of expected norms. Yet, above and beyond all of this none of them have sacrificed their music programs, each has what would be considered a successful program; participation grows each year, and the caliber of musicality grows as well. They sing, they play, they dance, they tour, they perform. These aren't just communities of young vibrant musicians of all kinds; rather, these are vibrant musicians who engage critically with the world around them and who realize potentiality beyond musical engagements. These are teachers and students, indeed people, who desire, in Dewey's (1916/1944) words to "take part in correcting unfair privilege and unfair deprivation, not to perpetuate them" (pp. 119–120).

SOME CONCLUDING REMARKS

Any inherited system, good for its time, when held to after its day, hampers social progress. (Bobbitt, 1918, p. 1)

Considering curriculum and curriculum making has often seemed to be a second thought for music educators, it's important to know about, but the acquisition of so many other "skills" demand our time and attention. Perhaps the "overwhelm" of addressing these issues has been our ticket out. Yet, we should consider that a reluctance or unwillingness, or even the inability to address these issues has not served us well, all of which speaks to ethical engagements that call to our attending. Historically, we have not consistently spoken of curriculum as an ethical engagement. Neither have we spoken of curriculum as performative; written documents that are acts of engagement, or the discrepancies between discourses and their enactments. Schmidt (September 2007) has addressed the curricular and pedagogical disconnect that plays out in different forms of discourses between what is proposed inside teacher preparation and how this is carried out into school programs. He is concerned with the ways in which teacher preparation programs often see enactment, placed outside the interactions of the moment, as a retelling of practice and curricular traditions, thus framing the educative process as one always already engaged in a discourse of "talk about" teaching rather than through an embodiment in/of the context and the moment. Bowman (2002) asks us to first consider "what we want education to do for our children and society" (p. 74) and then the ways in which musical engagements would further this. In the attempt to conceptualize curriculum as a series of steps that meet particular standards, in the attempt to simplify and find solutions to issues, or to create a one-size-fits-all curriculum in which processes give way to procedure, and understanding gives way to knowing, we are all—teachers, students, scholars—trapped in a rationality that does not provide for grappling with complexities and contractions. We have, in essence, framed the needs of our children, ourselves, and society as needs determined by forces outside of us, beyond our control.

Is there any possibility in curriculum? Giroux reminds us that schools are "contradictory sites; they reproduce the larger society while containing spaces to resist its dominating logic" (1988, p. xxxiii). There is immense and awful possibility in creating spaces of small and large insurrections. I would suggest that the inherited system of which Bobbitt speaks may never have been "good for" its own time and has indeed been "bad for" and hampered our progress. If as Pinar (2000) suggests, curriculum theory is the study of "how to have a learning environment" (p. 12), I would add that such learnings necessitate practices informed by the complexity of our relations, the relearning of what has been negated, as well as constant reengagement with the history of us. A history that makes all the difference and none; one that creates possibilities and alienates. A history not separate, detached, enclosed, but one always already implicated in and through life.

Class Discussion

1. Think back to your music classes (including performance based classes) and articulate your thoughts on the intent of the curriculum? Was there a sequenced curriculum? What was the purpose of the curriculum? What was absent in the curriculum?

2. In your own words, describe the relationship between society and curriculum. How does one affect the other? Why should we concern ourselves with this relationship?

3. How has the development of curriculum shaped the ways in which music education is viewed in the United States? What does curriculum development have to do with advocacy efforts? Can you imagine any ways this has prevented music education from being seen differently than it is?

4. How could you include parents and administration in discussing how curriculum in the music program may not be serving everyone? In what ways might it not be serving everyone? Should your program serve everyone? What about programs that are settled and anchored on performances and rankings. How will you engage with challenging and broadening these programs? Should you?

Projects

1. Visit a class in both a high school and elementary setting and ask the music teacher to describe their curriculum. Is the curriculum dictated by any guidelines? Were they able to contribute to the development of the curriculum? Do they follow the prescribed curriculum? Why or why not? Do they feel the curriculum speaks to their goals as music educators?

2. In a brief paper, compare and contrast the perspective of curriculum that the National Standards in Music represents with a more *reconceptualized* approach to curriculum. Can both visions coexist? How can music teachers resolve the apparent conflict in their music classrooms?

3. In a brief paper, describe ways that you can broaden "multiculturalism" and world musics to be something more than inclusion in your curriculum? What policy changes in your school might be necessary? What changes would be necessary in your classroom or ensemble?

SUGGESTED READINGS

Apple, M. (1990). *Ideology and curriculum* (2nd ed.). New York: Routledge.

Bobbitt, F. (1918). *The curriculum.* Cambridge, MA: The Riverside Press.

Freire, P. (1970/1993). *Pedagogy of the oppressed.* (Rev. ed.). New York: Continuum.

Wiggins, G. & McTighe, J. (1998). *Understanding by design.* Upper Saddle River, NJ: Prentice-Hall, Inc.

CHAPTER 8

~

Assessing Music Learning
Harold F. Abeles

INTRODUCTION

Formal and Informal Assessments

Assessment is an indispensable part of living. For many everyday decisions we make, assessment is a part of the process. When we decide to walk to an appointment, we typically determine the distance to location of the appointment and our average pace to decide when we should leave in order to arrive on time. Of course, we are likely to do this in one integrated process, rather than in a series of steps. When we decide we need a new couch, we are likely to consider practical issues, like measuring how big it can be and how much we are able spend, as well as aesthetic aspects before we go shopping.

Assessment is also in the music studio. We listen to our students' playing, assessing their strengths and weakness, then help them determine what additional experiences may strengthen their performance and develop them into well-rounded, independent musicians. Even the idea of developing into an "independent musician" focuses on the issue of assessment. An important quality of independent musicians is the ability to evaluate their own skills and make decisions regarding what they need to work on "independently" of a teacher or coach.

The point is that ongoing informal assessments are indispensable as part of living and learning. Assessment is a natural part of the teaching/learning process and is best practiced when it is a seamless part of teaching and learning that is well integrated into teachers' practice. When parents help their teenager learn to drive a car, both the teen and the parent are constantly assessing what skills are learned and what skills are still needed to reach the goal. The assessment/instruction process is well integrated. The teen isn't asked to stop, get out of the car and take a written test on the functions of the turn signal lever and rear window defroster. Instead, the parent(s) and teen both reflect on recent experience and decide on what the next appropriate driving experience should be.

An important aspect of teaching a teenager to drive a car is that it typically involves one or two teachers and one student driver so that the instructor(s) can devote all of their perceptive and cognitive skills, and maybe even a kinesthetic demonstration, to help the student driver develop the skills and understandings necessary to accomplish the complex task. In addition, learning to drive a car also is likely to occur in a relatively compact period of time. The initial stages might even occur in one afternoon, although practice, both guided and independent, may take place over several weeks, months, and years.

Studio instruction in music also typically takes place with one teacher and one student. In studio instruction, except for the end-of-semester juries, assessment is generally well integrated into learning. It is common for teachers to ask students to play a passage or etude, and while the student plays, the teacher assesses the quality of the performance. At times, studio teachers may focus on a particular quality such as intonation, as that particular aspect may be the skill the student has been trying to improve. Some teachers may help students develop their own assessment skills by asking them to reflect on certain qualities of the performance (Do you think that the Bb in the third measure was in tune? Was it sharp or flat?) and may encourage the student to develop sensitive listening and self-correcting practices (What adjustments did you make this time, so that the Bb was in tune?). Effective studio teachers are likely to be good at assessing student performances and at suggesting strategies to further develop students' skills. They are also likely to be good at encouraging students' own independent musicianship, by helping them develop sensitive ears and strategies for remedying performance challenges. Again, in effective studio instruction, assessment is often seamlessly integrated with instruction.

While informal assessments are indispensable to teaching and learning in many situations, there are circumstances that demand more formal assessments. Performance juries typically occur at a point where administrative decisions need to be made, such as assigning a grade at the end of a semester, determining whether a student should continue, or receive a degree or special recognition, such as a "performance certificate." Formal assessments, particularly those that result in a grade, allow teachers to communicate, in a summative manner, judgments about the overall quality of the work students have done. Teachers, students, and parents typically assume that a grade reflects teachers' judgment regarding students' achievement although, sometimes, it may reflect other characteristics such as effort or talent.

Formal assessments are necessary in an educational system that serves a large numbers of students. Both P-12 environments and colleges and universities have institutional characteristics that require formal assessments. Because students do not have *a single* tutor who helps them learn all disciplines throughout their schooling, it is necessary for teachers to communicate what students know to subsequent teachers. Ideally, this might be in detailed written reports illustrated with samples of students' work, but high student/teacher ratios necessitate briefer forms of communication, often just a single grade. The necessity to communicate profiles of students across institutions, either when students transfer from one school to another or move on to middle school or college, puts even more of a demand on the system. With the number of students our educational system has to manage, summary indexes, such as report cards and SAT scores, are the assessment tools that currently serve this purpose.

That doesn't mean that other kinds of important information aren't shared from teacher to teacher. A phone call or a conversation between a middle school instrumental music teacher and a high school instrumental teacher can provide a venue to share noteworthy qualities about an oboist who is matriculating from one school to another. More nuanced communication about assessment can also take place when written recommendations are completed by high school teachers for students' college applications.

The Functions of Assessment in Music Education

There are multiple reasons that assessment should be an integral part of the teaching/learning process in music. Most importantly, students need feedback to develop their own sense of their learning. *Formative assessment* provides feedback to students and teachers *during* instruction. For students, the goal of the feedback is to help refine and improve their learning, while for teachers the goal of the feedback is to help refine and improve instructional strategies. Formative assessment is part of a learning process that relies on feedback to progress. Its purpose is not to generate grades, but rather to improve learning. It can be systematic, for example, a college theory teacher might require students each week to submit a new section of a large analysis or a revision of a section of analysis previously submitted. The teacher's review of the submission might not result in a grade but rather comments on strategies to revise what was submitted. Even though, it is likely that the sections, when put together in a larger completed work, will be graded.

This assigning of an index or description of a student's level of attainment upon the completion of an assignment or unit or semester is considered to be *summative assessment*. A particular point in time is often the trigger for summative assessment, the occasion being dictated by the structure of schooling, such as the end of a grading period or a transition to a new learning circumstance. Summative assessments can also provide important feedback for students, helping them reflect on their musical strengths and areas that need improvement. They may also provide information to students on the quality of a performance or written analysis as judged by a teacher/mentor. Summative assessment may also describe how a student's work compares to other students' work. Summative assessments can help students discover what good work is. So, an effective assessment system should provide the opportunity for students to metacognitively develop an understanding of what the processes are that lead to good improvising, good singing, and good music problem-solving (Wiggins, 1989). To be effective in developing these understandings, summative assessments need to provide useful feedback. So a *single* grade after a performance jury or letter grade on a returned music history paper would be considered insufficient. Feedback that describes the strengths and weaknesses of a performance or paper, such as comments written in the margins of a paper, is what is necessary for students to develop an understanding of the processes that lead to good work.

Another function of assessment in music education is to communicate information regarding the students' performance to others. In school environments, that often means parents as well as other teachers and administrators. Ideally, communication between music teachers and students' parents is extensive and ongoing. Once again, providing information in the form of a single grade at the end of a marking period may generate the stereotypical query—What does the grade mean? Nevertheless, students, parents, other teachers, and administrators all share responsibilities in the music education of children and need to understand the nature and characteristics of students' musical achievement. Thus, clarifying the components that comprise a grade is critically important to enhance the process of communication among the different stakeholders in a child's musical education. A student might ask or assume the following: Does the grade mean I'm talented? Does it mean I worked hard in music? Does it mean I improved? Does it mean that I am more musical than most of my classmates? To maximize music education, effective communication is imperative.

Assessment versus Measurement versus Evaluation

The terms *assessment, measurement,* and *evaluation* often appear to be used interchangeably. Many thesauruses would list measurement and evaluation as synonyms of assessment. Nevertheless, they have specific meanings within the education community. *Assessment* is the broadest of the three terms. It is most often used to refer to all types of activities that result in generating an understanding of student learning, both informal and formal. Structured assessments, like tests and end-of-the-term performance juries represent a particular kind of assessment, as do the determinations that teachers may make during instructional experiences—informal assessments that are well integrated in the teacher-learning process. These different kinds of assessment may all be integrated into the same instructional experience.

Measurement, which might be considered a subset of assessment, narrowly refers to the assignment of numbers to qualities. When a tall person is measured with a measurement tool—a ruler, for example, the result is a quantity, for example, 74 inches. When a student's achievement is measured with a tool such as a test, the result is typically also a quantity, a score, for example—an 82. For example, in 2007, at the Illini Marching Band Festival Field Show Competition, one high school marching band received a score of 45.00 out of 50.00 for the music portion of the competition.

Evaluation includes judgment. We might think of evaluation as being the combination of assessment and judgment. An end-of-the-semester grade should be considered an evaluation while the score on a unit is an assessment. When a band receives a 45 on the music portion of a competition, adjudicators will often go through one additional step and assign that score, or sometimes combine several other scores for marching, percussion, and auxiliary groups, a summary label such as "Outstanding." This reflects a judgment about the overall performance of the group. In classrooms, teachers use scores to assign grades to students. Typically, the context of the score will affect the grade. If a score of 82 was the highest score achieved in the class, it might receive a different grade than if it was the lowest or in the middle.

CHARACTERISTICS OF ASSESSMENT TOOLS

Objective versus Subjective

When teachers think of qualities of good assessment, they may believe that the gold standard—in other words, what they should strive for—is traditional scientific measurement. Teachers want their assessments to be *objective*—when asked, this is the word they use (Shepard, 2000). Objective measures are those that strive to eliminate biases that may be part of the measurement tool. For a written test, such as an essay exam, bias may enter the assessment process when teachers score the essay. Different teachers may use different criteria for judging the same answer, resulting in different scores for the same essay. We might say that the different scores for the same essay suggest that the teachers were being *subjective*. The lack of objectivity, or *subjectivity*, may also affect the assessment of music performances. For example, when multiple judges are independently assessing an end-of-semester jury performance they may judge a performance differently based on their different music performance values. If one judge believes that for first semester freshmen cellists the most important performance issue is playing in tune, then any cello students who play with insecure intonation may receive low scores from this judge, regardless of the other qualities of their performances. If one of the other judges values musical interpretation above all other aspects of performance, then that judge may overlook occasional notes that are a little sharp or flat and score the performance differently—particularly if the performance was expressive.

Since subjectivity may enter the assessment process during the scoring of student performances, *objective* measures can work towards reducing this variability. For written assessments of cognitive achievement, objectivity is sought with fixed response tests, like multiple-choice or true-false tests. Several researchers (e.g., Bergee, 1987; Horowitz, 1994; Zdzinski & Barnes, 2002) have been able to demonstrate that the assessment of musical performances can be made somewhat objective by providing judges in performance juries with rating scales. The typical music performance rating scale might have categories representing several different dimensions of music performance, such as rhythmic accuracy, intonation, and interpretation, and asking judges to rate each dimension on a quantitative scale (e.g., 1 to 5).

Some measurement strategists and teachers, who might argue against an approach to assessment based on objectivity, would not necessarily advocate for subjective assessment, as they would likely be concerned that subjective assessment might not be equitable. Rather, they would more likely advocate an approach to assessment that would emphasis context, individualism, and a reduction of the power dynamic between teachers and students.

Reliability

Teachers strive to have the measures they use to assess achievement to be consistent. By consistent, measurement experts mean that scores generated by a measure should be reproducible. When a carpenter uses a tape measure to determine the length of a bookcase shelf that needs to be replaced, he/she expects that if he/she uses the same tape measure on the new board that he/she cuts for the shelf the board should fit. We expect that a tape measure is a consistent measurement tool. I've heard carpenters recommend that you should measure everything twice, which underscores their concern with the consistency and the reproducibility of their measurements. In educational settings, consistency of measurement tools is called *reliability*. Teachers want measurement tools to have high reliability, that is, to be very consistent.

Reliability is really an index of how much error is part of the measuring process. A measure that has high reliability will have little error. Consider that every score produced by a test is really comprised of two components, *the true score*—an index that represents what the student really knows, understands, or can demonstrate—and other factors that are uncontrollable. Those uncontrollable factors are referred to as *errors in the measurement*. Some of these errors in the measurement or inconsistencies are likely associated with the student, some with the testing environment, and others with how the test is constructed. For example, the student may not have slept well the night before the test, or have a cold, or may be taking the test in an uncomfortably warm room. These student factors are likely to reduce the student's score on the test. There may also be factors that might increase a student's score on a test, such as guessing right on a multiple choice test or having just reviewed information which appears in several questions on a test. Some of the errors that are part of the measurement might increase the score reported and other errors might decrease the reported score. Multiple measurements, as was illustrated in the tape measure example above, is a strategy for eliminating inconsistencies that creep into the measurement process. Such approaches can improve the reliability of assessments.

These same kinds of inconsistencies can be part of a music performance assessment. Certainly, students may not have slept well or may have a high level of performance anxiety that can limit their playing. It is also possible that a student's jury performance may be better than he or she ever played the piece in the practice room. Once again, the notion of having multiple examples to measure would give us a more reliable assessment of a student's true level of performance. In fact, isn't one of our goals as musicians to perform consistently well? Thus, hearing students perform the same work several times over a few weeks would likely improve the accuracy of teachers' assessment of students' performance.

While educators can have only a limited impact on several of the inconsistencies that can be part of the measurement process, they can try to reduce inconsistencies that are part of measurement instruments. There are different kinds of reliability that help us focus on the types of error that might be part of the measurement process. *Test-retest* reliability is concerned about the consistency or stability of measures over time. We expect that two administrations of the same test over periods of several days or a week or two would produce the similar results—in other words, assuming that there were no additional instructional experiences, we would expect students who performed well on the test to perform well again and students who did not perform well to again keep their relative position. We would expect this kind of consistency when assessing music performers.

Another type of reliability is *internal consistency*. Internal consistency focuses on the homogeneity of items on a test. A test that is internally consistent would be one on which students' performance on one half of a test—either the first half or last half, or the odd items versus the even items—would be similar to students' performance on the other half. A test that had high internal consistency would be a test comprised of more homogeneous items than a test with low internal consistency.

A third type of reliability is *interjudge reliability*, an important consideration in the assessment of music performance. Interjudge reliability refers to the agreement among judges when assigning a score to a student's performance, whether it is a written essay or a music performance. The example described in the objectivity/subjective section above suggests that judges who value different aspects of music performance may produce different ratings for the same music performance. Using rating scales to help judges focus on similar performance qualities may help improve interjudge reliability. Bergee (2003) reports that college music faculty members' interjudge reliability was generally good, when using rating scales to score students' performances.

What is good reliability? This question needs to be qualified by the type of measure being reviewed. Reliability indices range between 0 and 1.00. We should expect that published standardized tests, like intelligence tests or the SAT would have high reliabilities, around .90 or above, while a reasonable goal for teacher constructed classroom tests might be around .70. Measures with reliabilities below .60 would be considered to be unreliable. Bergee (2003) reports interjudge reliabilities around .80 for total scores for ratings of student performers by panels of judges comprised of college music faculty (p. 144). For panels of judges adjudicating music performances, reliabilities of .80 should be considered to be acceptable.

Validity

Validity is another quality of measurement tool that educators consider important. Validity answers the question, "Does an assessment measure what it claims to measure?" A measure must first be reliable before it can be valid. Validity is related to accuracy of a measure. An inexpensive home pregnancy test you bought indicates that you are pregnant. You purchase another identical test and once again it reports that you are pregnant. The results are consistent; in other words the measure is reliable. You then schedule an appointment with your primary care physician, who takes a blood sample and tests it. (Blood-based pregnancy tests have reliabilities rates above .99.) The result shows that you are not pregnant. Your home tests did not provide *valid* readings. While consistent, the home tests did not measure accurately what they were supposed to measure—pregnancy.

There are different types of validity to be considered by educators and psychologists. For teachers, *content validity* may be the most important. Content validity examines whether an assessment covers a particular area of content it is designed to measure. In a college music history class, a unit listening test on the Baroque style period would have lower content validity if it included listening examples composed by de Vitry, Machaut, or Mozart. In assessing music performance, if you were to ask students to be prepared to play all major scales and then during the jury asked them to play both major and natural and harmonic minor scales, the performance jury would have lower content validity. Content validity has become an important issue for teachers in disciplines like language arts and science with year-end state mandated mastery tests. Such high stakes tests are often based on state standards, which define the tests' content. Thus, teachers must adhere to standards-based curriculum content if they expect their students to perform well on the tests.

Another type of validity is *criterion-related validity*. Criterion-related validity examines the relationship between a test and other typically established measures of the same characteristic or quality. For example, the results of a new test of music aptitude that takes only 15 minutes to administer might be compared with the results of a more established measure of music aptitude, such as the 1995 *Musical Aptitude Profile (MAP)*, which requires three 50-minute sessions. If the new test had high criterion-related validity when compared to the *MAP*, then the new test might be substituted for the *MAP* when time for administration is limited.

Criterion-related validity can also be predictive in nature. For example, the *SAT* is marketed to college admissions offices as a good predictor of success in college. Aptitude tests like the *SAT* are designed to predict success. Therefore we would expect a test of music aptitude to have predictive criterion-related validity. Since aptitude tests are designed to predict success at something, "What would be an appropriate criterion for a music aptitude test?" A music aptitude test score for a third grader should predict the level of musical performance that the student achieves when he/she is a high school student. In one study of the predictive validity of the *MAP*, Harrison (1987) reported the test was an effective predictor for college music majors' course grades in music theory—in other words students who had high scores on the *MAP* had higher grades in music theory in college.

Construct Validity is a third kind of validity, which is often employed for validating psychological measures. It examines how well an assessment fits with a psychological or social construct or theory. For example, different theorists have written about their perspectives of intelligence. Gardner's (1983) popular perspective suggests that there are several different types of intelligences: bodily-kinesthetic intelligence, musical intelligence, logical-mathematical intelligence, linguistic intelligence, spatial intelligence, interpersonal intelligence, and intrapersonal intelligence. Therefore, a traditional IQ test, such as the Stanford-Binet that yields four subscores verbal reasoning, quantitative reasoning, abstract/visual reasoning, and short-term memory, would not fit well, in other words not have construct validity, with Gardner's theory view of IQ. Measures of psychological constructs such as *self-esteem* or *emotional intelligence* are likely to be validated with construct validity.

ASSESSING THE OUTCOMES OF MUSIC INSTRUCTION

The Relationship between Curriculum, Instruction, and Assessment

Curriculum, instruction, and assessment are inextricably intertwined. In other words, any assessment strategy used to measure student achievement should reflect both what is being taught and what approach to teaching is used. Hafeli (2008) underscores the strength of this relationship, stating, "Assessment criteria are arguably the most powerful communication of an individual teacher's philosophy of learning ..." (p. 8). For most students, what is assessed is what is important to learn.

This part of the chapter is organized into two sections, each describing different philosophical approaches to assessing the outcomes of music instruction—a traditional approach and an alternative approach. Shepard (2000) describes *traditional approaches* to classroom assessment as fitting well with a *behavioristic* model of instruction. She describes a behavioristic approach to instruction as one which is tightly sequenced and hierarchical, proceeds in small steps, employs external positive reinforcement and is driven by explicitly stated behavioral objectives.[1] This approach leads to a dominance of objective-type achievement tests, which use completion, multiple-choice, matching, and other objective testing strategies. These *traditional approaches* to assessment are well suited to assess the recall of information, which is a logical outcome of behavioristic instructional approaches.

Other instructional approaches which reconceptualized curriculum and instruction,[2] evolved out of the work of cognitive psychologists, such as Vygotsky (1978) and Bruner (1960). These instructional approaches can be grouped under the label *constructivism*. Constructivist instruction strives to develop deep understandings that are principled and support transfer across disciplines. Shepard (2000) summarizes attributes of constructivist instruction as acknowledging

---

[1] A behavioristic approach to instruction parallels what Benedict labels Scientific and Technical Rationality supported in the writings of Bobbitt and Tyler in Chapter 7.

[2] In Chapter 7, Benedict refers to this approach as reconceptualism.

that learning takes place in and is influenced by a social and cultural context, depends on students' dispositions and personal identity, involves metacognition, and is shaped by prior knowledge (p. 8). Constructivist teachers seek to develop higher order thinking and problem solving rather than simple recall in more democratically structured classrooms. Constructivist instructional strategies demand a broader range of assessment tools that go beyond objective tests. In this chapter, these assessment tools are referred to as *alternative approaches* to assessment (see page 178).

Traditional Measures of the Outcomes of Musical Instruction

There has been considerable work done by teachers and assessment specialists on the development of traditional measures of student achievement. Most of this work has been focused on students' cognitive outcomes—that is, their thinking. Cognitive outcomes include recalling of information, applying knowledge to new situations, analyzing, and evaluating materials and information based on specific criteria. Traditionally, college music history courses emphasize cognitive outcomes. In general, traditional measures are used at the end of a unit of instruction, and thus are typically summative assessments. In traditional approaches to instruction, there are often specific testing points, such as a unit test, mid-term, or final exam that are clearly distinct from the teaching/learning aspects of the instructional experience.

The repertory of objective cognitive objective tests includes multiple-choice, true/false, fill in the blank, and short answer. To reiterate, "objective" in this case means that the scorers will have a high degree of agreement on the right answer. Of course, many of these forms of tests will have answer keys that will insure scorers' agreement. Essay tests, another common measure of cognitive outcomes, are considered to be more subjective, as scorers of essay tests may focus on different strengths and weakness of the same essay, resulting in a range of scores for the same student's work. Because of the popularity of these different measures of cognitive achievement, there are several books that provide detailed recommendations for constructing cognitive tests (e.g., Osterlind, 1998).

One of the major criticisms of these traditional objective achievement tests is that they may focus on lower level learning, such as the simple recall of facts— "In what year was W.A. Mozart born?" Yet, it *is* possible to write multiple choice questions that measure more complex thinking. In music, listening questions often require more complex thinking to select a correct answer. For example, after playing an excerpt from the Allegro con brio section of the first movement of Beethoven's *Second Symphony*, asking students to decide which style period the excerpt represents, (a) baroque, (b) classical, (c) romantic, or (d) impressionistic, is likely to require students to at least apply, if not analyze, characteristics of style periods they have learned.

At times, the outcomes of music instruction focus on developing students' values. After all, we still teach courses titled "music appreciation." When teachers are interested in assessing the affective outcomes (attitudes, values, emotions) of their students, they may choose to use traditional measures of affective outcomes such as attitude scales. Typically, the format of an attitude scale includes a value statement paired with five-option response scale indicating how much the respondent agrees with the statement. For example,

SA A NN D SD[3] 1. I'd really rather listen to *Goth Rock* than *Techno.*

It is important to note that responses to statements on attitude scales are verbal indications of behaviors, not actual behaviors. Therefore, caution should be exercised when interpreting the results of attitude scales. There may be a variety of reasons for students to respond to statements on attitude scales in a particular way—such as how students view teachers' expectations for what the "right" answer is. Examining the distribution of music styles on students' MP3 playlists may be a more valid *behavioral measure* of students' listening tastes than an attitude scale score. While looking at actual students' behaviors is likely to produce the most reliable and valid measure of students' affect, such strategies are also likely to be labor and time intensive. It is important to acknowledge that verbal statements, such as "I love reggae!" are only approximations of actual behaviors, such as actually purchasing a reggae CD. Factors like the student's true value for reggae music and having the money with which to purchase a CD of reggae are likely to influence behavior. Multiple assessments can provide a more valid measure of affect than a single assessment. For further information about constructing attitude scales or other affective measures in educational settings, see Thorndike (2005) and Henerson, Morris, & Gibbon (1987).

Certainly, performance is a central outcome of music education. Traditional approaches to performance assessment conjure up images of judges sitting in the darkened audience section of a performance hall, while one performer after another mounts the stage to play their solos, etudes, and scales. Traditional performance assessments focus on strategies to improve both the reliability and the validity of the judges' ratings. Remember, for these assessment circumstances, the type of reliability that is most appropriate is "interjudge reliability"—in other words, examining the agreement about the quality of the performance among the judges. Most of the research and development (e.g., Abeles, 1973; Bergee, 1987; Horowitz, 1994; Zdzinski, 2002) that focused on improving traditional approaches to performance assessment have examined two issues—first, having all of the judges make judgments about the same dimensions of the performances (e.g., tone quality, interpretation), and second, increasing the number of judgments each judge makes. One of the strategies for having judges focus on the same performance dimensions is to have them evaluate the same characteristics of a performance (e.g., technique) rather than asking for a global undifferentiated judgment (How good was the performance?). A typical approach to increasing the number of judgments made is to increase the categories judges are evaluating

---

[3] SA—strong agree, A—agree, NN—neither agree nor disagree, D—disagree, SD—strongly disagree

or responding to. Instead of using a rating scale with five broad categories, rating scales are often comprised of a larger number of statements (25 to 40) describing aspects of performances (see Table 8.1). These efforts, in general, increase the interjudge reliability of performance assessment and also appear to increase the validity of the evaluations.

Several authors have published music performance rating scales that demonstrate high interjudge reliabilities. Many of these rating scales used four to six dimensions of performance, such as *intonation, interpretation, tone quality, rhythm accuracy,* and *articulation* to group specific descriptive statements about the performance. Each of the statements is typically paired with a response scale allowing the judge to rate the performance often using a five-option scale. Scales typically include both positive and negative statements to describe the performance.[4] Table 8.1 provides sample statements from several of these scales.

ALTERNATIVE APPROACHES TO THE ASSESSMENT OF THE OUTCOMES OF MUSIC INSTRUCTION

Recently, teachers have sought *alternative approaches* to assessment that fit better with newer philosophical and psychological perspectives of instruction. These alternative approaches appear to synchronize well with constructivist-based instructional strategies, which seek to develop higher order thinking and problem solving in more democratically structured classrooms. While there are several principles that serve as a foundation for alternative approaches to assessment, one key aspect is the attempt to have assessment be well integrated into instruction. Advocates of alternative approaches to assessment, such as Wiggins (1998), argue that we should not stop instruction to assess; instead, the assessment process should be a natural part of instruction. Wiggins labels such an approach *educative assessment.* There are several components of educative assessment that Wiggins suggests define the concept. The first is that assessment should *teach* by exposing students to meaningful authentic performance tasks, thereby engaging students. Another aspect is that assessment should be *open rather than secretive,* so that students have a clear understanding what is expected. Wiggins advocates that grades should "stand for something clear stable and valid" (p. 12) and that *assessment should take place over time* so that once seemingly unreachable high standards become reachable by many students. When discussing the characteristics of the feedback educative assessment should provide to students, teachers, and administrators, Wiggins uses terms like "useful," "clear and rich," and "direct," which will enable students to *self-assess* and *self-correct.* It is important that such systems provide many opportunities for timely feedback over long periods during which students might be working towards particular standards or

---

[4]   Both attitude and rating scales often include both positive and negative statements in an effort to encourage respondents to carefully read each statement and to avoid response set—the tendency of respondents to simply choose all responses in one column (e.g., all SAs).

Table 8.1 Sample Music Performance Rating Scale Statements

Zdzinski (2002)—String Performance
Maintains proper contact point.
Arm weight draws full sound from string and speed with bow.
Tone is full without harshness on forte.
Dry—too technical.

Bergee (1987)—Euphonium/Tuba Performance
Spiritless playing.
Poor synchronization of tongue and fingers.
Superior interpretation.
Good intonation at forte volume.

Cooksey (1974)—High School Choral Music
This choir projects the mood of the selection very well.
Articulation was clear and precise.
Inner parts balance the outer voices very well.
Sopranos sounded forced in upper pitch and dynamic ranges.
Overall effect is choppy and over-sectionalized.

DeCamp (1980)—High School Band
Crescendo and diminuendo are properly graduated.
Runs are played accurately and smoothly.
Entrances are not precise.
Performance lacks emotion.
Dotted rhythms played as triplets.

Horowitz (1994)—Jazz Guitar Improvisation
Sounds like just a bunch of licks over chord changes.
Plays with soul.
Solo builds to a climax.
Uses melodic motifs for sequences to hold solo together.
Solo is not developed logically.

Note: Typically these statements would be placed on a five-option response scale indicating how well the statement described the performance—often strongly agree that the statement is descriptive to strongly disagree that the statement is descriptive.

goals, so that teachers can provide intervention and adjustments to increase the likelihood of students' success in achieving the goals (Wiggins, 1998, pp. 12–13).

So, what would educative assessment look like in music? Alternative assessments in music should include authentic tasks for students to demonstrate their understandings and skills. In general, this means that assessment tasks should be significant and commonly done by people in the field—in other words, "real-world" tasks that parallel what musicians' do. Such tasks are generally more complex than what traditional testing approaches require.

If taking a multiple-choice test is not an authentic musical behavior, then what is it that musicians do? They sing, play music on instruments, compose music, improvise, and carefully listen to music. These musical behaviors require people to integrate multiple skills and understandings; so authentic music assessment tasks should do the same. When musicians prepare a piece for performance they spend many hours refining skills, reflecting on nuances, and making judgments about interpretations before they perform the piece for others. Performing a rehearsed piece provides an opportunity for students to demonstrate the ability to integrate different skills and understandings they have learned, both cognitively and kinesthetically. Thus, having students prepare music for performance is a more authentic task than to play a scale in an end-of-semester jury. While learning to play scales has a place in music instruction, performing a piece requires the integrated behavior more typically practiced by professional musicians. Making change with coins is a more authentic task for students learning subtraction than is completing a paper and pencil subtraction problem, although completing paper and pencil math problems may be a useful component of a math instruction.

In addition to being authentic, assessment tasks should clearly reflect instruction, so that the tasks can serve as a measure of the success of instruction. Authentic assessment tasks should also examine students' ability to use knowledge in other settings, in other words, to transfer the skills and understandings that they have acquired. When pianists learn to interpret a Chopin Prelude, there is the expectation that they will be able to apply what they have learned stylistically to other Chopin Preludes. Shepard (2000) states that teachers should strive to develop robust learning, that is, learning that is sufficiently secure so that it can be applied in new contexts. Authentic tasks should measure robust learning.

An important aspect of reconceptualizing assessment is that students are well informed about the tasks they are undertaking and about the criteria that will be used to evaluate the task. Often, in traditional testing, students try to "guess what is going to be on the test," so that they can better prepare. Such guessing is not a part of an educative approach to assessment, because in educative assessment students' projects are used both as part of the instructional and assessment process. In fact, in educative assessment, students are likely to apply the assessment criteria to their own work as well as to their peers' work.

For example, in a middle school, general music class students may undertake a month-long unit that asks them to compose a score for a five-minute video. Groups of three to five students are first asked to record an approximately five-minute video that depicts a typical part of their day. One group makes a recording of a student arriving home after school, being greeted by his dog, and then having a snack. The teams of students first edit the video with *iMovie* and then use *GarageBand* to compose an accompanying score. Projects with several stages or components provide multiple opportunities for assessment and parallel what Wolf and Pistone label as *domain projects* (1991).[5] During this project, there could be opportunities for students to determine criteria for what comprises an interesting video, as well as developing criteria for assessing a musical score for a video. They could use such criteria (possibly in the form of a scoring rubric) in both a formative and summative way, evaluating their own work as well as the work of other groups in the class.

This illustration provides an authentic task—students composing music for a video—in other words, the type of real-world task a musician might undertake. In addition, the students are asked to apply their understandings and skills in composing to a new undertaking, as well as develop self and peer evaluation skills, thus providing them the opportunity to demonstrate robust learning.

Scoring Rubrics

As suggested earlier, to meet the criteria outlined by Wiggins, educative assessment should provide students with the criteria by which their work will be evaluated. By providing evaluative criteria to students or by having them develop it themselves, as they become more independent learners, they are able to refine their ability to judge when their efforts represent desired qualities and to adjust their work to better meet stated criteria. Practicing self as well as peer evaluation quickly provides students with insights regarding what "good" work is.

Scoring rubrics also help students understand the target, or the standard or goal they are striving for. Rubrics are particularly appropriate for assessing complex authentic tasks, like music performance, that require judgment, rather than the right/wrong dichotomy inherent in objective testing. The performance rubric (Figure 8.1) is an exemplar provided by the Minnesota Music Educators Association.

By providing scoring rubrics, teachers are giving more insight into what they think are the important aspects of a project and the levels of quality that might be exhibited by student work. Rubrics are efforts to provide information, but are not a perfect form of communication, and students and teachers working with rubrics will find that rubrics provide a starting point to understand each other's notions of good work.

It is also important to provide students with a standard of what is expected for a particular assignment and to illustrate how a scoring rubric is applied to that standard. Thus, anonymous assignments from students in previous years who have done excellent work can serve as models for current students. In addition, to assist in refining students' understanding of the different levels of descriptions contained on scoring rubric, sample assignments that reflect different levels of achievement should also be provided to students.

For teachers, developing rubrics can provide the opportunity to reflect on what they value and how well a particular assignment helps fulfill instructional

---

⁵ Wolf and Pistone (1991) use the term domain projects to refer to long-term, open-ended projects that integrate production (making) with perception (learning to understand) and reflection (thinking about one's work and the works of others).

	4	3	2	1
Tone	The tone is consistently focused, clear, and centered throughout the range of the instrument.	The tone is focused, clear, and centered most of the time. Extremes in range cause the tone to become uncontrolled.	The tone is sometimes focused, clear, and centered. Some pitches within, the normal playing range are uncontrolled.	The tone is often not focused, clear, or centered regardless of the range being played.
Rhythm	The pulse is secure. Rhythms are accurate.	The pulse is steady. Rhythms are mostly accurate. A few duration errors.	The pulse is erratic. Some rhythms are accurate. Frequent or repeated duration errors.	No perceived pulse. Rhythms are seldom accurate.
Pitch	Virtually no errors. Very secure pitches.	A few isolated errors. Mostly accurate and secure pitches.	Frequent or repeated errors. Some accurate pitches.	Few accurate or secure pitches.
Articulation	Secure attacks. Markings (staccato, legato, slur, accents, etc.) are accurate and obvious.	Mostly secure attacks. Markings (staccato, legato, slur, accents, etc.) are mostly accurate and obvious.	Some secure attacks. Markings (staccato, legato, slur, accents, etc.) sometimes accurate and obvious.	Few secure attacks. Markings (staccato, legato, slur, accents, etc.) mostly not observed.
Dynamics	Dynamic levels are obvious, consistent, and an accurate interpretation of the style.	Dynamic levels are mostly accurate and consistent.	Dynamic levels can be discerned.	Dynamic levels not evident.
Phrasing	Musical nuance to indicate phrase structure is consistent and sensitive.	Musical nuance to indicate phrase structure is often obvious.	Musical nuance to indicate phrase structure is sometimes used but seldom obvious.	Musical nuance to indicate phrase structure is not used.
Expression and Style	Consistently performs with nuance and style in response to the score and coaching.	Often performs with nuance or style indicated in the score or suggested by the instructor or peer.	Sometimes responds to musical nuance indicated in the score.	Seldom evidence of musical nuance in musical phrases.

Figure 8.1. Rubric for assessing music skills (Schaefer, 2008).

goals. Different scoring rubrics are typically developed for different assignments, and while Hickey (1999) provides a more general rubric for evaluating music compositions, she encourages teachers to adapt and modify rubrics depending upon the particular assignment and the grade level of the students.

Scoring rubrics can be holistic—using one global dimension to focus on the quality of the entire work—or analytical. A holistic rubric designed to assess performance might employ just one of the six criteria in Figure 8.1. Analytical scoring rubrics, those having multiple articulated criteria, such as the one presented on page 182, are most useful to students as means of understanding different components that comprise a quality project. The effectiveness of a scoring rubric as part of learning is determined by how well it assists students to improve their work. There are two aspects of scoring rubrics that are key to their effectiveness. First, the criteria identified must get to the heart of what is important in student learning, not just what is superficial and easy to evaluate. Thus, most music teachers would agree that criteria like craftsmanship and creativity are at the heart of developing student compositions, while criteria such as the neatness of notation are not.

Effective rubrics should use rich descriptive language to specify quality levels of each criterion. It is also important to use unique language at each level rather than just "less than" or "more than" an adjacent box. Also, effective scoring rubrics do not use superficial or arbitrary quantitative criteria such as, "the composition uses at least four different chords, and the composition uses at least five different chords," as the number of chords a composition uses doesn't necessarily make it musical. When possible, strive for language that can be easily observed both by the teacher and student. When assessing vocal performances, it may be appropriate to consider "stage presence." Using descriptive behaviors, such as "posture," "demonstrates confidence," "makes eye contact with audience," and "engages the audience with gestures," is more effective and instructive than broad terms like "charismatic."

In some student centered learning environments, students not only have an understanding of the criteria by which their work will be judged but also provide input into the evaluation process. One way this can be accomplished is through having students participate in the development of scoring rubrics. Through these experiences students are likely to increase their ownership of the learning and evaluating process and produce better work. When students are involved in the assessment process, the process will become more meaningful. Having students participate in the development of scoring rubrics will also supply the teacher with insight into unique criteria that students themselves value in their learning experiences.

One approach to getting students involved is by simply providing groups of students with a blank grid and asking them as teams to list characteristics of a "good" result from the assignment (e.g., performance, composition). Once the different teams agree on different criteria, have the groups develop statements that describe the different levels of each criterion and have the entire class review what each group has produced. Depending on the amount of time available, the final rubric might result from an extended class discussion or from the teacher summarizing the class ideas and representing it to the students for review. As students become more experienced with using both teacher- and student-developed rubrics, producing new student-developed rubrics becomes more efficient.

Scoring rubrics are also a good means of having students become involved in self-assessment and peer assessment. Advocates of student centered learning reject the notion that the teacher is the one arbiter of what is "right." The opportunity for students to reflect on their own work and compare it with criteria articulated in a scoring rubric helps move them toward becoming independent learners. This is not likely to happen overnight. Students' initial self evaluations may be superficial, but over time, they are likely to be able to develop the depth and reflectiveness that characterizes independent learners.[6] Tierney, Carter, & Desai (1991) report that teachers describe that an additional benefit of self-evaluation is the moving away from the tendency to compare students with each other and toward evaluations that compare students with themselves (p. 110). It is particularly important for music students to develop their self-evaluative skills in performance classes and to move away from the tendency to compare themselves with other students who play the same instrument.

Peer evaluations can also play an educative role in assessment. Teachers often say that peer evaluations must be managed carefully, so that constructive recommendations are generated. Teachers should provide well crafted strategies for students to conduct peer evaluations, so that students develop appropriate skills to nurture each other's learning. Good opportunities for constructive peer evaluations exist in several music learning settings, including performance and composition classes. In both settings, the analytical skills necessary to evaluate others' performances or compositions will enhance students own musical development.

Reconceptualizing Assessment Assignments

In many ways, the arts have been in the vanguard of using authentic tasks to assess the achievement of students (Wolf, 1987/1988). After all, it is common for music teachers to use authentic performance tasks as means of assessing achievement. Are there ways that we can better incorporate authentic tasks to more fully reconceptualize assessment?

What does it mean to be successful or achieve in a music class? Certainly, it is more than just playing or singing well. A musically literate student should be able to play, listen critically, improvise, compose—in other words, all of the skills and understandings that are part of a comprehensive music educational experience. What evidence can music teachers gather to better understand all of what their music students are learning?

Portfolios

One approach to providing evidence of students' achievement in these areas is to use student portfolios. Portfolios can be used in a formative way to help students

---

6 It should be noted that the finds of several studies suggest that music students are inconsistent in evaluations of their own performances (Bergee, 1993, 1997; Hewitt, 2002; Kostka, 1997),

and teachers keep track of student learning and help students revise and improve their work. Such portfolios are typically called *process portfolios*. Other portfolios that are more cumulative and represent summative work are called *product portfolios*.

Process portfolios are places where students keep evidence of their achievement and growth *over time*. The evidence can take a variety of forms, but should reflect authentic music behavior. Davidson and Scripp (1990) recommend that comprehensive evidence for music learning should include performance, as well as evidence of perception, and reflection.[7] They argue that perception—specifically, a strong sensory discrimination—is critical to the refinement of artistic efforts and the appreciation of finished performances. Reflection is also a critical skill for musicians as they must have well-developed sense of self and of their strengths and weaknesses (p. 51).

A music process portfolio is likely to include evidence of performance. Practically, these might be audio tapes of student performances throughout the year, ideally demonstrating students' development of skills over time. In addition, evidence of perception and reflection should be included. There are several ways to include evidence of perception and reflection, such as written reflections on rehearsals or tapes of rehearsals. Music educators experienced with portfolios in choral (Stevens, 2001) and band (Dirth, 2000) ensemble settings include evidence such as written individual and ensemble critiques, tapes of performances, concert reviews, and questionnaires in student portfolios. The comments from a high school students' chamber group rehearsal is shown in Table 8.2.

Some teachers also provide music scores of works and ask students to listen to live performances or tapes of themselves or ensembles and then comment on passages that need to be improved or that show improvement (see Figure 8.2).

How can this kind of writing serve as useful documentation of music students' thinking? Some high school ensemble directors have asked students to write reviews of their concerts as shown in Table 8.3.

These kinds of assignments are designed to provide evidence of students' perception and self-reflection. If the assignment, such as the one in Table 8.2, focuses the student's attention on her own performance, it can be used as a tool to help the student focus her attention on self-adjusting her performance. If the assignment is focused more on an ensemble performance (Table 8.3 and Figure 8.2), it can provide evidence of students' perceptive learning as well as understanding of the context for their own performance.

Journals versus Assignments

Just because several assignments are collected in a notebook, does that comprise a journal? For many educators, journals have a narrow definition and objective. Journals can be places where students write reflections of their work in music, like their ideas for composing, or journals might be tied to evaluating performances,

---

[7] Production, perception and reflection are key components of the Arts Propel approach to assessment (see, Wolf & Pistone, 1991).

Table 8.2. Student Comment Sheet

Title of Piece: *Telemann Concerto in G- arr. For 2 vlns, viola, cello*

PITCH: *This is the first time I've played this piece from start to finish. Overall I think it sound terrible and very rusty. My 16th notes need to be cleaned up quite a bit. The best way for me to improve them would be to slow down, and gradually speed them up to tempo.*

RHYTHM: *My big problem here is my fourth finger stretch to the high "E". The only way for me to reach it is to shift my hand up. During this reading, however, I forgot to shift back down.*

TEMPO: _____

_____

_____

DYNAMICS: *I also need to be more aware of the dynamics notated in the music. I often played this piece as if it were a boring study.*

ARTICULATION: _____

_____

_____ (Dirth, 1994)

Table 8.3. High School Band Member's Concert Review

The concert band gave its last performance of the year. The concert fell far from short of the band's esteemed reputation, and compelled the delighted audience to rise for applause. The first selection was a piece entitled Symphonic Prelude to Adeste Fidelis. The first clear, balanced notes of the trumpet section were clear indications of the quality of music to follow. The most noticeable aspect of this piece was the articulation. The trumpets were especially impressive in the beginning, creating a sound nearly perfect in tone and phrasing so that all that was heard was pure music. The rolls between phrases on percussion instruments (such as the suspended cymbal at measure 21) were clear and even; and kept the interpretation and the feeling alive. In the section from 33 to 41, the saxes and clarinets were beautifully balanced, however it was here that the percussion made its first articulation error, that of the chimes not being quite loud enough. The second came at 53, where the down beat was missed by a fraction by the timpani and cymbals. These errors were made up in the end, however, when the climax of the piece was moved along by cutting cymbal crashes, bells, and excellent buzzed rolls on the snare drums....

(Dirth, 1994)

Figure 8.2. Sample high school band score comments (Dirth, 2004, p. 112).

rehearsals, or lessons. They are places where students can keep thinking about their music learning in a metacognitive way. They can be valuable assessment tools—as demonstrated in this high school students' journal (Table 8.4).

While journals are a powerful tool for educative assessment, particularly for encouraging students' self-assessment, teachers should consider the degree to which these personal reflections should be a part of an evaluation system. It may be that every item in a process portfolio will not be included in a final evaluation. Both the teacher and student might select some of the items in the process portfolio to be included in determining a grade, although certain assignments should be included for every student.

Scoring rubrics are an effective tool for evaluating evidence in a student's portfolio. Typically, music teachers will score each category of evidence, such as ensemble critiques, separately. Dirth (2000) asked each band student in his ensemble to independently evaluate each component of their portfolios. In a year-end interview, he compared his evaluation with theirs in an effort to support their development of self-assessment skills, although his evaluations were the grades that appeared on their report cards.

STANDARDIZED TESTING IN MUSIC

Paralleling the development of educative assessment approaches in classrooms, the use of standardized achievement testing in education, particularly testing

Table 8.4. High School Band Students' Lesson Journal Entry

December 14

Relief, my lesson went well yesterday. Combined with Amanda's lesson I got everything taken care of. I was really surprised that I had breathing mistakes in Hallo Chorus. It sounded right in band but when I was isolated I just couldn't get it. But finally I learned what to do. I just need to remind myself that breathing takes the place of a note. I just cant put a beat into a measure. I did recieve vindication when finally I played that rhythm at 11 in X-mas festival. I just needed to write down the rhythms in the repeats. I just couldn't visiulize the rhythum. (Dirth, 1994)

that focuses on year-end mastery of a few subject areas, increased in the last two decades. Part of this increase in testing is due to national education policies, such as the *standards movement* and the No Child Left Behind legislation. This is less true for music education. In fact, the use of standardized tests in music appears to have declined since the 1960s.

A standardized test is one that is typically developed by a test development company with both content and testing experts. Considerable information about the details of a standardized test is made available including reliability and validity reports and norms—which helps teachers compare the results for individual students or schools to test results for an age, geographical, or national comparison group. Standardized tests differ from classroom tests in that they are used to compare individual students, classes, schools, or school systems to others and measure more generalized areas (e.g., music achievement), while teacher-developed classroom tests are used mostly to provide feedback to students and measure more specific achievement areas, such as rhythm notation. Typically, in standardized testing, students do not receive feedback about specific items they answer correctly or incorrectly, while typically they do receive feedback about their performance on specific items on teachers developed tests.

Standardized tests can be categorized by the areas they measure. Some are designed to predict future behavior or capacities; these are called *aptitude* tests. IQ tests, for example, are designed to predict future behavior. If an aptitude test result indicates that a young student has a high aptitude for a particular field such as music, it would be expected in the future that the student would perform well in music classes.

There were many standardized music aptitude tests developed during the twentieth century. Some are of historical interest, such as the *Seashore Measures of Musical Talent* (1919) and others, such as the several music aptitude tests developed by Gordon—*Musical Aptitude Profile* (1965), *Primary Measures of Music Audiation* (1986), *and Intermediate Measures of Music Audiation* (1986)—are often used in research studies to measure music aptitude.

In contrast to predictive tests, *standardized achievement tests* are used to measure what students have learned in a particular discipline. The year-end tests administered by states to children in every public school are omnipresent examples of standardized achievement tests. The 20th century was also a time when several music standardized achievement tests were published, including, Colwell's *Music Achievement Test* (1965) and Gordon's *Iowa Tests of Music Literacy* (1991).

There are a few other measures of music achievement which, while never widely used beyond research applications, represent unique areas of assessment. *The Watkins-Farnum Performance Scale for All Band Instruments* (Watkins & Farnum, 1954) was constructed to measure performance on band instruments. It was an attempt to develop a standardized measure of instrumental performance, and primarily measures sight-reading and technique. In 1967, Long published the *Indiana—Oregon Music Discrimination Test*, a revision of an earlier test by Kate Hevner Mueller (1934). It was designed as a test of musical taste in which students choose between a musical phrase and a distorted version of the same phrase (Long, 1972). Other standardized tests not specifically in music but which may provide useful information to the music student include vocational interest measures, such as the *Strong Interest Inventory* (1994). These measures are traditionally used by guidance counselors to assist students in identifying possible vocational paths including music vocations.

STATE AND NATIONAL ASSESSMENTS OF ACHIEVEMENT IN MUSIC EDUCATION

The National Assessment of Educational Progress (NAEP) is designed to measure academic achievement in all disciplines of school children in the United States. NAEP was first designed and administered in the 1970s and includes assessments in several school subjects including the arts. More recently, it has been used to measure student outcomes related to the National Standards. The music assessment was designed to measure skills and knowledge in three areas of music learning— creating, performing, and responding to music. A description of a music exercise from the 1997 NAEP appears below:

> This task explored improvisation, creation, and evaluation activities in music using rock-style background music as stimulus material. Four tasks were included in this session as follows:
>
> improvising at the keyboard with a background tape to create an original melody;
>
> performing the original melody on the keyboard unaccompanied;
>
> singing a vocal improvisation with the background tape; and
>
> completing written self-evaluation questions about the performances.
>
> (NAEP, 1999)

In 1997, NAEP assessed the music achievement of eighth grade students in schools across the country. It was designed to provide a national overview of students' achievement in a variety of music competencies (Schneider, 2005). The results of the 1997 administration of the NAEP in music showed that for the responding items, items that asked students to listen to and then respond to questions about what they heard, most students performed at or above the national standards in music. In the performance area though, only 35% of the students were able to sing "America" at or above the "adequate level" on pitch, while 78% performed above the "limited level" in rhythm. As might be expected, students who are involved in music activities in or out of school performed better on the tests than those who do not participate in music activities (Lehmann, 1999).

With the state-level proliferation of achievement testing, typically in language arts, math, science, and social studies, some states have considered developing year-end achievement testing in music. States like California, concerned that school districts are ignoring state mandated music requirements, have considered establishing state tests to demonstrate how music standards are *not* being met (Asimov, 2007). Other states, like New York, have developed measures to assess students' attainment of the state standards in music. These assessments typically are designed to measure areas similar to the NAEP—creating, performing, and responding to music. Zuar (2006) reports that few states have been able to focus on the arts, as the testing required by NCLB requires such an extraordinary resource commitment that there are not resources left to support year-end testing in the arts. Those who advocate for including music in year-end testing, including MENC, suggest that including music achievement testing at the state level would likely improve the equality of instruction and make music more clearly part of the core curriculum. While NCLB legislation includes arts as part of the core curriculum, it does not require the arts to be part of the standardized testing requirements.

EVALUATING SCHOOL MUSIC PROGRAMS

Examining music achievement outcomes for individual students provides teachers with insight into the effectiveness of instruction. There are times when information beyond an individual music classroom is useful in helping shape and improve music curriculum and instruction for a district, region, state, or nation. NAEP may be conceived as a tool for evaluating the effectiveness of the nation's music instruction. Since education is organized locally, it is useful to examine the effectiveness of music instructional programs at the local level.

Most evaluations of district school music programs have specific goals in mind. They often focus on curriculum reform, as well as an examination of the resources available for implementing effective music instruction, including facilities, materials and equipment, and staffing. Such models of music program evaluations rely on a two-dimensional approach—identifying the *inputs* (curriculum, facilities, etc.) and assessing the *effect* of the resources on student outcomes. It is important to include the participation of those who are stakeholders in music program evaluations, including district administrators and members of the community—often parents of students, as they will be critical in implementing any changes recommended in an evaluation report.

A school district music program evaluation might begin with a description of the curriculum, staffing, materials and equipment, and facilities that enable the music program to offer instructional experiences for students. One challenge for many districts is to determine how to assess support for the music program. Is it enough? Is it "more than" enough? One approach is to compare resource allocations with neighboring districts. A valuable tool in this process is a monograph developed by MENC titled, *Opportunity-to-Learn Standards for Music Instruction: Grades PreK-12* (1994). It provides benchmarks for curriculum and scheduling, staffing, materials and equipment, and facilities for an effective music program.

Often administrators and parents employ the most visible outcomes, such as the quality of concerts and the number of students enrolled in elective music ensembles, as measures of the effectiveness of a music program. It is important for music educators to assist all members of the school community in understanding the breadth of music programs. In doing so, music educators should provide valid measures of student learning that reflect both state and national music standards and that are also sensitive to the uniqueness of a particular district's music program. It is very important that districts use multiple measures of outcomes. These might include the number of students participating in all-district or all-state performing groups and evaluations of ensemble at festivals. But, defining the success of a music program should include more than these measures. Assessments might include questionnaires that students complete about their view of what they have learned about music in school. If individual states have developed measures for student achievement in music, then the scores generated on those measures by students in a particular district might be used as one measure. Most importantly, a thorough evaluation of a music program should include examining students' work produced at all levels of instruction, in a wide range of music classes. This examination must reflect state and national standards *beyond* playing and singing. Many districts will hire an external consult to help in program evaluations and to present a report to the Board. This practice is often effective as "outside experts" may contribute an objective dimension to an evaluation.

CONCLUSION

This chapter was designed to increase your understanding and appreciation of the important role assessment plays in learning. It is anticipated that knowledge of assessment strategies and philosophical and political issues concerned with them are necessary for music teachers to effectively function in schools.

The debate focusing on assessment in education will continue to ferment as two markedly different philosophies of assessment underlie the traditional and alternative approaches described in this chapter. It is challenging for both approaches to assessment to exist within the same educational system. The emphasis on year-end testing, like the NCLB mandated achievement tests in literacy, math and science, is motivated by school management concerns driven by an "input → output" model, while alternative assessments are driven by pedagogical concerns that focus on helping students learn. Good management and strong pedagogy are necessary for educational systems to function well, yet tensions between the different approaches to assessment will continue, particularly when different results are produced by the different approaches. Understanding and reconciling the results of alternative assessment and traditional assessments must continue to be the focus of teachers and educational assessment specialists.

Issues like the evaluation of music programs and the judging of music teacher effectiveness continue to be modeled on strategies developed in general education. Music education professionals need to continue to emphasis the unique needs of effective music programs and the unique aspects of music teaching for music to thrive in the 21st century.

Class Discussions

1. Select an instructional area like studio music lessons or an ensemble class and a level of instruction, elementary school, middle school, high school, or college. For the teaching circumstance you've identified, a) give at least three examples of instructions/or types of activities that you would give your students to enable them to write in their journals; and b) describe how you would provide reactions to the journals during the year.

2. Place the following traits in order based on which might be the most reliably measured to which might be least reliably measured. Be able to defend your decisions: Musical Aptitude, Music Taste, Knowledge of Music Fundamentals, Music History, Aesthetic Sensitivity, An Aural test of Musical Styles (period, year, and composer).

3. For each of the following tests, identify at least one appropriate criterion you could use to establish the criterion-related validity of the test. Be able to defend your choices: Musical Aptitude, Music Taste, Rating Scale to judge a music performance, Knowledge of Music Fundamentals, Music History, Aesthetic Sensitivity, An Aural test of Musical Styles (period, year, composer).

4. Using a table (5 columns × 5–7 rows) with empty cells, develop a scoring rubric for one of the projects in this course. First, discuss with your classmates what criteria (categories) the project should be evaluated on. You should generate at least five criteria categories. Then develop descriptions of the four different levels of quality for each criterion.

Projects

1. Identify a performance area for either an individual instrument or an ensemble and a level of performance. For example, a middle school trumpet

performance or a high school choral performance. Identify from four to seven categories or dimensions appropriate for evaluating the performance (e.g., tone quality, interpretation, etc.) Generate at least five statements for each category that describe either a good or bad performance for that category. Place your statements on a five-option likert-type scale. Collect from three to five short recordings of individual or group performances to rating using your rating scale. Have at least three judges (e.g., members of your group) score the performances using your rating scale. Discuss items on the scale on which the judges agreed or disagreed.

2. For an ensemble class or individual lessons, have your students keep a reflective performance journal. Provide them with some content guidelines— such as aspects of the class or lesson they should comment about (e.g., things that I need to work on). Collect the journals after a month. Review them to see if there is evidence of students' ability to self-assess their own performance or to assess the performance of an ensemble of which they are a member. Reflect on how you might improve their ability to self-assess.

SUGGESTED READINGS

Wiggins, G. P. (1998). *Educative assessment: designing assessments to inform and improve student performance*. San Francisco, CA: Jossey-Bass.

Osterlind, S. J. (1998). *Constructing test items: Multiple-choice, constructed-response, performance and other formats (Evaluation in education and human services)*. Norwell, MA: Kluwer Academic Publishers.

Wolf, D., & Pistone, N. (1991). *Taking full measure: Rethinking assessment through the arts*. New York: College Board Publications.

CHAPTER 9

❧

Methods and Approaches

Cathy Benedict

> There is a time to admire the grace and persuasive power of an
> influential idea, and there is a time to fear its hold over us. The
> time to worry is when the idea is so widely shared that we no
> longer even notice it, when it is so deeply rooted that it feels to
> us like plain common sense. At the point when objections are
> not answered anymore because they are no longer even raised,
> we are not in control: we do not have the idea; it has us.
>
> (KOHN, 1991, P. 3)

INTRODUCTION

How often have we heard people describe themselves as Kodály, Orff, Suzuki, Gordon, or Dalcroze teachers? What exactly do they mean by this when they describe themselves as such? And perhaps more interestingly, what would the authors of these pedagogical approaches think of such identification? When contemplating the myriad of choices with which one is faced when considering the how and why of teaching music, one place people often begin is by choosing to "teach" a particular method. As such, it is consistent, and perhaps even necessary to include in books, such as this one, a chapter that addresses methods of teaching music. However, this chapter seeks to broaden the customary and conventional "how to" approach of presenting these methods and pose a series of questions that push not only our conceptualization of them but also the normative givens that seem such a part of them.

In the following chapter, several of these "methods" will be examined so that the reader may become familiar with the particular and salient points of each. However, as is consistent with the rest of this book, it is believed that in order to approach and enter a working familiarity with issues, it is important, and even incumbent upon us, to rethink and reengage with the issue in a broader context. It is never enough to just read about a particular "method." One must engage in experiencing each through perhaps summer programs and workshops. However, even the "doing" of a method is ineffectual if a broader contextualization of the forces that frame and continue to frame the "method" aren't explored and articulated.

In this chapter, an outline of each "method" will be articulated, as well as the genesis of each approach, including the historical, cultural, and philosophical issues embedded within each method. Questions will be posed that address, among others, the underlying assumptions about music learners and music, what it means to know, learn, and teach, the definition of musical literacy, and multiculturalism. Finally, as we attempt to understand and frame the implications of each of these approaches, we must be mindful of the ways in which each of these men engaged in setting and framing the intent, parameters, and processes. To that end, each section ends with content specific issues as well as a final section that addresses issues that are similar in each approach.

WHAT IS A METHOD?

Many of the "methods" that will be addressed in this chapter have been referred to as approaches, concepts, and even philosophies. Is it essential, then, to consider the philosophical grounding that frames and shapes each of these approaches. Each of the men who developed these approaches has very particular ideas as to what and how it means to know. Each of them also sees this particular musical knowing as serving the greater good, or humanity. What of these philosophies of knowing and have these philosophies morphed into very particular ideologies? Precisely because a continuum of interpretation for each of these approaches exists and is as varied as there are people who claim to "teach" them, we need also to consider how and what "methods" are.

What then is a method, and were any of these approaches intended as methods to be prescribed and followed? Thomas Regelski (2004) has warned the music education community to be mindful of "methodolatry," and an "uncritical devotion to, or worship of, technicist approaches" (p. 7). He suggests that a blind and unconditional reliance on methods to "train" a student musically masks and denies the possibility of seeing the "situatedness" of school cultures and environments and thus the limitations and constraints of the approaches and even the positioning of privilege go uninterrogated. Each of the men who will be reviewed in this chapter believed that sequential introduction of elements pulled from musical experiences would encourage and develop improvisation and creation. They each also believed that these approaches would allow all students of varying abilities and backgrounds access into the world of great art music. And even though each of these men lived to see how far reaching their approaches were embraced, one wonders how they would contend with the cottage industry that has emerged with the almost universal recognition of their names as music educators and their attendant approaches.

In what ways, then, have these approaches been turned into systematic procedures of distilling musical experiences into discrete and measurable units, and at what expense to the original vision and intent of the creator? And finally, what does it mean to be engaged meaningfully with music through and within these approaches?

In the following sections Dalcroze, Kodály, Orff, Suzuki, and Gordon will be examined in such a way as to allow the reader to become familiar with the cultural and sociological forces that informed each of the approaches. The practical application of each approach will also be detailed with the intent of examining how each approach may be applied throughout the spectrum of what makes up a school music program.

EMILE JAQUES-DALCROZE

When people first consider Emile Jaques-Dalcroze (1865–1950), they often think of Eurhythmics. While this is one aspect of the work of Dalcroze, as with any one of these pedagogical processes, taking on (or even more problematic "teaching to") this one characteristic without considering how Dalcroze conceptualized being in the world would be to deny and trivialize the greater significance of what Dalcroze saw as the purpose of education and thus the purpose of music education. Influenced by the work of Rousseau, Dalcroze believed that "Education ... should have as its chief aim the suppression of resistances of every nature which hamper the individual in the externalization of his character ..." (1921, p. xiii).

Trained in conservatory as a pianist, Dalcroze engaged in composition and improvisation processes that often grew out of improvised textual settings. It was in his work with his students, however, as Professor of Harmony at the Geneva Conservatoire (1892), that Dalcroze not only discovered in his students rhythm and pitch problems, but perhaps more disturbing was the discovery of their inability to express and engage musically. It was during these years that Dalcroze came to see musical perception, viewed thus as a cognitive reaction, as incomplete. Consequently, he came to believe that the "whole organism" needed to be engaged so that there could be harmonization between "mind and body" (1921, p. vii). For Dalcroze, the body was the "intermediary between sounds and thought" (p. 8); it was the object through and in which our feelings and intellect would manifest and transform. The cultivation of free play was integral to the process of developing individuals who were in tune with their own temperament rather than "isolated" individuals; it was for Dalcroze a way of knowing who we are. It was his desire that through self-mastery students would come to know themselves and thus take on the ability to place themselves in the world so that as contributing citizens they would "adapt themselves ... to individual and collective existence" (p. viii).

Dalcroze saw the individual as part of a larger collective through which participation in this collective, without the constraints of worry or inhibition, would bring a sense of joy. In joy he saw a kind of self-knowledge that would promote liberation and independence. Dalcroze saw this joy occurring when students became aware of the control over restraints; thus joy occurs as a "joint sense of emancipation and responsibility" (p. 175). For Dalcroze then, joy was a journey of inquiry that had the potential to affect all of those around.

The Process

The study of rhythm awakens 'feeling for bodily rhythm and aural perception of rhythm. The study of solfege awakens' the sense of pitch and tone-relations and the faculty of distinguishing tone-qualities. The study of improvisation combines the principles of rhythm and solfege and teaches pupils to interpret on the piano musical thoughts of a melodic, harmonic, and rhythmic nature. (1921, pp. 120–121)

For Dalcroze, being musical meant having consciousness of sound and consciousness of bodily rhythm (p. 79). Looking for exercises that would instill in his students a sense of musicality that connected mind and body in ways that would unite sound, thought, movement and feeling, Dalcroze searched for a series of exercises that would afford students the opportunity of engaging physically and intellectually with musical processes. Finding nothing suitable, he set about creating exercises that would constitute at once instruction *in* rhythm, and education *by* rhythm, or eurhythmics (p. 9).

Dalcroze saw the separation of curriculum and teaching as fragmentary and specialized (p. 6); for him, this was a false separation of engaging in and with music. He was not interested in teaching ear training as a set of segmented harmonic and melodic exercises. He believed rather, that inner hearing came as a result of connecting the body to the auditory processes; movement was seen as the intermediary between the physical nature of singing and hearing. As such, for Dalcroze, the realization of musical concepts comes in and through movement utilizing, ear training (solfege), improvisation, and eurhythmics. Always engaging in musical experiences students first internalize concepts by doing and embodying—never separate from the music—rhythm, structure and movement, solfege, pitch and tonality, and improvisation.

He believed that students first develop a sense of rhythm through training of the muscular system. Consequently, students first begin by internalizing rhythmic concepts through time and space. After spending a year in rhythmic training so that each student could "train his power of hearing, realizing and creating musical sounds in rhythm" (p. 131), students begin attending solfege classes while continuing to engage with rhythmic exercises. So that students would understand the direct connection between rhythm and melody, these solfege exercise corresponded directly to the rhythmic exercises. And finally, as the synthesis of rhythm and solfege, improvisatory exercises that also coincided with the exercise of rhythmic and solfege were introduced.

Application

The Dalcroze approach originated with college-age students; however, application to multiple ages seems inherent in the process. Facility on an insturment (more often than not piano) is integral to this appraoch. Teachers must be able to improvise on their insturment so that students will make the connection between body and mind as facilitated by the eurhythmic process. Adolescent students may be less than willing to move about the room in free improvisation, but perhaps with the use of more contemporary movements students could engage in the same ear training like exercises.

Content-Specific Issues

Dalcroze's main concern was that his students were coming out of a music education training program with technique and skills, but lacking in musicality and creativity. While Dalcroze saw eurhythmics, ear training, and improvisation as separate threads he did not conceive of them as separate and discrete entities. Eurhythmics is not an end in itself, nor is ear training and improvisation. The three areas are integral to the process. Therefore, if these three areas are broken down into teachable units so that the method or the steps become more important than the goal or purpose of the process itself, educators run the risk of accomplishing that which Dalcroze sought to challenge: students with technique and skills and little musicality. That said, it seems appropriate to consider the reverse: students who are musical and can improvise yet who do not posses the literacy skills Dalcroze desired.

Dalcroze believed that music could be used as a way to develop temperament and in some cases to "subdue the activities of too excitable temperaments" (1921, p. 8). He saw temperament as responsible for differing aptitudes in rhythmic actions and that the structure of the body was integral to "motor expression" (p. 320). As part of this, he notes that peoples of European descent have greater muscular capacity than those people of "savage races" (p. 320) and that it is "obvious that the influences of climate, customs, and historical and economic circumstances must have produced certain differences in the rhythmic sense of each people" (p. 320). But we need not concern ourselves, for subduing temperament can "easily be modified by training" (p. 321). Thus, Dalcroze believed so strongly in the possibilities of rhythmic training that such training could help to rectify, mollify, and even subjugate that which prevented "aesthetic development and attainment of intellectual and physical balance" (p. 333).

KODÁLY

In art bad taste is a real spiritual illness. It is the duty of the school to offer protection against this plague. The school of today does not only neglect to do this, it actually opens door and gates to the trash of music. In school, singing and music making must be taught in such a way that in the child for all his life a desire for noble music is awakened. (Kraus, 1990 p. 83)

Zoltán Kodály (1882–1967) was born in Kecskemét at a time and in a country in which social upheaval and national identity underscored and framed a lifetime of humanistic endeavor. Kodály played in the school orchestra, but his family environment provided the beginnings of his musical education: in order to complete a family chamber ensemble Kodály learned to play the cello after learning piano and violin. As the son of a stationmaster, at the age of 10, Kodály was entitled to an education at the local grammar school.

During the first half of the 20th century Kodály and Bartók were closely connected to what has been referred to as the "populist" trend in Hungary. The populist movement was an "intellectual and ideological trend sharply opposed to the great estates and capitalism..." (Lackó, 1987, p. 40). This was a movement that was concerned with social welfare and the transformation of society so that the conditions for the "peasantry" and the masses were raised. Kodály believed that the "cohesion of a community, depended on one language, one people" so that a "national unity" may be formed (Young, 1964, p. 105). This commitment to social welfare coupled with his love of literacy, language, and semantics provided a framework that would serve him as he became more engaged with collecting Hungarian folk songs and devising a classification system. Under this classification system, folk songs were analyzed according to their final note and tonal and melodic range.

Kodály knew the work of Dalcroze and yet chose to engage with the musical educative process differently. As a composer and musicologist, Kodály's engagement with these separate but interrelated fields shaped the vision of his approach. Departing from Dalcroze, Kodály believed first and foremost that musical engagement began with singing and the physicality embedded in that. Just as Dalcroze felt that movement was not only the way in which students should enter musical engagements, but also a way to inform citizenry, Kodály believed musicianship would lead toward intellectual development. Literacy meant being able to pick up a piece of music and read it as you would a newspaper. Thus, the beginnings of a lifelong enjoyment of music meant being able to read and write musical notation.

At no time in Kodály's life did he set out to develop a method of teaching music; he did not "make up" the method; his beliefs evolved from his focus on the material and repertoire.

The Process

Kodály borrowed tools of the process from pedagogies that were already in existence. The method incorporates the tonic solfa system of Guido d'Arezzo, the melodic hand signs are borrowed from John Curwen; movement evolved from the work of Dalcroze; the rhythmic syllables are based on a system of Emile Chêvé, and the educational grounding from the work of Swiss educator Pestalozzi.

Kodály saw this process not just as music education but also as a way in which to transmit culture. Thus, the Kodály process begins first and foremost with folk songs of the child's culture—the "music mother tongue." These folk songs, which serve multiple functions, and of which Kodály believed should be of only the highest quality, eventually lead and pave the way to art music. These folk songs, often centering around the pentatonic, prepare and lay the foundation from which a sequence of musical elements will be pulled, named, and then practiced. And finally, these folk songs and singing games provide access not only to the culture of the community but the skills necessary for musical literacy.

Kindergarten and first grade are often seen as the preparatory years in which students are engaging with activities that focus on phrasing, dynamics, tempo, beat/rhythm, high/low, and the descending minor third. When teachers feel that students have internalized in-tune singing and steady beat, they begin the process of naming, or making conscious musical elements. The sequencing of the musical elements is pulled from the music of the culture and the frequency with which certain elements occur. In North America, this process often first begins with students internalizing rhythm against beat. As students are led toward an understanding that there are places that have more than one sound, or syllables on a beat, teachers name this as "ta," and "ti, ti." After "naming" these rhythms syllables, teachers then plan lessons in which students can practice these rhythms in various ways, including sight reading, dictation, and singing known songs with rhythmic syllables. In these same lessons in which students are practicing these rhythm syllables, Kodály teachers include activities that prepare to make conscious sol and mi. Students internalize these pitches through hand signs and move toward an understanding that these notes are a skip apart. When teachers feel that students have internalized this skip, the notes are placed on the staff. At that point, students are now practicing ta and ti a well as sol and mi. Thus, the musical sequencing continues to progress as new elements are introduced, named, and practiced. As such, each lesson should include elements of preparation, practice, and when appropriate, naming or making conscious.

Applications

The tonic solfa system and accompanying hand signs, as well as rhythmic syllables can all be considered invaluable tools for any musical setting. Students who come to middle and secondary schools with a strong Kodály background may be able to engage with sophisticated harmonic and melodic structures. Teachers at the upper levels can incorporate the tools to engage students physically with the music-making process. The hand signs not only focus the ear but focus the body. Students who begin instrument and vocal training at this age often have not had a chance to internalize beat and rhythm in ways that facilitate the process of reading music. The Kodály process of moving from speech to body engages the whole body rather than a more traditional note and rhythm reading process that seems often disconnected from the musical experience. Band and orchestral students can benefit from first singing their parts through the use of hand sings and solfa, so that they may internalize the pitches and rhythms.

Content-Specific Issues

Kodály's concern was that after decades of occupation and control, Hungary was in the process of losing its "mother tongue." This, coupled with his deep and abiding love and interest in literacy, propelled him toward conceptualizing an approach to teaching music that would lead toward literacy and access to the great works of art. However, the systemization of this process, broken down into discrete units, provides a method so detailed that it can in many cases be entered, enacted, and construed as teacher proof curriculum, thus protecting the process from the teacher and alienating teacher and student from the music-making engagement. As such, the method (and literacy as it is defined by the western canon) can become a tool that serves and reproduces a very particular cultural capital.

For each nation that engaged with this process, Kodály intended that musical material should be of the people within that culture. However, we ought to consider that not only is this monocultural framing impossible in the United States but to engage in such a conceptualization could also be construed as signifying racial and ethnic biases. Kodály believed that the inclusion of other musics would allow for diverse representation. However, one might consider that music of the Native American culture (for instance) is transmitted aurally and to break down this music so that it might be used as a vehicle for literacy that leads toward the works of the great masters would be to subsume and appropriate the music of this culture. So, rather than honoring the people of that culture and the culture itself, this process could serve to reproduce and replicate the dominant status quo as represented by functional literary embedded in western music.

CARL ORFF

Carl Orff's (1895–1982) career spans a time in Germany that saw many changes, including the rise of his musical recognition that came during National Socialism and the Nazi regime. He is often remembered outside of the music education community as the composer of such works as Carmina Burana. Orff also held an interest in theater and dance that led him to collaborate with Dorothee Guenther in which the influences of Laban and Mary Wigman (a pupil of Dalcroze) could be seen. From this relationship with Dorothee Guenther, he began a school for training adult teachers in physical education. From the very beginning at the Guentherschule (as the school was called), Orff saw dance rhythm and music as inextricably connected. Orff sought to move away from the traditional piano music that had accompanied gymnasium training programs and move toward a model in which students would improvise their own music and create their own accompaniment to accompany the training. As part of this process, Orff wanted students to be playing this music on instruments that were primarily rhythmic. With the help of Karl Maendler, a set of wooden barred xylophones and metal-lophones were devised that were accompanied by glockenspiels, recorders. Other instruments, such as the cello and viola were also included in order to provide the drones needed for the improvisatory music.

Orff sought to use the experience of the Guentherschule as the model for music education of children. Poised, in 1931, to introduce the publications

(Schulwerk: Musik für Kinder) that emerged from this into Berlin schools, the ideas developed in the Guentherschule were unfortunately deemed as Orff suggested, "undesirable" under the new political regime. During the war, Orff set aside any educative work and concentrated on musical composition. However, in 1948, Orff was asked to compose music for children that children would play for a series of radio broadcasts. Out of the preparation for these broadcasts emerged a new Schulwerk focusing this time on the childrens' singing voice as well. The overwhelming response to these broadcasts led to information and requests for the instruments. The popularity of this work moved throughout the world, first through Canada and Sweden and then into places such as Portugal, Spain, and Japan. Concerned that Schulwerk was being "amateurishly and falsely interpreted" (1977, p. 8), Orff wrote five volumes of Schulwerk. He thus sought to establish in 1951 a training institution in Austria at the Mozarteum that included movement pieces that could not be included in the radio broadcasts. The new Schulwerk that emerged from this focused on a process as one in which the pupil would not just take part as a "listener" but as a participant, in which music would be a unity of movement, dance, and speech.

The Process

It is not exclusively a question of musical education; this can follow, but it does not have to. It is, rather, a question of developing the whole personality. This surpasses by far the aims of the so-called music and singing lessons found in the usual curriculum ... Everything that a child of this age experiences, everything in him that has been awakened and nurtured is a determining factor for the whole of his life. Much can be destroyed at this age that can never be regained; much can remain undeveloped that can never be reclaimed. (1977, p. 9)

Orff did not include a prescribed plan as to how the Schulwerk should be implemented. It is not a "rational, prescribed scheme or work" (Liess, 1966, p. 59), but rather a way in which to engage the child in the imaginative processes that derive from the natural self-expression of a child and the ways in which a child naturally learns and engages in music. Rather than begin with functional harmony, Orff begins with the ways in which music, speech and movement are inextricably linked through the engagement with language and the textual connection to nursery rhyme and folk song. Through music experiences that begin with the descending minor third moving through the pentatonic scale and modes, eventually through simple functional theory, children are able to experience the basis of all musics inevitably extending to "general culture and thus becomes education through music" (p. 61).

The process first begins with unstructured speech then moving into singing and speech as framed through nursery rhymes and chants, folk songs and game songs. These rhythms then become translated into body percussion sounds (snapping, clapping patchen—leg patting—and stomping) then onto nonpitched percussion instruments (such as wood block, finger cymbals, etc.) then finally onto the Orff instruments themselves. The process moves from simple to complex, always incorporating improvisation moving from the known to the unknown. The idea, then, is to begin simple, with simple songs from the child's culture and musical concepts more suitable to children and move through the process so that students experience success in consonance rather than failure in dissonance. To that end the pentatonic scale and the removable bars of the Orff instruments allow for improvisations within the bounds and parameters of open borduns and then simple harmonic construction. The melodic sequencing is predetermined beginning with the descending minor third (sol-mi) and then next adding la, re and do. The Orff process often begins with children exploring the rhythm of their names as canons and ostinato patterns and translating those sounds to body percussion, nonpitched percussion and then to the Orff instruments. These rhythm fragments then become sung and played melodic fragments (beginning with the descending minor third), ostinato patterns, and then parts of a larger melodic and (later) harmonic whole.

Movement is integral to the Orff process and begins in the same elemental way as does the music. Students begin with movements that come naturally to them, movements that emerge from play such as skipping, hopping, running, and twirling. Combining this free play of movement with improvisation, students engage much in the same way as the Dalcroze focus on Eurhythmics. However, what differs in the Orff approach is that speech and song, rather than rhythm, anchor the process. Thus, improvisation occurs throughout the process as children play with and create rhythmic and movement patterns that emerge from their own natural development. Notation came early as Orff saw this as an important step so that students may write down their compositions.

Orff actually saw this process as being most effective as part of the day and not necessarily as what we would now refer to as a special or a pullout program. He also articulated the possibilities of this process being used to connect with other subjects.

Applications
The creative process of Orff lends itself to applications in multiple settings. The choice of materials one chooses to engage with determines the appropriateness for each setting.

Music Appreciation Class
Many middle and upper school settings have a music appreciation course that students are required to take for a music credit. Many of these classes tend to focus on issues of music history. Using the Orff process to improvise and compose music that is of the period suggests an internalization of the musical processes of that period that is musical in understanding.

Integrated Curriculum
Incorporating an Orff curriculum with general education teachers opens up possibilities for greater connections among disciplines. Students may write original works that address topics and then compose and improvise music so that the

topic becomes a performance piece. Students may also take existing texts they have been studying and create compositions that bring a heightened sense of awareness to the social and contextual issues embedded in the text.

Choral and Instrumental Setting
The rhythm and melodic syllables lend themselves, in both instrumental and choral settings, to greater harmonic and melodic understanding. Rather than just playing or singing one's part, the use of the syllables can call attention to the greater whole of a work, as well as a tool for teaching and learning.

Many vocal arrangements have been created that incorporate the Orff instrumentarium. While this may seem the most obvious application of the process, one might consider the instruments as a way to compose and improvise original choral settings from existing or original texts. As with the choral setting, the Orff process and instruments could be used as an accompaniment to either existing or original instrumental settings.

Content-Specific Issues
From the very beginning of his conception of this process, Orff saw it as a way of engaging creatively and meaningfully in and with music/movement. The original compositions for the Guentherschule were all freely composed and improvised as an integral part of the movement. Thus, movement was as much, if not more, a part of this process, and as such the Orff instruments were seen as extensions of this process, one with movement and musician. The music that was being composed at that time was not (by its definition) high art or music of the masters; it was of and for the moment based on the ways in which both musicians and dancers were interacting, it was not an object nor a commodity. In the ensuing years, as the original process has often been codified into discrete steps, movement as the attendant focus has shifted to the process itself. Thus, the creativity in which Orff so believed can take a back seat to moving through the process itself: speech, transferred to body percussion, transferred to non-pitched, transferred to Orff instruments. As the process becomes more important, it can, in essence, become more real than the engagement with the music-making engagement.

SHINICHI SUZUKI

There arises, then, the inevitable question of how to live. (Suzuki, 1983, p. xi)

I was brought up in the violin factory, and, at times, when I had a fight with my brothers and sisters, we would hit one another with violins. I then thought of the violin as a sort of toy. (p. 68)

The details of Shinichi Suzuki's (1898–1998) life are numerous and celebrated. Whether through the myriad web sites, books, articles, testimonies, concerts, and presentations throughout the world, the work and beliefs of Suzuki are internationally known and commemorated. Born in Nagoya, Japan, one of

12 children, to parents of little musical background, and whose father founded (at the time) the largest violin factory in the world, Suzuki lived 99 years as a beloved friend and mentor to many. As the above quote points out, rather than being raised from day one as a string player with musical ambitions, the violin for Suzuki was a sort of toy, something he and his siblings spent holidays and summers building. It wasn't until his 17th year, after hearing a recording on a gramophone of Mishca Elman playing "Ave Maria," that Suzuki's "eyes were opened to music." After hearing this recording, he returned home from the factory with a violin and spent subsequent hours listening and imitating a Haydn minuet, eventually playing it so well that he thought of this as his "first" piece. In his early 20s, he began studying formally in post-WWI Germany, where he met and was befriended by Albert Einstein, from whom he says he learned the following:

> Harmony—in order to achieve it, one person must gracefully give in to the other, and it is nobler to be the one who gives in than the one who forces the other to give in. Harmony cannot be achieved any other way. (1983, p. 79)

The "talent education," or "mother-tongue" method of Suzuki cannot be separated from Suzuki, the man. Nor should the process ever simply be seen as a way to "teach violin" or even "music." This was a man not only shaped by two world wars but a man whose entire life was guided and greatly influenced by Tolstoy's words, "Conscience is the voice of God," which Suzuki later reframed as, "Life is the voice of God." His view of teaching was not just based on the observation that all children have ability (talent) and that learning music should be as simple as learning a language, or that incorporating varying sized instruments would be fundamental to success in learning. This was a man who believed in the significance of character, the importance and influence of noble adults in the lives of children, of the goodness and love of children that music could lead toward "a fine and pure heart" (p. 12) and indeed, world peace could be found through "good citizens" (p. 105). All of which can be achieved "if only the correct methods are used in training" (p. 1).

The Process

> It is in our power to educate all the children of the world to become a little better as people, a little happier. We have to work toward this. I ask no more than the love and happiness of mankind, and I believe that this is what everyone really wants. (Suzuki, 1983, p. 82)

Suzuki believed that everyone was born with the ability (talent) to learn; indeed, he is most often quoted as saying, "Talent is no accident of birth" (p. xi). And while he believed that every child had aptitude to be developed, he deliberately avoided aptitude tests. Repetition, imitation and modeling is at the heart of the method; beliefs that stemmed from his observations of how students learned to speak as well as his observations of a parakeet learning to speak. Yet, not only repetition and imitation, but all of this with the help, guidance, and modeling of the parent. Thus, from the very beginning of the method, a parent or parental figure is to take lessons for several months along with the child. Suzuki also believed that listening daily to the music one is learning, including multiple versions and interpretations, is integral to the study of the required music. Consequently, daily listening exercises as well as observations of teachers and other students, and frequent attendance at concerts and performances is required so that "good" music and performance is internalized. Because expressivity and musicality are fundamental to this method, note reading is not started from the beginning but rather delayed until the student has perfected a repertoire of set music. While some critics may be under the impression that note reading is totally neglected, it is simply postponed until it becomes necessary in the developmental process. As Suzuki observed, students learn to speak before they learn to read or write; thus, note reading at an early stage in the development of the musician, not only disregards and even prevents the expressive and analytic development of the musician but also impedes such skills as analytical listening and playing.

One such analytical method for mental preparation is referred to as the "stop and prepare" approach. After playing one pattern, and before moving to the next, the student is instructed to pause and think through, or analyze, the preparation for the following pattern. After much repetition, this pause is eventually shortened to the point that the music continues seamlessly, perfectly. Perfecting each piece before moving on is integral to the discipline process that Suzuki thought built character: "If a child hears good music from the day of his birth, and learns to play it himself, he develops sensitivity, discipline and endurance. He gets a beautiful heart" (p. 105).

Once a piece was perfected, it isn't left behind. Each piece is constantly returned to with new emphasis placed on musical ideas; as new pieces are learned, students continue to revisit older repertoire so that as new techniques are studied, they may be applied to what is already known. Therefore, it is also necessary to learn the repertoire in a structured order, presented without omissions, so that concepts and techniques are built upon. The repertoire, which is presented in a series of volumes, consists of "familiar folk melodies," baroque, classical and romantic music. Teachers have some leeway as to the presentation, but for the most part contemporary or modern music is not introduced at this stage. This repertoire and this choice of repertoire is reflected in the ways in which Suzuki's life was greatly influenced by the music of Mozart: "I am eternally a child on Mozart's bosom" (p. 81). Suzuki believed that through the music of Mozart and others, one could develop "superior abilities" (p. 1) and become a "finer" person. That said, Suzuki believed that "art" wasn't something out of reach; art was to be found and lived in our everyday lives, in our everyday actions.

Application

The development of ability is straightforward. This can be absolutely relied upon. People either become experts at doing the right thing, which is seen as a fine talent, or they become experts at doing something wrong and unacceptable, which is seen as lack of talent. So it behooves everyone to become expert in the right things, and the more training he or she receives the better. Depending on these two things—practice and practice of the right things—superior ability can be produced in anyone. (Suzuki, 1983, p. 98)

Suzuki never wavers from the "rightness" of his vision of training and ability and as such training, that was first conceptualized for the violin, was extended to other string instruments. Toward this goal, multiple sizes of the instruments, supplied and made by the Suzuki company, made and continue to make it possible for very young children to begin the talent education training early. The method has since been broadened to not only include flute and piano, but to other areas outside of music as well. Wondering why subjects such as mathematics, English, calligraphy, art, and so forth, could not be taught by the "talent education" method, Suzuki began the Early Development Association in Tokyo so that the "mother-tongue" method of education could be incorporated throughout all areas of education.

Closer to home, Cox (May 1985), suggests choral environments can benefit from what he refers to as the continual renewal process, in which pieces are revisited so that new vocal and choral techniques may be applied in familiar settings. Rather than learning a piece of music never to return to it, Cox believes there should be a deliberate focus on sequencing elements (and thus, returning to known music) so that students may grow musically. Cox suggests the use of continual guided listening to professional performances as well as the modeling of concepts to be taught. While not particularly innovative in the 21st century one might consider that very few choirs or instrumental ensembles revisit music as this is perhaps not viewed or constructed as progress.

Content-Specific Issues

More so than other methods of teaching, Suzuki seems to attract critiques of the most public kind. In today's society, the notion that it is a given that a parent could not only attend the lesson with the child, but also study the instrument for the first few months and then practice at home with the child seems overwhelming in its assumptions. Although, the Suzuki approach calls for specific focus on each individual as they progress and develop through the repertoire, there are some who have suggested that the issue of students having little to no say in the choice of repertoire, coupled with the focus on large group lessons and concerts, ignores and hinders the development of individuality and uniqueness. There are still others who express concern and dismay with the faces of children who are focused and not seemingly "happy" in their engagements. And yet, probably most articulated and most problematic for many is the issue of note reading, and consequently sight reading, and the threat this seems to pose. Clearly, Suzuki would point out, it is note reading that gets in the way of musical expressivity as well as careful and analytical listening, and yet, as literacy seems to be at the heart of what most people understand music education to be, this criticism alone seems to challenge the "validity" of this method.

When suggesting a possible strategy for sequencing note reading and sight reading, Landers (1980) cautions that "the introduction to note-reading should be taught mainly as a preparatory phase that helps the child to become aware of certain concepts" (p. 68). Note reading should come only after students have internalized by imitation and memorization, the music that will be reviewed and revisited for note reading. The following is an abbreviated sequence suggested by Landers (pp. 68–70):

First step: The student plays the music and follows along while the teacher points to the notes.

Second step: The student and teacher do the same with other well know pieces but this time as the teacher points, the teacher emphasizes "melodic direction." The teacher and/or student sing "up," "down," "same" for the intervals.

Third Step: More of the same, except this "short" and "long" are emphasis for duration.

Fourth Step: At this point emphasis is placed on "step," "skip" or "same."

Fifth Step: Interval names are replace "step" and "skip," and so forth.

Sixth Step: Rhythmic values are emphasized with words and gestures to indicate beat value.

Seventh Step: Absolute note names are added as the teacher and student sing and play.

This engagement with and procedure of teaching notes could be applied in any setting in which the music teacher thought it necessary to focus on western-centric literacy. This method is also concomitant with the beliefs of Orff, Kodály, Dalcroze and as we shall see, Gordon; musical experiences and expression are integral to preliteracy and literacy engagements.

EDWIN GORDON

It is axiomatic that to expose students to great works of art without proper readiness represents inefficient procedures, which in time can transform wishful and unrealistic thinking on the part of the teacher into negative attitudes on the part of frustrated students. (Gordon, 1971, p. 114)

When one observes photos of Edwin Gordon (1927-), one is immediately struck by the fact that he is always surrounded by children. Clearly, this love for children and his passion for music have driven his engagements in and with this field. As a scholar and researcher who has held numerous university positions, including the Carl E. Seashore Chair for Research in Music Education at Temple University, Gordon continues to write and conduct research in the field of music psychology. While it may be not the first thing mentioned about Edwin Gordon, nor even the most important aspect of Gordon's career, it is fascinating to note that for a time in his life he played bass with Gene Krupa. Yet, once one becomes aware of the construction of tonal patterns and his belief that engaging with rhythm isn't a matter of keeping time, but rather one of "feeling tempo and meter and relating to rhythm patterns" (Gordon, 1971, p. 122), one immediately senses the deep connection this relationship with Krupa and jazz must have had in the conception of how Gordon must see his life, has made meaning in his life, and the subsequent articulation of the Music Learning Theory.

While many of the musicians addressed in this chapter would not have referred to their conception of the musical learning process as method, the sequential and comprehensive curricular goals are for Gordon, part of a learning method that is applicable to, and can align with, the full spectrum of music programs including, early childhood, elementary general, instrumental, vocal, and private studio. Music Learning Theory is, at its most basic, an explanation of how we learn music. Based on research done in the field of music psychology, Gordon sees the method as an enhancement to those engagements that good music teachers already do well. So while there is a sequential basis to curriculum development, Music Learning Theory exercises, unlike for instance, Kodály and Suzuki, enhance rather than consist of the entire lesson or rehearsal.

At the heart of Music Learning Theory is the belief based on research that everyone is born with some degree and level of musical aptitude. Gordon defines aptitude as "a measure of a student's potential to learn" (1989, p. 1) and believes that words such as, "ability," "talent," and "musicianship" do not clearly articulate aptitude and even deflect attention away from the distinction between aptitude and achievement, or the "measure of what a student has learned" (p. 1). In the development of a series of tests, including the Musical Aptitude Profile, Gordon has looked at variables such as socioeconomic status, environment, race, religion, nationality, and even musical training and concluded that none of these affect positively or negatively the level of musical aptitude with which one is born. Musical aptitude may fluctuate between birth and age nine based on musical training, but after the age of nine the potential to learn music decreases and even diminishes. While some have criticized aptitude tests as a tool that can be used as a way to decide who can or can't be taught music, Gordon's views are clear on this aspect. Knowing the musical aptitude of a student allows the teacher to teach to each child's differences. As such, it is not a matter of teaching less musical skills or content to those with lower aptitude rather, the difficulty of the tonal and rhythm patters is altered during the music learning theory portion of the lesson so that each student is challenged and engaged.

> The higher the level of music aptitude with which children are born, the more varied early experiences are required if they are to maintain that level. The lower the level of music aptitude with which children are born, the fewer early experiences are required to sustain that aptitude. Effectively, innate aptitude must either be maintained or lost. (Gordon, Sept 1999, p. 44)

Consequently, in the view of Gordon, all of this is dependent on how well music is taught in the early years.

The Process

> What we merely recognize or imitate what we have heard, we live in the past. In audiation, the past lives in us. (Gordon, Sept 1999, p. 42)

At the heart of how music is taught in music learning theory is the belief that children learn music much the same way they learn language. While similar in belief to that of Kodály, Orff and Suzuki, that sound and aural must precede symbol, Gordon focuses on a systematic sequencing that prepares students to first audiate tonal and rhythmic patterns so that reading becomes a process of recognition rather than decoding the notes on a page.

Audiation is a concept that seems at face value a simple matter of inner hearing, or being able to hear the music in one's head. However, being able to imitate a pattern or sing back from memory is only a small part of the process. For Gordon (1999), "Audiation takes place when we hear and understand in our minds music that we have just heard performed or have performed sometime in the past" (p. 42). In order to move toward this understanding, the curriculum is thought of as a whole/part/whole process of developing audiation. All repertoire is considered the "whole" and "part" is the tonal and rhythm patterns that are introduced at the beginning of each class and provide the framing for the rest of the class. These tonal and rhythm patterns relate to the language learning process in that as we learn to speak we hear total sentences rather than single word utterances. The context of these utterances allows us to make meaning; thus the context of the tonal and rhythm patterns are established by tonal center and reinforced meter. Tonal is reinforced through establishing a resting tone and chordal progressions that establish the harmonic center. Meter is reinforced through movement that serves to internalize both macro and micro awareness. Consequently, these tonal and rhythmic patterns layer upon each other providing the framing and scaffolding that is similar to the learning of vocabulary. Neutral syllables for both tonal ('bum') and rhythmic ('bah') patterns are introduced. Eventually, solfege and rhythmic syllables become part of the tonal and rhythmic patterns that provide verbal associations that help to distinguish between patterns. Gordon believes that this naming of tonal and rhythmic patterns is much the same as naming objects and concepts in language. Consequently, these patterns not only provide a more fluid way of reading music, they also provide the framework for creativity and improvisation.

Context–Specific Issues

> The more a person knows about music, the more he is able to enjoy it, and the more he enjoys music, the more he is able to learn about it. (Gordon, 1971, p. 65)

As was addressed earlier, Gordon views music learning theory as a process that is at the heart of every school music encounter; whether general, choral or instrumental, this process provides an entry point to understand and thus enjoy music. In an instrumental classroom, learning theory is a way to help instrumentalists understand music at a level far deeper than simply putting one's finger down on the correct keys. For Gordon, imitating sounds is not the same as audiating.

> Many students learn to memorize what they see in notation without audiating what they are reading. They too are simply imitating…To imitate patterns is like memorizing only the sequence of a series of words. To audiate is like comprehending the syntax of that series of words. (1989, p. 290)

Learning sequence activities can be part of any context. It is simply a matter of devoting the first moments of the class or lesson after which choral or instrumental activities are taught the rest of the session. In a choral setting, Gordon believes the song is more important than the words; children are continually surrounded by words, but not so with learning music through their ears. If one teaches the text first the students pay more attention to the words than the music, thus, focusing on the melodic and tonal aspects of the music furthers the process of audiation. Calling attention to and teaching the bass line of a melody also furthers the audiating process by bringing attention to the harmonic foundation.

Instrumental and choral settings are important in this process but for Gordon, it is early childhood in which learning theory is most crucial. As was noted before, Gordon researched learning and aptitude and found that the first nine years of a child's life are the most crucial in developing one's aptitude. As such, it is important that young children are exposed to varied and multiple music so that the foundation for readiness is laid. Through informal guidance, which can take the form of either unstructured or structured guidance, young children experience music with the help of both teacher and parent. Subsequently, musical thinking moves out of the cumulative preparatory stages of random to purposeful response of early childhood engagements.

GENERAL ISSUES AND LINGERING THOUGHTS

Many of the issues raised in this chapter have been content (or method) specific issues. There are, however, issues that emerge that suggest assumptions to which one ought to attend. With the exception of Gordon, each of these men state that their engagement with musical processes is not a method, but rather an approach or a philosophy. One must then assume that their conceptualization of philosophy is based on what it means to "know" music, and thus what it means to teach and learn music. Hence it is important to recognize from where each of these men attributed the inception of their ideas of the educative process.

While each may have taken different aspects from his philosophy, the Swiss educator, Johann Heinrich Pestalozzi, influenced many of them as to how they envisioned the processes of their approach to music learning. Pestalozzi expanded and built upon the ideas of Rousseau who believed that if one were to begin first with signs, then students would be prevented from broader understandings. Pestalozzi also believed that children learn best through their senses and the use of objects rather than words, or lectures. He was concerned with the whole person and attending to (rather than separating and teaching to just one) the cognitive, the tactile and the heart. Thus, for both Rousseau and Pestalozzi, the learning process was best broken down into simple and manageable steps that moved from the simple to the complex, the known to the unknown, experience comes before names, and that teaching should proceed from the concrete to the abstract. Clearly, it is possible to recognize the ways in which the men in this chapter entered and interpreted the ideas of both Rousseau and Pestalozzi.

And while the process and even necessity of improvisation plays an integral role in most if not all of these approaches improvisation seems conceived of as a process bound by assembly-line constraints and of controlled environments and clearly delineated divisions of labor, often made arbitrary by the key of "folk music," and the (often limiting) melodic, rhythmic, and harmonic framework that frames the music. Many of these men suggest that the music content be that of the child's "culture," with movement from the musically simple to the musically complex, encompassing both melodic and rhythmic structures of, in many cases, "folk music of the mother tongue." This, however, not only suggests that the musical palate of students may be disregarded, but that the students' increasingly sophisticated sonorous and technical understandings of musics rooted in vast and multiple cultures and technologies will simply be dismissed.

While these approaches may seem practical and even obvious, what is less apparent are the unarticulated assumptions these men make about what learning music means and even what music is. What then does it mean to "understand music" for these men, and what does it mean to "teach" this understanding? Each of these men speaks of the importance of creating and improvising one's own music, yet how does this seemingly irrefutable simple, basic, and elemental sequencing that forever leads toward a very particular framing of literacy, lend itself to understanding and creativity? Literacy may have something to do with the ability to read and write, but what it means to be literate has been broadened to include comprehension and an understanding of the tension between self and the ways in which what it means to know and be literate are often driven by the dominant status quo and the accompanying cultural capital.

A philosophy of "understanding," as it has been construed by these men, seems often to be more about ideology than philosophy. So while it may seem that by including these methods, or that teaching these methods in one's classroom provides a space for all musics and a process of creating, we need to consider that in replicating these processes we are reproducing ways of engaging musically that seem common sense and natural. In doing so, these methods become tools for knowing the world through often appropriated cultures so that students may come to know "good" music, be appreciative audience members who may or may not have the skills to read a score. It also seems to be a given that these methods can either save all of human kind or at the very least build good citizens. Noble goals? One needs only to be reminded of the words of Bobbitt and the training of men and how curriculum can be made to eliminate "low character" through the right method. Ethical goals? Perhaps not, as they are most often defined through the engagement with and embracing of music of the "great" works and an aesthetic bounding of form and structure that anticipates and signifies moral import. Perhaps not, as their conception of authenticity as preconceived or predetermined ideas, rather than authenticity as reciprocal transactions with situated engagements, constructs very particular ways of being. And finally, perhaps not as these goals confer a vision of what it means to be a citizen that hierarchically positions form over interpretation, structure over cultural understandings and universality versus contextuality.

Over 40 years ago Marion Flagg wrote, "The simplicity of the Orff approach has the consoling appeal that the complexities of living in today's world can be pleasantly and safely ignored. Would that it were so!" (Dec. 1966, p. 30). Over 40 years ago, a reliance on method and the ways in which the these methods might allow the teacher to transcend the messiness of complex questions and inquiry was being embraced. Over 40 years ago, these methods entered our consciousness and became our deus ex machina; the palatable ending to all our worries. Many music educators have suggested that an eclectic approach to teaching music might be the answer to accommodating all of these different methods; that one could simply choose from each that which would serve them in their curriculum. Of course, this isn't so simple in the eyes of those who see only one method over the another. I am reminded of the Kraus (1990) quote from earlier in the chapter in which the issue of "spiritual illness" (p. 83) is addressed, an illness that only Kodály can remedy, and one wonders how easily this eclectic approach would sit with each of the of these men.

In a book published by the American Orff Schulwerk Association (1977), one author remarks that there is "no virtue in being complex" (as cited in McNeill, p. 77). It would seem then that virtue lie in embracing the simple. Yet, as Ms. Flagg points out, simple belies safety. Embracing, rather than ignoring complexity would mean realizing how we have replicated these methods disregarding the need to, while at the same time purporting to, attend to the core of such significant and ominous work. A critical engagement with what has historically been at the center of our profession goes beyond deconstruction or disregard, and affords the space to rethink and reengage so that we may interrogate what it might mean to know and how these processes as systematized ways of knowing prevent the constant process of becoming teacher/learner, learner/teacher.

Class Discussion

1. In this chapter, what is the relationship between ideology and philosophy?
2. Consider the Carder quote that speaks of "spiritual illness" and the "trash of music." What are the assumptions and implications embedded in this quote? What "common sense" and "normative" practices are implied?
3. Consider the issue of breaking down the learning experience into small manageable pieces that lead toward an accumulative end. How does this process

influence what the end can be? Can there be other "ends" and what might those be? What would your "method" of teaching and learning then look like?

4. What characteristics identify each of these methods? To what extent do you think proponents of these methods have claimed certain basic and universal strategies as their own (Dalcroze—movement and Orff- improvisation, for example)?

Projects

1. Visit elementary classrooms and describe what you see. What methods are being used? To what end? What are the underlying philosophical goals of the teacher that are made manifest in the teaching? How do methods look on different teachers?

2. Write a brief paper address the questions: What would teaching and learning look like that wasn't driven by a prescribed methodological and sequential approach? What would students "learn" or "not "learn"?

3. Reflect back on your own learning experiences and consider what methods or approaches might have been used in your classroom. What expectations were either explicitly or implicitly asked of you as a musical learner? What assumptions were embedded in the way you were taught? What were the philosophical goals of your teacher. Prepare a brief report of your reflections.

SUGGESTED READINGS

Dalcroze, E. J. (1921). *Rhythm, music and education.* New York: G.P. Putnam's Sons.

Gordon, E. (1971). *The psychology of music teaching.* Englewood Cliffs, NJ: Prentice Hall, Inc.

Suzuki, S. (1983). *Nurtured by love: The classic approach to talent education.* Miami, FL: Warner Bros. Publications Inc.

Wheeler, L. & Raebeck, L. (1977). *Orff and Kodály adapted for the elementary school.* Dubuque, IA: W.C. Brown Co.

CHAPTER 10

~

Choosing Music Literature
Randall Everett Allsup

INTRODUCTION

As was mentioned in Chapter 7, the decisions a teacher makes about what is included in a course of study (and what is not) form the very heart of a class curriculum. This chapter is about the *why* and *how* of choosing music literature. It is also about the *where* and *when*, the *whether* and *for whom*, and the *under what circumstances* and *in what manner*. While musical "instruction" can be defined as the function of dispensing knowledge or musical know-how, instruction alone does not define the limits of an education in music. Good teaching is not mechanical, nor is it a matter of simple transmission. The way an educator shapes learning experiences and the choices she makes about the content of what is taught are responsibilities weighted with care, requiring thoughtful deliberation and genuine feeling, a state of mind that Maxine Greene calls "wide-awakeness" (Greene, 1978, pp. 42–52).

The philosophy of responsible choosing is the philosophy of ethics. Whether one uses the term "ethics" or not, the practice of arriving at a well-considered decision is part and parcel of everyday teaching. Yet, simple choices about matters of music curricula do not become *ethical* choices until the educator grapples in a personal way with notions like tradition, history, biography, culture, context and change, as well as the values and beliefs that surround them. Greene reminds us that an ethically considered action "is usually between two goods, not between good and bad or right and wrong" (Greene, 1978, p. 48). Duty and custom, tradition and history: these are never more than partial rights or partial goods. This chapter will look at the underlying tensions that frame this discussion. Readers are invited to use John Dewey's *Experience and Education* as a companion reference, especially as this short treatise anchors the three main themes investigated: tradition, change, and choice.

THE PROBLEMS OF TRADITION

In choosing the right music to program in chorus or the right song to teach a third-grade class, there is often a tension between the tradition that the music teacher was trained in and the array of faces that stand before her. More than ever, today's music educator is confronted by the antinomies of pluralism: its difficulties and promise, its distance and contiguity, and the seemingly intractable conflict between tradition and change (Bowman, 2001). Suddenly, terms like multiculturalism, diversity, and pluralism stand in bold contrast to the singular teacher, standing alone at a podium, looking back at her class. Increasingly, students have very different expectations for what they want from a music class, and the teacher is reminded that there is nothing universal or inherent in the task at hand (Frierson-Campbell, 2006).

Confusion surrounds how we think about past and present. Chapter 3 reminds us that the past has often looked more traditional, more "ideal" than it ever really was. Recall the conflict between the representatives of Aristophanes, whose mythical ideas of well-behaved music students singing patriotic hymns in perfect marching order conflicted with the "new education" of Socrates, who was portrayed by his foes as arguing for an everything-goes child-centered relativism. In all likelihood, there never was a time when children were safely predictable (thank goodness) and perfectly teachable. And with regard to recent eras, perhaps there were too few times when students came to school asking for Beethoven or Paul Creston. But one thing is sure today: rare is the 21st century music educator who can confidently rely upon a shared cultural vocabulary from which to build assumptions about what to teach.

The Past and Public Schooling

The story of public schooling is the hapless, achingly beautiful quest to transmit the best of what went before us, while at the same time making the objects of our study a meaningful concern to the students in our charge. Acknowledging that there can be no fixed endpoints in a world that always changes, the charge John Dewey asked of public education was this: "How shall the young become acquainted with the past in such a way that the acquaintance is a potent agent in appreciation of the living present?" (Dewey, p. 11) A rich and growing experience, located in the "living present," seems the only measure by which an ethically considered curriculum can be judged. This is a simple truth that all experienced music educators know: a musical tradition will die unless its new charges care enough to take ownership of it. A so-called "living tradition" must allow for *new* methods of care, and Dewey would insist that the accumulation of traditional know-how is useful only insofar as it allows for modification. Because each school, each classroom, and each curriculum will look and sound different, the results of study—the various modifications that result from cultural adaptation—will also look and sound quite different (Allsup, 2006).

Notice where Dewey has focused his attention: experience. Not on standards, history, or handed-down books, but on the educational experience of the growing child. This poses a number of intractable problems. Asking teachers to locate learning in experience and meaning-making through the relative lens of culture threatens the very history such a philosophy is alleged to bring alive. Completely missing from this view is an accepted canon, a collection of agreed upon studies that all students should know and be able to do. What about national standards, the basics, and adequate yearly progress? How do we determine who is and who isn't a qualified teacher? How do we judge a band contest, or grade a student's work? This idea that a "growing and rich experience" is the criteria by which a teacher's work is judged sounds an awful lot like pandering. And concerning "modification," an oboist practicing the Ferling *Études* is no more allowed to pick which dynamic markings to perform than she can choose whether or not to play an octave in tune. The music teacher may respond to Dewey by saying, "there are indeed fixed endpoints, in fact my entire calendar is *fixed* around them! There are end-of-year concerts, for one, and exacting standards by which my all-state oboist will be rated."

These are frequently heard questions and critiques, with all the appearance of commonsense, even fact. For most music teachers, end-of-year concerts *are* a fact of life, so are auditions and etude books. But who makes the standards, and who picks the books? And why are the Ferling *Études* so important? For whom are the Ferling *Études* important? These questions seem rhetorical at first, but they deserve an answer. "Because I say so" or "Because I had to play Ferling when I was your age" are tempting replies, but intellectually shortsighted. To students for whom a curricular choice does not make sense, surely some order of defense is appropriate. Finding an ethical response to the commonsense of tradition is imperative, lest the traditions we value ossify and fall into simple custom or duty.

Habitus and Hegemony

Concerned with the ways in which cultures reproduce themselves silently, Pierre Bourdieu worried that certain habits of mind create beliefs so durable that they seem ridiculous to examine critically. These habituated beliefs are so widely shared that they appear natural or universal. "Because the subjective necessity and self-evidence of the commonsense world are validated by the objective consensus on the sense of the world, what is essential *goes without saying because it comes without saying*: the tradition is silent, not least about itself as a tradition" (Bourdieu, 1977, p. 167). Silence or "*habitus*" is a "natural" partner to the obvious and self-evident. The problem that concerns Bourdieu is that there is nothing "natural" about a culture's tradition. Although the sun will rise and the moon will set, the material events and activities that attend a teacher's calendar are neither fixed nor freely occurring. Schools, music programs, and marching bands are entirely humanly constructed. Yet, when asked to think critically about a topic that seems obvious or permanent, like an end-of-year concert or an all-state audition, notions of the "real world" are invoked to defend practices that seem as natural as the rising of the sun. When a situation is obvious, it validates itself. The more obvious and true the situation appears, the more difficult it is to imagine it differently.

The silent power of tradition and the habits of mind that protect the "real world" from scrutiny operate most efficaciously when there is, as Bourdieu reminds us, objective consensus, or an agreement that takes the form of commonsense. This silent agreement usually occurs in homogeneous cultures whose long-standing practices seem objectively "normal." It may take an outsider (or the mindset of a outsider) to help the custodians of a particular tradition see an experience differently. An observer, for example, uninitiated in the history and tradition of marching bands, might wonder why these groups dress in military garb or why their members are often seen tossing rifles. To the uninitiated observer, it may seem incumbent to ask whether these military symbols are congruent with the public school's civic mission, or even unnecessarily violent. Yet, such an inquiry is sure to provoke confusion among marching band fans who are habituated to the customs of the genre. This is not to suggest they are no explanations or even logical reasons for the traditions and practices of marching bands—or Ferling Études and all-state auditions, for that matter. It is to suggest, however, that we become wide-awake to the world around us, to break through the obvious and look for questions. For the ethical music educator determined to examine the habits of her practice, what "goes without saying," doesn't mean "it comes without asking."

Research on cultural practice often uses the term hegemony to describe the partite manner in which a cultural practice is maintained uncritically while at the same time winning the consent of the potentially disempowered voices for whom it speaks. Associated with the post-Marxist field of philosophy called "critical theory," and specifically with Antonio Gramsci [1891–1937], hegemony is the idea that a prevailing custom, social order, or belief does not need the machinery of explicit state, political, or professional power to control the operations of its participants, even and especially if the said custom, social order, or belief actually works *against* the participants' own interests (Gramsci, 1975). The term hegemony, broadly employed in the fields of sociology, political science, and education, denotes the *silent* oppression of a less powerful majority by a more powerful minority. When and how an oppressive belief or custom becomes "normalized" is rarely clear. The point is that no explicit coercion is necessary to control its exercises once a belief's ostensibly oppressive practices are made operational through convention or tradition.

What would an example of hegemony look like in today's schools? Although popular with most voters and politicians, the testing movement behind the No Child Left Behind (NCLB) Act of 2002 is *not* an example of hegemony because the effective operation of widespread high-stakes testing needs explicit federal enforcements and penalties for noncompliance (NCLB Act, 2001). It can be debated, however, that the contest and competition tradition that makes up a large and established aspect of North American music education is an apt example of hegemonic practice. The contention would be formulated like this:

- Competitions occur in almost every music discipline; they are an established aspect of the educational landscape.
- No one knows exactly when this tradition started, or why it has become so popular.
- The majority of music teachers participate in competitions; the minority who don't seem odd to the majority who do.
- There are many hardships associated with competitions, not the least of which is time and expense; their pedagogical value is dubious.
- Participates endure the hardships of competing—possibly taking short cuts and making compromises—because they believe it is the right thing to do; some participants win, but many more must lose.
- Normal, commonsensical, and with few "realistic" alternatives, the tradition continues; meanwhile an operational system evolves around the practice, supporting its continuance.

The readers of this chapter may find the scenario outlined above overly reductive or even biased. Others may resonate with its claims. Certainly, there are many opportunities for personal experience to refute or support a particular assertion. The point is not to accuse festival and competition adherents of being the unwilling victims of an oppressive educational system, or to suggest that the teachers who participate in competitions miseducate or oppress the students in their charge. Nor is the aforementioned example a polemic against the "realities" of competition and music education. Rather, it is to suggest, as Greene does in evoking author Virginia Wolf that "behind the cotton wool of daily life...is a token of some real thing behind appearances" (Greene, 1995, p. 27). Habits, customs, and everyday routines obscure our attempts to see what lies beyond the obvious. To ask ourselves to consider those aspects of our lives fall victim to "*habitus*" or lay checked within a quietly controlling system is to break with simple appearances and name the world we teach in (Freire, 1973).

How do we "see" beyond the appearances of the familiar world? How do we articulate the problems we find there? Estelle Jorgensen suggests dialectical analysis, the kind of Socratic irony practiced in Ancient Greece, and evidenced in disciplined philosophy (see chapter 3). She forcefully posits that in order to counteract the power of habit and custom, an educator must adopt a healthy dose of "teacher skepticism," the conviction "that there must be something wrong with the most cherished or plausible idea" (Jorgensen, 2003, p. 10). Like Greene, Jorgensen reminds us that ethical practice is *achieved*, its exercise "is an act of respect for the efforts expended and achievements of one's fellows, and a corrective to the tendency for unexamined assumptions to become dogma" (Jorgensen, 2003, p. 10). The lack of surprise that defines dogmatic teaching, its unchanging adherence to a particular belief or custom, is the very antithesis of teacher ethics.

The music educator must interrogate her practice, to ask whether words like duty, routine, predictability, and tradition are safe realms from which to carefully design an *evolving* class curriculum or whether such characteristics represent a *static* place, a state of disempowerment or silence. It serves all music educators to ask: when does tradition, like the cotton wool of custom, hide experience from examination?

Power, Ideology, and Official Knowledge

In all likelihood, it has become clear to the reader of this chapter that discussions of tradition and curriculum cannot be separated from discussions of politics and power. As soon as one considers the "who," "what," and "why" questions of music education—*Whose music? What makes this music good? Why this music, not that?*—one is confronted with problems that demand a great deal of self-reflection. The cultural forms and values of a dominant culture have a material effect upon all aspects of society, and anyone who has been outside the center of power knows that cultural know-how is not neutral. Ideology as such, "is the system of the ideas and representations which dominate the mind of a man [sic] or a social group" (Althusser, 1971). Like Bourdieu's notion of *habitus*, "ideology expends itself in the idolization of given experience" (Horkheimer & Adorno, 1999).

The field of critical theory argues that the main purpose of institutions like schools, families, and religious establishments is to reproduce, maintain, and extend the ideological trappings of dominant culture, thus normalizing as "given" certain beliefs and practices over others. As such, educational institutions produce a distinct form of "school ideology," what Michael Apple calls "official knowledge" (Apple, 1993). Schools, writes Apple, are "deeply implicated in the politics of culture. The curriculum is never simply a neutral assemblage of knowledge, somehow appearing in the texts and classrooms of a nation. It is always part of a *selective tradition*, someone's selection, some group's vision of legitimate knowledge" (Apple, 1993, p. 22).

Considering the diverse array of music that is accessible in today's global world, it is surprisingly easy to figure out what counts as official knowledge among music educators. A ranked compendium of suggested literature, scaled from easy to difficult, and usually accompanied by a standardized lesson plan, is available from any publisher's catalog or professional website. To win All-state honors at NYSSMA (New York State School Music Association), an oboist is expected to perform Vivaldi's *Concerto in F Major* or Ravel's *Sonatine* (NYSSMA, 2006). To garner acceptance at prestigious Schools of Music, most saxophonists audition on Paul Creston's *Sonata*, less often on Cannonball Adderly's *Sambop*. Institutions that represent and promote professional music education have likewise "institutionalized" popular music. A general music teacher who wishes to instruct her pupils in the study of popular music may, for example, work from an MENC-approved lesson plan to teach the song "Tearing Up My Heart" by NSync. These examples illustrate that contra Dewey's emphasis on process, official knowledge "pre-exists" experience. Its means are a handed-down canon of authorized or institutionalized works. Its ends are a reward, like a juried prize or medal, to which its participants are afforded access to some form of recognition or privilege.

Tradition and Teacher Agency

Because the same cultural institutions that generate official knowledge train, certify, and support music educators, it is hardly surprising that music teachers—adept at the skills for which they have been rewarded—pass on what they know (in the form of official knowledge) to a younger generation. It stands to reason that music educators will teach what they are good at, whether or not what they are good at reflects the needs and wishes of their students. Yet, it is important to emphasize that official knowledge is not commensurate with teacher agency, nor can ideology fully delimit the choices available to music teachers. The music educator is never hostage to thoughtless custom. Since no art form exists apart from tradition, and no artist exists independent of past accomplishments, the challenge that faces music educators is not *what* to hand down, but *how*; their challenge is the measure, quoting Dewey, through which "the young become acquainted with the past in such a way that the acquaintance is a potent agent in appreciation of the living present" (Dewey, p. 11). Teachers face the difficult task of claiming a tradition, making it relevant, and crafting an appropriate curriculum.

Identifying the ideological structures that impede a relevant and exciting musical education is the point of this section. Problems occur when musical texts deemed canonical begin to stand apart from the students for whom they are designed. Marked off from the living present, a type of "school-only" music invents itself. Since students can bring little of themselves to the experience of music-educationalized music making or "school-only" music, a passivity is built into the teacher-student relationship. "Since the subject matter as well as standards of proper conduct are handed down from the past," wrote Dewey, "the attitude of the pupils must, upon the whole, be one of docility, reception, and obedience" (Dewey, p. 3). This does not mean, of course, that an ethically crafted music curriculum is one in which students alone choose the music they wish to study. For Dewey, that would evince a poor understanding of the very purpose of education; nor does this perspective hold great faith in the judgment of teachers (Dewey, 1902). If, however, the problem of tradition hinges on how well history informs and assists the present, the enemy of a meaningful and humanistic education is docility and obedience.

THE PROBLEMS OF CHANGE

Agreeing that the formative objectives of school and schooling are to provide students with the skills, values, and knowledge to tackle the unfolding historical conditions of their time, the great educational challenge of the 21st century is the problem of rapid change and cultural pluralism. School, perhaps more than any public institution invented, is the primary site where the cultivation of the individual and the cultivation of the citizen occur in tandem. The pluralistic and rapidly changing nature of contemporary society deeply challenges this two-fold directive. Teachers must attend to the flourishing of every child, but there is a collective struggle, too. It is the latter mandate, at the communal and cultural level, where educators part company. Do we teach to assimilate, recognize, honor, discover, propagate, expose, induct, or liberate? A little of each? Or more of just one? Do we speak of a common community, or an expanding one? When we speak of the public good, do we speak of one thing or many?

What does it mean, for example, that a choir director can render an historically correct version of Mozart's *Te Diem*, and still know that the work is heard differently by each performer? "Any object—a classroom, a neighborhood street, a field of flowers—shows itself differently to each spectator. The reality of that object arises out of the sum total of its appearances to all who view it" (Greene, 1995, p. 156). Greene, in this excerpt, recounts the beautiful dialectic of location and knowledge. We know the meaning of our world through our individual lens or location. But that meaning must be constructed with others, others who see what we see differently. The promise of pluralism is an expansion of meaning or knowing. The problem of pluralism is its promise—that the increasingly multiple vantages points from which to name our world makes knowing any one thing contestable or open to revision.

If an educator begins to see the world as unstable or culturally relative, it deserves asking how one genre or tradition of music can be chosen for study over another. The skeptical music educator might ask, are there *any* criteria to follow when all cultures are equal and all voices are to be heard? In debates about multiculturalism and tradition, the cliché of a "slippery slope" is evoked to suggest that once we begin a critical accounting of an historical text, say Mozart's *Te Deum*, we will soon descend into a pit of relativism, a place where Mozart is indistinguishable from the very lowest forms of music (usually that which is popular with teenagers and played loudly). The manner in which educators debate these questions reveals a great deal about their hopes and fears. Tempted by unsophisticated or exaggerated arguments, we can choose to be afraid and defensive. Or, we can see that debates about who we are as individuals and as citizens renew us and hold promise for a better future.

Multicultural Education

What necessitates "multicultural education?" Why modify the word "education" with the adjective "multicultural?" Aren't all children taught the facts of school regardless of the multiplicity of cultures from whence they come? Isn't multicultural education redundant with the notion of "public" education? If it sounds odd that there is a special kind of education called "multicultural education" that is distinct from plain or generic education, one needs reminding that there preexists precious few neutral or universal concepts from which teachers can safely invoke. For much of the 20th century, this neutrality hid what was the default educational paradigm of the United States: assimilation and nativism. Conceived as a method to bring disparate immigrant cultures together, the "melting pot" paradigm of education is today seen by many scholars as a hegemonic practice that normalized the teaching of so-called native cultures [white, male, hetero-, Anglo-American] over the beliefs, values, and practices of participating minority groups. Recognizing the gap that existed between the democratic ideals of the dominant culture and the social realities that silenced those students outside the margins, an ethnic revitalization movement emerged post-*Brown vs. the Board of Ed* that led to the development of what is today called multicultural education (Banks, 1985). Distinct from traditional education and its picture of objective knowledge, multicultural education holds the view that a singular culture's way of knowing or "epistemology" is never the *only* way of knowing.

"Each age, it is found, must write its own books," concluded Ralph Waldo Emerson a century and a half ago (Emerson, 1983, p. 56). Like Dewey, Emerson spoke to the deliberative process of education more than the disciplined receptivity from which traditional knowledge is engendered. Process words—"ing-words" like *doing, making, debating, searching*—call attention to how meanings are created in common, and how ideas are understood through association. Assimilated facts and handed-down learning mean much less than the ability to apply said facts in a contemporary context. An over-emphasis on book-learning and rote memorization produces a class of learners that Emerson called the "bookworms," those "who value books...not as related to nature and the human constitution" but those who pursue knowledge apart from an appreciation of the living present (Emerson, p. 57). Perhaps anticipating the argument for multiple ways of knowing and the canon wars that such a cosmopolitan epistemology would provoke, Emerson wrote, "Books are the best of things, well used; abused, among the worst. What is the right use? What is the one end, which all means go to effect? *They are for nothing but to inspire*" (p. 57).

In James A. Banks' conception of multicultural education, the contents of study (books, scores, aural artifacts, etc.) are understood as integrated with the active construction of multiple ways of knowing and finding. A preeminent scholar in this field, Banks defines multicultural education along five process domains:

1. **Content integration**. This dimension deals with the manner in which teachers choose "examples and content from a variety of cultures or groups to illustrate key concepts, principles, generalizations, or theories."
2. **Knowledge construction**. This process concerns the methods teachers choose "to help students to understand, investigate, and determine how implicit cultural assumptions, frames of references, perspectives, and biases within a discipline influence the ways in which knowledge is constructed." Multiple ways of knowing are encouraged; knowledge is constructed dialogically rather than handed down.

3. **Prejudice reduction**. Teachers help students develop an open and inclusive attitude toward the unfamiliar, culminating in "more positive attitudes toward different racial and ethnic groups."

4. **Equity pedagogy**. "Teachers modify their teaching in ways that will facilitate the academic achievement of students from diverse racial, cultural, ethnic, language, and gender groups." Teachers adapt a wide range of teaching styles to reflect the diversity of their classroom.

5. **Empowerment and school structure**. All members of the teaching community work collaboratively to restructure and reimagine the school as a space where students are empowered and treated with dignity (Banks, 2006, pp. 4–18).

Few educators would publicly argue against the process ideals that are presented in dimensions 3–5 above: radicals and conservatives alike see the school as a place where all are treated equitably and every student is given a fair shake (their means differ, of course). For traditionalists, the problem with multicultural education hinges on the objects of study (dimension 1) and the seemingly anti-intellectual embrace of cultural relativism (dimension 2). If the multicultural mandate suggests greater inclusion of diverse readings and activities, an important question remains: what gets included in a course of study and what gets left out? With a finite supply of instructional time available in any given school calendar, the culturally responsive music teacher may be forced to give up standard offerings in favor of the so-called non-traditional. With what texts do we replace our tradition? The Fauré *Requiem* with selections from *"Cats?"* Recitatives with rap? (For some, my interpretation of tradition and *non*-tradition could well be reversed).

Essentialism and the Crisis of Schooling

For "essentialists," those scholars who wish to protect a singular view of the truth, multiculturalists' anti-essentialist embrace of heuristic epistemology has turned the humanities into a "laughingstock." (Kronman, 2007, p. 139). In the postmodern mindset, for example, musical "works of art" dissolve into mere "listenables" (Elliott, 1995) and the aesthetic criteria that have historically informed musical quality and taste are reduced to a given music's "use function" (Regelski, 2005). Defenders of the "Great Works" or the masterpieces of Western culture contend that the pursuit of perfection, beauty, truth, and knowledge should look the same in contemporary Chicago as it once did in Ancient Greece. The essentialist logic goes something like this:

All education involves a search for truth.
All truth is universal.
Therefore, one universal course of study should apply to all students everywhere.

In this view, teachers collapse difference under one common vision of community, through one common view of truth—*we assimilate*. Whereas multiculturalists speak of many things and not one, essentialists speak of one thing, not many.

Conservative critics argue that without fixed truths and endpoints to guide us, schools and colleges have become increasingly balkanized and timid (Bloom, 1987). "The more a classroom resembles a gathering of delegates speaking on behalf of the groups they represent," writes Anthony Kronman, director of humanities at Yale University, the more difficult it is "to explore questions of a personally meaningful kind. In such a classroom, students encounter each other not as individuals but as spokespersons...and the works they study are regarded more as statements of group membership than as the creations of men and women with viewpoints uniquely their own—with the depressing result that great works...are unjustly neglected on account of a shameful discrimination" (Kronman, 2007, p. 139). According to this view, the liberal arts, which took their name two millennia ago from the ancient Greek ideal that education liberates the mind, have suddenly become entirely *un*-free places, postmodern realms of "political correctness" and "identity politics." Rather than engaging in the difficult task of judgment, analysis, and critique, multiculturalists celebrate everything equally. The result, accordingly, is that little is learned, but much is affirmed.

Born of the *Brown vs. the Board Education* decision and the civil rights advances of the 1960s (including those of women), multicultural education slowed considerably in the 1980s and 1990s. Critics claimed that schools could no longer be trusted to educate students equally and non-ideologically, thus the movement toward national standards and high stakes testing—the essentialists' reaction to runaway relativism—was born. By lumping multicultural education together with clichés of permissiveness, relativism, and non-rigorous coursework, the idea of "school" became synonymous with "crisis." And with schools in perpetual crisis, federal control or takeover of education logically followed. National standards and national testing were designed to *de*-power local stakeholders, from the school boards, parents, and principals to the teachers whose traditional role it has been to design and implement the curriculum they wish to teach. What is good for rural Texas must likewise be good for urban Chicago or suburban Virginia.

Ironically, *democracy* was the culprit. By choosing to include and integrate non-Western or nontraditional curricular offerings equally, and by cultivating openness with regard to the texts studied (Bank's dimension 1) and the means for understanding them (dimension 2), multicultural educators were accused of removing core requirements to favor ethnic and gender demands, suspending critical judgments about value and taste, lowering academic standards, and celebrating self-esteem over rigorous examination (Schlessinger, 1991). The famous Reagan-era critique *A Nation at Risk* quipped, "we have a cafeteria-style curriculum in which the appetizers and desserts can easily be mistaken for the main course" (Lazerson, 1987, p. 198). "At risk" was more than just a nation's children and their education, but the very survival of its economy—the American way of life. The "educational foundations of our society are presently being eroded by a rising tide of mediocrity," *A Nation at Risk* concluded (Lazerson, 1987, p. 197). Its primary author, William Bennett, brilliantly conflated the idea of tradition with a rigorous manner of teaching based on standards and testable measures (the inverse of Bank's dimension 2) with an education in "classical" content like historical texts and hard sciences (the inverse of dimension 1).

Diversity and the National Standards

The report gave birth to a national standards movement that affected every teachable (and testable) discipline, including music and the arts. Neither dessert, nor appetizer, the National Standards for Music Education (1994) claimed main course status for the arts:

> The standards say that arts have "academic" standing. They say there is such a thing as achievement, that knowledge and skills matter, and that mere willing participation is not the same thing as education. They affirm that discipline and rigor are the road to achievement. And they state emphatically that all these things can in some ways be measured... (Consortium of National Arts Education Associations, 1994)

Official knowledge became testable knowledge. Thus, even in the arts, an epistemological shift occurred. *Knowing* concepts replaced *understanding* concepts. If standardization is an educational priority, it is easier, for example, to test what students know about sonata-allegro form than to ask for an *understanding* of sonata-allegro form. "Standardization," writes Jorgensen, "deflects attention from the needs and interests of the people who are the central concern of educators, does not go to the heart of education, and can be subverted easily by teachers and students alike" (Jorgensen, 2003, p. 128). Beyond the cynical teaching-to-the-test temptation that deforms educational practice and narrows teachable opportunities, Jorgensen worries that the standards movement depersonalizes children, homogenizes difference, and removes teachers from larger conversations about the role of education and schools in public life. "Instead of teaching every young person to know and do certain musical things, music education can ensure that every young person experiences music in ways that are relevant to, and meaningful in, her or his particular reality... Rather than being funneled toward predetermined ends and prosaic means, diversity can be encouraged and celebrated" (Jorgensen, 2003, p. 128).

Product words, nouns like achievement, knowledge, skill, discipline, rigor, and measurement (taken from the brief excerpt above) can be read in many ways. For former president George W. Bush, they were ideals that protect children against the "soft bigotry of low expectations." They assure that allowances aren't made through misguided welfare. Yet an emphasis on product words, like an emphasis on the objects of our studies, mask the real location of learning—the learning that occurs in the motion, in the relationship, between the books of a given curriculum, the ideals we hold out for their engagement, and the instructional methods we choose. While battles between traditionalists and multiculturalists tend to be fought over the inclusion or exclusion of the objects of study, we can safely say that books alone do not substantiate learning. Nor do abstract ideals of excellence, rigor, and adequate yearly progress.

In thinking of education and the mind in terms of verbs (or gerunds) more than nouns, Dewey's notion of education as process—that a "growing and rich experience" is both the criteria and location of learning—helps educators come to terms with the perennial issues of relativism and anti-intellectualism that are leveled against multiculturalists. In many ways, the question of relativism is a red herring; like the problem of standards and hierarchies, relativism must yield to *knowing more*. The conscientious educator is always weighing matters of relative value, whether the choices are intertraditional or intratraditional. The traditionalist may "judge" one Beethoven string quartet to be of more educational value than another because (say) *Opus 135* yields the greatest potential for educational growth for *these* students at *this* time.

But musical growth, if it is to be purposeful and enriching (in other words *educative*), is never just the ability to translate the notes on the page to a corresponding historically-correct musical rendition. A choir director may choose to include South African freedom songs because they too, like Beethoven string quartets, yield great potential for musical growing. But the latter experience would be hollow if the choir director's conception of educational growth failed to include a critical evaluation of both the historic and contemporary contexts from which freedom songs emerged, if this curricular choice failed to enlighten previous performance experience, and if this musical encounter did not purposefully lead to richer understandings of the very meaning of "choir" and "choir music." Diversity and challenge are thus preconditions for growth. The musical mind is expanded when we interact expressively, deliberately, and knowledgeably in the multiple ways in which we musically find ourselves.

TEACHER JUDGMENT

Too often when the obligations of tradition meet up with the imperatives of change, cultural conflict occurs. Schools, as noted, are endowed by all appearances with mutually contradictory aims; being the primary site where culture is learned and negotiated, they are thus poorly served by a public that is itself ill-reconciled to the dialectics of tradition and change. Teachers bare the brunt of navigating this conflict, hewing to the demands of product words like excellence, achievement, and objectivity, while holding out hope for the ways in which a well-designed curriculum may open, inspire, connect, and empower the students in their charge. To the degree that it is possible, teachers must resist the simplification that the aforementioned binaries appear to enforce. Critical judgments—acts of freedom—are required.

Living Traditions and Freedom

In spite of the formative role that traditions play in shaping who we are, even a highly codified and custodial tradition is never shared and experienced identically with all its participants. Writes David Hansen, no musician, artist, or educator has ever had the same "initial encounter" with a particular art form and "nobody's subsequent history...will ever be identical with another's" (Hansen, 2001, p. 122). Conceptualizing tradition as something that moves, a place in which each of us swims for a short period of time, creates enormous possibility for arts instruction. Writing about the generative capacity of tradition, Hansen posits, "tradition does not describe that which remains identical or frozen or that which should be blindly accepted. Tradition, once again, is not traditionalism. Everyone in a practice begins as an imitator, but what they imitate and, with effort and luck, grow beyond is always on the move, whether subtly or dramatically. In this light, the sense of tradition funds freedom..." (p. 122)

We cannot talk about instruction without talk of freedom. We cannot talk about growth without freedom, nor curriculum, nor choice. When we speak of freedom, we speak of beginnings and initiatives—present and future powers. Tradition funds freedom by giving students a place to start, their own "initial encounter." Yet too often music teachers treat the future voyage of their music students as expectations predicated on their own past. They may treat all their students to the same method; they may prepare all their students for the same future. What begins necessarily as imitation, continues as imitation—or ends when the music student enacts his own freedom by declaring irrelevant the present method of instruction for meeting the hopes and needs of *his* future. This is a dismal view of music education, but one that captures the frozen obedience of traditionalism. It can be said that teachers are not educators who teach from scripted lessons or hide behind the predictability of routines, method books, and unchanging lesson units. Rather, they are the functionaries or custodians of a past cultural practice. Objectifying instruction, removing one's self from the contingencies of life and life's problems, seeing children monolithically rather than in all their messy plurality is inherently self-alienating. Can dialogue exist in such settings? Is there anything new to be known?

For the music teacher moved to embrace a living tradition, it would be remiss to consider her freedom "negatively," as the simple absence of restrictions, or as the naïve unanchoring of all of her life's previous musical work. Dewey speaks very carefully about the responsibility of teacher freedom, seeing "freedom of outward action as a means to freedom of judgment and of power to carry deliberately chosen ends into execution" (Dewey, p. 73). If we are to eschew the safe predictability of a learning method or scripted rehearsal, it is our responsibility in turn to make wise judgments. These choices may have to do with the problems that particular students are facing. *What learning goals are appropriate for this classroom at this period of their musical growth? What alternatives are there to the understanding of polyrhythms, seventh chords, or the pentatonic scale?* Ethically arrived at curricular choices may have to do with the lived lives of one's students.

How might my instruction in classical technique help you play better jazz? I under-
stand your goals and I will help you to meet them, though your future path looks
different than mine did when I was at your age.

Freedom from restriction—the freedom to teach differently from way we were
taught, the freedom to work in the order of one's choosing, the freedom to tinker
with one's tradition—"is to be prized only as a means...to power," writes Dewey,
"power to frame [new] purposes, to judge wisely, to evaluate desires...power to
select and order means to carry chosen ends into operation" (p. 74). This conception of power is different from earlier accounts as it is tied to mutual responsibility and growth; it is not an appeal to teacher-centered learning or new forms
of manipulation. And, unlike contemporary discourses that seek to de-power
teachers through the mechanics of testing and standards, preplanned curricula,
and the punitive markers that designate the "highly qualified" from the "low,"
this stance believes in the power of teachers to interact wisely within the unique
populations they are entrusted to educate.

The result of conceptualizing our tradition as evolving and alive is the kind
of positive freedom, for both students and teachers, that is most worth having.
It does not necessitate a moving *away* from tradition, but the movement toward,
the movement forward and together. "The only freedom of enduring importance," writes Dewey, "is freedom of intelligence...freedom of observation and
of judgment exercised in behalf of purposes that are intrinsically worth while"
(Dewey, p. 69). A young oboist who studies the Ferling *Études* does so on behalf
of an inner need, to participate in the lived tradition of her teacher, or to procure
new ways of knowing in a realm or tradition that may be evolving differently.
The cultivation of multiple excellencies, the cultivation of a diverse musical mind
is made manifest through the trials she puts her new learning through, and the
rewards that attend them. The oboe teacher likewise experiences exponential
rewards, some that attend to the growth of himself as an instructor, some as an
evolving musician, some that connect him to new sides of himself. The following
quote from Greene is an implicit critique of orthodoxies, traditionalists, dogmas,
and the way "official knowledge" fixes the participants of its study. Her voice lays
claim to the freedom of self-knowing, and the importance of diversity:

> To be yourself is to be in process of creating a self, an identity. If it were not
> a process, there would be no surprise. The surprise comes along with being
> different—consciously different as one finds ways of acting on envisioned pos-
> sibility. It comes along with hearing different words and music, seeing from
> unaccustomed angles, realizing that the world perceived from one place is not
> the world. (Greene, 1995, p. 20)

With freedom comes some amount of fear, most certainly; fear of misinter-
pretation, fear of surprises, fear of the unseen. Concerning the choices teachers
make regarding literature and methods of instruction, this chapter holds the view
that we needn't fear a movement *away* from the traditions we love; rather, freedom creates the possibility of new unions, new inductees, and new encounters

(Dewey 1910; Greene 1995; Hansen, 2008). This conception of teaching captures both the existential "aliveness" of being wide-awake in the world, and the sense that a "living" tradition "draws students *into* worlds of knowledge, experience, and outlook that extend beyond what the family or local community can normally provide alone" (Hansen, 2001, p. 119).

Representing Difference

Recall the image of the singular music educator, standing alone at a podium, looking back at a class that may appear to all intents and purposes to be a room full of strangers. Her musical mandate is complicated, even contradictory. She may wish to induct her choir into the tradition of Mozart, but she may fear "assimilating" difference. She knows that the classical Western art form that she has been inducted into and to which she is highly trained (and which she loves profoundly) has been applied reflexively, even hegemonically, as the standard or essentially true object of study: *have its abuses excluded some from its participation?* Wide-awake to the changing world around her, she may wonder whether Mozart means anything today, whether Mozart is relevant in the musical world of the students staring back at her. Yet, she strongly believes that it is the educator's job to teach the unknown and unfamiliar, to bring students into new realms of knowledge, and she can say with some certainty that Mozart is not a part of the local community she teaches in. She believes Mozart is beautiful, just as other musics are beautiful, but what is the right choice?

If a curriculum is that which an older generation wishes to pass on to a newer one, and if ethics is the practice whereby choices are fairly made between competing "right answers," an ostensibly sensible solution to the demands of a pluralistic classroom is to represent all participants equally. Yet imagine not only the difficulty of such endeavor, but its potential to label and misidentify. Can we really say that one particular music is Mexican and another American, Mexican-American, Canadian, French, or French-Canadian? Could we possibly "single out one American musical work to represent the nation?" Patricia Shehan Campbell asked facetiously; and if so, just what would it be?

> . . . a shape-note song, a choral hymn by William Billings, Duke Ellington's "Take the A-Train," Charles Ives's *New England Triptych*, a Sioux Indian social dance song, "Yankee Doodle," a croon-tune by Elvis Presley, Leonard Bernstein's "(I'd Like to Be in) America," a segment of Aaron Copland's *Appalachian Spring*, an African American spiritual, or Bruce Springsteen's "Born in the USA?" (Campbell, 1996, p. 68)

American music is also salsa and reggaeton (at least in this author's neighborhood). It is likewise Swedish dance music sung in English, and Disney's *Beauty and the Beast* recorded in Spanish. When issues of representation, consumerism, and nationality intersect, the questions become increasingly convoluted. Is Ray Charles's *I Got a Woman* still American when it is performed by Japanese musicians? How does it change when an all-girl band sings the words? If a Wisconsin toddler grows up listening to Baby Mozart, is the music still considered Austrian? Is Broadway's *Les Miserables* French or American?

Regarding questions of cultural heritage, schools, and educational purpose, the questions become more serious. Can we agree, in principle, that Harlem children should have the chance to experience jazz music, even if they have never listened to it at home or heard it on the way to school? Shouldn't the Chinese children adopted by American parents have the opportunity to learn mandarin folksongs as part of a family project? (Lee, 2002) Shouldn't predominantly-white children in homogenous Illinois communities have the opportunity to learn mandarin folksongs as part of their community project? The degree to which these questions can be answered without patronizing paternalism or patriotism is the very heart of the problem. But the logic of diversity, Greene reminds us, is contradictory:

> ...we need openness and variety as well as inclusion. We need to avoid fixities, even the stereotypes linked to multiculturalism. To view a person as in some sense "representative" of Asian culture (too frequently grouping together those of Japanese, Korean, Chinese, and Vietnamese culture in addition to ignoring each individual's differences) or Hispanic, Afro-American, or Euro-American culture is to presume an objective reality called "culture," a homogenous and fixed presence that *can* be adequately represented by existing subjects. (Greene, 1995, p. 163)

Without recourse to normative platitudes, the reader of this chapter is asked to consider: *what is the use of multicultural music?* To honor and celebrate? To equalize and make socially just? To ration fairly? To represent who we think we are teaching? Are our engagements with multiculturalism a cynical response to the exigent demands of nervous administrators? To use as an instrumental lure—as a bridge to "serious" music, as is often the case with popular music? Is multicultural music (including popular music) a brush with the exotic, a gift to our students, like a John Williams arrangement in band, or the sing-along finale? Is multicultural music just a chance to give the drum section something to do? Or do our platitudes about multicultural music speak to abstractions about global citizenship and world engagement? Is multiculturalism the bourgeois privilege of exposure and the cultivation of new tastes?

The Emergent Curriculum

Surely, the case for an ethically constructed curriculum is needed, one that resists the stereotyping of representational pluralism on the one hand and the oppressive universality of traditionalists on the other. While the following assertion may appear to be oxymoronic, perhaps the single largest impediment to the problem of choosing music literature is an overemphasis on the objects of study: *the problem with choosing music is that we think too much about the music.* When we speak of traditional music education, we speak of established works like the Creston *Sonata*, the Ferling *Études* or Mozart's *Te Deum*; we may speak less often their educational purpose. Likewise, given the pluralistic mandate that is an ever-increasing expectation in public schools and music education research, the problem of choosing multicultural music literature reflects an analogous overemphasis on the *objects* of study. Well-intentioned conductors consider adding the works of female composers to already crowded concert programs. Songs about Harriet Tubman are sung during Black History Month, and odes to Japanese cherry trees resurface every May. But what do these figurative choices represent? The results of logical, well-planned, and integrated instruction, or objects of representation, emptied of meaning?

What if the emphasis of our judgment is focused on the choice of instructional aims, as much or in some cases more than the choice of an instructional object? It is worth underscoring that an object of study alone—a score, an etude, a song—serves no intrinsically educational purpose. Selecting music without explicit consideration for the progressive growth and enrichment of further experiences reduces Education (with a capital E) to its merest sociological function. In traditionalist conceptions of education, this is the way dominant culture is replicated. In the clichés of multiculturalism, this is the child-centered relativism that sees teenagers as only interested in rap, and Spanish-speaking children as contented to sing *La Bamba*. Dewey, ever disdainful of the 'isms that bifurcate education, found the latter just as problematic as the former. Critiquing the laissez-faire manner in which progressive education celebrates spontaneity and self-esteem at the expense of instruction, Dewey wrote "many of the newer schools tend to make little or nothing of organized subject matter...to proceed as if any form of direction and guidance by adults were an invasion of individual freedom, and if the idea that education should be concerned with the present and future meant that acquaintance with the past has little or no role to play in education" (Dewey, pp. 9–10). A living tradition is the stuff of "*organized* subject matter;" neither pure process nor pure product, but the mindful, judicial amalgam that defines what it means to educate.

If an object of study alone serves no intrinsic educational purpose, then it is the organized educational process that is attached to said object that brings to life the kind of emerging and world-revealing experience that teachers hold out for their students. In such a view of curriculum and instruction, the teacher is funded with tremendous power and responsibility. Good judgment is an ethical imperative because the choice of instruction and instructional content resides squarely in what is good for one's student or students. It is unclear whether the problem of judgment makes life easier or more difficult for teachers, but a sense of aliveness attends not just the developing curriculum but the very lives of all involved. "Wide-awake," the music educator lends abiding attention to the manner in which students are seen, listened to, and understood, resisting residence in the abstract, or in aggregation or stereotype. This manner of seeing the world requires experience, maturity, insight, the willingness to make mistakes, intuition, and an almost forswearing of certainty, a stance that Dewey calls "doubtful possibility" (Dewey, 1910, pp. 101–115). Because the *why* and *how* questions of choosing music literature—the *where* and *when*, the *whether* and *for whom*, and the *under what circumstances* and *in what manner*—are never questions that can be answered with a simple yes or no, it is only through an orientation toward instruction that is part doubt and part hope that educators can do their work in rapidly changing times.

SUMMARY

There is no inherent dichotomy between the music literature that forms the backbone of our curricula and the educational experiences and aims we attach to its unfolding. Nor is there a recommended order in which curricular decisions are made: instruction goals do not need to precede the selection of music, and the selection of music needn't precede the method of instruction. The tension occurs in the ideals we hold for the experience at hand. If, for example, there is only one way to envision a band program, then such a band director is under no obligation to worry about who his students are, what music to perform, or how to rehearse. As mentioned earlier, there are plenty of systems in place that officiate the practice of band, and the interested director needs only to subscribe to an available professional method or follow his state's adjudication manual.

For those educators who wish to encourage multiple ways of knowing and experiencing music, who wish to create conversations across cultures and traditions, instructional aims can be a way of ordering experience without resorting to the superficiality and feel-good relativism that is often associated with the multicultural agenda. Recall Banks' process domains of multicultural education. The content of a general music classroom or a middle school choir can be integrated from a variety of sources, some familiar, some not, "to illustrate key concepts, principles, generalizations, or theories" (Banks, 2006, p. 4). Of course, choosing music literature with experience in mind complicates matters of concert programming and curriculum design. Simply performing the work of a female composer, without consideration for the work's educational purpose, or historic and contextual meanings is at best of dubious value and at worst patronizing and paternalistic. Similarly, a song about Harriet Tubman should not suddenly appear every February as if falling from the sky; but if the work has educational merit, it should be folded into a larger organization of study. Choosing music literature with experience in mind means being intimately aware of our students' "expert-ness" and then effecting subsequent relationships between the known and unknown.

Using Bank's model of integrated instruction is not an argument to universalize music, or to suggest that there are musical principles and ways of knowing that speak directly across every culture. Nor is this a naïve assertion on the part of this chapter's author that all music educators are willing or equally equipped to culturally integrate music across multiple contexts. It is to suggest, however, that in spite of the difficulty such an instructional approach would entail and its potential for misuse, only two options are available: 1) we can remain frozen in a traditionalist curricula, never venturing beyond the realms of our initial encounters, or 2) we can attempt to communicate between cultures and accept the difficulties and rewards that will ensue. Educators whose expertise has narrowed and deepened since the days of their initial encounters are not asked to give up what they love and are good at. Quite the contrary, they are expected to share what they do well. However, adopting an orientation that seeks to bring alive the multiple traditions available for study requires a willingness to learn new things, new musics and new ways of seeing and hearing, even as we preserve the traditions we love (Greene 1995; Hansen, 2008).

The key aspect of a living tradition is that it serves a deeply humanistic project. For teachers, the imperative to connect—the complicated conversations we engage in across cultures and contexts—is more than a way of staying "fresh," it deepens our own values as we learn more about who we are and what we think we can do. "If one conceives of oneself as working in a practice whose origins reside far in the past, and whose value will persist long into the future, one can derive additional sources of strength and perhaps even of imagination as a teacher," writes Hansen (1995, p. 133). Keeping a tradition alive, "discovering the connection which actually exists *within* experience between the achievements of the past and the issues of the present" (Dewey, p. 11) is an act of imagination that feeds both teacher and student—and possibly propels a tradition long into the future. Take note of the existential component to this project, this quest to connect, this philosophical and ethical orientation. By way of contrast, Dewey brings to mind the *de*-humanization of traditionalism, "the traditional school could get along without any consistently developed philosophy of education. About all it required in that line was a set of abstract words like culture, discipline, our great cultural heritage and so forth, actual guidance being derived not from them but from custom and established routines" (Dewey, p. 18). Imagine the extra difficulty of drawing students into new realms of knowledge through established routines and rote procedures. Routines, after all, are mindless, conversations are mindful. Routines invoke conformity, all students are different. It is only when the music educator conceives of each choice of music literature as the beginning of a conversation that a musical encounter, initial or otherwise, can grow in life and appreciation.

Class Discussion

1. What does "the choosing of musical repertoire is an ethical endeavor" mean? How does an ethical framework help music teachers make "right" decisions? How might it complicate matters? Cite an example of an ethically considered choice of music literature.

2. Consider John Dewey's question, "How shall the young become acquainted with the past in such a way that the acquaintance is a potent agent in appreciation of the living present?" What is another way of saying this? What is Dewey asking us to think about?

3. What does musical citizenship mean? How is it related to ethics and choice of musical repertoire? Make a list of ideals that you hold out for your students. What kind of music would you choose to realize these goals? What would your teaching look like?

4. What strategies have you used to create relevance in your classroom? How can the careful choice of music literature create openings? How might some choices inhibit connectedness and culturally-relevant learning? Cite some examples from your own experience when you succeeded and when you failed—what did you learn, and what would you do differently?

Projects

1. Imagine that you are the high school choral, band, or orchestra director (choose one) in a community in your state (choose one). You are planning your spring semester's work that will culminate in a concert. For the concert you plan to perform six pieces. Considering the issues raised in this chapter, choose six pieces that you are familiar with to work on during the spring and perform in the concert. How has the community you selected influenced your decisions? Provide a rationale for the overall program and/or the individual pieces you select.

2. Review James Banks's five-process domains of multicultural education. Explain how each domain can be understood and integrated into a music classroom. Cite examples of music literature that might be used to illustrate each objective and how the musical aim might be taught. Write a brief report summarizing your reflections.

SUGGESTED READINGS

Dewey, J. (1930/1997). *Experience and education.* New York: Touchstone.

Greene, M. (1988). *The dialectic of freedom.* New York: Teachers College Press.

Hansen, David T. (2001). *Exploring the moral heart of teaching: toward a teacher's creed.* New York: Teachers College Press.

Jorgensen, Estelle (2008). *The art of teaching music.* Indianapolis: Indiana University Press.

CHAPTER 11

⁓

Music Education Technology
James Frankel

INTRODUCTION

This chapter serves to develop an understanding of the manner in which technology may influence the ways we define music and how technology may impact what it means to make music. These perspectives will influence both what music is taught and how that music is taught. This chapter will review traditional educational applications of computers in music, including computer-aided instruction (CAI), drill and practice, simulations and gaming, as well as the role of the Internet as a resource for music educators. The potential impact of new musical instruments such as synthesizers, drum controllers, and wind controllers will be examined. The chapter will also explore how new music-sequencing software has developed a new generation of GarageBand composers. The effect of the interaction of music technology and popular culture will be explored, including issues of copyright and digital music, with suggestions for how such developments may influence music curriculum.

TECHNOLOGY IN THE MUSIC CLASSROOM

Technology and music have had a close relationship throughout history. Composers and musicians have always been at the forefront of technological advances in terms of both new instruments and new outlets for the distribution of their music for others to experience (Williams & Webster, 2006). Whether one thinks of Beethoven and the invention of the modern piano, the impact of the printing press on publishing music, the impact of the phonograph on making recordings of music performances available for home enjoyment, or the impact of synthesizer and the completely new palette of sounds available to composers in the late 20th century, technology has had an integral role in the history of music and will continue to do so for many years to come. Likewise, musicians are often the first to embrace new directions in technology. This can clearly be seen with the recent developments in the digital music age. No longer are record companies the exclusive avenue for record production, promotion, and distribution (Kusek & Leonhard, 2005). Music production software and the Internet have created entirely new ways for musicians to record, promote, and sell their music to fans they may never have reached with the more antiquated model of the record label as the sole outlet for distribution.

Music classrooms and music teachers have been typically less willing to embrace these new technologies as educational tools (Jassmann, 2004), often falling back on more traditional methods of instruction, especially in terms of teaching performance and music theory skills. This trend is not exclusive to the music classroom or even other arts subjects. It is often clearly evident throughout the core curriculum subjects as well (Cuban, 2001). Technology in the music classroom, when facilitated with sufficient teacher training and appropriate curricular integration, has the potential for having a very positive impact on the music education the students receive. Research suggests that the pedagogical impact on a teacher who uses the technology effectively can also be very positive, creating opportunities for students and teachers to explore their creativity in ways difficult to achieve without technology (Reese 1995, Rudolph 2004, Williams & Webster 2006, Davidson 1990, Frankel 2002).

One of the many pedagogical implications of technology in the music classroom is that it can afford teachers and students opportunities for more student-centered learning and alternative assessment. In an educational landscape that emphasizes the importance of differentiated instruction and the value of the constructivist approach to learning, technology can facilitate assessment models that embrace these methodologies. For example, teachers might assign their students a project where the objective is to provide biographical information about an important composer from the Baroque period. In the past, students would be expected to research the life of the composer and create a formal written report that might include a portrait of the composer. With technology, students can create projects in a number of different formats that include multimedia examples including audio, video, images, hyperlinks to relevant web sites, interactive games, and more. For example, a student could create a podcast about the composer that includes images of the composer, their instrument, audio or MIDI files of their most famous compositions, and suggested links to web sites about the composer. If the student would rather present the same information in a different way, a movie for example, readily available technology can facilitate this. Pink (2005) points out that in order for students to succeed in the 21st Century, these types of opportunities (student-centered, creative experiences) for students are critical.

Technology can help solve some of the many problems that face music educators today. For example, if a teacher needs music for their students to perform but has a limited budget, they can create arrangements, at no cost, of any music within the public domain for any type of ensemble simply by downloading a MIDI file from a web site, opening that MIDI file in a piece of notation software, and using an algorithm within that software to create customized arrangement for their students to perform. If teachers need to encourage their students to practice, or need a way to assess student practice, they can incorporate technology that allows students to perform assigned musical exercises at home and use software along with a microphone and an Internet connection to record and submit their performances directly to their music directors' computer for assessment. If a teacher needs to provide parents with an accurate assessment of their child's work, teachers can post students' work online so that parents can download and listen to podcasts created in school by their children through the iTunes Music Store. If a teacher wants to communicate quickly and efficiently to all of the students in their music program, they can easily create a web site for their music program. These advances seem to accelerate with each school year, and many teachers are finding it difficult to keep up with them (Jassmann, 2004). Some teachers long for the days when phonographs and LPs were cutting-edge technology, while others wonder what direction music will take in the future and what affect it will have on live performance and music education.

Software

The birth of MIDI (Musical Instrument Digital Interface) in 1983 made it possible for computers and synthesizers to communicate with one another. Early music software primarily revolved around two categories that took advantage of MIDI: sequencing software and notation software. Sequencing software did just that: sequence musical events. These events included pitch, duration (rhythmic value), tempo, dynamics, and desired sound (patch). Early sequencers allowed users to record performances on a synthesizer that could then be played back and edited. Editing could include changing the pitch and duration of each note entered. Sequencers also allowed users to input notes one at a time (step entry), eliminating mistakes in the performance of that particular musical passage. Once a performance was recorded, users could then save the file as a Standard MIDI File that could then be shared with others. Early sequencers could only handle MIDI information. It would be nearly twenty years until the next major advance in sequencing technology—the incorporation of digital audio and video.

Early notation software titles were also somewhat limited compared to their modern counterparts. These titles could create simple scores with little or limited capability, but dot-matrix printers could note yet produce high-resolution scores (Williams & Webster, 2006). Most composers continued to use written manuscript, music typewriters, or nongraphic programs like *Score* to create their music, rather than use these early versions. It was not until the mid-1980s when HP and Apple Computer released the first laser printers that desktop music publishing truly took off. Soon after the invention of the mouse and the graphical user interface, but not until the release of *Finale* in 1988, and after both *Overture* and *Sibelius* most music composers and music publishers began to utilize notation software titles. Today notation software is the most common way for composers and arrangers to both input their music and publish it. The advances seen in the past decade with the arrival of Sibelius and the subsequent competition between Sibelius and Finale have been truly remarkable. Each title has unique features that allow them to stand out: the incorporation of video directly into the score; an expanded palette of virtual instruments; the ability to scan music into the computer and have it open as a notation file; and the ability to convert Standard MIDI Files (SMFs) to notated scores. Imagining what composers like Bach, Mozart, and Beethoven would have been able to do with the aid of notation software is somewhat frightening—each perhaps doubling or tripling their output within their lifetime.

It is important to note that there is a fundamental difference between these two types of software that music educators should bear in mind. The original intent of sequencing software was to capture musical performances and play them back. Notation software's intent was to create music that would be played by live musicians. While advances in notation software playback functionality have been great, they can never replace live performance—one of the cornerstones of music education. We will explore ways to use both sequencing and notation software in the music classroom in the fourth section of this chapter.

In addition to sequencing and notation software, CAI titles have been around since the early 1980s. Most early titles centered on music theory skills. Simple drill and practice exercises helped students learn note names, rhythms, key signatures, intervals, chord qualities, and even the principles of voice leading. Companies such as ECS, PG Music, Harmonic Vision, and Ars Nova released software titles specifically created for use in the music classroom—and for many teachers these early software titles were their first experiences using technology in their music classrooms.

Today the Internet is playing a larger role in terms of delivering music software to students, much of it available at little or no cost. Many of the advances in Internet content have come about primarily from advanced animation programs like Flash. Flash allows programmers to create interactive content for web sites. This content can include almost all of the features that traditional CAI titles typically have. Users can answer questions about music in a variety of ways, compose music online, play interactive games, listen to music examples, watch videos about music from various cultures, and even use their computer as an accompanist while they practice a given piece of music. Flash has revolutionized what can be done on a web site—incorporating all aspects of the multimedia experience. With the ever-changing world of the Internet will certainly come major advances in the years to come; advances that will certainly include more interactivity and improved audio playback and recording functionality.

CLASSROOM ENVIRONMENTS

A study conducted in 2002 by the United States Department of Education's National Center for Educational Statistics found that 99% of public schools in the United States had Internet access, and perhaps, more impressively, 92% of all classrooms in the United States had computers with Internet access (Kleiner and Lewis, 2003). This study is now six years old, and if the trends illustrated in the study have continued, that number is almost certainly already higher in 2009. MENC published the Opportunity-to-Learn Standards for Music Technology in 1999 that clearly state that technology should be in every music classroom. While this might not be the case yet in every music classroom, researchers and standard writers are working together to advocate that every music educator in the United States has, at the very least, access to a computer.

Technology often changes the physical environment of a classroom. This is especially the case with music classrooms. Whether the classroom is used for performance or classroom instruction, computers and their related peripherals (LCD projectors, synthesizers, amplification systems, MIDI interfaces, cables, headphones, etc.) need to have adequate space to be used effectively. With this in mind, a number of different classroom environments can be envisioned and a related index of specific strategies and recommendations can be created to maximize the effective use of technology to be found in each. The environments include what we call: (1) The No Computer Classroom, (2) The One-Computer Classroom, and (3) The Networked Music Technology Lab.

The No-Computer Classroom

Although certainly the least ideal of environments for the effective integration of technology into the music curriculum, it is still possible to make use of what technology there is in a school within a music class. Oppenheimer (2003) points out that the vast majority of schools across the United States have dedicated computer labs staffed with full-time teachers serving as facilitators to integrate technology into any curriculum taught within the school. If a music teacher does not have access to a computer within the classroom (assuming that the teacher has a classroom), that teacher should make use of the school computer lab to enhance instruction.

Today, there are many music education software titles and Internet-based activities that do not require any of the peripheral equipment. For example, most notation software titles do not require an external keyboard to enter information. The user interface on both *Finale* and *Sibelius* has a Qwerty keyboard entry option that actually allows the user to input musical information by typing in the desired notes that is often faster than recording it in by playing it on a musical keyboard. Some loop-based sequencing software titles like *GarageBand* and *Acid* have keyboard entry functions using a graphic user interface (GUI) that displays an on-screen keyboard allowing users to "play" melodies on the keyboard by either clicking the notes with a mouse, or by using the qwerty keyboard in a manner similar to the notation titles mentioned earlier. More recently, the web development software known as *Flash* has made it possible to include interactive software on a web site provided they have installed the free plug-in application *Shockwave* on their computer. One such web site, www.musictheory.net, includes many useful lessons, trainers, assessments, and utilities that help both teachers and students in terms of teaching and learning music theory concepts. This web site, like many education-oriented web sites on the Internet, is free and is the perfect resource for the music educator who is looking to enhance a music theory course with technology, but has neither the budget or the technology available within the classroom.

If a school does not have a computer lab, teachers can still make effective use of their own personal computers to make teaching materials for their classes including: music theory exercises and worksheets; sheet music including warm-up exercises, scales, and musical arrangements; finding free listening examples (either MIDI files or digital audio files) to play for the students; as well as utilizing the Internet for research to assist in planning lessons. A personal computer can also greatly assist with common administrative tasks that music educators have including creating schedules; publishing concert programs; creating department newsletters and web sites; creating detailed databases to organize music libraries, inventories, and other student information; maintaining a digital plan book and grade book; and corresponding with students, parents, colleagues, and administrators.

The One-Computer Classroom

Teaching music in a One-Computer Classroom as opposed to a No-Computer Classroom poses some significant differences that should be considered before deciding whether to purchase technology for a classroom. First, the fact that there is a dedicated music classroom within a school and a computer within that classroom speaks to the level of commitment from the school district toward the music program. Second, a computer with a projection device, speakers, and Internet access has the capability of completely changing the way that a teacher presents information to their students on a daily basis, and can dramatically shift the pedagogical style of the educator. Third, and perhaps most importantly from a pedagogical standpoint, teaching in a One-Computer Classroom as opposed to a No-Computer Classroom affords teachers the opportunity to teach with technology in a transparent manner. Transparency occurs when the teacher uses technology to enhance instruction in the same manner as other teaching tools including the chalkboard, stereo, and VCR rather than using the technology just for the sake of using it (Rudolph, 2004). When a teacher brings a music class to the computer lab, the students are conscious of the fact that this is a special occasion—it's "computer time" rather than music time. When technology is used on a regular basis to enhance instruction, the students view the technology as a tool to help them learn that concept, rather than a novelty.

Before we examine specific strategies for teaching in a One-Computer Classroom, it is important to note that the only way to make a One-Computer Classroom effective is to have some method of projecting the computer screen so that students can easily see the information being presented to them. There are two basic ways to project the images from a computer: an interactive whiteboard and an LCD projector. An interactive whiteboard is by far the better option but it can be expensive and sometimes cost prohibitive. The interactive whiteboard allows the teacher to project the images from their computer desktop onto a large whiteboard that includes special tools that allow teachers to interact with the images on their computer screens. For example, a teacher can project an image of a notation file and then use a special pen that allows them to click on menu items on the whiteboard. This is very helpful in showing students how to use the various functions of the software as well as for highlighting the musical concepts that are being taught. LCD Projectors are certainly more affordable than interactive whiteboards but are cost prohibitive for many. If these options are unavailable, it is possible to have students in small groups gather around the computer monitor, but it can lead to classroom management issues that might outweigh the benefits that technology can bring (Frankel, 2005).

According to Kleiner and Lewis (2003), 92% of all classrooms have at least one computer. While this certainly sounds promising, that figure does not necessarily mean that the computers in those classrooms are being used directly to instruct students. Many teachers designate that one computer for exclusive teacher use, often administrative in nature. In order to make best use of a computer in a music classroom, it is essential that the teacher use the computer (along with a projection device) as an integral part of their daily instruction. This can include the following: creating customized *PowerPoint* presentations to integrate audio, visual, and Internet web sites into a lesson; creating class compositions that use the new concepts taught in the lesson; recording and archiving student performances; having legal access and playback capability to thousands of free MIDI and digital audio files of important musical compositions in the public domain; and facilitating differentiated instruction within the small group lesson.

The Networked Music Technology Lab

The most ideal teaching situation for the effective integration of technology into a music curriculum is a Networked Music Technology Lab. By networked, we are referring to two types of networks: (1) a system that connects each workstation to a central teaching station, with a method of enabling each station to transmit an audio signal to the rest of the class and a method of verbal communication through a microphone; and (2) a system that allows data transfer via a central file server that teachers and students can access to post and submit files of various formats. The most common pieces of equipment in a Networked Music Technology Lab include: a computer with Internet access, a synthesizer with a MIDI interface, a student interface device that allows students to communicate with the teacher via headphones, and music software titles including sequencing, notation, and CAI titles. Networked Music Technology Labs can have anywhere from four to thirty-two stations—all connected to a central teacher console. The teacher console typically allows the teacher to communicate with each station, and allows external audio devices and computers to be connected to it.

When a Networked Music Technology Lab is paired with a teacher station connected to an LCD Projector, the transparent integration of technology is easily possible. Teachers can teach mini-lessons at the beginning of the period and then assign tasks for the students to complete with the technology. This ensures that students learn only specific aspects of the software at any one time and are thereby able to focus more on the musical concepts being taught. Classroom management in a Networked Music Technology Lab is quite different than a traditional music classroom. When used effectively, the teacher console can be a powerful classroom management tool. Programs like *Apple Remote Desktop* (Mac) and *Vision* (PC) give teachers the ability to view each computer monitor on their own computer monitor, take over the mouse of each computer if a student has a question about software functionality, and transfer files to each computer in the lab. When the teacher console and monitoring software are used in tandem, a teacher can be far more effective in quickly resolving any technical issues that might arise during any given lesson. When a file server is employed in a Networked Music Technology Lab, classroom management becomes even easier. Teachers can create folders on a file server that the students can then save their work to directly. This eliminates files getting lost and allows the teacher the ability to access those files from any computer. Having all students' work saved in one location rather than locally on individual computers saves a great deal of time.

Each one of the classroom environments listed in this section is geared more toward the General Music classroom rather than the performance-based classroom. It is important to note that while students in performance ensembles can benefit greatly from effective technology integration, it is perhaps better integrated into small group lessons rather than large ensemble rehearsals for obvious logistical and music reasons. However, the One-Computer Classroom model can be used effectively by an ensemble director to take attendance, play recordings for the students, create warm-up exercises for the students using notation software, highlight certain music theory concepts contained within the repertoire, and to record portions of the rehearsal for playback and critique. Software titles like *SmartMusic* that encourage students' practice can also have a positive impact on an instrumental music program. Although giving time to take your performance ensemble to the computer lab is certainly not feasible or recommended, selectively integrating technology into the performance-based aspect of your music program to improve overall musicianship skills is.

COMPUTER-AIDED INSTRUCTION

Rudolph (2004) describes three distinct categories of music software: *tool, tutor,* and *tutee.* The definition of each of these categories is quite simple. Software in the *tool* category includes any program where the main function is to create music. This category includes music production software such as sequencing, notation, and audio editing programs. This category of software and their effective integration into a music curriculum is discussed in the next section of this chapter. The second category of software, *tutor,* includes all computer aided instruction (CAI) programs available to music educators. CAI titles can vary greatly: some are primarily assessment tools that test previously learned skills, and some are complete packages—both teaching and assessing comprehension of musical concepts. As mentioned above, CAI titles have been around since the early 1980s and are commonly used in General Music classrooms. Software from the third category, *tutee*, includes programs like *PowerPoint, Flash*, and web site design packages such as *Dreamweaver*. This category of software is intended for teachers and students to create educational materials that others can learn from. The focus of this chapter centers on the second category—*tutor*. There are many CAI software titles available for educators and many ways to use them in the classroom. The following is brief description of the various titles available and how one might integrate them into a music classroom.

Pedagogical Software and Hardware

Before reviewing some of the CAI titles available, it is important to note that technology does not always provide an effective teaching tool for certain aspects of music. There are times when its use is cumbersome and ineffective. Curricular integration of technology in the music classroom should always occur *after* the music curriculum has been created. Music educators must identify the musical concepts that they would like their students to learn and then decide how to effectively convey that content to their students. The Technology Institute for Music Educators (TI:ME) has published *Technology Strategies for Music Education* in order to give examples of how technology can be used effectively in the music classroom. The authors agree that some aspects of a music curriculum are well served by technology and others are not (Rudolph, Richmond, Mash, Webster, Bauer & Walls, 2005). It is up to the individual teacher to identify opportunities for effective technology integration.

A Review of CAI Software

Richmond (in Watson, 2005) reviewed CAI software titles for the *Technology Guide for Music Educators* created by the Technology Institute for Music Educators (TI:ME). The author categorized these titles into two types of software: web based programs and software titles in the traditional CD-ROM format. The purpose of the review was to provide music educators with a brief synopsis of the functions of each software title. In an effort to provide readers with ideas on how to integrate different types of CAI software rather than list each specific title (which can quickly become obsolete), we have broken down these CAI titles into four categories: Drill & Practice, Tutorial, Creativity, and Assistive Technologies. Along with some suggested software titles and web sites for each category, what follows is an effort to provide examples of how each type of CAI software could be integrated into a music curriculum.

Drill & Practice Software

Early music software titles relied heavily on the drill and practice concept. The fundamentals of music are concepts that can be easily assessed using simple questions: display a note on a staff and ask the student to name it. It is certainly ironic that many current software titles rely heavily on traditional models of assessment. Some might argue that nothing has really changed from a pedagogical perspective if the new teaching tools rely heavily on the pedagogical models of the past. Because of the inherent nature of software design, drill and practice software titles are very common. The software presents a question, and the user responds. What is certainly very different than the drill and practice models of the past, however, are the ways in which the materials are presented. With high quality colorful graphics and digital sound quality that is reminiscent of the video games that so many of our students play in their leisure time, perhaps drill and practice is more exciting than the traditional methods of the not-so-distant past.

There are many software titles available that assess a student's knowledge of these concepts. They differ from the category that follows in that they do not attempt to teach the concepts they are assessing; they simply drill them. These titles include *Practica Musica* (Hybrid), *Auralia* (Hybrid), Alfred's *Interactive Musician* (Hybrid), *SmartMusic* (Hybrid), and *Musition* (PC). Each of these titles offer to cover a wide variety of music skills for various age levels. Most have methods of recording student progress and allow teachers to create their own customized assessments.

Effective integration of drill and practice software into the music curriculum depends on the grade level and the type of classroom environment. For example, using drill and practice software in a general music classroom at the elementary level can be effective depending on how it is used. In a One-Computer Classroom with an interactive whiteboard, a teacher could use the software to assess their student's understanding of note names by showing the exercise on the screen and having students respond by raising their hands and speaking the answer. Activities like this may make these concepts more exciting for the students— especially if it is framed as a game. In a performance-based classroom at the middle school level, drill and practice software might be used to reinforce theory concepts during group lessons or sectionals. Students could be asked to complete theory exercises individually over the course of a few lessons—especially those students who find the concepts difficult to grasp. In a high school music theory course, drill and practice software can be used as an assessment device throughout the year. Teachers can assign each student a certain number of exercises that must be completed during the course. Quizzes and tests can also be generated using many of these titles, and those results can be stored directly over the network to the teacher's computer.

Tutorial Software
Software in this category often features drill and practice exercises similar to those mentioned above but also includes instructional material and lessons that can serve as a self-guiding course for the students. Teachers need to decide whether or not the instruction contained on the software should replace traditional

teaching. While the lessons included on the software are often very comprehensive, there may be fundamental differences between the pedagogical approach employed by the software and the approach of the teacher. Teachers can use titles from this category as supplemental materials to reinforce concepts already taught, or to serve as differentiated instruction tools for those students who are either beginners or advanced students. These titles include: Alfred's *Essentials of Music Theory Volumes 1–3* (Hybrid), Sibelius *Instruments* (Hybrid), *Music Ace Maestro* (Hybrid), and eMedia's *Piano and Keyboard Method* (Hybrid). Each of these titles features comprehensive lessons covering most of the fundamentals of music, impressive animations and graphics, high quality audio examples, customization features as well as game-like assessment devices similar to those in the drill and practice category. Each title is specifically targeted to a certain age level; so be sure to select software that is age appropriate.

Possibilities for effective integration into the music curriculum are similar to those mentioned for drill and practice software. Again, teachers can select one lesson or game to use with their class that helps to reinforce any concept that is being taught. In some cases, the teacher might prefer to have the software explain the concept to the class and then use the appropriate assessment exercise check for understanding. In a performance-based classroom, students can use titles from this category to either sharpen their theory skills or to learn new concepts.

Creativity Software

The creativity category of CAI software titles available includes programs that specifically target the exploration of composition and student creativity. These titles differ from notation programs in that they combine drill and practice exercises, multimedia lessons, interactive games, and opportunities for students to compose in an environment that does not include traditional notation. Software titles in this category include the following: Sibelius *Groovy* (Hybrid), Sibelius *Compass* and *Compass Tracker* (Hybrid), *Making Music* and *Making More Music* (Hybrid). Curricular integration strategies for this category centers mainly on the general music classroom setting for elementary and middle schools and music theory or music appreciation courses at the high school level. In these settings, it is preferable to have enough copies of the software for the students to use it on an individual basis, but a creative teacher can adapt their lessons to incorporate the software using the One-Computer Classroom model discussed earlier. Students can create class compositions, and the many games and activities included can be completed as a class.

The MENC National Standards in Music Education specifically require all students to be able to compose or arrange music within specified guidelines. MENC has published *Strategies for Teaching: Technology* as a guide for how to implement each of the nine National Standards in Music, including composition. Utilizing these software titles allows students who do not have strong music theory skills to compose music. By utilizing concepts like iconic notation, students can manipulate music in a variety of environments that encourage creativity.

Most of these titles use concepts such as using shapes and different colors to create different timbres and melodic motives. Sibelius *Compass* is geared more toward middle and high school students and includes more advanced exercises that can be tied directly to scores within the notation program by Sibelius. This bridge from iconic notation to traditional notation is a powerful tool for any music teacher incorporating composition into their general music classes. Fostering and facilitating student creativity is one of the major strengths of music technology (Rudolph, 2004). Effectively utilizing software titles from this category can greatly enhance any music program.

Assistive Technologies for Special Learners

The final category of CAI software titles also includes hardware that can create successful music-making experiences for students with special needs. Recent advances in technology have created some wonderful ways for students to make music that may not have been possible in the past. These technologies include *Dancing Dots* (Hybrid) software that converts standard music notation to Braille for students who are blind or visually impaired; *Sibelius Speaking* (Hybrid) that allows blind or visually impaired composers to utilize a MIDI keyboard and a computer keyboard to input music into *Sibelius* with the aid of a software program that uses a computerized voice that speaks the chosen commands, and a hardware device called *SoundBeam* that converts body movement to sound. The *SoundBeam* device has been found to be very effective with students who are either autistic or severely physically disabled. In addition to these technologies, strides have been made in adaptive technologies that allow students with physical disabilities to play traditional instruments. Assistive technology can afford students the opportunity to fully participate in a traditional music program.

Online Resources

The Internet is one of the fastest growing resources for music educators (Rudolph, 2004), with web sites serving in a number of different capacities: resources for research, preparation, and lesson plans; online music educator communities; showcases for student compositions; archives for sheet music and MIDI files that can be converted to notation files; and web sites for use in the music classroom. Many symphony orchestras have created web sites that teach students about the instruments of the orchestra, biographical information about famous composers, basic principles of orchestration, form, and highlight the repertoire that an orchestra might play at a young people's concert. Many university programs are turning to the Internet to deliver online music courses and even online degrees. As mentioned above, software programs like *Flash* have made it possible to create interactive online content that can be used in similar ways to the CAI titles already discussed.

The interactivity of the online experience greatly increased during the first decade of the 21st century to what many refer to as Web 2.0. This term can be defined as the shift from users being passive readers of content to active publishers of content. Blogs, podcasts, wikis, instant messaging services, and social networking sites have created a space for Internet users to publish anything and everything. Web sites such as *MySpace* and *Facebook* have hundreds of millions of users worldwide, each sharing aspects of their personal lives. Blogs allow users to post their viewpoints on issues and allow readers to comment. This discourse can have great implications for music education. Teachers at the K-12 and university levels can have their students respond to questions outside of class time, ranging from critiques about musical examples played during class to discussion questions from a course textbook. Podcasts allow teachers to record their lessons for their students to listen to outside of class time, and allow students to present projects in a whole new medium. Wikis allow users to edit online content. Although there has been great debate about the efficacy of sites such as *Wikipedia*, a powerful opportunity for learning can be having students research and edit musical entries. Cooperative learning opportunities can also be enhanced using wikis as groups of students can work on a project simultaneously using sites such as Google docs. Instant messaging services that incorporate audio and video, such as *iChat* and *Skype*, can have great implications for distance learning and for bringing content area experts directly into the classroom. University level teachers can have virtual office hours by communicating with students using these services. Students in rural areas can take lessons online with an instructor who lives a few states away. Finally, social networking sites that are specifically set up for educators, such as *NING*, can use the typical functions of one of these sites to create an online class community where students can connect to discuss issues concerning the class. The functionality of Web 2.0 has tremendous potential for education in general and its role will certainly grow in the near future.

MUSIC PRODUCTION SOFTWARE

In addition to the numerous software titles in the CAI category, music instruction can be enhanced by music production software. Software in this category would fall under what Rudolph (2004) calls *tools*. These tools enable users to edit, create, notate, and record music in a variety of ways. There are three type of music production software: sequencing, notation, and audio editing software. Sequencing and notation software programs have been around since the earliest days of music software, and the improvements made over the past twenty years have been substantial—including the ability to incorporate digital audio and video. Digital audio editing software is a more recent addition as audio files typically require a large amount of memory to store and edit. Modern computer hard drives are exponentially larger than ten years ago, and this increase in computer RAM and ROM has facilitated the growth in digital audio editing software market (Watson, 2005).

Music production software can be incorporated into a music curriculum in a number of ways including: creating original compositions; writing customized arrangements for any performing ensemble; recording individual student and ensemble rehearsals and performances for critique and assessment; creating accompaniments for classroom or performance ensemble use; creating listening examples; and many other projects that involve the recording and creation of music. The following illustrates how each aspect of music production software could be incorporated into a music curriculum.

Sequencing Software

Music sequencers simply sequence musical events over time. Those events include a pitch being played by a certain instrument for a certain length of time, dynamic and tempo changes, recording audio, and playing external digital audio files. Sequencers capture both live performances and musical information that has been inputted using a mouse. A typical interface for a sequencer resembles a multitrack tape recorder. Each track can record an instrumental or vocal performance. Users can then add effects, transpose, change the timbre, adjust the volume, and edit the performance. Sequencers have varying amounts of tracks available, depending on the available memory and the sequencing software being used. Once a performance has been captured, sequencers can save the files as MIDI files or audio files that can then be transferred to CD burning software programs.

As a teaching tool, sequencers can be utilized in a variety of ways in a music classroom. One of the most common uses for a sequencer is when it is used as an accompanist for a performing ensemble. Teachers can input the sheet music and orchestrate it any way they want. In the vocal music-setting, individual voice parts can be brought out by increasing the track volume, different versions (including one where the melody played and one without) can be created easily by muting the desired track, accompaniment tapes can be made for students to take home to practice, and the final version can be played while the director focuses on conducting rather than accompanying. In the instrumental music setting, many of the same concepts from the vocal music setting can be used, including making accompaniment CDs for their students to take home to practice. Most sequencers also have audio recording capabilities. This feature allows teachers to make recordings of rehearsals and performances directly to the hard drive of the computer for assessment and CD creation. In the general music setting, sequencers can be used to facilitate student composition. Loop-based sequencers allow nonmusic students to employ short audio and MIDI clips to create new works by layering them and adding their own tracks. Teachers can use a variety of prompts to inspire composition, including visual images, stories and poems, current events, and movies. Students can record themselves singing assigned songs over imported MIDI files for assessment. Students can use MIDI keyboards with sequencers to record themselves performing simple melodies and songs on the keyboard. Students can create podcasts on a variety of topics for posting on *iTunes* or the school web site. Teachers can create listening guides to masterworks that include visual images and video clips.

As an example of one of these projects, teachers can have their students research a given week in musical history and then create a podcast that highlights the events that happened during that week. Called "This Week In Music" students are assigned some web resources where they can find reliable information about music history that is presented in a calendar fashion. Using those resources the students then write a script that includes the events in musical history from their assigned week and gather multimedia examples (including images, video clips, and audio examples) that help to illustrate their podcasts. Using sequencing software that includes video integration, students then compile their podcasts and present them during their assigned week. The teacher can create a podcasting web site (using either district hosting services or one of many free podcast hosting sites on the Internet) where student work can be posted.

Notation Software

Notation software allows users to compose, arrange, transcribe, and edit music. It also allows users to scan in already published sheet music and to download MIDI files to convert them to notated scores. Once in the notation program, users can edit, transpose, simplify, and arrange that music for performance. Notation software affords teachers and students the opportunity to print out high-quality scores for live performance.

There are two major companies that produce notation software: MakeMusic— the creators of *Finale* and the family of *Finale* notation software titles, and *Sibelius*. Both products are extremely useful in the classroom. *Finale* has a number of scaled-down versions of the software including *PrintMusic*, *Allegro*, and *NotePad*. *Sibelius* also has a student version of the software. In addition, both programs have the capability of producing worksheets for students.

There are many ways to use notation software in the music classroom. In the performance-based music class, teachers can not only compose and arrange music for their ensembles but can also create warm-up exercises, theory worksheets, listening examples, ear training exercises, accompaniments, and using the HTML file saving capabilities teachers can create all of these materials for an online environment. Students in these performance ensembles should be encouraged to write for the ensemble as well. Assigning a Bach chorale for every student to arrange for the band, chorus, or orchestra will give them an opportunity to think about orchestration, balance, dynamics, texture, and range. In the general music classroom, notation software affords students the opportunity to compose music within specified guidelines. Teaching the fundamentals of music can be made more meaningful by having the students apply their knowledge by completing short exercises with notation software. Instead of teaching about two-part inventions, have the students write them. If you are teaching major and minor triads, have the students create short compositions that utilize both. If you are teaching students about theme and variations, have them compose simple variations on a well-known tune. Form a "Young Composers Club," and teach interested students about the process of composition. There are many ways to incorporate notation software into a music curriculum. The ideas listed above are intended to illustrate some of them and inspire others.

Audio Editing Software

The third category of music production software is primarily for teacher use but can be utilized by students in certain settings. Audio editing software is intended for use with recording and editing live performances—although existing digital music files can also be imported for editing. digital audio workstations (DAW) can be either software- or hardware-based, or a combination of the two. Software-based DAWs usually consist of a computer running audio editing software, an audio interface device that allows users to convert analog audio signals (microphones, electronic instruments) to digital data, microphones, and a CD burner. Hardware-based DAWs are stand-alone units that allow users to record multiple tracks of audio simultaneously. These stand-alone DAWs also have many of the same editing capabilities as audio editing software. Using hardware- and software-based DAWs in combination allows users to record performances using hardware and then edit those performances on the computer. DAWs have a variety of different features—some are intended for use with a computer and some are complete stand-alone recorders. Because many of the hardware-based DAWs are expensive in comparison to their software-based counterparts, teachers should closely examine these units and the features they need to successfully integrate digital audio into their curriculum.

Audio editing software can be integrated into a music curriculum in a variety of ways. First, portfolio assessment can be facilitated with audio editing software. Teachers can record performances of their students and burn them to a CD so that students can have a record of their progress. Audio editing software allows teachers to select only certain passages from performances for inclusion on the CD. This means that a teacher can record an entire lesson, with multiple student performances, and then break the recording up into smaller segments containing each individual student performance. These segments can then be stored in a folder created for each student, and can be compiled at a later date for burning. At the high school level, students can compile their work throughout their high school years and include recordings of required audition pieces when auditioning for college music programs. Second, audio editing software allows teachers to create CDs containing listening examples for critique and analysis. Audio editing software can import recordings from CDs or audio files obtained on the Internet. These audio files can then be edited so that small selections of the imported audio can be taken from the original recording for inclusion on a listening example CD. Third, audio editing software can be a tool for creativity for the students. Loop-based compositions and sampling are a major part of the popular music culture. Many hip-hop and rap artists use the same audio editing software titles mentioned above. Students can create compositions that sound remarkably similar to their favorite music. This musical connection can be a powerful learning experience for both students and teachers. Finally, there are examples of how music programs have integrated digital audio recording into their curriculum—creating student-run record labels at the high school level that produce high quality recordings of student ensembles. The knowledge and skills obtained using the software and hardware are often transferable to future employment opportunities in the music industry (Williams & Webster, 2006).

An example of a project where students are asked to create loop-based compositions could include a film-scoring lesson where students are given a short film clip to write a script for as well as the musical scoring. Another idea might be to have the students create a commercial jingle for a fictitious product or service—perhaps as an interdisciplinary lesson with either a language arts teacher or a video technology teacher. And yet another project idea would be to create a soundtrack for a video game. There are many video clips available online from popular video games. Students could use the loops from the software to create their own music, as well as create original compositions and loops that could be incorporated into the project.

NEW INSTRUMENTS

Electronic musical instruments come in all shapes and sizes, each with different functions and purposes. These instruments include electronic keyboards, synthesizers, and many various types of controllers. Controllers don't produce sound themselves—they trigger sounds from an external MIDI synthesizer. Types of controllers include the following: keyboard, wind, percussion, mallet, guitar, hand chimes, and orchestral controllers. A more recent category of electronic music instrument is not a physical instrument at all. Virtual instruments are software-based synthesizer that can be programmed and triggered using either sequencers or external controllers. These virtual instruments take up only hard drive space thereby eliminating the need for obtaining rack-mounted synthesizers to expand a musician's sound palette. Many vintage synthesizer sounds are now available as virtual instruments as well as newer synthesizers. The seamless integration of virtual instruments into many of the music production software titles available makes the days of owning multiple keyboards unnecessary. Music technology workstations need only one keyboard for note entry. It is a matter of personal preference in selecting a keyboard for a music technology workstation. An inexpensive MIDI controller can be just as useful as expensive synthesizer—it is truly a matter of taste.

Electronic Keyboards and Synthesizers

When used effectively, electronic keyboards and synthesizers can be invaluable teaching tools for music educators (Rudolph, 2004). In most music technology labs, MIDI keyboards are the instruments of choice. The terms electronic keyboards and synthesizers are essentially synonymous. Electronic keyboards can be defined as a keyboard instrument that requires electricity to produce a sound—including digital pianos. Synthesizers can be defined as electronic keyboards that re-create the sounds of acoustic instruments as well as create new sounds. For the music technology lab setting, both electronic keyboards and synthesizers are used equally.

When selecting a keyboard, there are a number of features to consider before determining which model is appropriate for your needs. Important features include: General MIDI compatibility (an industry standard set of 128 sounds), type of MIDI interface (USB or MIDI), quality of the sounds, polyphony (number of voices at a given time), number of keys (typically ranging from 25 to 88), whether the keys are weighted, touch-sensitivity, audio output/input options, programmability, and others. For most classroom settings, a basic 61 key General MIDI synthesizer with good sounds and a MIDI interface is acceptable. Higher end synthesizers often include onboard workstations that allow users to create sequences directly into the memory of the keyboard. Some synthesizer models also include digital audio inputs that allow for sampling and advanced synthesis features. If the primary use of the music technology lab is for piano instruction, teachers should consider utilizing digital pianos that closely resemble the feel and sound of an acoustic piano.

Electronic keyboards and synthesizers can be integrated into a music curriculum in a variety of ways. As stand-alone instruments, keyboards can be utilized in performance ensembles such as band and orchestra to perform parts from a score where there is no one playing the part. Utilizing piano players in band and orchestra affords students an opportunity to perform in an ensemble. In addition, there are many examples of MIDI ensembles at the high school and university level that perform music specifically written for them. While it may not be feasible to disassemble a music technology lab to perform with the synthesizers on stage, MIDI ensembles can include student instruments brought in from home, various types of controllers, and school-owned synthesizers purchased specifically for the ensemble. Outside of the performance setting, keyboards are commonly used in music technology labs as input devices for sequencing and notation software programs. They can also be used to teach students piano skills.

Why electronic keyboards and synthesizers over acoustic pianos? In a classroom or group instruction setting, it is impractical to teach multiple students simultaneously as it is extremely difficult to hear each individual student while others are playing. Because electronic keyboards and synthesizers require amplification to be heard, teachers can incorporate the audio signals of these instruments into a networked keyboard lab setting as described earlier in this chapter.

Controllers

The most common type of controller is the keyboard controller. There are three major advantages of utilizing keyboard controllers over synthesizers: they are less expensive; they are portable; and they typically require less desktop space. In addition, keyboard controllers that are USB ready can be connected to a computer with a USB cable and eliminate the need to purchase a MIDI interface device (many synthesizers are also USB ready). Disadvantages include the fact that keyboard controllers do not make any sound on their own and that there is often less control over editing sounds than with a synthesizer.

There are two types of wind controllers: electronic wind instruments (EWIs) that employ woodwind fingering systems and are played with a virtual reed, and electronic valve instruments (EVIs) that employ the brass fingering system and a reed-like mouthpiece. EWIs and EVIs trigger external synthesizers. Musicians can select any timbre on the synthesizer to perform with. Wind velocity controls the volume on both types of wind controllers, and there are pitch bend and modulation wheels to create a more human-like performance. Wind controllers are not as common in school settings as keyboard controllers and are rarely used in a lab setting (Williams & Webster, 2006). Some possible advantages of using wind controllers over traditional wind instruments include the fact that wind controllers do not have intonation issues; they are more affordable than traditional acoustic instruments, and wind controllers can play an infinite number of different timbres. Some might argue, however, that wind controllers are not a substitute to acoustic instruments and should not replace them in a performance or classroom setting.

Percussion controllers include electronic drum sets, drum pads, and mallet-like instruments. Like their wind controller counterparts, percussion controllers trigger external synthesizers, and performance techniques create variations in the instruments sound. The velocity that the musician strikes the instrument with controls the volume. Individual drum pads can be programmed to trigger different timbres. For example, a pad designated as a snare drum can have a rim shot programmed into the outer edge of the pad. Percussion controllers can either emulate traditional percussion instruments or can be used to trigger short melodic sequences and chord progressions. Both EWIs and electronic drum sets were very popular with bands in the 1980s but fell out of favor during the 1990s. They are making resurgence in the early 21st century as instruments in MIDI ensembles, and advances in technology might encourage teachers to consider their inclusion in traditional performing ensembles as well (Watson, 2005).

Other types of controllers include guitar, hand chime, and orchestral instrument controllers. Each of these controllers is very similar to wind and percussion controllers in that they use the structure of a traditional instrument as a means to trigger external synthesizers. Their use in the music education setting is less common than wind and percussion controllers, although their inclusion in any performance ensemble is possible.

Virtual Instruments

Virtual instruments have been around for quite some time. Both Macintosh and Windows operating systems are equipped with virtual instruments—Macintosh utilizes *QuickTime Musical Instruments,* and Windows utilizes Microsoft's *GS Wavetable SW Synthesizer* (Watson, 2005). These software-based sounds allow these operating systems to playback MIDI files. More recently, with the advent of large capacity hard drives, synthesizer manufacturers are selling virtual equivalents of their hardware-based products. These virtual synthesizers are fully functioning instruments that can be manipulated with a mouse and triggered with a USB keyboard controller, external synthesizer, or a sequencing or notation program. Virtual synthesizers (softsynths) come in a variety of proprietary plug-in formats allowing specific music production software titles to use certain softsynths. Not all softsynths are compatible.

From a curricular integration standpoint, virtual instruments significantly improve the playback of notation files and significantly broaden the sound palette available for composition using sequencers. In a music technology lab with limited space, virtual synthesizers can be used with USB keyboard controllers instead of hardware-based synthesizers. For labs that already have hardware-based synthesizers, virtual synthesizers can serve as an additional source of high-quality sounds for the playback of notation files (that typically do not use hardware-based synthesizers) and sequencer files.

NEW MEDIA—NEW DIRECTIONS

The first years of the 21st Century have raised some complex issues and questions about the way we listen to and obtain music. When compact discs were first brought to the market in 1982, the amount of information held on one CD was more than most computer hard drives could store. Record companies could not imagine the changes that the digital music revolution would bring to their industry only twenty years later. With early peer-to-peer file sharing services such as *Napster*, computer users were able to upload entire CDs on to their computer and share those files with anyone. Faster modem speeds made it possible to download an entire CD in less than a minute—and individual tracks in seconds. With compression formats such as MP3s, AAC, and WAV, music can be compressed into much smaller file sizes than the AIFF format used by CDs.

The actions of P2P file sharing service users violate copyright law. Users do not pay for the files they download—making their actions equivalent to theft—punishable by up to $250,000 in fines and five years in prison for first-time offenders (Lessig, 2004). The Recording Industry Association of America (RIAA) has made the prosecution of users who download music illegally a top priority, having filed over 8,000 lawsuits since 2003. The public dismantling of the original *Napster* in 2001 did little to deter online P2P file sharing services like *LimeWire* and *KaZaa* from continuing to operate.

Legal music downloading sites such as the Apple *iTunes Music Store* are demonstrating how people are now obtaining their music—the *iTunes Music Store* has sold billions of songs on their service since being launched in April of 2003. Music playback devices such as the *iPod* are now able to play television shows and movies in addition to music files. This recent advance in technology, along with video sharing web sites like *Google Video* and *YouTube*, has many network television and film studios rethinking the future of content delivery. The coming of *Internet II* and widespread broadband access will enable high-speed content delivery—making it possible for all known media to eventually converge for web delivery (Kusek & Leonhard, 2005). These advances in technology will certainly have an impact on the way one thinks about music in the future.

Teacher Training

Students in classrooms today are often more tech-savvy than their teachers (Bobowick, 2001). One of the biggest obstacles for the effective integration of technology in education is the need for professional development (Cuban, 2001). Music teachers often cite the lack of adequate and effective training as a reason for not integrating technology into their curriculum (Jassmann, 2004). Reninger (2000) points out that while the technology available to music educators can greatly enhance instruction, little good will come of it if they don't feel comfortable using it. Lowther, Jones and Plants (2000) found that most of today's teacher education programs do not meet the standards set by the International Society of Technology in Education (ISTE) and the National Council for Accreditation of Teacher Education.

Professional organizations such as the Technology Institute for Music Educators (TI:ME) and the Association for Music Technology Instruction (ATMI) are dedicated to training teachers and researching methods for improving technology use in the music classroom. While TI:ME is targeted primarily toward K-12 music teachers, ATMI serves the collegiate community, focusing on the investigation of technology as a pedagogical tool and its impact on music learning.

CONCLUSION

Music technology, when used effectively, can have a tremendous impact on the way students learn about music. Students in the 21st century are "wired" to technology in a way that their teachers simply did not experience as students themselves. Cell phones, text messaging, blogging, online chat rooms, video games, iPods, and networking web sites like MySpace are changing the way students communicate and learn. While traditional teaching methods are certainly valuable, adapting those methods to meet the learning styles of the "wired" student in our classroom can yield very positive results. Music technology hardware and software, in the hands of a creative and well-trained teacher, have the potential to foster student creativity in ways unachievable in the past. Today, students can create musical scores to selected film clips; create podcasts about musical concepts that can be shared with the world; create loop-based compositions with software that allows nonmusicians to have successful music-making experiences; have access to any piece of music in the public domain in a variety of file formats for appreciation, analysis, or arrangement; and learn about musical concepts in a multimedia format that relates to the way they experience information outside of the classroom environment. In addition, with the widespread success of video games such as Guitar Hero and RockBand, teachers should look for ways to incorporate the functionalities of these games to teach fundamental music concepts. Students' interest in music is stronger than ever; technology can facilitate music-making experiences in a classroom setting that take advantage of the learning styles of the "wired" students.

As Rudolph (2004) states, "computers and computer-controlled instruments are the crayons for music class" (p. 6). They afford students music-making opportunities in a way similar to when young children color with crayons. The process of drawing and coloring with crayons can be an art-making experience with no wrong answers. When young children color, they are exploring their creativity. Notation and sequencing software can be used as "sketch pads" for a student's musical ideas—a place where "wrong answers" can create opportunities for learning. Why does my music sound the way it does? What would happen if I changed the chord in this measure? What if a different instrument played this melody? How can I make music that sounds like Bach? These questions, and the lessons that can be learned from them are powerful creative experiences—experiences that can be greatly enhanced by music technology.

Class Discussion

1. What might be the role of music technology in the traditional performance ensemble (band, chorus, orchestra)? Do electronic instruments have a place in a traditional performance ensemble?

2. What are the implications for urban schools with regard to music technology? In your opinion, is the *Digital Divide* getting larger when it comes to the integration of technology into urban school music programs compared to their suburban counterparts?

3. Are there certain musical skills and/or understandings better developed with technology than without technology?

4. Do video games such as *Guitar Hero* and *Rock Band* have a place in a music classroom?

Projects

1. Visit a nearby music classroom that uses technology. What hardware are they using? What software are they using? Observe students using the technology. What kinds of musical skills and understandings are they developing? How would you describe the role of the teacher? Write a brief report summarizing your visit.

2. Consider a music teaching circumstance in an elementary or secondary school. Select two pieces of software for developing a particular music skill or understanding that you are interested in. Tryout the software. Find reviews of the software online or in print. Compare and contrast the software considering how effective each will be in developing the skill or understanding you initially identified with the level of students you selected.

3. Develop a plan to increase the music technology resources at your school. First, identify the musical goals you hope to accomplish with your plan. List the hardware and software necessary to help your students meet the musical goals. Find out the costs for the resources and develop a strategy for purchasing the technology resources over several years.

SUGGESTED READINGS

Cuban, L. (2001). *Oversold and underused: Computers in the classroom*. Cambridge, MA: Harvard University Press.

Rudolph, T. E. (2004). *Teaching music with technology (2nd Edition)* Chicago: GIA Publications.

Watson, S. (Ed). (2005). *Technology Guide for Music Educators*. Belmont, CA: Thomson Higher Education.

Williams, D. B., Webster, P. R. (2006). *Experiencing Music Technology (3rd Edition)*. Belmont, CA: Thomson Higher Education.

CHAPTER 12

~

Issues Facing Music Teacher Education in the 21st Century: Developing Leaders in the Field

Colleen Conway

INTRODUCTION

In 1987, MENC published the document *Music Teacher Education: Partnership and Process* that was the report of a task force on music teacher education. The report discussed the following: (a) recruitment, selection, and retention of music teachers; (b) design and structure of music teacher certification programs; and (c) professional development of the music teacher. The introduction to the teacher certification section suggests: "A partnership of music professors, music education professors, and school music educators clearly provides the key to a successful program in music teacher certification" (p. 29). The authors challenged all members of the partnership at the time to "...declare our commitment to this process and reach out to other members of the partnership" (p. 55).

When Colwell edited the first *Handbook of Research on Music Teaching and Learning* in 1992 there was just one chapter in the book that addressed issues of teacher education (Verrastro & Leglar, 1992). Verrastro and Leglar suggested that although some research had been done in the 70s and 80s, the body of research in music teacher education had little focus: "The establishment of a clearinghouse for research in teacher training would make a lasting contribution to the profession. An effort is needed to establish research priorities in order to build a coherent body of knowledge about the questions deemed most vital" (p. 691). In *The New Handbook of Research on Music Teaching and Learning* (Colwell & Richardson, 2002), Liz Wing and Janet Barrett edited a complete section of the book that included eight chapters devoted to issues of teacher education. Each chapter in the *Handbook* was coauthored with a researcher from general teacher education. However, only some of the research discussed in these chapters comes from music teacher education. This resource does serve as an introduction to the larger field of research in teacher education and served as somewhat of a springboard for a more focused research agenda in music teacher education. Music teacher education has seen considerable attention from researchers and policy-makers since *No Child Left Behind in 2003* (Conway, Albert, Hibbard, & Hourigan, 2005). However, even with this deepened level of research and scholarship, the issues surrounding entry to the music education profession, preparation of music teachers at the preservice level, and support of music teachers at the in-service level, continue to challenge the profession.

The goal of this chapter is to outline the major challenges in music teacher education and suggest ways in which P-12 teachers can collaborate with teacher educators to affect positive change. I begin by describing the research and policy context for music teacher education giving special attention to recent national initiatives. I then examine the important role of the P-12 music teacher in the recruitment of music education majors into the preservice program. The middle section of the chapter addresses preservice music teacher education including the following: general issues in music teacher education; observation of teaching with a teacher's lens; preservice fieldwork; music education methods courses; student teaching; and alternative certification models. Throughout this section I highlight the importance of P-12 teachers as role models, cooperating teachers and visitors to music education classes. I conclude the chapter with a consideration of the challenges experienced by music teachers in the first years of teaching and suggest that in-service music teachers are important links in the teacher education process as they advise and mentor these new teachers in informal and formal ways.

MUSIC TEACHER EDUCATION RESEARCH CONTEXT

There are several organizations within music education that direct their attention to the development of the preservice music teacher and issues concerning music teacher education overall. The Society for Music Teacher Education (SMTE) was founded in 1982, and its membership includes all higher education members in MENC—The National Association for Music Education (http://smte. us). The *Journal of Music Teacher Education* (begun in 1990) publishes much of the work of the Society. Since 2005, SMTE has become active in studying teacher education, presenting best practices in teacher education, and setting agendas for research. The first SMTE Symposium was held in 2005. At that first meeting the organization developed a variety of smaller teams of scholars and researchers. Figure 12.1 includes the SMTE Areas of Strategic Planning and Action (ASPA). SMTE group members meet at National MENC meetings as well as at a SMTE Symposium every other year.

General music teacher educators have met since 1991 at the Mountain Lake Colloquia held every other year in West Virginia. Years of discussion and collaboration have led to the publication of a journal called the Mountain Lake Reader associated with the Colloquia. Members of this group focus their time together on the sharing of research and experiences on the teaching of elementary and secondary general music methods courses. More information regarding Mountain Lake is available at http://www.mtsu.edu/%7Enboone/index.html

Teacher Recruitment
Assessment and Alignment
Preservice Teacher Development
Restructuring the Curriculum
Cultural Diversity in Music Teacher Education
School and University Partnerships
Policy and Association Partnerships
Professional Development for the Beginning Music Teacher
Professional Development for the Experienced Teacher
Teacher Retention
Preparing Music Teacher Educators and Supporting Current Music Teacher Educators
Alternative Licensure

Figure 12.1 SMTE Areas of Strategic Planning and Action.

Instrumental music teacher educators met at the first Instrumental Music Teacher Educators (IMTE) retreat in Deer Creek, Ohio, in 2005 and also continue to meet every other year. The most recent Call for Proposals for the retreat outlines the following topics of interest to the organization:

- Student-centered instruction
- Developing comprehensive musical understandings in every student
- Changing the culture of instrumental music education
- The importance of the teaching/learning process in a product-driven profession
- Lifelong musical participation
- Increasing the influence of instrumental music education methods instruction/instructors
- Defining/describing pedagogical content knowledge in instrumental music teacher education
- Recruiting instrumental music teachers and instrumental music teacher educators
- The ongoing professional development of teachers in ways that move them beyond the traditional instrumental music education paradigm

For more information regarding IMTE see: http://imte.webhop.org.

There are several research organizations that devote their energies to teacher education in general. The largest division within the American Educational Research Association (AERA) is Division K—Teacher Education (http://www.aera.net/divisions). Members of AERA meet every year, and Division K meetings focus solely on issues of teacher education. The American Association of Colleges of Teacher Education (AACTE, http://www.aacte.org/) also meets annually to explore topics related to teacher education. AACTE publishes the *Journal of Teacher Education* (JTE, http://www.aacte.org/Publications/journal_teacher.aspx).

MUSIC TEACHER EDUCATION POLICY CONTEXT

AACTE (discussed above) was one of five organizations responsible for the founding of the National Council on the Accreditation of Teacher Education (NCATE, http://www.ncate.org). There are currently 632 colleges of education in the country accredited by NCATE. The primary accrediting organization for music education is the National Association of Schools of Music (NASM, http://nasm.arts-accredit.org). There are approximately 610 schools and departments of music accredited by NASM. Some music education programs must be accredited by both NASM and NCATE in addition to state-level licensure policies. Others may be NASM and not NCATE or may be part of any number of other smaller teacher education accrediting associations. NASM, NCATE (or another teacher education accrediting body), and state education departments represent the major policy stakeholders for preservice education. I turn now to ways in which the P-12 teacher can work to recruit music education majors into the profession.

RECRUITMENT OF MUSIC EDUCATION MAJORS INTO THE PRESERVICE PROGRAM

Most music teachers begin their development as teachers long before they ever enter into an undergraduate music education program. Some have known that they wanted to be music teachers since elementary school. Most of them have taught some private lessons and held leadership roles in their high school music programs as section leaders, drum majors, and peer teachers. Research tells us that music education majors regularly credit a music teacher from their past as their primary reason for majoring in music. Fredrickson and Burton (2005) suggest that "Current music teachers may be the best recruiters the profession has. They exert a great deal of influence that could positively affect the recruiting of future music teachers (Bergee, Coffman, Demorest, Humphreys, & Thornton, (2001)" (pp. 30–31).

Music teachers are encouraged to promote the positive aspects of being a music teacher to their students. Music teachers lead such crazy and busy lives that middle school and high school students are not always made fully aware of the advantages of the music teacher career. The literature also states some concern that many of the current music education recruits come from well-established suburban large-ensemble programs and yet the high need in the music education job market is in urban and rural settings that often offer diverse courses in music. Attracting music education majors from diverse racial, socioeconomic, and geographical backgrounds is a challenge as well.

P-12 music teachers are encouraged to work with local Tri–M Chapters (the MENC organization for middle and high school students) to attract students into music education. Music teachers can also help incoming music education majors to be prepared for the comprehensive work of the degree. Encouraging study in piano, voice, sight-singing and aural skills, written theory, music history, composition, and improvisation will help the potential music student to succeed once they arrive on campus.

One final issue regarding "recruitment and retention" concerns what researchers refer to as the "apprenticeship of observation" (Lortie, 1975; Cochran-Smith, Feiman-Nemster, & McIntyre, 2008). Teachers enter into a preservice teacher preparation program after many years as students in P-12 music programs. The influence that P-12 music teachers have over the type of music teacher that a former student will "become" is substantial. Research suggests that the observations of teaching that teacher candidates have done previous to entering a teacher education program are at least as powerful as what is learned in coursework. The concept of the "apprenticeship of observation" highlights another important role of the P-12 educator in teacher education.

GENERAL ISSUES IN MUSIC TEACHER EDUCATION CURRICULUM

Once music education students arrive on campus, the biggest challenge in most certification programs is managing to fit all the coursework deemed necessary into the degree program along with general music requirements as well as general studies requirements. In many music education programs, coursework has been added as NASM, NCATE, and state regulations have required, but, very often little has been "taken away" from the curriculum. Most music education students take longer than four years or attend in the summers to complete the degree. Research on socialization of the preservice music student suggests that most music students experience a conflict of identity as they try to develop as a musician and a teacher simultaneously. The musician identity is more prevalent during the degree as applied lessons and small and large-ensemble preparation represent "immediate needs." The skills needed for success in music teaching (piano skills, aural skills, conducting, and pedagogy) are somewhat removed from the day-to-day life of the undergraduate student. Most music teacher education programs attempt to address this conflict by sequencing curricula so that students are in at least one music education course each semester. These courses often include observations of teaching as a way to highlight the importance of the music teacher skills.

Observation of Teaching with a Teacher's Lens

One of the most challenging times in the journey to become a teacher occurs early in the undergraduate experience as the music education student grapples with the comparison between what they are learning about teaching and what they think they already know. Feiman-Nemser (2001) suggests:

> The images and beliefs that prospective teachers bring to their preservice preparation serve as filters for making sense of the knowledge and experiences they

encounter. They may also function as barriers to change by limiting the ideas that teacher education students are able and willing to entertain...These taken-for-granted beliefs may mislead prospective teachers into thinking that they know more about teaching than they actually do and make it harder for them to form new ideas and new habits of thought and action. (p. 1016)

In addressing this concern, one of the most positive changes teacher education has seen in the past decades is a focus on getting music education students out to schools early in their teacher education experience. It was not uncommon even 15 years ago for the first experiences in schools for many music education students to be during student teaching. It is now common practice for freshmen and sophomore students to be required to observe music teaching and learning as well as do some limited fieldwork previous to the student teaching semester.

Fieldwork observations are often cited by beginning music teachers as both the most and the least valuable requirements in the music teacher education program. When observations are well structured and the music education students understand the goal of the observation, they suggest that getting in to schools early is an incredibly valuable aspect of preservice music education. However, many times, students are told to go to schools to do an observation with little preparation and beginning teachers cite these sorts of requirements as not valuable. One of the ways in which a P-12 teacher can collaborate with teacher educators at this juncture is by inviting underclass music education students into your classroom and helping them consider their own previous experience in relation to what they are seeing and hearing in your classroom.

Learning to view the classroom from the teacher's perspective is an important benchmark in the journey to become a teacher. Feiman-Nemser (2001) suggests:

The studying of teaching requires skills of observation, interpretation, and analysis. Preservice students can begin developing theses skills by analyzing samples of student work, comparing different curricular models, interviewing students to uncover their thinking, studying how different teachers work towards the same goals, and observing what impact their instruction has on students. Carried out in the company of others these activities can foster norms for professional discourse such as respect for evidence, openness to questions, valuing of alternative perspectives, a search for common understandings, and shared standards. (p. 1019)

P-12 music educators are encouraged to engage preservice student visitors in discussion about the observation, interpretation, and analysis of teaching. Logistics of observations within the already overloaded schedule of the University faculty member often results in the University faculty member not attending student observation fieldwork. P-12 teachers are needed at this phase to provide positive role models, to begin to speak to the preservice teacher as if they were a "teacher," and to encourage "thinking" like a teacher.

Preservice Fieldwork

Early fieldwork for preservice teachers can take many different forms. Student may go out to a school once a week for one or multiple semesters. They may do an extended experience where they are in a school for a full week or two. All students in a course may attend fieldwork together with their instructor or the student may go out to a school alone. There is no one "right" way to design these early fieldwork experiences. Faculty loads, student schedules, availability of local schools, and other resources affect the nature of field placements.

Students may teach a short portion of a lesson in a P-5 general music class or they may provide a warm-up for a large secondary ensemble. Very often, preservice fieldwork includes working with groups of children in sections or small ensembles. There is a delicate balance between fieldwork that provides good first teaching experiences and fieldwork that is a "trial by fire" approach to the profession. Owing to faculty loads, class sizes, and logistics, it is sometimes difficult for college and university faculty to get out to schools to observe preservice teachers in fieldwork, and without feedback the early fieldwork is not useful in helping the beginning teachers understand their role as the teacher. Thus, providing constructive feedback to music education interns is another role for the P-12 teacher in the teacher education "partnership."

Music educators have documented successful partnerships between P-12 schools and universities in a variety of diverse collaborations for fieldwork including professional development schools, service-learning models, immersion fieldwork, and fieldwork with diverse learners. In the "professional development school" model, a university professor and a P-12 teacher collaborate and share the teaching of both the P-12 students and the university students (Henry, 2001). In this type of fieldwork, the lines between University faculty and P-12 teachers become blurred and preservice students get to interact simultaneously with children, in-service teachers, and university professors.

In a "service-learning" model music education students provide music instruction in a school where there is no music program. The students and the university faculty member are the music program. "Immersion fieldwork" (Emmanuel, 2002) refers to placing students in a diverse setting for an extended time period during which they live in the community as well as teach. Hourigan (2007) examined the experiences of participants involved in fieldwork in self-contained special education classrooms. Music education researchers encourage fieldwork that fosters reflection and provides time for the beginning music teachers to interact with college professors and P-12 music teachers working with children. There is not a single "perfect" model of fieldwork, but we know that those empowered with assisting preservice students in their first work with children have an extremely important role in the process of teacher education.

Music Education Methods Courses

P-12 music teachers are often asked to teach, assist, or visit music education methods classes. In the next section, we focus on some of the issues inherent in

Teaching music in higher education (Conway & Hodgman, 2009) so as to help P-12 teachers in their roles as teachers, assistants, or visitors to a methods class. In designing music education methods classes, educators need to be informed by the research in adult learning styles. Attention needs to be given to designing small group/cooperative learning projects and discussion and problem-solving activities in the effort to encourage reflection. Music education students need to learn to reflect "in" and "on" (Schon, 1983, 1987) the action in music classrooms, and they must consider multiple strategies for solving classroom dilemmas. Questioning techniques need to be practiced by methods instructors and skills for facilitating classroom dialogue explored. Students need to feel that they are learning in a "safe" environment. In order to accomplish this, methods class instructors need to encourage students to disagree and state their feelings and opinions openly in class. Methods courses are so "jam packed" with content that it is often difficult to remember that adult learners need these interactive strategies and that lectures or stories of "what has worked in the past" are less useful in these courses.

Student journals have been shown to encourage the learning of reflective thinking skills when used in preservice methods courses. In addition, the use of case studies, role plays, and simulations are recommended as instructional techniques for the music methods course instructor. Reflection is different for every student; thus, attention to individualized instruction based on a student's prior knowledge, experience, and interests is suggested in the literature.

More frequent testing (as opposed to a midterm and final only) and the use of alternative grading procedures (portfolios, teaching demonstrations, interviews, projects, presentations) will provide a methods course atmosphere more conducive to the learning of reflective thinking skills. The assessment procedures used by the methods instructor will affect the student's perception of "safe environment" in the class as well as the type of thinking he/she uses to complete the course work.

In order for reflection to occur, a methods course must provide a place where a student can discover, share, discuss, and recognize the influence of his/her prior knowledge and experience in music on his/her teaching orientation. If the development of reflective thinking skills is a desirable outcome in teacher education, then the methods instructor must model these processes.

Student Teaching

Student teaching has been documented as the most valuable component of the teacher education process. Beginning music teachers often state they learned more in student teaching than in any other time in teacher education. This research finding supports the important role of the P-12 teacher in the process of teacher education. Although it is impossible to generalize needs and characteristics of all student teachers, there are some common themes that arise when thinking about music student teachers. It is often difficult for the student teacher to think broadly beyond the setting they are working in. It may seem as if they want the cooperating teacher to tell them "how to do it." Cooperating teachers can help the student teacher to think beyond the given context by asking the student teacher questions and avoiding "telling" them how to teach or what to do. Most music student teachers are nervous, but also excited and curious. If the cooperating teacher recognizes the need for building confidence early in the experience and understands that student teachers need assistance in planning lessons, choosing scores and managing a class, the student teacher will get through the nerves and begin to grow. Co-op teachers should see the student teaching time period as a process that starts slowly (working with small groups of students, or teaching 4–5 minute sections of a lesson) and then gradually increases in responsibility until at the end of the experience the student teacher is teaching most of the lessons. Some student teachers will succeed with a "throw them to the wolves" approach but most learn best when the process is gradual.

It is important to have open lines of communication between the co-op teacher and the university supervisor regarding the student and the placement details. It is also important for the co-op to remember that the student teacher needs to have positive interactions with you as well as the university supervisor. Regarding this phenomena, Podsen and Denmark (2000) suggest:

> They [student teachers] find themselves in unfamiliar territory faced with two taskmasters-you, the cooperating teacher, and their college supervisor. Even under the best circumstances, student interns constantly question their ability to successfully complete the experience, asking such questions as: "How can I make my cooperating teacher happy? What am I expected to do? Will I get a good recommendation from my mentor teacher? How can I get all of my coursework done and still plan and teach lessons? Is my college supervisor satisfied with my progress? What happens if I don't do well? Will I still be able to graduate?" Depending on the intern's confidence level and current skills, and the consistency among the taskmasters, these questions get answered or they multiply. (p. xvi)

It is important for the profession to view student teaching as a "spot" on the continuum of learning to teach and not as the "end point." Teachers learn to teach once they have students of their own. Student teaching is an important benchmark in the process of becoming but not the "end" of the process.

In one of my recent beginning teachers studies (Conway, Micheel-Mays, & Micheel Mays, 2006) we compared the stages and struggles of student teaching to the stages and struggles of the first year in order to get a better sense of the transition between these two phases of the developmental continuum. The most disturbing finding in this study was that both the student teacher and beginning teacher data included concern about teacher "voice." Both teachers felt as if their ideas and opinions were not valued by others, and they articulated this feeling in the study. This issue of beginning teacher voice will be addressed in the upcoming section on beginning teachers; however, it is important to consider the implications of this issue at the student teaching level as well.

Graduate Certification Models and Alternative Certification

Although the large majority of music teachers are prepared in undergraduate teacher education programs, there are a variety of graduate certification models as well. Some schools and departments of music offer a master of music education degree with teacher certification or a post-bachelors certification. These programs typically have the same coursework and sequence as an undergraduate degree including preservice fieldwork, methods courses, and student teaching. There is no research within music education on the developmental differences for these students who are somewhat older and have more life experience than the traditional undergraduate student.

There are also a number of alternative certification programs in music education. Robinson (2003) states: "These programs, referred to as 'alternative routes to certification' (ARC), have proliferated in recent years with the number of states allowing such programs doubling from eighteen in 1986 to forty in 1992" (pp. 139–140). He goes on to discuss the great diversity in types of offerings considered "alternative" and presents the advantages and disadvantages of alternative certification in music education. He suggests that a major advantage to ARC may be the potential for alternative routes to attract a more diverse teaching force. However, Robinson points out that there is no research in music education on alternative routes, and it is unclear in the general research if ARC teachers stay in the field in the long term.

Regardless of how a teacher gets to the first year, it is clear that much of the learning of "music teacher education" happens on the job. The P-12 teachers who hire, mentor, and support beginning teachers are a crucial link in the music teacher education process.

SUPPORTING BEGINNING MUSIC TEACHERS

New teachers have two jobs—they have to teach and they have to learn to teach. No matter how good a preservice program may be, there are some things that can only be learned on the job. The preservice experience lays a foundation and offers practice in teaching. The first encounter with real teaching occurs when beginning teachers step into their own classroom. Then learning to teach begins in earnest. The first years of teaching are an intense and formative time in learning to teach, influencing not only whether people remain in teaching but what kind of teacher they become. (Feiman-Nemster, 2001, p. 1026)

Although the quote above comes from the general beginning teacher literature, I have reported similar findings in a number of case studies to document the experiences of beginning music teachers and attempt to capture their voice and emerging identity. All of my work supports the concept that most of the learning to teach music occurs in the first years and preservice education can only do so much to prepare music teachers for the realities of schools. Most beginning teachers arrive at their first year with some "heads-up" that the first year of teaching is difficult. Beginning music teachers are usually aware of statistics on teacher retention. It would be rare for a teacher to not have heard the comment: "Oh, most beginning music teachers don't last five years." However, actually living through the difficulties still seems to surprise beginning teachers.

Early research in the 1970s on beginning music teachers documented the following experiences: isolation, loneliness, culture-shock, in-service help, administrative help, community relations, feelings of failure, feelings of being in a "sink or swim" situation, feeling overworked, feeling overburdened, feeling overtired, being confused by or in disagreement with administrative policies and evaluations, dealing with parents, and feeling threatened, insecure and vulnerable. These same challenges appear in the recent first year teacher research. One of the key concerns regarding beginning teachers is that the goal of this "spot" on the continuum of "becoming a teacher" is to provide a place for a teacher to become the best teacher he/she can be. However, much of the energy put forth towards beginning teachers centers on the concept of "induction" for the goal of teacher retention. Sometimes the goal of retention and the goal of teacher learning work in opposition to one another. Beginning teacher programs that focus on retention do not always encourage teachers to reflect on the hard questions about teacher identity.

There has been recent effort at the national level to focus on the mentoring and induction of the beginning teacher. Although most states have some sort of beginning teacher initiative, there is great variation from the national perspective regarding policies for beginning teachers. In many states, funding for beginning teacher programs is the responsibility of the local districts. For the most part, wealthier suburban districts often have detailed beginning teacher programs while other types of districts do not. These wealthier districts often provide induction workshops that are specific to beginning teacher needs as well as trained mentors who are paid for their work. In districts that cannot provide such support, the beginning teacher is left on his/her own to secure appropriate professional development as well as mentor support. Of special concern to music education is the sense that many beginning music teachers begin their teaching careers in urban and rural schools that do not have as many financial resources for providing beginning teacher support.

I begin this section with a discussion of beginning teacher professional development and induction, in general, and then will conclude the chapter with a focus on mentoring as mentoring is considered a "part" of induction. Research on induction has documented that music teachers need music content support as well as music mentors. Induction and mentor programs provided by state music organizations are growing in response to this but are yet to be studied by researchers. If real growth is to take place within music education, then new teachers are the key to this reform and change. P-12 music educators must continue to explore strategies for supporting teachers and sustaining teacher growth in the first years of music teaching.

The first step in supporting beginning music teachers is to recognize the inability of many school districts to provide appropriate support. School district administrators need to be educated regarding the value of content-specific professional development experiences for music teachers. In addition, music educators must become more active in the policy arena so that music teachers may receive professional development credit (also called in-service credit) for participation in professional development programs that can be provided by state, school district, and music department level organizations. It is difficult for the beginning teacher to advocate for these policy issues. Mentors and experienced music teachers can make this case.

Securing content-specific induction for music teachers is one of the challenges for beginning teacher induction. Another challenge is the nature of induction itself. Beginning music teachers are often "inducted" into a school by being provided with "this is how it works around here" information. This comes from administrators, parents, and students just as often as it comes from other teachers. More formal induction programs sometimes exhibit the same attitude (even the music content ones). I worry that in our effort to support beginning music teachers, we may be robbing them of the opportunity to make change both inside the profession and in society at large. Although they have not been in a situation to try out their ideas in teaching practice, most music teachers graduate from preservice programs with some ideas regarding music teaching and learning. If their only experiences with colleagues in early professional development programs center around meeting the status quo, then the profession is losing the opportunity to continue improving music teaching and learning.

If beginning music teacher induction is seen as a first-year survival program, then the kind of effect that the program can have on real teacher growth is minimal. This is not to say that music teacher "survival days" should be removed from the teacher's experience. However, all of us in the profession must recognize that merely presenting short-term survival strategies is not enough.

Many states recognize that the period of growth for a beginning teacher goes beyond the first year. However, I have observed that beginning teacher programs are primarily geared toward the first-year teacher. Teachers in their second-, third-, and fourth-years are often troubled by issues that go beyond survival. All good teachers know that learning to teach is a career-long endeavor. However, many teachers leave the profession in the first five years due to frustration. If the profession can help support teachers throughout this five-year period of concern, we may have a better chance of retaining them.

I have worked with beginning teachers who are not asking questions about improving themselves and their classrooms. Some of these teachers get through the survival stage of the first year and settle into a "teaching groove" that works for them. It is hard to watch beginning teachers teach their second year for the rest of their career. These teachers mean well, they like kids, they try to make connections for students. However, they lack the reflective capacity to continue to grow. Recognizing the need for professional development support beyond the first year will help not only to retain the reflective teachers, but it may also help foster more reflective teachers.

Mentoring Beginning Music Teachers

As suggested above, mentoring is "part" of the beginning teacher induction process. Most formal induction programs include mentoring but not all mentoring programs include induction or professional development workshops and experiences. Researchers typically study mentoring separately from induction. Some P-12 teachers may work as "formal" mentors for a beginning teacher, but the research literature suggests that many beginning music teachers secure "informal" mentors through their buildings, state music organizations, and other contacts. Whether you are working as a "formal" or an "informal" mentor, the literature on mentoring the beginning music teacher may provide some guidance as to how you can best collaborate and provide leadership in the field.

We know from research that beginning music teachers value mentors who are also music teachers. If a beginning teacher is assigned to a nonmusic mentor, he/she will most likely look to secure an "informal" music mentor. We know that beginning teachers state that regularly scheduled contact with a mentor is one of the characteristics of a successful relationship. Also important is that the mentor and mentee meet early in the school year. Beginning teachers state that it is in those first few days and weeks of school that they need the most help. Studies have suggested that beginning teachers value the mentor more if they have had an opportunity to interact in informal ways (social gatherings) at the start of the mentoring experience. Most importantly, music mentoring research highlights the importance of the mentor being available to observe the classroom of the beginning teacher.

Although the beginning teacher may feel nervous to invite an experienced teacher into the classroom, it is absolutely crucial that the mentor have a sense of the teaching context for the beginner. The beginning teacher might start the year by observing the mentor in the mentor's classroom first. Then, the mentor might come to the beginner's classroom and do some teaching. Depending on the teaching context, some team teaching may be appropriate.

Logistics of mentoring. Sometimes mentors and mentees are required to meet and document their conversations. In other settings the mentor/mentee interaction is more informal. Mentors and mentees who have regularly scheduled interactions (whether formal or informal) perceive the relationship as more valuable. In some settings, mentors are prepared for their role as mentors through professional development offerings, and in other settings no preparation is provided. The same is true for paying a stipend to mentors. In some cases a mentor is paid a stipend for his/her work with the mentee and in other cases, not. Payment for the mentor is provided by the school. Mentors who are prepared for their role as mentors are usually more successful. Also, if they are paid even a small amount for their work, they feel a greater responsibility to assist the beginning teacher. Mentor teachers are encouraged to share these research results with administrators and advocate for mentor preparation, music specific, when possible. University music teacher educators must work in conjunction with K-12 music educators and with state music organizations to advocate for appropriate mentor programs for beginning music teachers.

Mentor programs designed and implemented by state music organizations may be the answer to providing content support. However, these programs should be designed based on research on beginning teachers and not just on the wisdom of leaders of state music organizations.

Characteristics of Mentors

Building a relationship with a mentee is much like any other sort of relationship. Some experienced teachers make good mentors while others are good with children but not good in working with adults (which is essentially what mentoring is). The next section includes a variety of criteria that beginning music teachers have suggested may be important for a music mentor. Each is discussed in relation to how the beginning music teacher might consider the characteristic. Whether experienced teachers agree with this perspective or not, it is important to understand the perspective of the beginning music teacher.

Excellent musician. Since many beginning music teachers are just coming from a teacher education program in a school or department of music, we have found that they often desire a music mentor that they consider to be an excellent musician. What the beginning teacher must be reminded of is how this is defined for a veteran music teacher. Many music teachers are still actively involved as performing musicians, but others model their musicianship from the podium or in other ways. Beginning music teachers often make snap judgments regarding a mentor based on their applied performance work. Musicianship for a music teacher evolves over the career. The mentor may need to help the beginning music teacher broaden his/her understanding of the field in this area.

Strong knowledge of music subject matter. Beginning music teachers have documented that the music mentor must have a strong knowledge of the music content. Once again, the definition of this may be different for the beginning music teacher than it is in the real world. Although the new teacher may be able to rattle off details from music theory or music history class, they may find that what the mentor knows (and what they need to know) is how to teach this subject matter.

Exemplary teacher. Being an exemplary teacher has been documented as an important criteria for a mentor. Even a nonmusic mentor who is an exemplary teacher can be perceived as helpful to the beginning music teacher. An exemplary teacher (in any content area) is able to motivate students while providing developmentally appropriate instruction and empowering students to guide their own learning. Exemplary teachers talk about teaching and learning in a passionate way and are always ready to try new ways of reaching students. There are many exemplary teachers in every school building. Encourage your mentee to observe them in many fields of study.

Similar philosophy of music education. Some new teachers have been prepared with quite specific methodologies and ideas regarding music teaching and learning. Some mentors go into a mentoring relationship with the thought that they may have the opportunity to learn about new ways of teaching music that the beginning teacher may bring. Others have their "tried and true" way of teaching and want the mentee to embrace that. Mentees are often the same. Some come into the teaching situation ready to learn other ways of teaching music, and others believe that the way they learned in their college or university is the "best" or maybe the "only" way. Both the music mentor and the mentee must be open-minded and flexible regarding these issues if the relationship is to be successful. Of course, just as in any relationship, the issues of philosophical differences may be so great that no healthy growth can occur. This is why it is important for beginning teachers to have a variety of mentors.

Proactive in establishing relationship. Successful mentor relationships include a "two-way street" in terms of communication. Studies have suggested that mentors need to be proactive in contacting the mentee. Many beginning teachers will ignore the mentor at the beginning of the year as they are just too overwhelmed to even be in touch. Mentors are encouraged to stick with the beginner and stay in touch.

Good listener. Being a "good listener" has been defined as one of the important characteristics of a mentor. Sometimes the beginning teacher just needs to talk about what has happened in the classroom. They may not be looking for feedback and suggestions. They may just need to talk.

Organized. Some beginning teachers have suggested that the mentor must be "organized." If the beginning teacher is a very organized person then he/she wants a mentor who is the same way. Again, how one defines "organized" can affect the relationship match. Many music teachers are very organized but they still may have a stack of papers on their desks. I think the need for this concept of organization is closely related to the next category of "strong knowledge of policies and procedures."

Strong knowledge of policies and procedures (building, district, and state). Music teachers need mentors who can help them with the paperwork required by the job and who can help them to know deadlines for state music organizations or district-level dates. The mentors should share parent letters and handbooks with the new music teacher, as the administrative duties of the new music teacher have been documented as some of the most troublesome aspects of the position.

Personable but professional. This final characteristic is again related to a personality match between mentor and mentee. Finding a comfortable balance between being personal and yet professional is important. Some beginning music teachers want a mentor who will support them in life as well as music teaching and others will seek a music mentor only and rely on family and friends for other sorts of support. It is important for the mentor teacher to be clear about the level and type of mentor support that they can provide.

CONCLUSION

Music teacher education is often the brunt of attacks regarding lack of preparation for teaching. However, induction and mentoring research indicates that beginning music teachers need assistance in grappling with the messy issues in school change and curriculum reform that they encounter once they begin working in schools (Conway, Krueger, Robinson, Haack, & Smith, 2002). In many ways, we have come a long way since the 1987 call to action in *Partnership and Process*. However, true collaboration in music teacher education (at all levels including recruitment, preservice, and in-service education) between higher education faculty, policy-makers in music education, and P-12 music educators is still in its infancy.

Class Discussion

1. Reflect on your own teacher preparation. Consider your course work in music, music education, education, and general college requirements as well as other experiences such as observations and student teaching. How would you change it? Consider that most colleges and universities limit degree requirements to 120 credits.

2. Consider the music performance requirements for undergraduate music majors. Should the requirements be identical for music education majors and other majors in music, such as performance majors or music theory majors?

3. What are the issues associated with preparing teachers for culturally diverse music teaching settings. Consider courses as well as other experiences, such as observations and student teaching. Consider that you really cannot add additional courses given that most colleges and universities limit degree requirements to 120 credits.

4. Who are the "policy stakeholders" that oversee music teacher education? Discuss the issues associated with meeting the demands of these various groups.

Projects

1. Select four colleges or universities in four geographically dispersed states. Through their web sites describe the music education degree and examine the course sequence. How are they similar? How are they different?

2. Search for web sites of organizations that have stated positions on music teacher education. Report what you find.

3. Organizations like NASM and NCATE have established positions on music teacher certification. Compare the music teacher education program at your college or university with the guidelines of these two influential accrediting associations.

SUGGESTED READINGS

Conway, C. M. (Ed.). (2003). *Great beginnings for music teachers: Mentoring and supporting new teachers*. Reston, VA: MENC.

Conway, C., M., & Hodgman, T. M. (2006). *Handbook for the beginning music teacher*. Chicago: GIA.

Darling-Hammond, L., & Bransford, J. (2005). *Preparing teachers for a changing world*. San Francisco: Jossey-Bass.

Wing, L. & Barrett, J. R. (2002). Music teacher education. In R. Colwell and C. P. Richardson (Eds.). *The new handbook of research on music teaching and learning* (pp. 757–904). New York: Oxford University Press.

~

CHAPTER 13

The Inquiring Music Teacher

Harold F. Abeles and Colleen Conway

INTRODUCTION

It is challenging for music teachers to keep up with changes in the field. As teachers become initiated into the profession, juggling the demands of their students, the curriculum, and their evolving professional identity can seem all-consuming. However, being a professional music teacher includes the responsibility for continuing to develop new understandings both about music and about teaching. While both undergraduate and graduate programs can provide a strong base, music educators need to continue learning to be effective teachers. As our contexts for teaching evolve and as students' characteristics change, new knowledge about teaching and learning is critical.

Music teachers use experience, traditions, and authorities to develop teaching strategies. As experienced professionals, teachers often rely on patterns that develop from their teaching practice. Through experiences, patterns become refined, even nuanced, so that we are able to make reasonable pedagogical decisions based on patterns of decisions developed (learned) through our own teaching. That is, we gain new pedagogical knowledge.

Tradition is also a valued source of knowledge. Because music is so intertwined with culture, it has a strong component of knowledge based on tradition. Methods for teaching many instruments and singing are based on tradition, as is singing songs about animals with young children. In some cases, traditional knowledge may be a useful source of information while in other cases the circumstances that led to the tradition may have changed, so that the tradition may be less applicable. Consider how we think about school song repertory now as compared with 50 years ago. As we have become a more diverse society, what we consider traditional repertory has changed.

Music teachers also often turn to *authorities* as a source to refine our teaching. At professional meetings, clinicians address questions and challenges that are common in the practice of teaching music, often providing ideas useful for implementing refining classroom strategies. While each of these sources, experience, tradition, and authority, has both value and limits, research provides another source of knowledge that can provide an alternative source for decision making.

Research as a Source of Pedagogical Knowledge

Belonging to professional associations such as MENC provides music teachers with access to current research in the field through journals. While some of us might imagine sitting by a fireplace after a day of work, sipping a favorite beverage and settling down with the latest journal in our field, most of us have difficulty finding the time to make that image a reality. More typically, teachers seek out research when they need an answer to something that comes up in their teaching. Whether it is an answer to a pedagogy question, such as "What strategies should I use to assign grades to my middle school band students?," or a content question, "What 19th century women composers wrote choral pieces that I could use with my high school mixed choir?," most of the time teachers are motivated to seek out research when they need to answer questions related to specific work issues.

Just as music teachers define and seek answers to pedagogical problems, researchers in music education typically initiate studies by examining and defining problems related to the teaching of music. To the extent that the problems identified are relevant to an individual teacher's situation, the results of the study may be useful in systematically addressing the teacher's problems or questions. What are musical characteristics of preschoolers (see for example Sims, 2001)? How should students structure their practice sessions to be effective (see for example Miksza, 2006)? These questions, and many more, have been studied by music education researchers.

For new research-based knowledge to change practice, some degree of consensus must develop around it. Uncertainty about new strategies must be reduced if they are to be adopted widely. Music teachers who are steeped in tradition are likely to ask, "How convincing is the evidence for new knowledge—why should we change what we are doing?" Testing and retesting seem imperative to gain consensus or confidence that new approaches are viable.

It is also important to acknowledge that our field is comfortable with the notion that there are multiple solutions to problems and many ways of thinking about teaching. There is not *one* best way. There is not *one* way to effectively develop a strong high school choir program; there are many. There is not a single best method for developing improvisational skills in third and fourth graders. Teaching professionals acknowledge that a range of factors influence what strategies may be effective for particular teachers in particular teaching circumstances.

Much of the research in music education is conducted as part of graduate studies and as a part of some college and university faculty members' professional responsibilities. The amount of research produced in music education is small when compared with other fields like physics and chemistry as well as sociology and psychology. As a consequence, it takes a long time to reduce uncertainty regarding new research findings and still longer to actually implement them in music classrooms. So compared to other disciplines, new research-based knowledge in music education develops very slowly. Nevertheless, for the field of music education to grow in its sophistication of content and practice, research must continue to be an important part of our knowledge base.

Models, Conceptual Frameworks, and Theory

Researchers are interested in is how sets of ideas or concepts are linked together to form knowledge. The relationship between how a student practices and how well he or she plays is a prototypical relationship of interest to music educators. Uncovering how ideas or phenomena are linked to each other is an important part of understanding research. It is the part of the process that provides the connections between theorists, researchers, and practitioners.

For the moment, let's assume that a particular researcher is interested in examining effective practicing strategies. Does previous research (see for example Miksza, 2006) have implications for her current study? Does the researcher's own teaching experience have implications for her thinking about the topic? Does what she has been told by authorities, such as her own performance teachers, enter into her thinking as well?

When planning a research study, researchers often find it useful to describe the context of the problem being examined and any understandings suggested by experience, research, or other sources of knowledge. These interactions can be depicted in *conceptual frameworks* or *models* which might be presented in written or visual formats. They are speculative depictions designed to guide research, often one particular study, with the expectation that they will be modified once new knowledge is developed through additional research. For example, the conceptual framework depicted in Figure 13.1, based both on previous research and experience, represents the relationship among factors that affect students' choice of instrument.

Theories are generalizations that depict systematic views of concepts in a research domain and should be considered less tentative than models or conceptual frameworks. While theories serve many of the same functions as models or conceptual frameworks, they typically are based on a larger number of research studies over a longer period of time. Research projects in music education sometimes adopt theories in related areas upon which to base studies in music education (see for example, Attribution Theory of Motivation—Asmus [1986]).

SOURCES OF RESEARCH IN MUSIC EDUCATION

To understand the results of research in applied areas like music education, teachers need practical experience as well as the knowledge of previous research. Research syntheses are particularly useful for practitioners who are beginning to investigate an area that they are not very familiar with. Two collections of syntheses focus on research issues in music education. *The Handbook of Research on Music Teaching and Learning*, published in 1992, has 55 chapters, many of which

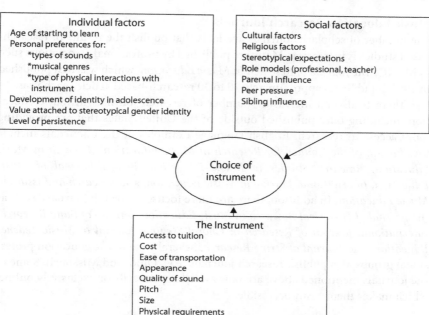

Figure 13.1. Hallam et al.'s Conceptual Framework for Factors Affecting Instrument Choice. (From Hallam, Rogers, & Creech, *International Journal of Music Education* **Vol 26(1) p. 15 Copyright © 2008 International Society for Music Education. Reprinted by Permission of SAGE.)**

are research syntheses. The *Handbook* includes syntheses in areas, such as music perception and cognition, curriculum, multicultural music education, giftedness, creativity, vocal and instrumental pedagogy, technology, and aesthetics. *The New Handbook of Research on Music Teaching and Learning,* published in 2002, is larger and includes sections on arts advocacy, music and medicine, teacher education, and studio instruction as well as other subjects. Other chapters provide more practical information on maintaining musicians' health, educating music teachers, and evaluating music education programs. One synthesis chapter, Azzara's (2002) on improvisation, reviews more than 130 sources, including theoretical writings on improvisation in music, dissertations and published research articles. He includes sections on social aspects, psychological aspects, world and western music performance, preschool/classroom improvisation, instrumental music improvisation, and jazz improvisation. Certainly, any teacher interested in knowing more about the research on improvisation or any researcher interested in undertaking the study of music improvisation would find this chapter a helpful place to begin.

Another source of research syntheses is the online journal published by MENC, *Update: Applications of Research in Music.* It strives to connect research in music teaching and learning to practice in music classrooms and rehearsal halls.

Music Education Research Journals

The number of scholarly journals available that publish the results of research-based studies is increasing. Many are published by professional associations such as MENC. The *Journal of Research in Music Education,* which was first published in 1953, it publishes approximately 25 to 30 research-based articles each year.

There is also an increasing number of research journals in music education, including ones published outside of the United States that are providing more access to research. English language examples of these journals include the *Bulletin of the Council for Research in Music Education, Research in Music Education, Research Studies in Music Education, British Journal of Music Education, International Journal of Music Education,* and *Research and Issues in Music Education.* In addition, there are more focused research journals, such as the *Journal of Historical Research in Music Education, Journal of Band Research, International Journal of Research in Choral Singing, Journal of Music Teacher Education,* and *Journal of String Research.* Several state music education professional groups also publish research journals (e.g., Ohio, and Missouri). Some of the journals mentioned above are now available primarily or exclusively online, which makes them easily accessible.

Searching Databases

Searching databases of research sources has become a very efficient means of finding literature related to your research questions. While there are several popular search engines for general web-surfing, such as Google, Yahoo, and MSN, music education researchers should rely primarily on academic search engines that search specific academically oriented databases.

As with any bibliographical source, it is important for the researcher to know what periodicals, books, newspapers or other information resources a database includes. Most databases focus on a particular field such as education (*Education Full Text*), music (*The Music Index Online*), or psychology (*psycINFO*), while others specialize in types of sources, such as *Digital Dissertations.* Within a particular discipline, databases often limit the sources they include. For example, a database called *Education Full Text* includes over 600 journals, but only three music education journals. Another shortcoming researchers should consider when using databases is the time limits of the sources. For example as of this writing, *Education Full Text* includes articles from the *Journal of Research in Music Education* from 1983 to the present. You should use several databases and seek assistance from library staff in selecting databases for efficient searches.

APPROACHES TO RESEARCH METHODS

There are several approaches to systematically investigating pedagogical or content problems in music education. These approaches, based on different philosophical perspectives, lead to different methods that researchers use to investigate problems.

The two broad research paradigms in music education, quantitative and qualitative, are based on research traditions and perspectives in different disciplines such as psychology and anthropology. Research traditions in educational research most closely parallel those used by researchers in music education.

Relationship between Philosophy and Research

Music education researchers recognize the important relationship between philosophy and approaches to research. How one thinks about the world may affect different aspects of a research study. Decisions about research design as well as ways of interpreting research can both be influenced by philosophical beliefs.

Epistemology is the branch of philosophy that examines of the nature of knowledge. Most researchers focus on two epistemological positions, *positivist* traditions and *post-positivist* traditions. Researchers in the *positivist* tradition are interested in discovering or uncovering <u>the</u> single truth about a phenomenon. They support a concept of inquiry that is objective and study observable behavior as the foundation for building scientific knowledge. Post-positivist researchers believe that reality is constructed within a social context and that it may be constructed differently by different participants—that is, there is not one single truth. Post-positivist researchers are interested in closely examining issues of context in relation to any given phenomenon.

Philosophical Inquiry: A Research Method?

An examination of research methods textbooks in education and music education reveals that some writers consider philosophical inquiry to be a research method (e.g., Phillips, 2008) while others do not (e.g., Wiersma & Jurs, 2005). In fact, experienced scholars in music education take quite diverse positions on the issue. Heller and O'Connor (2002), for example, do not consider philosophy a research method, although they do consider philosophical discourse an important scholarly activity and foundational in the research process (p. 1090). Their definition of research focuses on knowledge acquisition that is supported by empirical evidence—that is, evidence that is observed through one of the senses—rather than systematic logic. In another chapter in the same volume, Elliott (2002) challenges that position, suggesting that Heller and O'Connor's view is based on a particular ideology, empiricism, and represents a narrow perspective (p. 89).

Philosophical inquiry strives to provide deep analysis of ideas in music education. It strives to develop critical interpretations and explore alternative perspectives, as well as suggest new ways of thinking in an effort to encourage new insights. Often, philosophical dialogues may focus on value issues, such as "What should be included in the preparation of music educators?" More relevant to this chapter, they may focus on debates around research methodology, highlighting logical consistency in or conflicts with the assumptions of the research methods described later in this chapter. Some recent philosophical inquiries in education and music education have focused on policy issues, such as school choice, educational equity, social justice, feminism, the role of music in curriculum, the aesthetic experience, what musics should be part of school music, and what should be the relationship between music educators and the music industry.

Philosophical inquiry involves the attempt to think clearly and rigorously about difficult questions. Disagreement and criticism are characteristic of the work, thus it is often carried out in seminars and colloquia.[1] Philosophical work may analyze the work of other philosophers, of either historical or contemporary relevance.

Philosophical researchers talk about "doing philosophy" and there is a systematic approach that is used. Philosophical inquiry may proceed with the identification of a problem in the field and the posing of a thesis or theses to be examined. The data collected in philosophical research are texts from other researchers, authors, and philosophers. These are compared and contrasted, examined and analyzed. Philosophical inquiry uses inductive and deductive logic as tools for analysis. Conclusions are developed rationally to support the thesis. Other writers may, of course, point to flaws in the arguments used to support the thesis, underscoring the critical debate nature of philosophical inquiry. Because philosophical inquiry is not empirical, it is different from other approaches to the production of new knowledge presented in this chapter. That does not mean that it should be valued more or less, just that it presents a unique source. The journal *Philosophy of Music Education Review* includes examples of philosophical research.

QUANTITATIVE APPROACHES TO RESEARCH

Quantitative research methods, which primarily rely on numbers to organize and summarize findings, are united by a positivist philosophical perspective. Quantitative research is often categorized into two broad groups, experimental methods and nonexperimental methods. These different quantitative research methods address different types of research questions.

Experimental researchers are broadly interested in the question, "What will be under certain conditions?"—that is, cause and effect questions. In fact, the word "effect" is often found in the titles of experimental research reports, for example, The Effect of Music Instruction on Phonemic Awareness in Beginning Readers (Gromko, 2005). The goal of establishing causal relationships makes experimental research methods a valuable tool in the music education researcher's toolbox. It is the only research method that is designed to establish causal relationships.

Nonexperimental quantitative strategies include *descriptive* methods and *correlational*, and *causal-comparative* methods. Researchers using descriptive strategies are interested in answering the question "What is?," as in "What is the average amount of contact time elementary music specialists have with students each week?"

---

[1]   It should be noted that the journal *Philosophy of Music Education Review* often includes alternative perspectives of articles published in the same issue.

Researchers interested in answering relationship questions use correlational research methods. Questions they seek to investigate might include something like, "Is there a relationship between the number of hours a student practices per week and end of the semester applied jury grades?"

Researchers using causal-comparative strategies are seeking to establish trends that imply causal relationships. This approach examines how factors that are already in place, such socioeconomic status or gender, are related to other factors like musical taste or music instrument choice. Understanding what research strategy is used helps to interpret research reports.

Experimental Research Methods

For much of the 20th century, the randomized controlled experiment has been the "true experiment" when examining educational problems (Dehue, 2001). She writes that " ... promoted as the apogee of both rationality and reliability" (p. 286) it became the favorite of administrators who, intimidated by charges of arbitrariness, sought to justify their decisions in impersonal objective terms. Ultimately, randomized controlled experiments were advocated as "proof of overall good thinking and moral creditability" (p. 296).[2]

Experimental research methods in education closely parallel research paradigms in the natural sciences where experiments are conducted in controlled environments. If a chemist is interested in how a particular metal is affected by two different acids, he/she might take a strip of the metal, cut it in half, weigh each piece to ensure that they have identical masses, and then immerse each piece in a different flask, one with five milliliters of hydrochloric acid and another with five milliliters of sulfuric acid. He/she would likely measure immersion time by a stop watch, and control the temperature and the amount of light exposure for each flask. At the end of the immersion period, she would weigh each piece of metal to see how the different acids affected the mass of each metal piece.

The issue for music education researchers using experimental methods is how to translate the control that chemists have when conducting their experiments to music pedagogical settings. What compromises have to be made with the experimental research model when the "material" of interest for a music educator is not a piece of metal, but fourth graders playing recorders in music class? What kind of control over the environment does a music education researcher have during the day in a school building, when unimagined and unplanned events are part of what schooling often is?

How do music education researchers approximate the control that researchers in physical sciences can? In an experimental study, Rosenthal (1988) examined how different practice conditions affect the performance of advanced instrumental students.

---

[2] The No Child Left Behind (NCLB) legislation in 2001 specifically mentions scientifically based research as the strategy for demonstrating the effectiveness of educational interventions. NCLB defines scientifically based research as using rigorous, systematic, and objective procedures, specifically citing experimental or quasi-experimental designs.

Table 13.1 Experimental Research Abstract

1. Rosenthal, R., Wilson, M., Evans, M. Greenwalt, L. (1988). Effects of different practice conditions on advanced instrumentalists' performance accuracy. *Journal of Research in Music Education, 36* (4) 250–257.
2. Method: Experimental
3. Purpose: To examine the effectiveness of five different practice conditions on the performances of instrumentals.
4. Research Questions: "The specific research questions addressed were: (a) Are modeling, singing, and silent analysis effective practice techniques when compared with free practice or simply sight-reading? (b) Do modeling, singing, and silent analysis differ in their effectiveness as aids to practice (p. 251)?
5. Sample: 60 graduate and upper-level undergraduate students majoring on a woodwind or brass instrument. The students were randomly assigned to one of the five practice conditions.
6. Procedures: Five practice conditions were examined, modeling—students listened to a recording of the target selection, but does not actually play, singing—students sang the target selection and did not play, silent analysis—students studied the score of the target selection, but did not play the piece, free practice—students practiced the target selection, playing continuously, and control—students practiced a composition unrelated to the target selection. The target composition was selected to be challenging for the students and was transposed to suit the different instruments' range and. The study was conducted in a small room with recording equipment. Each student was read instructions depending on which group they were assigned to. Students in all groups were given three minutes to practice the piece by themselves using the condition they had been assigned. The researcher then returned to the room, asked the students to play through the piece once, played six beats on a metronome, asked the students to perform the piece and then left the room—returning when the student had finished playing. Each performance was analyzed by a trained musician, examining correct notes, rhythms, articulation, phrasing or dynamics, and tempo. The performances the scorers listened to were randomly ordered.
7. Results: First the accuracy of the scorers' judgment was examined. The agreement quotients between evaluators were quite high, all above .84. The results were then analyzed to determine if the different practice strategies affected the students' performance. The researchers reported that there were significant differences in the performance of phrasing or dynamics and tempo, but not for notes, articulation and rhythm. The modeling and practice groups produced the most accurate scores, while the control and singing groups generally produced the least accurate scores. The scores of the students in the silent analysis group were low on all of the measures except tempo.
8. Conclusion: The authors concluded that providing a model of the music may be a good strategy for instructors given the positive outcomes of observed even though the practice period was limited to just three minutes.

Rosenthal et al. used a generally agreed upon approach in the behavioral and social sciences to try to equate the five different practice groups in their study. The strategy typically employed by researchers is to *randomly* assign the students to two or more research groups. Random assignment means that the grouping is done by a process in which *chance* (or *probability*) is the only factor considered in the formation of the groups. Researchers expect this process to equate the groups, so that there is no systematic difference between them—just like when we cut a piece of metal in half, we don't expect there to be differences in the resulting two pieces. If there are differences, they would be due to chance. And that's what Rosenthal and her colleagues did. They randomly assigned the instrumentalists to different five practice conditions, so that the only difference between the students, to begin with, would be due to chance.

In the laboratory research example, the researcher managed factors like time, amounts, and temperature. In the Rosenthal et al study, the researchers control the research setting by, using the same room, having all the students practice for the same period of time—three minutes, and having all the students play the same target selection. The researcher's objective in this process is to remove alternative explanations for any difference in the responses of the five groups, other than the focus of the research—the difference practice conditions. When designing strategies for controlling experimental conditions in music education settings, researchers use logic and commonsense, with the goal being to eliminate possible explanations, other than what the research is focused on.

As stated earlier, the goal of experimental research, whether in a laboratory or classroom setting, is to discover "the truth"—to be able to describe a causal relationship and have confidence that the relationship will exist beyond the specific experimental circumstances to other similar circumstances. Experimental researchers are interested in generalizing the results of studies. Just like the laboratory researcher would expect that if he/she immersed the metal strips in the two acids 15 days later, the same effect would be observed, the music education researcher is expecting that if one practice strategy appears to be more successful in a study, then it will also be more successful should the study be repeated with other students. That is what motivated Rosenthal and her colleagues in the first place, the goal of finding a good practice strategy to improve the playing of instrumentalists.

To gain confidence in the generalizability of results, experimental researchers typically employ two strategies. The first strategy, statistical inference, is considered a benchmark analysis approach to determine if it is reasonable to have confidence in the results of a study. The foundation of statistical techniques is probability. Therefore, to apply statistical techniques to the results of research, chance—or the random process used to assign students to different experimental groups—must be in place. If there is random assignment of students, then inferential statistical techniques can be used to determine if the difference between the groups at the end of an experiment is large enough to be confident that the results would likely occur if the experiment was replicated. In fact, the amount of confidence placed in the difference is expressed with the phrase, *a statistically significant difference*. Statistical significance is further refined with an index of probability, most often *.05*. The .05 level of statistical significance means that there is a low probability (5 out of 100) that the result is due to chance. Therefore, in a well-designed experiment (one in which control was effectively used to manage alternative explanations for the results) when the results are statistically significant, they are likely to be due to the variable that was the focus of the study or experimental variable. In our example, this variable of focus was different practice strategies. Rosenthal et al. reports that there were significant differences in the performance of phrasing or dynamics and tempo as a result of the different practice conditions.

The second strategy for gaining confidence in the results of an experiment is to replicate the experiment. For example, Rosenthal's work might encourage other researchers to repeat her study in different colleges with different instrumentalists. If the results are similar, we have more confidence that they represent reality, or "the truth." If the results are different, then confidence may be lost. Ideally, several replications would occur before we would have sufficient confidence to implement the results in practice. Before music educators are convinced that one practice strategy is better than another, a case must be built both through inferential statistics and through replication, particularly if the new strategy is a departure from what music educators know—based on their experiences, tradition, or what authorities in the field advocate.

One of the challenges in applying laboratory experimental research methods in applied settings, like instrumental music practice, is what might be labeled the uniqueness versus the commonality issue. Experimental researchers use randomization to allow only chance differences to occur between research groups. As educators, we know that each learner is unique and brings to the music classroom different skills, different learning styles, different levels of confidence, and so forth. In fact, the uniqueness of our students is what makes teaching a challenging and interesting profession. So while randomization will distribute these different student qualities by chance, we expect that they may still influence the outcomes of research. In addition to the unique qualities of the students, each setting that the experimental researcher may want to apply his/her results to is also unique. Differences in communities, curriculum, facilities, and scheduling—frequency and length of lessons—all might differentially affect the influence of a practice strategy. While the experimental researcher's perspective (positivist) is that the "treatment effect" will trump all of this uniqueness (there is one truth, one strategy that will work in all circumstances), the qualitative researcher's approach (discussed in detail later in this chapter) is one that focuses on the uniqueness, and perceives individual qualities to be *more important* than the commonalities across groups that may or may not allow the strategy to work in several settings.

Quasi-Experimental Studies

When music educators undertake research projects in education settings they are often limited in their ability to implement all of the conditions of true experimental designs. One common problem when undertaking research in schools is the inability to randomly assign students to different research groups. Consequently, researchers have identified several strategies to manage the realities of collecting data in non-laboratory settings like schools. These strategies are labeled "quasi-experimental." While there are several different quasi-experimental strategies, only the most common will be reviewed here.

Nonequivalent control group studies are a frequently used alternative to randomized controlled experiment research strategies. In a nonequivalent control group study, there are at least two groups, and the groups have different experiences (treatments). One group is typically designated as the treatment group and the other the comparison or control group. In this approach, students are not randomly assigned to the two groups. Studies that take place in school settings often employ intact classrooms as their *nonequivalent* comparison groups. As school policies and procedures often constrain researchers' ability to employ true random procedures, nonequivalent control group designs are good options.

Researchers undertaking nonequivalent control group studies can increase confidence in the results by helping to eliminate alternative reasons for any differences in the results. For example, researchers should endeavor to make the experiences of each group equivalent, except of the aspect(s) being examined.

Time-series are also quasi-experimental designs. In time-series approaches, researchers use the same students for one or more treatments. Sims (2005), in her investigation of free versus directed listening with prekindergarten children, labeled her research design as a "subject-as-their-own-control design" (p. 81). Each prekindergartener participated in both the free as well as the directed listening condition. First, the students listened with no prescribed activity and then with a researcher designed activity approximately two weeks later. Sims' criterion to compare the two conditions was the amount of time each student listened to the two musical selections. She found that surprisingly there was not a significant difference in the amount of time the children listened to the selections in the two different listening conditions. It is possible that responses could be explained by an order effect, Sims suggests, with the children less interested in listening to the pieces the second time, although she points out that has not been the case in previous studies using the same research design.

Researchers employing quasi-experimental designs need to be aware of strategies to build confidence in their results. Replication, such as using the same design in different setting, helps to build a stronger knowledge base. Sims' research was extending previous research, which provided a context to understand the results. For example, she speculates that the children may have found the activity they did during the directed listening experience less appealing, which may have lead to shorter listening times for that condition (p. 84).

Causal-Comparative or Ex Post Facto Strategies

Causal-Comparative or *ex post facto* approaches to research examine conditions that are already in place, conditions that cannot be manipulated by the researcher (*ex post facto* is Latin for "after the fact"). For example, gender, the age when a student began to study an instrument, or instrument played are often variables of interest to music educators, and are typically pre-existing attributes. In causal comparative studies, the impact or relationship of a pre-existing factor on another variable is examined. Fitzpatrick's examination of the effect of instrumental music participation and socioeconomic status (SES) on the proficiency test scores of fourth-, sixth-, and ninth-grade students in Ohio (2006) illustrates this design. In her study, she examined the test scores of students who played instruments and compared them with the test scores of students who did not play instruments. She also considered students' SES in her analysis. She found that students who come from high SES families had consistently higher proficiency test scores, and for almost all of the proficiency tests, students participating in instrumental music within the two different SES groups had higher scores than their noninstrumentalist classmates. When considering Fitzpatrick's study, it is important to remember that she did not manipulate either of the variables being examined. Students in her study were already part of the instrumental music program in Columbus, and the family's socioeconomic status was already established. While it is typical to analyze the results of causal-comparative studies to determine if there are statistical significant differences, caution must be taken in interpreting the results as one of the assumptions of statistical testing has not been met, random assignment to groups.

While causal comparative research is a useful strategy available for examining pre-existing variables, it does not establish cause-effect relationships, despite its name. While a causal comparative analysis might yield a statistical relationship between variables, other variables not included in the design of the study may be competing explanations for any effect observed. In the Fitzpatrick study, it may be that the school district only allows students to participate in instrumental music if they maintain a certain grade point average. Consequently, when examining pre-existing variables, researchers must make efforts to incorporate possible alternative explanations into the study—either by controlling for them or by making them part of the analysis strategy—to increase confidence in the results.

Nonexperimental Quantitative Methods

Research methods that use quantitative approaches, but do not explore causality, fall into this category. While there are many subtypes of descriptive research, this section will focus on the more frequently used methods.

Questionnaires and Surveys

The questionnaire, or survey, is a frequently used research method designed to gather information from a group of people. The sample might be comprised of individuals, such as high school orchestra directors, or groups, such as drum and bugle corps, or institutions, such as, music departments. We are exposed to surveys in varied settings, including polls that are taken prior to elections designed to predict the winner.

When reading survey research, teachers should consider two methodological issues, how the content of the survey is designed and who is being surveyed. The content of a survey might seek to gather *facts* about music programs, such as the proportion of students involved in secondary school music programs in the United States. In one example of a survey of facts, Gregory (1995) surveyed 204 colleges and universities offering music education degrees to determine the amount and kinds of collaboration that existed between K-12 schools and higher education institutions. He reported that more than 96% of the higher education institutions collaborated with schools in some form, but the degree of collaboration varied widely and was somewhat related to the number of music education majors, the size of the institution, and the presence of a graduate program in music education.

Other surveys may focus on attitudes. Political polls are often surveys of attitudes towards certain political positions. A survey that examines the value elementary school principals place on music in the curriculum would be an example of an attitude survey. Gaines (1996) conducted a survey of high school band directors who were members of MENC. The survey posed the research questions, "Do high school band directors agree on a core repertoire for high school band?" and "If so, what compositions constitute this core repertoire?" (p. 7). Responses from 432 high school band directors indicated that there was strong agreement that certain compositions should be considered part of the core repertoire for high school band. The results generated several lists of repertoire for high school band directors to consult.

Another important issue for survey research is who comprises the sample. Sampling should be systematic. The population from which the sample is selected, such as elementary school principals, must be clearly defined. The results of a survey can only be generalized to the populations from which the sample was drawn; so if a survey randomly samples 100 elementary school principals in Indiana, the results can only be generalized to that state's elementary schools. Larger samples generate more confidence that the results will accurately represent the population.

How sampling is conducted can be an important factor in the accuracy of the results. If a survey is given in-person, or by mail, or phone, or via the internet—the strategy used is a factor which may limit or enhance the percentage of those sampled who actually respond to the survey. Having a high response rate adds to confidence in the results. Conversely, if only 20% of a sample responds to a mailed survey, questions regarding the characteristics of those who did not respond will cast doubt on the survey's results (Ferber et al., 2007).

Correlational Research
Correlational research seeks to determine the relationship between two or more characteristics of a group. The variables or characteristics are often the qualities

of an individual. For example, Woody and Burns (2001) examined the relationship between college-level music appreciation students' musical backgrounds, preferences, and beliefs and their responsiveness to classical music.

It is important to remember that use of the term "relationship" *does not* mean a causal relationship, that is, a relationship where one characteristic affects another characteristic. In correlational research, there is no attempt by the researcher to influence the research setting by manipulating a variable, such as practice strategy, to determine its effect on another variable, performance quality. Rather, the goal of the researcher is simply to describe the relationship between variables. An example of this issue is found in the relationship between the number of years high school students study the arts and higher SAT test scores. While correlational studies have found a positive relationship between these two variables, there are several possible explanations for the result (Vaughn & Winner, 2000). It could be that studying the arts develops good study habits, what some might call discipline, such as that required when practicing a performance skill. It may also be that students speculate that participating in the arts along with high academic achievement increases their chances to attend highly selective colleges (Winner & Hetland, 2000). The point is that the correlation does not help us in selecting or eliminating any of the possible reasons for the relationship that exists.

Correlational research results are reported with a family of statistics that yield *correlation coefficients*. Correlation coefficients can range from +1.00 to −1.00. In a positive relationship, where one variable increases as the other increases, such as height and weight, the correlation coefficient could vary from just above zero to +1.00. The stronger the relationship, the closer the correlation coefficient will be to +1.00. There can also be negative relationships, where one variable increases as the other decreases, such as between the number of hours spent watching television and middle school students' GPAs (Texas Education Agency, 1978). A correlation coefficient of 0.00 indicates no relationship between the variables, such as you might expect to find between the number of concerts performed annually by a high school orchestra and the number of tropical fish owned by the orchestra's director.

HISTORICAL RESEARCH

Historical research can yield valuable information for music educators. Certainly, one of the roles of historical research is to provide a basis for understanding the past. However, it can also provide a perspective for making decisions and formulating policies and help us to understand the antecedents for current circumstances. Through helping to identify trends, historical research may provide insights into likely future events and assist the profession in avoiding mistakes of the past.

Historical research may use both quantitative and qualitative strategies for examining issues, events, movements, or concepts of the past. Rather than collecting information from individuals or groups, historical researchers use other sources. Historical *documents* include newspapers, periodicals, diaries and journals, and letters. Quantitative records, such as school enrollments and music program budget records, can be important documents for historical researchers. Historical researchers also examine *relics*, or objects that provide information about the past. These might include musical instruments, textbooks, or recordings. A third source of information is oral history, including interviews the researcher gathers, or previously recorded oral comments, like testimony advocating music in the curriculum given to members of a board of education.

Historical information may be from primary or secondary sources. Good historical research relies on primary sources, which are first-hand accounts of events, such as a review of a performance or a recording of a live performance. Secondary sources are records or reports from individuals who did not witness the event. Secondary sources are useful in providing a broad picture of an historical period or issue, while primary sources are sought for establishing validity.

For example, many educators and music educators have written about the No Child Left Behind (NCLB) legislation providing their interpretation of how the legislation has affected educational practice. Music educators, for example, have written that the NCLB has constrained music programs. While it is informative to read these articles, historical researchers would seek to examine the original legislation, as well as policy statements from the US Department of Education, to develop a first-hand perspective on the legislation.

Historical researchers use the methods of *external* and *internal criticism* to help increase confidence in their work. Through external criticism, the researcher tries to determine the authenticity of the historical evidence. Is the document or relic what it appears to be? Issues regarding a document's author, as well as when or where it was written, lead to questions raised by external criticism. For example, was a particular recording made in a studio and carefully engineered or live in a hall in front of an audience? Methods of internal criticism help determine the accuracy or truthfulness of what is written in documents. Internal criticism checks for the dependability of reports as well as for bias. Examining and comparing multiple sources of information help establish trustworthiness. Both types of criticism are a part of the methodology of, and should be evident in, reports of historical research.

By examining multiple historical cases, researchers may be able to establish confidence in a conclusion. For example, music educators may see patterns between the rise and fall of the US economy and the resources available for music programs. Over time, observing multiple instances of this relationship suggests a possible causal relationship, although the historical researcher can never completely eliminate alternative or intervening influences. Such research may help music educators to anticipate events and prepare for challenges.

QUALITATIVE RESEARCH

Post-positivist researchers are interested in studying music teaching and learning as it exists in the natural context of classrooms. Qualitative research is well suited to studying and describing the qualities of phenomena as they occur in natural settings and contexts—so, researchers who are interested in the perceptions of music teachers or students about phenomena related to teaching and learning in music often do qualitative research. Qualitative research is descriptive. It does not aim to predict or establish cause.

Just as there are a variety of designs and approaches in quantitative research, there are also a variety of approaches within qualitative research. It is beyond the scope of this chapter to examine the variety of qualitative approaches in detail, but it is important to know that not all qualitative research is the same. The relationship between philosophy, particularly epistemology, and research affects research designs within qualitative research, just as it does within quantitative research.

Qualitative research approaches include the following: ethnography, phenomenology, heuristic inquiry, symbolic interaction, hermeneutics, narrative analysis, grounded theory, feminist inquiry, and critical theory. Although similar, each approach attempts to answer a slightly different question. Patton (2002) provides an excellent introduction to these traditions. His foundational question for phenomenology is: "What is the meaning, structure, and essence of the lived experience of the phenomenon for this person or group of people?" (p. 104). His foundational question for heuristic inquiry is: "What is my experience of this phenomenon and the essential experience of others who also experience this phenomenon intensely?" (p. 107). His question for symbolic interaction is: "What common set of symbols and understandings has emerged to give meaning to people's interactions?" (p. 112). As one can see, there are fine shades of meaning in each approach.

Research Questions

When reading qualitative research studies, look for research questions, which are typically found at the beginning of a report and help to define the purpose of the inquiry. Typically, researchers have reviewed past research literature and developed research questions based on that literature. However, in some studies, researchers outline research questions before a search of past literature. In these types of studies, literature is consulted after data have been collected so that knowledge of what past researchers have found in relation to a phenomenon does not hinder the researchers' ability to see what is most meaningful in the data. Regardless of which comes first, the literature review or the development of research questions, the research questions represent an important aspect of the study. All aspects of a study—design, data collection, and analysis—are guided by the initial research questions. For example, in an interview study, a researcher may ask: How many participants need to be interviewed? How many interviews should I conduct with each participant? Are individual interviews or focus group interviews better for this study? The best way to address these important research issues is to reflect on the study's research questions.

Types of Designs

Each of the approaches to qualitative research mentioned above may lead to different sorts of research strategies or designs. Some qualitative studies follow a *case study* design. Merriam (1998) and Stake (1995) discuss various types of case study designs including single case studies, multiple case studies, comparative case studies, and more. In most case study designs, the researcher collects as much information as possible on a small number of participants in an effort to provide a rich description of the participants' experiences. Case studies often include observations and interviews as well as document analysis. While the various case designs are not examined here, it is important for researchers to consider the diverse approaches when designing studies.

Silvey (2005) examined the way high school students perceived and experienced a choral composition they were learning to perform. This case study, conducted over a period of five months, chronicled the experiences and perceptions of three mixed choir members as they learned to perform the extended choral composition *Rejoice in the Lamb* by Britten. Results indicated that while the singers tended to focus on the technical skills needed to perform the music, deeper levels of understanding were apparently contingent on each participant's personal history, openness, and effort in relation to the composition.

In some qualitative designs, interviews are the primary source of data. Seidman (2006) makes a case for interview as a qualitative research design, suggesting that for certain information, such as what is it like to be a student in an ensemble, interviews may be the best avenue of inquiry (p. 5). Many qualitative studies in music education follow an interview design, employing interviews as the primary source of information. For example, in Flowers and Murphy's (2001) study of the music preferences, music activities, and music reflections of older adults (> 65), they used interviews as their only source of information. They reported that what their interviewees learned in music classes had a lasting effect on the participants and that music-making skill on an instrument was valued throughout their lives. In another example, Ferguson (2003) used interviews along with observations to examine the relationship between preservice teachers' experiences in a university String Project and their understandings of themselves as teachers. Ferguson's analysis suggested that the participants' perceptions were influenced by factors, such as previous teaching and performance experiences and family background, and she concluded that it is important to recognize individual differences in designing experiences for preservice teachers.

In recent years, music educators have begun to explore narrative inquiry and teachers' stories as a research design. Carter and Doyle (1996) emphasize that "the act of teaching, teachers' experiences and the choices they make … are inexorably linked to one's identity and, thus, one's life story" (p. 120). Thus they suggest that focusing on telling teacher's stories should be central to developing policies school reform and the education of teachers. Both at conferences and in journal articles, narrative studies in music education have often focused on capturing the voice of music teachers and students through journal writing and interviews. Leading scholars in this approach are Clandinin and Connelly (1995, 2000).

In their examination of the challenges and struggles described by a music student teacher and a first-year music teacher, Conway, Micheel-Mays, and

Micheel-Mays (2005) employed narrative inquiry, using data from teacher journals, observations, and interviews. They report that struggles common to both teachers included time management, issues of job security, the need to be validated, and the silencing of the beginning teacher.

Creswell (2007) outlines five approaches to qualitative inquiry including case study and narrative as listed here. He outlines phenomenological inquiry, ethnography, and grounded theory as additional key approaches. In some studies, researchers draw from characteristics in more than one approach. It is beyond the scope of this chapter to address all approaches, but readers should seek to develop an understanding of the diverse ways of approaching qualitative research.

Sampling

Sampling is an important issue for researchers using either quantitative or qualitative methods. For the quantitative researcher, sampling focuses on the question, "To whom can the results of the study be generalized?"

When reading qualitative studies, you will find that other approaches to sampling are used, such as *purposeful sampling*. Purposeful sampling allows the researcher to intentionally select information-rich, illuminative cases for in-depth study. The validity of qualitative research with regards to sampling depends more on the richness of the case(s) studied and the researcher's approach observation and analysis than on the size of the sample.

Patton (2002) provides a comprehensive discussion of 16 variations of purposeful sampling strategies used in qualitative research. Common purposeful sampling strategies used in music education include: "typical case sampling" to "illustrate or highlight what is typical, normal, average" (p. 243); "critical case sampling" which permits logical generalization and maximum application of information to other cases because "if it's true of this one case, it's likely to be true of all other cases" (p. 243); and "extreme or deviant case sampling," meaning "learning from unusual manifestations of the phenomenon intensely, but not extremely, for example, outstanding successes/notable failures" (p. 243). For example, in Shaddy's (2003) study of the mentoring of conservatory students, purposeful sampling was used to select the five mentors and four protégés on which the study focused. (Shaddy reported that protégés emulated their mentors' artistic and personal characteristics and displayed commitment to their work in efforts to continue to receive attention from their mentors.) Regardless of the sampling strategy used, researchers should justify why particular participants were chosen and how the reader should consider them in relation to others.

Types of Data

As mentioned earlier, decisions about the types of data to be gathered are guided by the research questions for a study. Qualitative researchers use a variety of strategies to collect information relevant to their research questions. Because qualitative researchers are often concerned about studying individuals, actions, or events in their natural settings, they must be sensitive to how obtrusive their data gathering approaches will be. Often, qualitative studies include multiple types of data (e.g., Ferguson, 2003) while others do not (e.g., Flowers & Murphy, 2001).

Observations are often used as a data collection strategy in qualitative studies. Concern about disturbing the natural setting of the research may influence the observation approach used. In school settings, it is seldom possible to watch a classroom from the outside, that is, without being *in* the classroom. If the research takes place in a classroom, the researcher may choose to maintain a passive presence, being as unobtrusive as possible and not interacting with students in the class. In such cases, the researcher is considered a *nonparticipant observer.* The researcher can also be a *participant observer,* when she actually participates in the music class on which she is gathering data. There may be different levels of researcher engagement depending upon the data being sought. The strategy used should be justified in any report of the study and once again be guided by the research question(s).

Observational researchers will most often record their observations with *field notes*—running descriptions of settings, people, activities, and sounds. Researchers may use videotapes and/or audio tapes to help accurately capture the details of their observations. For example, Duke and Simmons (2006) reviewed 25 hours of video-taped lessons of three distinguished artist-teachers in their search for common elements of expert studio teaching.

Interviews may be a primary strategy for collecting data or used in conjunction with observation, document analysis, or other techniques. Interviews may be very structured (i.e. researcher asks a set number of specific questions to several participants to compare responses) or quite un-structured and more conversational. *Interview guides or protocols*, a list of questions that interviewers want to exploring during each interview, provide focus and help make interviewing multiple subjects more systematic. Researchers may conduct both individual interviews and focus group interviews with multiple participants. Interviews are typically audio-recorded, to capture what is said, and then transcribed for analysis purposes.

Another data source often used in qualitative studies are written documents. For studies focusing on music learning, the documents analyzed may be written journals generated by teachers or students, students' writing samples, class assignments, and email communication among participants. Researchers may also use documents such as official records, curriculum guides, and newspaper accounts, as well as data from other research reports. Stavrou's (2006) examination of the current music curriculum for primary schools in Cyprus relies exclusively on her review of official curriculum documents as well as government reports. (She concludes that a prospectus that emphasizes the context of music teaching and learning in Cyprus should be more reflected in the curriculum.)

Approaches to Analysis and Reporting in Qualitative Studies

Qualitative researchers tend to use an inductive approach to the analysis of data, meaning that the critical themes emerge out of the data (Patton, 2002). Qualitative analysis requires some creativity, for the challenge is to place the raw data into logical, meaningful categories; to examine them in a holistic manner; and to find a way to communicate this interpretation to others. As has been the common thread in the discussion of qualitative research, issues of epistemology enter into decisions regarding qualitative analysis as well.

Each of the qualitative traditions (e.g., narrative research) has a slightly different approach to analysis of data. However, there are some common traits. Researchers begin analysis with a review of all data. They create transcripts for interviews and may enter transcripts and field notes into software if the analysis is to be supported with technology. The first step in most analysis procedures is to begin to code the data. During coding, the researcher typically identifies and tentatively names the conceptual categories into which the events observed will be grouped. The goal is to create descriptive categories which form a preliminary framework for analysis. Words, phrases, or events that appear to be similar can be grouped into the same category. These categories may be gradually modified or replaced during the subsequent stages of analysis that follow. Once the data has been coded, the researcher can begin to combine codes to create larger categories. Next, categories are re-examined to determine if and how they are linked, comparing and combining them in new ways in an effort to develop an integrated understanding (Hoepfl, 1997).

The results of qualitative studies are usually represented as findings or themes from the data. There is no template for the reporting of qualitative data. The story-like nature of the types of data collected can lead to any number of formats for reporting. The goal of the researcher is to provide a report that will be rich in detail and authentic.

While the process of analysis has been described as a linear one, the individual steps may occur simultaneously and repeatedly. The process should be thought of as iterative. During the analysis, additional data may be collected if the researcher uncovers gaps in the data. In qualitative research, the analysis and data collection are really commingled, with one serving as a guide to the other.

Criteria for Evaluating Research

How do we know when we read a report of project that good research has been carried out? Although research traditions vary greatly, there are some overarching concepts considered important when evaluating all types of research. Some of these concepts are considered more important than others in specific designs. Disagreement over these concepts and their definitions often has created what researchers call the *paradigm debate* between quantitative and qualitative researchers. In recent years, there has been considerable energy in the education profession put toward the concept of complementary methods of research (Green, Camilli, & Elmore, 2006), which underscores how diverse approaches to research can provide important and different insights into research problems. The following section reviews different criteria that are often used when evaluating research and suggests how they might be applied to different research approaches.

Objectivity

Quantitative researchers are interested in finding the single truth about a phenomenon. They support a concept of inquiry that is objective. For the quantitative researcher, subjectivity is something to eliminate, as it leads to results that are both unreliable and invalid (Hoepfl, 1997).

Patton (2002) believes that objectivity and subjectivity have become "ideological ammunition in the paradigms debate." Instead, he strives for "empathic neutrality" (p. 55). Patton rationalizes this perspective by citing the need for the qualitative researcher to develop a closeness with the research environment while maintaining a neutral stance toward the reporting of findings, presenting them in a non-judgmental balanced way.

Lincoln and Guba (1985) refer to the degree to which the researcher can demonstrate the neutrality of the research interpretations as *confirmability*, by examining the relationship between the raw data, analysis notes, coding categories notes, and preliminary findings.

Reliability and Validity

In quantitative studies, reliability and validity are criteria that researchers may use as indices of the quality of research. Reliability refers to the consistency of measures. High reliability, that is, measures that are consistent, is desirable within the context of quantitative studies. A consistent survey would be one that would produce similar results if respondents complete it more than once. Quantitative researchers think of the validity of a measurement as the degree to which a measurement tool measures what it is intended to measure. Test validity can be concerned with the degree to which a test is a good predictor, so questions about scores on the SAT predicting success, academic success at college would can be a question of validity.[3]

Many research scholars (Denzin & Lincoln, 2005; Patton, 2002) argue that the traditional definitions of reliability and validity as used in positivist research approaches may not be the correct terms to consider when evaluating other types of research. If qualitative researchers (a) recognize that there is no constant truth and (b) are interested in a better understanding of context, then we begin to blur the lines between the researcher and the "researched" (traditionally referred to in quantitative research as "subjects"). In these types of studies the issues of consistency (reliability) and authenticity (validity) take on a different form. Qualitative researchers often use the terms *dependability* and *credibility* when addressing issues of validity in their work. Patton (2002) states: "The credibility of qualitative methods, therefore, hinges to a great extent on the skill, competence, and rigor of the person doing the fieldwork—as well as things in a person's life that might prove a distraction" (p. 14). Qualitative researchers often report their own background and expertise in the area being studied, as they consider themselves the research *tool*. Thus it is reasonable for the reader of qualitative research to

---

[3] For a more detailed discussion of reliability and validity, see Chapter 8.

develop confidence in the results when the reader is convinced of the dependability and credibility of the information reported.

Triangulation. When quantitative researchers discuss *internal validity,* they are concerned with the accuracy of the findings (Are there alternative explanations for the results?). Quantitative researchers use experimental controls and randomization to improve internal validity. Qualitative researchers are, of course, also concerned with accuracy of their findings—but they are not aiming to discover a single truth in their investigations. They are instead committed to describing divergent views or perceptions of their study participants as well as those that may be shared among members of the group. One approach that qualitative researchers use to demonstrate trust in their results is to present evidence of *triangulation* (viewing a phenomenon through more than one lens) in their data collection, their analysis approaches, their conceptual frameworks, or a combination of all three. The use of multiple angles for examining a setting can strengthen claims about findings linked to shared points of view among participants. Using multiple angles of approach (or "crystallization," as Richardson [2000] describes it) can at the same time provide qualitative researchers with a way to compare and contrast findings that are different across participants. Observations, interviews, journals, researcher's logs are all data sources that may be triangulated, that is provide different views of a phenomenon. Having multiple people code the same data or using different coding techniques represent different analysis strategies that build confidence in findings. Conceptual framework triangulation might include examining the data through the lens of chaos theory, critical theory, feminist theory, or any other theoretical perspective that can be used to look at a data set.

Validity questions in qualitative studies can also be addressed with *member checks.* Study participants are provided with transcripts and/or analyses of the data and asked to corroborate the findings. This allows for the voice of participants to be included throughout the research process.

Generalizability

Quantitative researchers use research design, statistical techniques, and replication to demonstrate that their findings can be applied to other settings, that is, generalized. The idea of generalization is wedded to the philosophical foundation upon which quantitative research is based—seeking one solution to a problem regardless of context.

Qualitative researchers carefully discuss their conceptual frameworks and their interactions with research participants in order for readers to have enough information to consider the possible *transferability* (used in qualitative research in place of the quantitative term "generalizability") of findings to other contexts. According to Lincoln and Guba (1985), transferability is defined as the "similarity between two contexts" or the "fittingness" or congruence between two contexts (p. 124). The researcher is responsible for providing a thick, rich description of the phenomena and the contextual variables to allow the reader to determine transferability of the findings.

Schawartz (1996) uses the idea of *logical situational generalizability* (p. 7). If the reader can logically assume that participants in another population are in a situation similar to the one described in the study, it may be possible that results from the study are relevant in other contexts.

ACTION RESEARCH AND TEACHERS AS RESEARCHERS

The last decade has shown a renewed interest in the concept of music teachers/practitioners conducting their own research in their own classrooms (Conway & Jeffers, 2004; & Robbins, Burbank, & Dunkle, 2007). This concept of action research or teacher-research requires a shift in the power structure of research—from a relationship between the researchers, typically university professors, and the researched, P-12 music teachers or students, to collaborations between equal partners or work by the music teacher alone. Although teacher-researchers may use any research design to answer their research questions, qualitative research often are well suited to the practical questions that are of concern to teachers.

Action research refers specifically to a research design in which teaching practice is likely to change as a result of the study. Action researchers discuss a cycle of action including a reflective research spiral "wherein critical inquiry, based on experience followed by reflection, [is] used to continually improve the practice of teaching" (McMahon, 1999, p. 165). The reflective research spiral includes four steps—plan, act, observe, and reflect. The term "teacher-research" refers more generally to the teacher and the researcher being the same person, and the design may or may not include change "in action" during data collection.

Developing a Purpose and Research Questions

As in most types of research, the first step for teacher-researchers is to identify a problem or formulate a question regarding music teaching or learning. Since the goal of teacher-research is to affect change, the most important aspect to consider is the usefulness of the inquiry in terms of one's own teaching. While teacher-researchers are less concerned with generalizations to populations outside of their own context, results documented in one study may be transferable to other contexts. It is important that the teacher-researcher carefully describe the setting of the research and the participants involved in the study so that other music teachers may consider how findings may relate to other contexts.

Once a problem has been identified, the teacher-researcher begins to gather information and create documentation of the issues relating to the problem. Many researchers find it valuable to keep a diary or a teaching journal so that they may keep track of daily incidents that may relate to the research. In some cases, a teacher may want to videotape his classroom and use the videotape transcript as a form of observation data. Interviews with students, parents, and colleagues may also be appropriate data. Existing documents such as student grade reports, student compositions, portfolios, practice records, concert programs, audiotapes of performances, and so forth may also be used as data in the inquiry.

In studies done in collaboration with university researchers or other teachers, observations of a classroom performed by the collaborative partner may provide valuable insight for the study.

The teacher-researcher should reflect throughout the research process to determine when enough data has been collected. The data collection and analysis phases of a teacher-research project meld together so that thoughts regarding the meaning of the data begin to emerge during the process of the project. The researcher searches for meaning in the data collected by coding the data and developing categories that help to describe and organize the themes presented in the observations, diary notes, interviews, and so forth. Teachers and university researchers may analyze the data together, which adds another important dimension of reflection to the research process.

The final steps for the teacher-researcher include making decisions regarding teaching and learning based on the results of the study. Good teachers make these kinds of decisions every day, although often less systematically. What teacher-research does is provide a model for teachers to use in reflecting on their work. The documentation of these decisions and reflections contributes to the knowledge base of teaching. Collaboration with university researchers may be particularly helpful for documenting and dissemination.

Conway and Jeffers (2004) collaborated in an action research process to examine assessment procedures in beginning instrumental music. They developed a research partnership with each researcher focusing on particular aspects of the project. For example, Conway, a university professor, searched for related literature and Jeffers, an instrumental music teacher, developed the assessment tool, with reflections from colleagues as well as his university-based collaborator. The collaboration resulted in an effective assessment tool and a positive perspective of action research for both researchers.

SUMMARY

So what are the main messages in this chapter? First, it is important for music teachers to consider research as a source to help solve problems they confront, realizing that there is a limited amount of research in music education and that music teachers will also have to rely on other sources of knowledge, including their own experiences, to solve problems. Nevertheless, it is important to be aware of what the latest research-based information is.

This leads to the question, "Is it important that music education becomes more research-based?" Because almost all music educators, including those working in colleges and universities, spend so much of their time teaching rather than researching, for the field to become more like physics or psychology seems unlikely. Remember, each of us also needs time to make music! Yet, using approaches like action research, described above, more of us might become involved in generating research and as a consequence for some music educators, our positions might take on new and interesting dimensions. Developing more of a research-based understanding of our field may be particularly useful when working with policymakers or administrators who do not have the personal understanding that we have developed regarding music teaching and learning, and want documentation to help them develop policy or make decisions. Research-based documentation can be much more persuasive than anecdotes from teachers' personal experience.

It is also important to keep in mind that the results of one research study can only marginally increase our confidence that the "truth" has been uncovered. For music educators to really develop a satisfyingly confident understanding of a music teaching/learning circumstance, we must have multiple perspectives. Often, different perspectives help build confidence so that using what some researchers call *mixed methods*—combining both quantitative and qualitative approaches in the investigation of music teaching/learning situations—would add to the research-based knowledge of our work.

In regard to the issue of policymakers seeking evidence to inform their decisions, it is interesting to note that in the last decade, educational research has taken on a political dimension. The implementation of the No Child Left Behind (NCLB) legislation in 2001 (U.S. Congress, 2001) served as a catalyst for education researchers to debate causation and the research methods that might be used to establish it. NCLB legislation, when addressing the development of "evidence-based" educational interventions, uses the term "scientifically based" research 110 times (Slavin, 2002). NCLB defines scientifically based research as using rigorous, systematic, and objective procedures, and specifically cites experimental or quasi-experimental designs, preferably with random assignment (Slavin, 2002, p. 15). While researchers may agree that rigorous experimentation is ideal for making causal inferences, they also understand that studies that randomly assign students to an experimental or control group often are not feasible or ethical, particularly in schools. This is an important issue for some researchers, as the NCLB legislation controls a considerable amount of educational funding. As a consequence, professional associations like the *American Educational Research Association*, through their publications and presentations, have emphasized the importance of employing multiple approaches to research, arguing that this strategy that will ultimately provide policymakers and practitioners with the most complete picture of educational issues. We expect that this debate, which represents the basic tension between the two philosophical perspectives at the foundation of qualitative and quantitative research paradigms presented in this chapter, will continue to ferment.

Class Discussion

1. For each of the following studies, identify the research approach likely to have been used. There may be more than one answer. Discuss your classifications with other students in the class.

   a. Beginning instrumental music students were assigned either to heterogeneous class lessons or to private lessons in order that the best method of starting students on an instrument could be assessed.

    b. A study was made of the musical attitudes of rural socio-economically deprived students in Central Oklahoma.

    c. An assessment of the appropriateness of Formalism as an aesthetic theory for music education.

    d. A survey of principals' attitudes toward music in the curriculum.

    e. Observations of Three Expert Wind Conductors in College Rehearsals.

    2. Invite a graduate student or faculty member to come to your class to share a research project that he/she has completed with you.

    3. Select one volume (four issues) of the *Journal of Research in Music Education* to review. For each of the articles in the volume, classify the research method used, using the categories presented in this chapter. Discuss your decisions with other students in the class.

Projects

    1. Identity two different electronic databases from your college or university library, such as JSTOR, Education Full Text, ERIC, or the Music Index Online. Select two of the databases and search for the same keywords, for example, "music," "improvisation," "vocal," or "multicultural," "music," "elementary grades" in each. Compare the results. Note what music journals are included in each database.

    2. Select one of the research articles briefly described in this chapter, for example, Gregory (1995), Silvey (2005), Flowers' & Murphy (2001), or Conway & Jaffers (2004) and find it online or at the library. Then write a one- to two-page abstract of the article. Be sure to include the purpose, the research questions, a brief description of the method and the results, and the conclusion.

    3. Select an article from a research journal (one mentioned in the chapter) that interests you and write a one- or two-page abstract of the article. Be sure to include the purpose, the research questions, a brief description of the method and the results, and the conclusion.

SUGGESTED READINGS

Bogden, R., & Bicklin, S. (2006). *Qualitative research for education: An introduction to theory and methods. Needham* Heights, MA: Allyn and Bacon.

Colwell, R. (2006). *MENC Handbook of research methodologies.* New York: Oxford University Press.

Henson, K. T. (1996). Teachers as researchers. In J. Sikula (Ed.). *Handbook of research on teacher education* (2nd Ed.). 53–64.

Phillips, K. H. (2008). *Exploring research in music education & music therapy.* New York: Oxford University Press.

~

CHAPTER 14

Framing a Professional Life: Music Teacher Development through Collaboration and Leadership

Harold F. Abeles, Colleen Conway,
and Lori A. Custodero

INTRODUCTION

What is a professional life in music education? Most would agree that the ideal career would be rewarding both personally and musically that it would also be generative, leading to our own development as musicians and as teachers, and that through educating, we would continue to be educated. As you imagine sustaining a career in music education consider what led you to this path. We began as musicians and were moved to become teachers by a passion for sharing the joy of creative mastery—of being fluent in the language of tones and rhythms. Teaching is a collaborative act, defined by an interdependent relationship. We respond to student needs as a way to keep our pedagogy meaningful; we also seek out our own teachers with whom we share an artistic kinship in order to "strengthen, deepen, and refresh [our] craft" (John-Steiner, 2000, p. 95). Collaboration, then, is organic to the work of teachers and musicians, and the suggestions that fill this chapter should extend the ramifications of your influence.

Both collaboration and leadership nurture professional growth. Leadership is not typically sought; it is what follows the pursuit of excellence in the work we do. Gardner, Csikszenmihalyi, and Damon (2001) have been studying professional lives in what they call the Good Work Project. Based on hundreds of interviews with professionals in a variety of disciplines, they offer advice for those who feel they need a change to sustain their earlier enjoyment and feeling of contribution. Three broad suggestions include the following:

1. Expanding the domain—that is, providing access to music education to those who may not have had it before;
2. Reconfiguring the field—changing the spaces in which music education is usually taught; and
3. Taking a stand—perhaps working on advocacy issues. Additionally, the authors advocate for continuing education as key to a successful and rewarding career.

As our society changes, the educational needs of its citizens change. In response to globalization, greater disciplinary specialization, the exploding accessibility of information, and the creative potential of technological innovations what it means to be a music teacher has changed over the last two decades. Music teachers are more in control of their professional lives and have more influence in defining what it means to be musically educated. Music teachers' roles have changed. To be professional music educator now means to be a mentor, a school leader, and a professional whose experiences and expertise are acknowledged. Throughout this chapter, we invite you to imagine yourself as an evolving professional, utilizing your experience in teaching and musicianship—participating in professional opportunities that include mentoring novice music teachers, serving as a master or lead teacher, consulting for community music organizations and building a career that includes engaging in school-based management and shared decision-making, among many other professional initiatives.

Collaborations—Networking: In Schools

Successful music teachers collaborate with education professionals and a variety of community members to help musically educate children. Music teachers typically work in settings with many other educational professionals. As music educators develop into effective teachers, they have the opportunity to share their knowledge about students with other educational professionals. Classroom teachers are excellent sources of information regarding students' performance in their nonmusic classes, which can assist music teachers in developing a better understanding of effective teaching/learning approaches. There are other very practical interactions that music teachers have with other teachers in their schools. For example, music teachers rely extensively on the cooperation of other teachers to help schedule field trips or extra rehearsals for performances. Developing collaborative, collegial relationships with other teachers at your school is a critical component of any effective music program.

In addition, music teachers need to seek out formal and informal ways to interact with other music teachers. Designing professional development opportunities to enable music teachers to collaboratively support one another is one approach advocated by those who study teachers' careers. *Teacher learning communities*[1], more fully described later in the chapter, can provide important opportunities for collaborative support. At times, computer mediated communication, such as a discussion board, chat room, or wiki might also serve to help facilitate early career music teachers' interactions.

For a school district to establish and sustain a strong music program, collaboration among different music educators in the district is essential. Such collaborations are key to building a cohesive music curriculum. How do teachers

---

[1] Kanold, Toncheff, & Douglas (2008) describe a professional learning community as creating a collaborative teacher work environment where the capacity of teachers is developed with the goal of bringing coherence to school professionals' work with students (p. 263).

in different schools in the same district coordinate the experiences they provide for their students so that they complement what other teachers in the district are doing? Some districts will have a written music curriculum while others will not. If your district has a written music curriculum, it is likely to be one of the first documents you receive when you are hired. Districts' music curriculums should be revised periodically to reflect new understandings about teaching and learning and to reflect the best ideas of the current teachers in the district. Having the opportunity to participate in the collaborative process of revising a district's curriculum is a beneficial development experience for early career music education professionals.

Often music teachers have multiple administrators with whom they must work. Building principals often have direct responsibility for the supervision of all teachers in their school. These responsibilities can include scheduling and assignments of nonteaching responsibilities, like homeroom supervision. Principals' responsibilities are also likely to include observing and evaluating teachers' competence in the classroom, although if there is a Music Supervisor or Director of Fine Arts in the school district these functions may be shared among administrators or may be the sole responsibility of the arts supervisor.

It is unusual for principals to have an extensive background in music education, although they may be aware of general instructional documents like a state's music standards. Thus, it is essential to keep your school's principal well informed about your program and about your goals for student learning, how your curriculum will enable your students to reach those goals, and how your curriculum fits with the school's mission and state standards.

If your district has a supervisor for the arts, then that individual's responsibility is likely to include coordinating the curriculum for the district as well as planning professional development days for the music teachers in the district. Professional days provide opportunities to meet with colleagues from other schools and to understand how the "bigger picture" in the district curriculum provides a context for your work in your school. It is likely that the supervisor for the arts or music will have some responsibility for helping you grow and develop as a teacher, so she or he will likely also observe and evaluate your teaching.

Collaborations—Networking: In the Community

Depending on where you live and work, there is likely to be a variety of other musicians in your community. These community musicians provide a plethora of opportunities that effective school-based music educators regularly integrate into their curricular programs. Independent studio teachers, community music schools, church musicians, and professional musicians who play in a variety of venues—from concert halls to night clubs—are essential sources for educating students about the rich music culture in their own community.

Randall (2008) describes strategies for how school music specialists and independent music teachers can work together. He writes about the challenges of both the school music educator and the independent studio teacher having busy lives with little time to explore mutually beneficial arrangements. Randall emphasizes that the time students need for the development of specialized skills that is possible with independent studio instructors is seldom available within schools. Ensemble directors can provide lists of independent music teachers to their students as a means of encouraging students to take private lessons and/or studio instructors can volunteer to offer a master class at a local school to assist music specialists in preparing for a performance. Good communication can lead to independent teachers assisting students in preparing challenging sections of school ensemble pieces. Effective collaborations with independent music teachers in your community is likely to benefit your school music program in a variety of ways.

Collaborative partnerships with community-based music organizations can be another important resource for a school music program. Historically, these kinds of partnerships began with the establishment of the National Endowment for the Arts and state arts agencies in the 1960s, which provided funding for community-based music activities in schools. Today, in some schools across the country, partnerships function in isolation from school-based music specialists, so that the music instruction provided by the community-based group is parallel, rather than complementary, to the ongoing music curriculum. There is clearly a key leadership role for school-based music specialists to play in initiating, planning for, and implementing these partnerships and in an increasing number of schools, community music providers work collaboratively with music specialists. In these schools, music specialists may coordinate their curricula so that activities provided by community-based groups extend and deepen student learning in music.

Collaborations involving neighborhoods, schools, and school districts can strengthen programs by providing interactive opportunities and visibility to your programs; by resourcing the socializing characteristics of music, you may build bridges between and among constituencies. High school musicians may invite local elementary school to a rehearsal or even plan a concert designed just for them. At a southwestern US high school, the concert band performed a "pajama" concert for which student members wrote arrangements of children's tunes and wore the proper attire for the performances. Class projects that involve parents and other stake holders in the learners' lives will build musical connections— have a "guest conductor" day once a month and feature a younger child in the school or a parent or the mayor. As you learn more about the people in your local communities, you will better serve your students.

There are various relationships that may exist between music teachers and college faculty members. To some extent, the type of relationship may depend on the proximity of music teachers to colleges and universities. One relationship could be a new music teacher's interaction with faculty from their alma mater. Increasingly, teacher education programs are working with their recent graduates to facilitate and support the transition from preparing to be a teacher to professional practice. These efforts, often labeled *induction programs*, are designed to support a seamless transition from a teacher preparation program to the beginning teacher's own classroom (Stanulis, Burrill, & Ames, 2007).[2] Induction programs are based on the belief that the first few years of teaching are an important transition for professional educators, a period during which teachers decide if they will remain in the profession or leave. Such university/school partnerships can have other benefits to both partners, providing resources and expertise that can be shared. If you are teaching close to your alma mater, or another institution that prepares music teachers, even an occasional informal dinner with several recent graduates working in the area and a music education faculty member or two can provide an opportunity for sharing successful strategies and discussing the challenges of early career music teachers.

Music teachers may also collaborate with college-based music faculty on research projects. Chapter 13 described how action research projects provide excellent opportunities for collaboration among music teachers and music education faculty. Included in the section on action research are several published examples of research projects (e.g., Conway & Borst, 1999), which may serve as models for these collaborations.

As you gain more experience, you may be called upon to participate in the professional development of other music teachers. Serving as a cooperating teacher further cements partnerships between universities and schools and these kinds of relationships are a necessity for the continuation of the profession. In addition, college music education faculty members may invite you to talk with undergraduate music education students about your experiences as a teacher and may send preservice students to observe your teaching. To be successful, music teacher education programs need to be the responsibility of not only faculty members in higher education but also practicing professional music educators.

Involvement in Local, State, Regional, and National Professional Music Organizations

Another means of collaboration and making connections can be through membership in one of the many professional music organizations. These groups often sponsor professional development workshops and mentoring programs, and they provide web-based and print journals, articles, and other resource materials. The following list of music education professional associations is not comprehensive but provides links to many of the most well known national professional organizations. There may be other excellent music organizations in your state or local community.

Music Educators National Conference: The National Association for Music Education www.menc.org
American String Teachers Association www.astaweb.com
American Choral Directors Association www.acdaonline.org

---

[2] Induction programs are also discussed in detail in Chapter 12.

American School Band Directors Association www.asbda.com
Midwest Band and Orchestra Clinic www.midwestclinic.com
Gordon Institute for Music Learning www.giml.org
American Orff-Schulwerk Association www.aosa.org
Organization of American Kodaly Educators www.oake.org

It may be possible to attend clinics and workshops sponsored by any of these organizations and to apply for professional development or graduate credit for your participation in these events. Always check with your school district regarding whether the district will honor certain types of professional development options.

INTERNATIONAL OPPORTUNITIES FOR PROFESSIONAL DEVELOPMENT

Several of the organizations listed above have international programs as well, for example the Orff institute housed at the Mozarteum in Salzburg. You may also search out special interest summer courses offering experiences in multicultural music, or even travel with a group of music educators abroad. Programs that provide international experiences tend to be powerful catalysts for self-discovery through opportunities for cross-cultural collaboration. An example is *Umculo! Kimberley*, a 2-month summer program in Kimberley, South Africa, for choral and general music specialists that began in 1996.

The International Society for Music Education has five-day conferences every two years, usually during the month of July. The organization is comprised of seven commissions serving special interests in music education: early childhood, research, music and medicine, music teacher preparation, community music, the professional musician, and music and the media. These commissions typically hold their own seminars the week before the world conference at a location in the same vicinity. Activities at these conferences tend to be a balance between workshops, research talks, and student performances, which are quite extraordinary.

Several foundations have grant programs that involve study abroad. Guggenheim fellowships are to support creative work and rarely have limitations about where the work is done. Fulbright awards are usually connected with specific places that have agreements with the foundation. For information check the web sites.

Umculo! Kimberley: http://www.education.ualberta.ca/umculo/
Universitat Mozarteum Salzburg- Orff Schulwerk: http://www.moz.ac.at/german/orff/orff.shtml
International Society for Music Education: http://www.isme.org
Guggenheim Fellowships: http://www.gf.org/
Fulbright Grants: http://us.fulbrightonline.org/thinking_general.html

ENVISIONING A CAREER PATH

At the beginning of your career as a music teacher, it may be hard to envision what your professional role might be 10 or 20 years in the future. In this section, we present broad descriptions of how music teachers might develop from their first years of teaching through developing into mature, successful professionals. We believe that working toward the goal of becoming a mature professional music educator is a necessity in order for the music education of children to thrive.

As you approach your first job, your focus should be on your teaching—becoming successful in your music classroom or ensemble rehearsal space. This will require developing a sense of who you are as a teacher in your own classroom, beyond what you were able to do in your cooperating teacher's classroom when you were student teaching.

What does it take to feel comfortable as a music teacher? Of course, for each one of us, there may be a different answer, but there are some common elements, which can be inferred by systematically asking early career teachers about their challenges (see for example, Crocco, 2007). Studies suggest that beginning teachers are concerned about influencing what they teach, having autonomy, and being able to use their creativity. New teachers also want to forge positive relationships with their students and grow both professionally and personally (Crocco, 2007). Ingersoll (2003) reports that new, highly qualified teachers particularly resented losing control over curriculum decisions. While his study did not include music teachers, the analogy in a music setting would be to not have the freedom to choose repertory or other materials that you would use in your music classroom or ensembles.

Scholars concerned about teachers' careers often focus on the first five years as a critical initial period, as many new teachers leave the profession during this time. During these first five years, teachers need to feel valued by their administrators, their fellow teachers, and students, and by the fact that the work they are doing is important and successful (Dyal & Sewell, 2002). In many ways, the first part of a teaching career focuses on personal as well as professional growth. Music teachers who are perceived by their colleagues and students as effective in the classroom are likely to gain the respect required to begin to influence schooling more broadly.

ADVOCATING AND INITIATING CHANGE:
PROVIDING LEADERSHIP

As music teachers become effective and secure in their classrooms, they should take on new responsibilities, including leadership roles. While leadership roles for teachers may mean different things, *teacher leadership* as a construct has become more focused as a result of education/teacher reform movements begun in the 1980s. When teachers take on leadership responsibilities, it is expected that instruction will improve.

Why should music teachers seek leadership responsibilities? Certainly, one of the reasons to adopt leadership roles is that when teachers participate in school decision-making, their commitment to carry out those decisions increases (Weiss, Cambone, & Wyeth, 1992). Another reason for music teachers to participate as leaders in the school is that their expertise can contribute to the quality of their colleagues' teaching. A third reason often cited in support of teachers taking on leadership roles is for teachers' own growth and development (York-Barr & Duke, 2004). In some circumstances, teachers may take on formal leadership roles by participating in specific committee assignments, such as the development of an elementary school music curriculum. In other circumstances, teachers' participation in leadership may be more informal, such as helping a new colleague at another school plan a holiday concert.

As music teachers move towards mid-career, they may wish to seek out more variety in their work. For some, this may include moving to a different teaching setting, such as from a middle school instrumental position to a high school instrumental position. Others will be able to provide leadership roles in curriculum and staff development in specific areas, like music technology, where individual teachers may have developed a specialized expertise.

Still, other music teachers may seek out opportunities to work in *shared governance* within schools. While shared governance can be defined in a variety of ways, in general, it means a shift towards a more collaborative, distributive model of decision-making in schools and a shift away from emphasis on a more formal, one-person, principal-directed decision-making model (York-Barr & Duke, 2004, p. 264). Shared governance in schools, which is intended to incorporate teacher expertise in decisions that influence instruction, classroom, and school organizational issues, can provide interesting school leadership opportunities for music teachers.

What does it take to become a school leader? Snell and Swanson (2002) report that teachers who become leaders are those who demonstrate high levels of instructional expertise, collaboration, reflection, and a sense of empowerment, while Wilson (1993) includes being viewed as learning-oriented, being willing to take risks, and being willing to assume responsibility.

Why take on these responsibilities? Teachers take on leadership for the successful evolution and advancement of the profession. For schools to function effectively, teachers must help provide vision and collaborate on the work necessary to reach the vision. Collay (2006) suggests that assumptions of men (administrators) leading women (teachers) and children are sorely dated and have been soundly rejected. A shared leadership model is more widely accepted and fits with concepts of how teachers view their professional roles and their teacher identities.

As music teachers grow as professionals, their personal values and professional skills are merged. Music teachers' professional identities take on personal, intellectual, and moral components. While early career music teachers bring to their classrooms or rehearsal halls the beliefs that children can learn and teachers can improve society, in order to sustain a career as a music teacher additional skills and values need to be cultivated. These include being effective in the classroom, collaborating with colleagues, *and* having influence over decisions that affect one's professional life (Collay, 2006).

Taking on leadership responsibilities has an activist dimension. A fully functioning professional music educator is not passive but rather initiates actions, and one way to do this is in the area of interdisciplinary curriculum development. What might these actions look like for a mid-career teacher? Often, interdisciplinary curriculum projects in schools are developed with music as an afterthought (Bresler, 2002; Snyder, 2001). An all-too-common scenario would have fourth grade level teachers' planning time scheduled when the music teacher is scheduled to teach the fourth grade classes—leaving the music professional out of the core planning process. Questions like, "Do you know a song for my fourth graders that mentions teeth in the lyrics?" accompanied with an explanation that the fourth grade classes are undertaking an interdisciplinary unit on dental hygiene might be the consequence of such planning. Interdisciplinary curriculum design is clearly an opportunity for music teachers to take on a leadership role. Why not have music at the core of a fourth grade curriculum unit? Why not have a musical genre, like the blues, serve as the focus of an interdisciplinary unit? Or an historical period rich in music tradition, like the Harlem Renaissance? Leading an interdisciplinary planning team benefits not only your students' musical development but also that of the collaborating classroom teachers and your own professional growth!

Music is one curriculum area that requires advocates to champion its centrality and importance. Math, science and language arts teachers rarely are asked to justify why their discipline should be part of the school curriculum. Yet, in certain school districts, particularly in difficult economic times, the importance of music in the schools is questioned. One leadership role the professional music educator must take on is that of an advocate for the place of music in the curriculum. The "professional music educator advocate" must be multidimensional. Of course, advocacy begins with having a strong music program, one that obviously contributes to the musical education of children in the school district.

Advocacy includes helping administrators in your school district understand the importance of music in the curriculum, not only at times when it is questioned but also through ongoing enculturation. Unfortunately, many of the graduate programs that prepare administrators neglect educating them about the role of the arts in a comprehensive school curriculum. Introducing school administrators to professional materials such as the state arts standards can be part of a useful strategy for helping principals and central district administrators to more clearly understand the role of music in schools and to refine criteria with which they use to judge the quality of a music program. One effective way to communicate with school administrators is through written reports, underscoring the basic philosophy/mission of the music program, plans for attaining goals, and the strengths and weaknesses that may exist. Such reports should be submitted even if they are not required, as they are important means for systematically communicating with school administrators. While such reports should include important details, providing a one-page executive summary of reports can be a successful strategy to ensure that at least the major points of the report are communicated.

To be effective with school officials or board members, music educators must be well informed about the issues and questions on which administrators and school boards focus. This means understanding local issues like enrollment trends, details of financial support, curriculum, and accreditation as well as national issues like the No Child Left Behind legislation and year-end achievement testing.

Music education advocacy can also involve interactions with both parents of children in your school and members of the community who are not parents. Building on the foundation of a strong music program, it is important for parents to gain an appreciation for the many aspects that comprise an effective program. While performance aspects of music programs are often the most visible to community members, comprehensive music programs have many other components, like broadening students' exposure to music from around the world, that are important to a well rounded music education. Likewise, while elementary and middle school general music programs often have little visibility, they are the building blocks that serve as the foundation for the district's performing groups.

There are also opportunities to be a responsible, proactive leader in music education beyond your school district. While interactions with local government officials may include inviting them to performances or having performing groups appear at local government events, finding opportunities to inform local officials about the goals of music education programs in schools should also be part of your agenda. At the state level, state music education professional associations often organize opportunities to speak with state officials, such as the state legislators for your district. Most state associations that are affiliated with MENC have government relations committees, which are "responsible for studying problems and issues at the state level, framing position papers for adoption by the executive board of the association, [and] planning appropriate courses of action" (MENC, 1987, p. 84). Taking on leadership responsibilities in various state or regional professional organizations are important ways for fully professional music educators to contribute to continuing the profession.

Developing as a Professional

What should professional development in music education look like? "Is it about a one-day 'let's get pumped' experience led by 'experts' in the field, or can we expand our experiences to be more meaningful?" (Conway, Albert, Hibbard, & Hourigan, 2005, p. 8). Conway et al. advocate developing communities of music teachers who get together to share ideas and solve problems. Why not schedule regular meetings for music educators to work together on changing classrooms and improving practice? It is important for the profession to move from

intermittently scheduled meetings where teachers are talked at, to more frequent, systematic, and meaningful encounters where the experience of teachers
is acknowledged and valued.

The Importance of Teachers Securing Their Own Professional Development

One of the key findings from research on music teacher professional development
has been that music teachers need music specific professional development (see
Special Focus issue of the *Journal of Music Teacher Education* in Fall 2007 for a
complete discussion of the research in music teacher professional development).
This same research has also documented that music teachers are often frustrated
that district professional development offerings are often generic and not situated
within music.

Music teachers need be proactive in securing music-specific professional
development. Sometimes, this is as simple as approaching a building principal or
district administrator and offering to organize an upcoming in-service day for
all of the music teachers in a school district or county. There will be some administrators who insist that teachers attend a generic professional development program, but often many administrators will welcome music teacher suggestions.

Some districts are likely to still be grounded in a model of "expert-driven"
professional development. Teachers in such districts may need to write a proposal
to bring in a clinician or facilitator. However, with the current focus on *teacher
learning communities,* a carefully designed proposal that allows for teachers to
share and discuss issues of music teaching and learning may be accepted.

In addition to designing music-specific professional development, teachers
can show real leadership for the profession by studying their own best practice
models and documenting professional development experiences. Researchers
(e.g., Conway et al., 2005) make the case that little is known about teachers' professional development in the arts, and that what *is* known is that school administrators need to support and encourage music teachers to seek out professional
development. They suggest that it is important that music teachers are able to
select art-centered professional development activities that support their individual needs. They write: "In an effort to provide meaningful experiences for teachers, professional development organizers need to better reflect the needs of arts
teachers in the content of their sessions and offerings. Research points to the conclusion that the quality and contentment of teachers, as well as their programs,
are reflected in the merit of their ongoing professional development" (Conway
et al., 2005, p. 7). Chapter 13 provides some suggestions for teacher involvement
in action research and teacher research. Music teachers' professional development is a ripe area for that sort of inquiry.

Developing as Musicians

Your students need to see you as a musician. Students need to understand that
music teachers are musicians. Music education professionals should fulfill this

dimension of our professional lives in many and diverse ways. Obviously, music teachers must demonstrate their musicianship daily in their classrooms. This is done in several different ways as teachers use their technical expertise and artistic judgment to listen, compose, and perform music with their students.

It is also important for music education professionals to find opportunities to demonstrate their musicianship outside of the classroom or ensemble rehearsal room. It may be in the context of a recital at school or another community venue. It may be as a conductor or member of a community band or choir, or as an organist in a local church. Performance opportunities for professional music educators should not be limited to traditional western art music venues, as students should see their teachers in a variety of venues demonstrating their musicianship. In a club, at a wedding, or in a restaurant—all are places that provide occasions for us to be musicians.

Not only should our music making be visible to our students, but we also need to nurture our musicianship by finding new and challenging opportunities for us to grow as musicians. It is important for each of us to remember that it was *making music* that was *the* primary factor in choosing our career.

The Power of Community and Collaboration

As mentioned above, *teacher learning communities* (TLC) have become a popular way for public schools and districts to think about teacher professional development. The notion of TLC has evolved since the 1980s. Some "are social groupings of new and experienced educators who come together over time for the purpose of gaining new information, reconsidering previous knowledge and beliefs, and building on their own and others' ideas and experiences in order to work on a specific agenda intended to improve practice and enhance students' learning in K-12 schools and other educational settings (StateUniversity.com, 2008)." TLC can both be intellectual, as well as physical or social spaces for teachers. They provide the space for thinking, sharing, and better understanding teachers' work, as well as for placing teachers' work in a political and/or social/cultural context. One of the key tenets of the TLC movement is the term "communities of practice" popularized by Etienne Wenger and Jean Lave (Wenger, 2008). Wenger suggests that "[c]ommunities of practice are groups of people who share a concern or a passion for something they do and learn how to do it better as they interact regularly" (para. 2). Music teachers who learn and develop within a "community of practice" or in a "teacher learning community" have opportunities to share their thoughts and reflections on music teaching. They are empowered to bring their own issues of teaching and learning to the learning community. Although this concept has become popular within school districts, music teachers are often invited to part of a "teacher learning community" in which they are the only music teacher.

The music education profession needs to use the powerful concepts of teacher learning communities and communities of learning in planning and organizing professional development within state music education organizations and other music education contexts. Unfortunately, as mentioned earlier, music teacher professional development within music organizations often follow an expert "stand and deliver" model. Research (Conway & Holcomb, 2008) on music teacher professional development experiences has documented that informal interactions with colleagues is perceived as one as the most important element of teacher growth. The studies of graduate education mentioned below also include findings related to the positive impact of "learning from others" and "community." It is essential that teachers and leaders of music organizations explore models for meetings and conferences that will allow teacher interaction and development of community. This requires breaking the mold of the traditional expert-driven professional development model.

Changing Needs of Music Teachers Throughout Their Careers

As described earlier in this chapter, the roles of teachers change at different stages of their careers. The needs of music teachers for different types of professional development are also likely to change throughout their careers. Early in the career, beginning music teachers need assistance with the "nitty gritty" issues of teaching like choosing repertoire, planning lessons, and classroom management. While some support for these issues can be found on professional associations' web sites (see, for example, MENC position paper on program sacred music on school concerts, for beginning teachers), getting advice from a colleague in the community where you teach is often more meaningful. Mid-career teachers begin to broaden their understanding of what it means to be a teacher, and professional development that focuses on teaching to individual differences, sequencing curriculum, authentic assessment, and theories of learning and development may be better utilized by these teachers than by beginning teachers. In a 2008 study, Conway examined teacher perceptions of professional development within the framework of the *Life Cycle of the Career Teacher* model (Steffy, Wolfe, Pasch, & Enz, 2000). She concludes that the career stage of music teachers impacts the kind of professional development they seek (pp. 15–16).

Recent research (Bauer, Forsythe, & Kinney, 2007) has also suggested that the professional development needs of music teachers change in relation to their teaching levels such that elementary music teachers have different needs for growth than secondary teachers. In addition, music teacher needs are likely to vary in relation to their primary teaching area—band, orchestra, choral, or general music teaching. Music teachers must be proactive in securing appropriate development. They need to educate administrators regarding their changing and diverse needs throughout their careers and advocate for appropriate professional development experiences.

Graduate School and Continuing Education

Most states and school districts award professional development credits or pay scale increases to teachers who attend graduate school. Some states require a graduate degree for permanent certification, and some districts will even pay for the graduate degree. Barrett (2006) points to graduate work's potential for creating a productive two-way movement between teaching theory and class-room practice and states that master's degree courses "can be especially strong in their capacities to engage teachers in the study of music and music teaching, which builds disciplinary depth, and also in fostering teacher-directed inquiry" (p. 26). Attending graduate school, whether in a degree program or as a "life-long education" student, may be a powerful form of professional development.

There are many varieties of graduate programs for teachers, including exclusively distance-learning options as well as summer and academic year programs with different focuses. And research is just beginning to document the motivations for graduate school as well as the experiences in different types of programs. Conway, Eros, and Stanley (in press) compared the experiences of summer-only versus academic year master's degree students and found that master's graduates had various initial motivations for the degree ranging from the need to complete continuing education credits to maintaining their teacher certification to beginning a journey towards a doctoral degree. Graduates from both types of programs expressed concern about the time involved in graduate study including the time to complete assignments, time to reflect on learning, and time to plan new lessons for their P-12 students and incorporate new understandings developed from graduate study.

Although it is difficult to make a direct connection between earning a graduate degree and changes in graduates' teaching practice and/or changes in their P-12 students' learning, Conway, Eros, and Stanley (in review) studied the perceived effects of graduate education on student achievement in music. They found that master's degree graduates perceived that their master's degree education did impact their P-12 teaching. Yet it is still unclear how *different* aspects of graduate education may impact P-12 teaching. Does course work or the experience of writing a thesis have different effects on P-12 teaching? How do the collaborative relationships developed among graduate students from different school districts affect their own learning and their teaching? According to Conway et al., future research needs to unpack these issues so that those who plan graduate music education programs can better understand how to meet the needs of schools and teachers.

As has been mentioned throughout this section, there are many questions regarding teacher professional development that have yet to be examined. Music teachers' participation in action research and teacher research inquiries may lead to answers to these important questions.

Providing for Others and Learning from Others as Professional Development

As teachers gain more experience, they begin to learn from everyone around them. Conway (2008) found that experienced teachers "recognize the opportunity to learn from their own students or from student teachers as a form of professional development" (p. 14). Experienced teachers are also likely to be called upon to provide professional development, and they perceive these experiences as fostering their own professional growth. Conway also reported that students and colleagues, as well as good and bad administrators, provided useful sources of learning for experienced music teachers.

Some music mentoring research suggests that mentoring may be a form of professional development (Conway & Holcomb, 2007). Teachers engaged in teacher-research projects state that they learn from their students (Robbins, Burbank, & Dunkle, 2007) or co-researchers (Conway & Jeffers, 2004). Robinson (2005) concludes his presentation of the experiences of veteran teachers in a Connecticut teacher assessment program with the following: "Perhaps the opportunity to become involved with beginning teacher mentoring, induction, and assessment initiatives can be the means through which our more experienced colleagues can find the room to grow without leaving the classroom entirely" (p. 58). There are tremendous opportunities for professional growth if music teachers willingly take a leadership role within the school building, school district, or local/regional/national music organization. As has been the theme throughout this section, we encourage this involvement as well as related teacher-research or action research that might provide the profession with much-needed information about music teaching and learning.

CONCLUSION

In this chapter, we have posed questions and issues to consider as music teachers enter the classroom and grow as professionals. When new to the profession, there is still much to learn to be successful. Achieving the status of "successful or mature professional" involves the development of confidence and the respect that comes from being effective in the classroom and ensemble rehearsal room as well as in schools, communities, and beyond.

We conceived of this book, and the course in which you are likely enrolled, as an initial step in an expedition that will lead you to being a successful professional music educator. As you develop, you will need to refine your networking skills, seek out a variety of ways to help you develop as a professional, and envision different paths of professional growth.

Professions are comprised of groups of individuals whose work is connected. While each of our positions within music education may be unique, there are many things that we have in common, including the love of music and music making. There is not a single recipe to move along the path toward being a successful professional, but it is imperative that each one of us continues to grow in order to provide the very best music experiences for the students with whom we are fortunate to work.

Gardner, Csikszentmihalti, and Damon, the scholars involved with the Good Work Project, end their first book on the subject with the following advice for early career people, although we find them useful across the realm of experience:

> Without strong foundations that give meaning to the future, it is hard to keep up professional values under the pressure of countervailing forces. And so, as

often as needed, unclutter you mind: Revisit those codes, documents and exemplars that are integral to your domain—whether they are as ancient as the words of Moses, Hammurabi or Hippocrates, or as recent as the mission statement of your favorite organization. Next, seek the support of others that chare the same purpose...., find allies inside or outside the job, or, in the style of a social entrepreneur, consider starting an organization of like-minded peers ... You will also need a third vital ingredient—the resolve to stick by your principles. Knowing what should be done and having the means to do it are useless without personal commitment. (2001, pp. 248–249)

During the next 20 years, more will be expected from music teachers—to participate in school-based management, to plan their own professional development, and to plan their own professional pathways. For music teachers during this time, many doors will be open, and many will lead to invigorating professional lives.

Class Discussion

1. Discuss your own professional development experiences in building, district, state, and music organization. What did they focus on? How would you design a professional development experience for teachers in your district that is collaborative and works toward developing a community of learners?

2. Describe what you perceive to be the ideal qualities that you would seek in school administrator. How would your ideal school administrator do? How would her or his actions differ from a less-than-ideal school administrator?

3. Identify several content rich topics or themes that could serve as organizers for interdisciplinary education units with music at the core. Speculate how various discipline areas could develop instructional strategies that would compliment the focus of music at the core of the unit.

4. What role should graduate programs play in the career development of teachers. What should comprise the curriculum of graduate education for music teachers? At what point(s) in music teachers' careers might graduate education be most advantageous?

Projects

1. Explore one or more of the professional association web sites mentioned in this chapter. Write a critique of the web site, citing what you find particularly useful and content or tools that are not included that you think should be.

2. Write a five-year professional development plan for yourself. The plan should answer questions such as who you are as a music educator and where your strengths might take you?

3. Identify colleges and/or universities in your area that prepare music educators. Describe partnerships that they may have with your school district, such as student teaching placements or teacher induction programs.

4. Write a proposal for music-specific professional development in your school or district. Include a focus on community and collaboration in your approach.

SUGGESTED READINGS

Bowman, R. F. (2004). Teachers as leaders. *The Clearing House, 77* (5), 187–191.

Music Educators National Conference (2007). Special focus issue on music teacher professional development. *Journal of Music Teacher Education, 17* (1), 3–90.

Steffy, B. E., Wolfe, M. P., Pasch, S. H., & Enz, B. J. (2000). *Life cycle of the career teacher.* Thousand Oaks, CA: Corwin.

Lieberman, A. & Miller, L. (2004). *Teacher leadership.* San Francisco: Jossey-Bass.

REFERENCES

~

Abeles, H. F. (1973). Development and validation of a clarinet performance adjudication scale. *Journal of Research in Music Education, 21*, 246–255.

Adam, A. & Mowers, H. (2007). Listen Up! *School Library Journal, 53*(12), 44–46.

Adderley, C., Kennedy, M., & Berz, W. (2003). "A home away from home": The world of the high school music classroom. *Journal of Research in Music Education, 51*(3), 190–205.

Addo, A. O. (1997). Children's idiomatic expressions of cultural knowledge. *International Journal of Music Education, 30*, 15–25.

Adorno, T. (1963). *Introduction to the sociology of music.* (E.B. Ashton, Trans.). New York: Seabury Press.

Alperson, P. (1991). What should one expect from a philosophy of music education? *Journal of Aesthetic Education, 25*(3), 215–242.

Allsup, R. E. (Spring, 2003). Mutual learning and democratic action in instrumental music education. *Journal of Research in Music Education, 51*(1), 24–37.

Allsup, R. E. (2006). Species counterpoint: Darwin and the evolution of forms. *Philosophy of Music Education Review, 14*(2), 159–174.

Allsup, R. E. (2007). Democracy and one hundred years of music education. *Music Educators Journal, 93*(5), 52–57.

Altenmüller, E., Kesselring, J., & Wiesendanger, M. (2006). *Music, motor control, and the brain.* Oxford, UK; New York: Oxford University Press.

Althusser, L. (1971). *Lenin and philosophy.* New York: Monthly Review Press.

Anderson, L. W., & Krathwohl, D. R. (2001). *A Taxonomy for learning, teaching, and assessing: A revision of Bloom's taxonomy of educational objectives.* New York: Longman.

Andrews, B. W. (1996). Student team learning in music instruction: Restructuring the traditional task-incentive system. *McGill Journal of Education, 31*, 159–177.

Apple, M. W. (1990). *Ideology and curriculum* (2nd ed.). New York: Routledge.

Apple, M. W. (1993). *Official knowledge: Democratic education in a conservative age.* New York: Routledge.

Apple, M. W. (1995). *Education and power* (2nd ed.). New York: Routledge.

Apple, M. & King, N. (1977). What do schools teach? *Curriculum Inquiry, 6*(4), Curriculum Theorizing since 1947: Rhetoric or Progress?, 341–358.

Aristophanes. *The Clouds*. (Anonymous, Trans.). In *The complete Greek drama*. New York: Random House.

Armstrong, V. (2001). Theorizing gender and musical composition in the computerized classroom. *Women: A cultural review, 12*(1) 35–43.

Armstrong, V. (2008). Hard bargaining on the hard drive: Gender bias in the music technology classroom. *Gender and Education, 20*(4), 375–386.

Asimov, N. (2007, March 2). Study finds students lacking in arts education. It suggests achievement tests, more funding to meet state's goals. *San Francisco Chronicle*.

Aslin, R. N. (1981). Experimental influences and sensitive periods in perceptual development: A unified model. In R. N. Aslin, J. R. Alberts, & M. R. Peterson (Eds.). *Development of perception: Psychobiological perspectives. Vol. 2: The visual system*. New York: Academic Press.

Asmus, E. (1986). Achievement motivation characteristics of music education and music therapy students as identified by attribution theory. *Bulletin of the Council for Research in Music Education, 86,* 71–85.

Association of American Universities. (AAU). (2006). *National defense and education initiative: Meeting America's economic and security challenges in the 21st century*. Retrieved June 25, 2006, from http://www.aau.edu/reports/NDEII.pdf.

Atterbury, B. (1989). Being involved in mainstreaming decisions. *Music Educators Journal, 75*(6), 32–35.

Ayers, M. D. (Ed.) (2006). *Cybersounds: Essays on virtual music culture*. New York: Peter Lang.

Azmitia, M. (1988). Peer interaction and problem solving: When are two heads better than one? *Child Development, 59,* 87–96.

Azzara, C. D. (2002). Improvisation. In R. Colwell & C. Richardson (Eds.). *The new handbook of research on music teaching and learning* (p. 1219). New York: Oxford University Press.

Babbitt, M. (1958). Who cares if you listen? *High Fidelity, 8*(2), 38–40, 126–127.

Bailey, D. (1993). *Improvisation: Its nature and practice in music* (2nd ed.). New York: Da Capo Press.

Bandura, A. (1977). *Social learning theory*. New Jersey: Prentice Hall.

Banks, J. A. (1985). Ethnic revitalization movements and education. *Educational Review, 37*(2), 131–139.

Banks, J. A. (2006). *Cultural diversity and education: Foundations, curriculum, and teaching*. Boston: Pearson Education, Inc.

Barrett, J. (Mar., 2005). Planning for understanding: A reconceptualized view of the music curriculum. *Music Educators Journal, 91*(4), 21–25.

Barrett, M. (1999). Modal dissonances: An analysis of children's invented notations of known songs, original songs, and instrumental compositions. *Bulletin of the Council for Research in Music education, 141,* 14–20.

Barron, F., Montuori, A., & Barron, A. (Eds.) (1997). *Creators on creating: Awakening and cultivating the imaginative mind*. New York: Jeremy P. Tarcher.

Benedict, C. (2006). Defining ourselves as other: Envisioning transformative possibilities. In C. Freierson-Campbell (Ed.). *Teaching Music in Urban Classrooms: A Guide to Survival, Success, and Reform*. Lanham, MD: Rowman & Littlefield Education.

Benedict, C. K. (2004). *Chasing legitimacy: The national music standards viewed through a critical theorist framewor*. Unpublished Dissertation. New York: Teachers College, Columbia University.

Bergee, M. J. (1987). *An application of the facet-factorial approach to scale construction in the development of a rating scale for euphonium and tuba music performance.* Ph.D. Dissertation, University of Kansas.

Bergee, M. J. (1993). A comparison of faculty, peer, and self-evaluation of applied brass jury performances. *Journal of Research in Music Education, 41,* 19–27.

Bergee, M. J. (1997). Relationships among faculty, peer, and self-evaluations of applied performances. *Journal of Research in Music Education, 45,* 601–612.

Bergee, M. J., & Cecconi-Roberts, L. (2002). Effects of small-group peer interaction on self-evaluation of music performance. *Journal of Research in Music Education, 50*(3), 256–268.

Bergee, M. J. (2003). Faculty interjudge reliability of music performance evaluation. *Journal of Research in Music Education, 51,* 2, 137–150.

Bergee, M. J., Coffman, D. D., Demorest, S. M., Humphreys, J. T., & Thornton, L. P. (2001). *Influences on Collegiate Students' Decision to Become a Music Teacher.* Report sponsored by MENC: The National Association for Music Education.

Bergeson, T. R., & Trehub, S. E. (1999). Mothers' singing to infants and preschool children. *Infant Behavior and Development, 22*(1), 51–64.

Berliner, P. (1994) *Thinking in jazz: The infinite art of improvisation.* Chicago: The University of Chicago Press.

Bernstein, L. (2005). *Leonard Bernstein's young people's concerts* (Ed. J. Gottlieb). Pompton Plains, NJ: Amadeus Press.

Birge, E. B. (1928). *History of public school music in the United States.* Reston, VA: Music Educators National Conference.

Birge, E. B. (1984). *History of public school music in the United States.* Reston, VA: Music Educators National Conference.

Blacking, J. (1990). Music in children's cognitive and affective development. In F. R.Wilson & F. L. Roehman (Eds.). *Music and child development* (pp. 68–78). St. Louis, MO: MMB.

Blacking, J. (1995). *Music, culture, and experience: Selected papers of John Blacking.* Chicago: University of Chicago Press.

Blacking, J. (1995/1967). *Venda children's songs: A study in ethnomusicological analysis.* Chicago: University of Chicago Press.

Bliem, C. L., & Davinroy, K. H. (1997). *Teachers' beliefs about assessment and instruction in literacy.* Unpublished manuscript, University of Colorado at Boulder.

Bloom, A. (1987). *The closing of the American mind.* New York: Simon & Schuster.

Bloom, B. S. (1956). *Taxonomy of educational objectives; the classification of educational goals* (1st ed.). New York: Longmans, Green & Co.

Bloom, B. S. (Ed.). (1985). *Developing talent in young people.* New York: Ballantine Books.

Bloom, B. S. E., Engelhart, M. D., Furst, E. J., Hill, W. H., & Krathwohl, D. R. (1956). *Taxonomy of educational objectives: The classification of educational goals. Handbook 1: Cognitive domain.* New York: David McKay.

Bobbitt, F. (1918). *The curriculum.* Cambridge, MA: The Riverside Press.

Bobbitt, F. (Apr., 1921). A significant tendency in curriculum-making. *The Elementary School Journal, 21*(8), 607–615.

Bobbitt, F. (Sep., 1924). The new technique of curriculum-making. *The ElementarySchool Journal, 25*(1), 45–54.

Bobbitt, F. (Dec., 1934). The trend of the activity curriculum. *The Elementary School Journal, 35*(4), 257–266.

Bobo, J., Hudley, C., & Michel, C. (2004). *The Black studies reader.* New York: Routledge.

Bobowick (2001). *Information Technology for Schools: Creating Practical Knowledge to Improve Student Performance.* In Bena Kallick & James M. Wilson III (Eds.). San Francisco, CA: Jossey-Bass.

Bourdieu, P. (1977). *Outline of a theory of practice.* (Richard Nice, Trans.). Cambridge: Cambridge University Press.

Bowman, W. D. (1998). *Philosophical perspectives on music.* New York: Oxford University Press.

Bowman, W. (2002). Educating musically. In R. Colwell & C. Richardson (Eds.). *The new handbook of research in music teaching and learning.* New York: Oxford University Press.

Boyd, J. (1992). *Musicians in tune: Seventy-five contemporary musicians discuss the creative process.* New York: Simon & Schuster.

Boyd, W. & King, E. (1995[1921]). *The History of Western Education* (12th ed). Lanham, MD: Barnes & Noble Inc.

Bradley, D. (2005). Music Education, Multiculturalism, and Anti-Racism—Can We Talk? *Action, Criticism, and Theory for Music Education 5/2.* http://act.maydaygroup.org/articles/Bradley5_2.pdf

Bradley, D. (2007). The sounds of silence: Talking race in music education, *Action, Criticism, and Theory for Music Education 6/4*: 132–162. http://act.maydaygroup.org/articles/Bradley6_4.pdf

Bradley (2008). Oh that magic feeling! Multicultural human subjectivity, community, and fascism's footprints. *Philosophy of Music Education Review, 17*(1), 56–74.

Branscome, E. (2005). A historical analysis of textbook development in American Music: Education and the impetus for the national standards for music education. *Arts Education Policy Review, 107*(2).

Brett, P., Wood, C., & Thomas, G. C. (Eds.) (2006). *Queering the pitch,* 2nd ed. New York: Routledge.

Britton, A. P. W. (1989). The how and why of teaching singing schools in eighteenth century America. *Council for Research in Music Education Bulletin (99)*, 23–41.

Bronfenbrenner, U. (1974). Developmental research, public policy, and the ecology of childhood. *Child Development 45*(1), 1–5.

Bronfenbrenner, U. (1976). The experimental ecology of education. *Teachers College Record 78*(2), 157–204.

Bronfenbrenner, U. (1977). Toward an experimental ecology of human development. *American Psychology 32*, 515–531.

Bronfenbrenner, U. (1979). *The ecology of human development.* Cambridge: Harvard University Press.

Bronfenbrenner, U. (1986). The ecology of the family as a context for human development. *Developmental Psychology, 22*, 723–742.

Bronfenbrenner, U. (2005). Ecological models of human development. In M. Gauvain & M. Cole (Eds.). *Readings on the development of childhood* (4th ed.), 3–8. New York: Worth Publishers.

Bronfenbrenner, U. & cusCeci, S. J. (1993). Heredity, environment, and the question "how?": A new theoretical perspective for the 1990s. In R. Plomin and G. E. McClearn (Eds.). *Nature, nurture, and psychology.* Washington, DC: American Psychological Association.

Brown, A. L., Ash, D., Rutherford, M. Nakagawa, A. & Campione, J. C. (1993). Distributed expertise in the classroom. In G. Salomon (Ed.), *Distributed cognitions: Psychological and educational considerations* (pp. 188–228). New York: Cambridge University Press.

Bruner, J. (1960). *The process of education*. New York: Oxford University Press.

Bruner, J. (1996). *The culture of education*. Cambridge, MA: Harvard University Press.

Buckingham, D. & Rebekah, W. (Eds.) (2006). *Digital generations: Children, young people, and new media*. Mahwah, NJ: Lawrence Erlbaum Associates.

Bruner, J. S. (1990). *Acts of meaning*. Cambridge, MA.: Harvard University Press.

Butler, A., Lind, V. R. & McKoy, C. L. (2007). Equity and access in music education: Conceptualizing culture as barriers to and supports for music learning. *Music Education Research 9/2*, 241–253.

Campbell, D. T., & Stanley, J. C. (1966). *Experimental and quasi-experimental designs for research*. Chicago: Rand McNally.

Campbell, P. (1995). Of garage bands and song-getting: The musical development of young rock musicians. *Research Studies in Music Education, 4*, 12–20.

Campbell, P. S. (1996). *Music in cultural context*. Reston, VA: Music Educators National Conference.

Campbell, P. S. (1998). *Songs in their heads: Music and its meaning in children's lives*. New York: Oxford University Press.

Canadian Music Educators Association (2006, November 12) *Past CMEA/ACME conferences*. Retrieved November 23, 2008, from http://www.cmea.ca/about/History/PastConferences.htm

Carnegie Forum on Education and the Economy Task Force on Teaching as a Profession. (1986). *A Nation Prepared: Teachers for the 21st Century: The Report of the Task Force on Teaching as a Profession*: Carnegie Forum on Education and the Economy Task Force on Teaching as a Profession.

Carnegie Foundation for the Advancement of Teaching. (n.d.). *Carnegie foundation for the advancement of teaching*. Retrieved April 21, 2007, from http://www.carnegiefoundation.org/index.asp.

Carter, K., & Doyle, W. (1996). Personal narrative and life history in learning to teach. In J. Sikula, T. Buttery, & E. Guyton (Eds.). *Handbook of research on teacher education* (2nd ed. pp. 120–142). New York: Macmillan.

Chapidos, C., & Levitin, D. J. (2008). Cross-modal interactions in the experience of musical performances: Physiological correlates. *Cognition, 108*(3), 639–651.

Chin, H. (2006). *Doing less to learn more: Stories of music learning and teaching with the Alexander technique*. New York: Teachers College, Columbia University.

Choate, R. A. (Ed.) (1968). *Documentary report of the Tanglewood Symposium*. Washington, DC: Music Educators National Conference.

Chung, Jin Won (2006). *Self-regulated learning in piano practice of middle-school piano majors in Korea*. Ed.D. dissertation, Columbia University Teachers College, United States—New York. Retrieved August 15, 2008, from Dissertations & Theses: Full Text database. (Publication No. AAT 3205330).

Clandinin, D. J., & Connelly, F. M. (1995). *Teachers' professional knowledge landscapes*. New York: Teachers College Press.

Clandinin, D. J., & Connelly, F. M. (2000). *Narrative inquiry: Experience and story in qualitative research*. San Francisco: Jossey-Bass.

Clemmons, M. J. (2007). *Rapport in the applied voice studio*. Unpublished Doctoral Dissertation. New York: Teachers College, Columbia University.

Coalition for Music Education in Canada (CMEC) website (http://coalitionformusiced. ca/cmecindex.php, accessed November 23, 2008)

Cobb, E. (1977). *The ecology of imagination in childhood*. New York: Columbia University Press.

Cochran-Smith, S., Feiman-Nemser, S., & McIntyre, D. J. (2008). *Handbook of research on teacher education: Enduring questions in changing contexts (3rd. ed.)*. New York: Routledge.

College Board. (1983). *Academic preparation for college: What students need to know and be able to do*. New York: College Board.

Colwell, R. (1969). *Music achievement test (MAT)*. Chicago: Follett Educational Corp.

Colwell, R., Colwell, R. A., & Colwell, R. (1974). *Concepts for a musical foundation*. Upper Saddle River, NJ: Prentice-Hall.

Colwell, R. (Ed.) (1992). *Handbook of research on music teaching and learning*. New York: Schirmer Books.

Colwell, R., & Richardson, C. (Eds.) (2002). *The new handbook of research on music teaching and learning*. New York: Oxford University Press.

Committee on Basic Concepts in Music Education. (1958). *Basic concepts in music education*. Chicago: National Society for the Study of Education.

Condon, W. S. & Sander, L. W. (1974). Neonate movement is synchronized with adult speech: Interactional participation and language acquisition. *Science, 183*, 99–101.

Consortium of National Arts Education Associations. (1994). *National Standards for arts education: What every young American should know and be able to do in the arts*. Reston, VA: Music Educators National Conference.

Conway, C. M. (2006). Special mentoring series: Navigating through induction: How a mentor can help. *Music Educators Journal, 92(5)*, pp. 56–60.

Conway, C. M. (2008). Experienced music teacher perceptions of professional development throughout their careers. *Bulletin of the Council for Research in Music Education, 176*, 7–18.

Conway, C. M., Krueger, P., Robinson, M., Haack, P. & Smith, M. V. (2002). Beginning music teacher mentor and induction policy: A cross-state perspective, *Arts Education Policy Review, 104(2)*, 9–17.

Conway, C. M., Albert, D., Hibbard, S., & Hourigan, R. (2005). Arts education and professional development. *Arts Education Policy Review, 107(1)*, 3–9.

Conway, C. M. & Hodgman, T. M. (2009). *Teaching music in higher education*. New York: Oxford University Press.

Conway, C. M., & Jaffers, T. (2004). The teacher as researcher in beginning instrumental music. *Update: Applications of Research in Music Education, 22(2)*, 35–45.

Conway, C. M., Micheel-Mays, C., Micheel-Mays, L. (2005). A narrative study of student teaching and the first year of teaching: Common issues and struggles. *Bulletin of the Council for Research in Music Education, 165*, 65–77.

Conway, C. M., Micheel-Mays, C., & Micheel-Mays, L. (2006). Student teaching and the first year of teaching: A comparison of stages and struggles. *Bulletin of the Council for Research in Music Education. 165*, 65–78.

Cooksey, J. M. (1974). An application of the facet-factorial approach to scale construction in the development of a rating scale for high school choral music performance. Ed. D. Dissertation, University of Illinois at Urbana-Champaign. 280 pages.

Coon, H. & Carey, G. (1989). Genetic and environmental determinants of musical ability in twins. *Behavior Genetics, 19(2)*, 183–193.

Cope, P. & Smith, H. (1997). Cultural context in musical instrument learning. *British Journal of Music Education, 14*(3), 283–289.

Copland, A. (1939). *What to listen for in music.* New York: McGraw-Hill Inc.

Cox, Dennis (May 1985). Suzuki, Chorally speaking. *Music Educators Journal, 71*(9), 43–45.

Cremin, L. A. (1961). *The transformation of the school: Progressivism in American education 1876–1957.* New York: Knopf.

Creswell, J. W. (2007). *Qualitative inquiry and research design.* Thousand Oaks, CA: Sage Publications.

Csikszentmihalyi, M. (1975). *Beyond boredom and anxiety.* San Francisco: Jossey-Bass.

Csikszentmihalyi, M. (1979). The concept of flow. In Sutton-Smith, B. (Ed.). *Play and learning* (pp. 335–358). New York: Wiley.

Csikszentmihalyi, M. (1990). *Flow: The psychology of optimal experience.* New York: Harper and Row.

Csikszentmihalyi, M. (1996). *Creativity: Flow and the psychology of discovery and invention.* New York: Basic Books.

Csikszentmihalyi, M. (1997). *Finding flow: The psychology of engagement in everyday life.* New York: Basic Books.

Csikszentmihalyi, M., & Csikszentmihalyi, I. S. (1988). *Optimal experience: Psychological studies of flow in consciousness.* New York: Cambridge University Press.

Csikszentmihalyi, M., Rathunde, K., & Whalen, S. (1993). *Talented teenagers: The roots of success failure.* New York: Cambridge University Press.

Cuban, L. (2001). *Oversold and underused: Computers in the classroom.* Cambridge, MA: Harvard University Press.

Custodero, L. A. (1998). Observing flow in young children's music learning. *General Music Today 12*(1), 21–27.

Custodero, L. A. (2000). Engagement and experience: A model for the study of children's musical cognition. Paper presented at the Sixth Annual Conference on Music Perception and Cognition, Keele, UK.

Custodero, L.A. (2002). Seeking challenge, finding skill: Flow experience and music education. *Arts Education and Policy Review, 103*(3), January/February 2002, 3–9.

Custodero, L. A. (2003). Perspectives on challenge: A longitudinal investigation of children's music learning. *Arts and Learning, 19,* 23–53.

Custodero, L. A. (2005). Observable indicators of flow experience: A developmental perspective on musical engagement in young children from infancy to school age. *Music Education Research, 7*(2), 185–209.

Custodero, L. A. (2006). Singing practices in 10 families with young children. *Journal of Research in Music Education, 54*(1), 37–56.

Custodero, L. A. (2008). Intimacy and reciprocity in improvisatory musical performance: Pedagogical lessons from adult artists and young children. In S. Malloch and C. Trevarthen (Eds.). *Communicative musicality.* (pp. 513–530). Oxford, UK: Oxford University Press.

Custodero, L. & Johnson-Green, E. A. (2003). Passing the cultural torch: Musical experience and musical parenting of infants. *Journal of Research in Music Education, 51,* 102–115.

Custodero, L. A. & Johnson-Green, E. A. (2008). Caregiving in counterpoint: Reciprocal influences in the musical parenting of younger and older infants. *Early Childhood Development and Care, 178* (1), 15–39.

Custodero, L. & Williams, L. (2000). Music for everyone: Creating contexts for possibility in early childhood education. *Early Childhood Connection, 6*(4), 36–43.

D'Ausilio, A., Althenmuller, E., Belardinelli, M. O., & Lotze, M. (2006). Cross-modal plasticity of the motor cortex while listening to a rehearsed musical piece. *European Journal of Neuroscience, 24,* 955–958.

Dalcroze, E. J. (1921). *Rhythm, music and education.* New York: G.P. Putnam's Sons.

Damasio, A. (1999). *The feeling of what happens: Body and emotion in the making of consiousness.* New York: Harcourt.

Damasio, A. (2003). *Looking for Spinoza: Joy, sorrow, and feeling brain.* New York: Harcourt.

Darling-Hammond, L. (2008). *Closing the achievement gap through P-16 strategies.* Paper presented at the University-Assisted Public Schools as a Model for P-16 Education in New York State. New York: Teachers College, Columbia University, October.

Darrow, A., Johnson, C., & Ghetti, C. (2001). An analysis of music therapy student practicum behaviors and their relationship to clinical effectiveness: An exploratory investigation. *The Journal of Music Therapy, 38*(4), 307–320.

David, M. & Clegg, S. (2008). Power, pedagogy and personalization in global higher education: The occlusion of second-wave feminism? *Discourse: Studies in the Cultural Politics of Education 29,* 4, December 2008, 483–498.

Davidson, J. & Malloch, S. (2009). Musical communication: The body movements of performance. In S. Malloch, and Trevarthen, C. (Eds.), *Communicative Musicality* (pp. 565–583). New York: Oxford University Press.

Davidson, J., Sloboda, J., & Howe, M. (1995). The role of parents and teachers in the success and failure of instrumental learners. *Bulletin of the Council of Research in Music Education, 127,* 40–44.

Davidson, L. (1990). Tools and environments for musical creativity. *Music Educators Journal, 76*(9), 47–51.

Davidson, L. (1994). Songsinging by young and old: A developmental approach to music, In R. Aiello & J. Sloboda. (Eds.). *Musical perceptions* (pp. 99–130). New York: Oxford University Press.

Davidson, L., McKernon, P. & Gardner, H. (1981). The acquisition of song: A developmental approach. In J. A. Mason, et al. (Eds.). *Documentary report of the Ann Arbor Symposium,* (pp. 301–315). Reston: Music Educators National Conference.

Davidson, L. & Scripp, L. (1988). Young children's representation: Windows on music cognition. In J. Sloboda (Ed.), *Generative processes in music: The psychology of performance, improvisation, and composition* (pp. 195–230). Oxford, UK: Clarendon Press.

Davidson, L., & Scripp, L. (1990). Tracing reflective thinking in the performance ensemble. *The Quarterly of Music Teaching and Learning, 1*(1&2), 49–62.

Dcamp, C. B. (1980). An application of the facet-factorial approach to scale construction in the development of a rating scale for high school band music performance. Ph.D. Dissertation, The University of Iowa. 127 pages.

Dehue, T. (2001). Establishing the experimenting society: The historical origin of social experimentation according to the randomized controlled design. *The American Journal of Psychology, 114*(2), 283–302.

Dei, G. J. S. (1996). *Anti-Racism education: Theory and practice.* Halifax, NS: Fernwood.

Dei, G. J. S., & Kempf, A. (Eds.) (2006). *Anti-colonialism and education: The politics of resistance.* Rotterdam: Sense Publishers.

Dietrich, A. (2004). Neurocognitive mechanisms underlying the experience of flow. *Conciousness and Cognition, 13*, 746–761.

DeLorenzo, L. (Nov., 2003). Teaching music as democratic practice. *Music Educators Journal, 90*(2), 35–40.

Delpit, L. (1995). *Other people's children: Cultural conflict in the classroom.* New York: The New Press.

DeNora, T. (2000). *Music in everyday life.* Cambridge, UK: Cambridge University Press.

DeNora, T. (2003). *After Adorno: Rethinking music sociology* [online]. Cambridge University Press. Retrieved http://www.myilibrary.com.proxy.queensu.ca/Browse/open.asp?ID=42171

Denzin, N. K., & Lincoln, Y. S. (Eds.) (2005). *Handbook of qualitative research, 3rd ed.* Thousand Oaks, CA: Sage Publications.

Dewey, J. (1902). *The Curriculum and the Child.* Chicago: University of Chicago Press.

Dewey, J. (1910). *How we think.* Boston: D. C. Heath & Co. Publishers.

Dewey, J. (1916/1944). *Democracy and education.* New York: Macmillan, Inc.

Dewey, J. (1938). *Art as experience.* New York: Minton, Balch & Company.

Dewey, J. (1930/1997). *Experience and education.* New York: Touchstone.

Dillard, C. B. (2006). When the music changes, so should the dance: cultural and spiritual considerations in paradigm "proliferation," *International Journal of Qualitative Studies in Education 19*(1), 59–76.

Dirth, K. (1994). Portfolio assessment in music. Paper presented at MENC National Convention, Cincinnati, OH, April 1994.

Dirth, K. A. (2000). *Implementing portfolio assessment in the music performance classroom.* Ed.D. dissertation, Columbia University Teachers College, United States—New York. Retrieved June 26, 2008, from Dissertations & Theses: Full Text database. (Publication No. AAT 9976711).

Dissanayake, E. (1992). *Homo aestheticus: Where art comes from and why.* New York: The Free Press.

Dissanayake, E. (2000a). Antecedents of the temporal arts in early mother-infant interactions. In N. L. Wallin, B. Merker, & S. Brown (Eds.). *The origins of music* (pp. 389–410). Cambridge, MA: MIT Press.

Dissanayake, E. (2000b). *Art and intimacy: How the arts began.* Seattle: University of Washington Press.

Doll, Jr., W. (1993). *A post-modern perspective on curriculum.* New York: Teachers College, Columbia University.

Dow, P. B. (1991). *Schoolhouse politics: Lessons from the Sputnik era.* Cambridge, MA: Harvard University Press.

Duke, R. A., & Simmons, A. L. (2006). The nature of expertise: Narrative descriptions of 19 common elements observed in the lessons of three renowned artist-teachers. *Bulletin of the Council for Research in Music Education, 170,* 7–20.

Eisner, E. (1985). *The educational imagination: On the design and evaluation of school programs* (2nd ed.). New York: Macmillan.

Elliott, D. J. (1995). *Music matters: A new philosophy of music education.* New York: Oxford University Press.

Elliott, D. (Ed.) (2005). *Praxial music education: Reflections and dialogues,* New York: Oxford University Press.

Ellison, M. (2001). The Marsalis family and the democratic imperative in jazz. *Race and Class, 43*(1), 1–28.

Ellsworth, E. A. (1989). Why doesn't this feel empowering? Working through the repressive myths of critical pedagogy. *Harvard Educational Review, 59* (3), 297–324.

Emerson, R. W. (1983). *The American scholar, Selected Essays and Lectures*. Washington, DC: The Library of Congress.

Emmanuel, D. (2002). *A music education immersion internship: Pre-service teachers' beliefs concerning teaching music in a culturally diverse setting*. Unpublished doctoral dissertation, East Lansing, MI: Michigan State University.

Erikson, E. (1968). *Identity, youth and crisis*. New York: Norton.

Erlich, S. B., Levine, S. C. & Goldin-Meadow, S. (2006). The importance of gesture in children's spatial reasoning. *Developmental Psychology, 42*(6), 1259–1268.

Feiman-Nemser. S. (2001). From preparation to practice: Designing a continuum to strengthen and sustain teaching. *Teachers College Record, 103(6),* 1013–1055.

Feld, S. (1974). Linguistic models in ethnomusicology. *Ethnomusicology, 18,* 197–218.

Feldman, D. H. (1988). Dreams, insights and transformations. In R. J. Steinberg (Ed.), *The nature of creativity* (pp. 271–297). Cambridge, UK: Cambridge University Press.

Feldman, D. H. (1994). Creativity: Proof that development occurs. In D. H. Feldman, M. Csikszentmihalyi, & H. Gardner (Eds.). *Changing the world: A framework for the study of creativity* (pp. 85–101). Westport, CT: Praeger.

Feldman, D. H. (2000). Was Mozart at risk? A developmentalist looks at extreme talent. In R. C. Feldman & B. M. Shore (Eds.). *Talents unfolding: Cognition and development* (pp. 251–264). Washington, DC: American Psychological Association.

Feldman, D. H., Csikszentmihalyi, M., & Gardner, H. (1994). *Changing the world: A framework for the study of creativity*. Westport, CT: Praeger.

Ferber, R., Sheatsley, P., Turner, A., Waksberg, J. (2007). What is a survey, 2nd ed. *The American Statistical Association* Retrieved October 10, 2007, from http://www.whatisasurvey.info/

Ferguson, K. (2003). Becoming a String Teacher. *Bulletin of the Council for Research in Music Education*, 8–48.

Field, T. (1998). Maternal depression effects on infants and early interventions. *Preventive Medicine, 27*(2), 200–203.

Fitzpatrick, K. R. (2006). The effect of instrumental music participation and socioeconomic status on Ohio fourth-, sixth-, and ninth-grade proficiency test performance. *Journal of Research in Music Education 54*(1), 73–84.

Flagg, M. (Dec., 1966). The Orff system in today's world. *Music Educators Journal, 53*(4), 30.

Flowers, P., & Murphy, J. (2001). Talking about music: Interviews with older adults about their music education, preferences, activities, and reflections. *Update: Applications of Research in Music Education, 20*(1), 26–32.

Frankel, J. (2002). An evaluation of a web-based model of assessment for the New Jersey State Core Curriculum Content Standards in music. Unpublished doctoral dissertation. New York: Teachers College, Columbia University.

Frankel, J. (2005). Teaching in a one-computer classroom. *Music Education Technology Magazine, 3*(3), 12–17.

Fredrickson, W. E., & Burton, B. (2005). Where will the supply of new teachers come from, where shall we recruit, and who will teach these prospective teachers? *Journal of Music Teacher Education, 14*(2), 30–36.

Freire, P. (1973). *Education for critical consciousness*. New York: The Seabury Press.

Freire, P. (1995). *Pedagogy of the oppressed*. New York: Continuum.

Friedan, B. (2002). *The feminine mystique*. New York; London: W. W. Norton.

Frierson-Campbell C. (Ed.) (2006). *Teaching Music in the Urban Classroom, Volume 1: A Guide to Survival, Success, and Reform*. Lanham, MD: Rowman & Littlefield Education.

Froehlich, H. (2006). Mirror, mirror on the wall...Or the challenge of jumping over our own shadows. *Action, Criticism, and Theory for Music Education*, 5/2: http://act.maydaygroup.org/articles/Froehlich5_2.pdf

Froehlich, H. C. (2007). *Sociology for Music Teachers: Perspectives for practice* (2007) Upper Saddle River, NJ : Pearson Prentice Hall.

Gaines, D. A. (1996). *A core repertoire of concert music for high school band: A descriptive study*. Unpublished doctoral dissertation. New York: Teachers College, Columbia University.

Gardner, H. (1982). *Art, mind, and brain: A cognitive approach to creativity*. New York: Basic Books.

Gardner, H. (1983). *Frames of mind: The theory of multiple intelligences*. New York: Basic Books.

Gardner, H. (1994). *Creating minds*. New York: Basic Books.

Gardner, H. (1997). Keynote address: Is musical intelligence special? In V. Brummett (Ed.), *Ithaca Conference '96, Music as intelligence: A sourcebook* (pp. 1–12). Ithaca, NY: Ithaca College.

Geertz, C. (1973). *The Interpretation of cultures*. New York: Basic Books.

Geertz, C. (1983). *Local knowledge*. New York: Basic Books.

Gergen, K. J. (1994). *Realities and relationships: soundings in social construction*. Cambridge, MA: Harvard University Press.

Getzels, J. W., & Csikszentmihalyi, M. (1976). *The creative vision: A longitudinal study of problem finding in art*. New York: Wiley.

Gfeller, K., & Darrow, A. (1988). Mainstreaming problems for music teachers. *The Education Digest, 53*(9), 46–48.

Gibson, E. J. (1988). Exploratory behavior in the development of perceiving, acting, and the acquiring of knowledge. *Annual Review of Psychology, 39*, 1–41.

Gibson, J. J. (1977). The theory of affordances. In R. Shaw & J. Bransford (Eds.). *Perceiving, acting, knowing: Toward an ecological psychology* (pp. 67–82). Hillsdale, NJ: Erlbaum.

Gilligan, C. (1993). *In a different voice: Psychological theory and women's development* (2nd ed.). Cambridge, MA: Harvard University Press.

Giroux, H. (1981). *Ideology, culture and the process of schooling*. Philadelphhia, PA: Temple University Press.

Giroux, H. (1988). *Teachers as intellectuals: Toward a critical pedagogy of learning*. New York: Bergin & Garvey.

Giroux, H. (December 1992). Curriculum, multiculturalism, and the politics of identity. *NASSP Bulletin, 76*(548), 1–11.

Giulianotti, R. & Robertson, R. (2007). Forms of glocalization: Globalization and the migration strategies of Scottish football fans in North America. *Sociology, 41*(1), 133–152.

Gutek, G. L. (1995). *A history of the Western educational experience* (2nd ed.). New York: Random House.

Goals 2000: Educate America Act of 1994, H.R. 1804, 103d Cong., 2nd sess. (1994).

Goldin-Meadow, S. (2000). Beyond words: The importance of gesture to researchers and learners. *Child Development, 71*(1), 231–239.

Goldin-Meadow, S., & Singer, M. (2003). From children's hands to adults' ears: Gesture's role in the learning process. *Developmental Psychology, 39*(3), 509–520.

Gordon, E. (1971). *The psychology of music teaching.* Englewood Cliffs, NJ: Prentice Hall, Inc.

Gordon, E. (1989 edition). *Learning sequences in music: Skill, content and pattern.* Chicago, IL: G.I.A. Publications.

Gordon, E. (Sept., 1999). Audiation and music aptitudes. *Music Educators Journal 86*(2), 41–44.

Gordon, E. E. (1986). Intermediate measures of music audiation. Chicago: GIA Publications.

Gordon, E. E. (1986). Primary measures of music audiation: A music aptitude test for kindergarten and primary grade children. Chicago: GIA Publications.

Gordon, E. E. (1991). Iowa tests of music literacy. Chicago: GIA Publications.

Gordon, E. E. (1995). Musical aptitude profile (3rd ed). Chicago: GIA Publications.

Gordon, E. E. (1998). *Introduction to research and the psychology of music.* Chicago: GIA Publications.

Gould, E. (September 2005). Desperately seeking Marsha: Music and lesbian imagination. *Action, Criticism & Theory for Music Education, 4*(3), 1–17.

Gould, E. (2007). Thinking (as) difference: Lesbian imagination and music, *Women & Music, (11),* 17–28.

Gould, E. (2008). Devouring the other: Democracy in music education. *Action, Criticism, and Theory for Music Education 7*/1, 29–44. http://act.maydaygroup.org/articles/Gould7_1.pdf

Gould, E. (2008). Feminist imperative(s) in music and education: Philosophy, theory, or what matters most. *Educational philosophy and theory,* Retrieved November, 28, 2008, from http://www3.interscience.wiley.com/search/allsearch?mode=quicksearch&products=journal&WISsearch2=1469-5812&WISindexid2=issn&contentTitle=Educational+Philosophy+and+Theory&contextLink=blah&contentOID=118509536&WISsearch1=gould&WISindexid1=WISauthor&articleGo.x=17&articleGo.y=7

Gould, E. (Spring 2009). Music education desire(ing): Language, literacy, and lieder. *Philosophy of Music Education Review, 17*(1), 41–55.

Gramsci, A. (1975). *Prison notebooks.* New York: Columbia University Press.

Green, L. (2002). *How popular musicians learn: A way ahead for music education.* England: Ashgate Publishing Limited.

Green, L. (March 2005). The music curriculum as lived experience. *Music Educators Journal, 91*(4), 27–32.

Green, L. (2008). *Music, informal learning and the school: A new classroom pedagogy.* England: Ashgate Publishing Limited.

Green, L. (2008). Group cooperation, inclusion and disaffected pupils: Some responses to informal learning in the music classroom. Presented at the RIME Conference 2007, Exeter, UK, *Music Education Research, 10*(2), 177–192.

Green, J. L., Camilli, G., & Elmore, P. B. (2006). *Handbook of complementary methods in education research.* Mahway, MJ: Erlbaum.

Greene, M. (1995). *Releasing the imagination: Essays in education, the arts, and social change.* San Francisco: Jossey-Bass.

Greene, M. (1971). Curriculum and consciousness. In D. Fliners & S. Thorton (Eds.). *The Curriculum Studies Reader.* New York: Routledge.

Greene, M. (1978). Landscapes of Learning. New York: Teachers College Press.

Greene, M. (2000). *Releasing the imagination: Essays on education, the arts, and social change*. New York: John Wiley & Sons.

Greene, M. (2001). *Variations on a blue guitar: The Lincoln Center Institute lectures on aesthetic education*. New York: Teachers College Press.

Gregory, M. K. (1995). Collaboration for music teacher education between higher education institutions and K-12 schools. *Journal of Research in Music Education, 43*(1), 47–59.

Gromko, J. E. (1994). Children's invented notations as measures of musical understanding. *Psychology Today, 22,* 136–147.

Gromko, J. E. (2005). The effect of music instruction on phonemic awareness in beginning readers. *Journal of Research in Music Education, 53*(3), 199–209.

Gruber, H. E., Davis, S. N. (1993). Inching our way up Mount Olympus: The evolving-systems approach to creative thinking. In R. Sternberg (Ed.), *The nature of creativity* (pp. 243–270). New York: Cambridge University Press.

Guilbault, D. M. (2004). The effect of harmonic accompaniment on the tonal achievement and tonal improvisations of children in kindergarten and first grade. *Journal of Research in Music Education, 52*(1), 64–76.

Guilford, J. P. (1950). Creativity. *American Psychologist, 5*(9), 444–454.

Guilford, J. P. (1957). Creative Abilities in the Arts. *Psychological Review, 64*(2), 110–118.

Guillemette, R. (2003). *Sputnik and the crisis that followed*. Retrieved June 25, 2006, from http://www.centennialofflight.gov/essay/SPACEFLIGHT/Sputnik/SP16.htm.

Hadot, P. (2002). *What is ancient philosophy?* (Michael Chase, Trans.). Cambridge, MA: Harvard University Press.

Hafeli, M. C. (2008). What happened to authenticity? Students' progress and achievement in art revisited. In R. Sable & M. Manifold (Eds.). Through the prism: Looking at the spectrum of writings by Enid Zimmerman. Reston, VA: National Art Education Association.

Hallam, S. (1997). What do we know about practice? In H. Jorgensen & A. C. Lehmann (Eds.). *Does practice make perfect? Current theory and research on instrumental music practice* (pp. 179–229). Oslo, Norway: Norges Musik Khogskole.

Hallam, S., Rogers, L. & Creech, A. (2008) Gender differences in musical instrument choice. *International Society for Music Education, 26*(1) 7–19

Hammel, A. M. (2001). Preparation for teaching special learners: Twenty years of practice. *Journal of Music Teacher Education, 11,* 5–11.

Hanley, B. & Montgomery, J. (Mar., 2005). Challenges to music educators: Curriculum reconceptualized. *Music Educators Journal, 91,* (4), 17–20.

Hanna, P. R. (1962). Education: An instrument of national purpose and policy. In P. R. Hanna (Ed.), *An instrument of national goals* (pp. 1–10). New York: McGraw-Hill.

Hansen, D. T. (1995). *The call to teach*. New York: Teachers College Press.

Hansen, D. T. (2001). *Exploring the moral heart of teaching*. New York: Teachers College Press.

Hansen, D. T. (2008). Curriculum and the idea of a cosmopolitan inheritance, *Journal of Curriculum Studies, 40*(3), 289–312.

Hansen, R. K. (2005). *The American wind band: A cultural history*. Chicago: GIA Publications, Inc

Hanslick, E. (1957). *The beautiful in music*. (Gustav Cohen, Trans.). New York: The Liberal Arts Press.

Hanson, H. (1958). Music looks forward. *Music Educators Journal 44*(6), 28–32.

Harman, A. E. (2001). National Board for Professional Teaching Standards' National Teacher Certification [Electronic Version]. *ERIC Digest, ED460126.*

Harris, W. M. (1962). Music in the Space Age. *Music Educators Journal, 49*(2), 79–81.

Harrison, C. S. (1987). The long-term predictive validity of the Musical Aptitude Profile relative to criteria of grades in music theory and applied music. *Educational and Psychological Measurement, 47*(4), 1107–1112.

Heller, J. J. & Edward J. P. O'Connor, E. J. (2002). "Maintaining quality in research and reporting," in R. Colwell and C. Richardson (Eds.). *The new handbook of research on music teaching and learning.* New York: Oxford University Press.

Henerson, M. E., Morris, L. L., & Fitz-Gibbon, C. T. (1987). *How to measure attitudes (CSE Program Evaluation Kit).* Newbury Park, CA: Sage Publications.

Hennessey, B. A., & Amabile, T. M. (1993). The conditions of creativity. In R. J. Sternberg (Ed.), *The nature of creativity* (pp. 11–38). New York: Cambridge University Press.

Henry, W. (2001). Music teacher education and the professional development school. *Journal of Music Teacher Education, 10*(2), 23–28.

Herndon, M & McLeod, N. (1990). *Music as culture.* Point Richmond, CA: MRI Press.

Herszenhorn, D. M. (2003, July 23). Basic skills forcing cuts in art classes. *New York Times.*

Hess, F. M., & Finn, C. E. (Eds.) (2004). *Leaving No Child Behind?: Options for kids in failing schools.* New York: Palgrave Macmillan.

Hevner, K. (1934). Appreciation of music and tests for the appreciation of music. *Studies in Appreciation of Art.* Eugene, OR: University of Oregon Publication, IV, 6, 83–151

Heward, W. L. (2006). *Exceptional children: An introduction to special education.* Upper Saddle River, NJ Prentice-Hall.

Hewitt, M. P. (2002). Self-evaluation tendencies of junior high instrumentalists. *Journal of Research in Music Education, 50,* 215–226.

Hewitt, M. P. (2005). Self-evaluation accuracy among high school and middle school instrumentalists. *Journal of Research in Music Education, 53*(2), 148–161.

Hickey, M. (1999). Assessment rubrics for music composition. *Music Educators Journal, 85*(4), 26–32, 52 & 33.

Hindemith, P. (1942). *Craft of musical composition.* (A. Mendel, Trans.) New York: Associated Music Publishers.

Hoepfl, M. C. (1997). Choosing qualitative research: A primer for technology education researchers. *Journal of Technology Education, 9*(1), 47–63.

Holmes Group. (1986). *Tomorrow's teachers : A report of the Holmes Group.* East Lansing, MI: The Holmes Group.

Holmes Partnership. (n.d.). *The Holmes Partnership.* Retrieved April 22, 2007, from http://www.holmespartnership.org/

Hope, S. (1994). An open letter on standards. *Arts Education Policy Review, 95,* 36–39.

Horkheimer, M. & Adorno, T. W. (1999). *Dialectic of enlightenment.* New York: Continuum.

Horowitz, R. A. (1994). The development of a rating scale for jazz guitar improvisation performance, Ed.D., Columbia University Teachers College, 101 pages; AAT 9511046.

Hourigan, R. M. (2007). *Teaching music to students with special needs: A phenomenological examination of participants in a fieldwork experience.* Doctoral Dissertation,

The University of Michigan (ISBN# 9780549174868/VDM Verlag (2008) ISBN#: 978-3-8364-7663-8).

Howe, F., & Buhle, M. J. (2000). *The politics of women's studies: Testimony from thirty founding mothers.* New York: Feminist Press.

Howe, K. R. & Berv, J. (2000). Constructing constructivism, epistemological and pedagogical. In D. C. Phillips, (Ed.), *Constructivism in education: Opinions and second opinions on controversial issues* (pp. 19–40). Chicago: University of Chicago Press.

Howe, M. J. & Sloboda, J. A. (1991). Young musicians' accounts of significant influences in their early lives. 1. The family and the musical background. *British Journal of Music Education, 8,* 39–63.

Howe, N. & Strauss, W. (2000). *Millennials rising: The next great generation.* New York: Vintage Books.

Hubard, O. M. (2007). Complete engagement: Embodied response in art museum education. *Art Education, 60*(6), 46–53.

Huebner, D. (1976). The Moribund Curriculum Field: Its wake and our work. *Curriculum Inquiry, 6*(2), 153–167.

Inglis, D. & Robertson, R. (2008). The elementary forms of globality: Durkheim and the emergence and nature of global life of classical sociology. *SAGE Publications 8*(1): 5–25.

Jackson, P. (1975). Shifting Visions of the Curriculum: Notes on the Aging of Franklin Bobbitt. *The Elementary School Journal, 75,* (75th Anniversary Issue), pp. 118–133.

Jackson, P. (1968). Shifting visions of the curriculum: Notes on the aging of Franklin Bobbitt. *The Elementary School Journal, 75,* 118–133.

Jackson, P. (Summer, 1980). Curriculum and its discontents. *Curriculum Inquiry, 10*(2), 159–172.

Jackson, P. (1990). *Life in classrooms.* New York: Teachers College Press.

Jassmann, A. E. (2004). The status of music technology in the K–12 curriculum of South Dakota public schools. *Dissertation Abstracts International, 654, 1294A.*

Johnson, C. M., & Stewart, E. E. (2005). Effect of sex and race identification on instrument assignment by music educators. *Journal of Research in Music Education, 53*(4), 348–357.

John-Steiner, V. (1997). *Notebooks of the mind.* New York: Oxford University Press.

John-Steiner, V. (2000). *Creative collaboration.* New York: Oxford University Press.

John-Steiner, V., Meehan, T., & Mahn, H. (1998). A functional systems approach to concept development. *Mind, Culture, and Activity, 5*(2), 127–134.

Jones, P. (2005). Music education and the knowledge economy: Developing creativity, strengthening communities. *Arts Education Policy Review, 106*(4), March/April, 2005, 5–12.

Jorgensen, E. (1995). Music education as community. *Journal of Aesthetic Education, 29*(3), 71–84.

Jorgensen, E. R. (1997). *In search of music education.* Urbana, IL: University of Illinois Press.

Jorgensen, E. R. (2003). *Transforming music education.* Bloomington, IN: Indiana University Press.

Jorgensen, E. R. (2008). *Art of teaching music.* Indianapolis, IN: Indiana University Press.

Joseph, D. & Southcott, J. (2007). Retaining a frisson of the 'other': imperialism, assimilation, integration and multiculturalism in Australian schools, *Music Education Research, 9*(1), 35–48.

Kaemmer, J. E. (1980). Between the event and the tradition: A new look at music in sociocultural systems. *Ethnomusicology, 24*(1), 61–73.

Kahane, J. C. (1978). A morphological study of the human prepubertal and pubertal larynx. *The American Journal of Anatomy, 151*(1), 11–19.

Kantor, H. (1991). Education, social reform, and the state: ESEA and federal education policy in the 1960s. *American Journal of Education, 100*(1), 47–83.

Kaplan, M. (1966). *Foundations and Frontiers of Music Education*. New York: Holt, Rinehart and Winston.

Karlsen, S. & Brändström, S. (2008). Exploring the music festival as a music educational project. *International Journal of Music Education, 26*(4), 363–373.

Kastner, M. P., & Crowder, R. G. (1990). Perception of the major/minor distinction IV: Emotional connotations in young children. *Music Perception, 8*(2), 189–202.

Keddie, A. (2005). A framework for gender justice: Evaluating the transformative capacities of three key Australian schooling initiatives, *The Australian Educational Researcher 32*(3), 83–102.

Keene, J. A. (1982). *A history of music education in the United States*. Hanover, [N.H.]: University Press of New England.

Keil, C. & Feld, S. (2005). *Music grooves*. (2nd ed.). Arizona: Fenestra Books.

Keller, H. (1957). *The open door*. Garden City, NJ: Doubleday.

Kemp, A. (1995). Aspects of upbringing as revealed in the personalities of musicians. *Quarterly Journal of Music Teaching and Learning, 5*(4), 34–41.

Kennell, R. (1992). Toward a theory of applied instruction. *The Quarterly Journal of Music Teaching and Learning, 3*(2), 5–16.

Kennell, R. (2002). Systematic research in studio instruction in music. In R. Colwell & C. Richardson (Eds.). *The new handbook of research on music teaching and learning: A project of the Music Educators National Conference* (pp. 243–256). New York: Oxford Univeristy Press.

Kennell, R. & Marks, V. (1992). Student motivation in the applied music studio. *American Music Teacher, June/July, 26–29*.

Kerz-Welzel, A. (2005). The pied piper of Hamelin: Adorno on music Education. *Research Studies in Music Education, 25, & 11.*

Killian, J. R. (1962). New goals for science and engineering education. In P. R. Hanna (Ed.), *Education : An instrument of national goals* (pp. 72–98). New York: McGraw-Hill.

Kim-Cassie, V. (2008). Teaching strategies for beginner orchestra class: Integrating seating arrangements and flow experience. *Canadian Music Educator, 49*(4), 50–51.

Kivy, P. (1997). *Philosophies of arts: An essay in differences*. Cambridge, UK: Cambridge University Press.

Kjeldgaard, D. & Askegaard, S. (2006). The glocalization of youth culture: the global youth segment as structures of common difference. Journal of Consumer Research. Retrieved November 23, 2008, from http://find.galegroup.com.proxy.queensu.ca/itx/start.do?prodId=AONE

Kliebard, H. (1977). Curriculum theory: Give me a "for instance". *Curriculum Inquiry, 6*(4), 257–269.

Kleiner, A., Lewis, L. (2003). *Internet access in U.S. public schools and classrooms: 1994–2002*. Washington, DC: U.S. Department of Education Institute of Education Sciences, NCES 2004–011.

Kohn, A. (1991). *Punished by rewards: The trouble with gold stars, incentive plans, A's, praise and other bribes*. New York, NY: Houghton Mifflin Company.

Kostka, M. J. (1997). Effects of self-assessment and successive approximations on "knowing" and "valuing" selected keyboard skills. Journal of Research in Music Education, 45, 273–281.

Krathwohl, D. R. (2002). A revision of Bloom's taxonomy: An overview. Theory Into Practice, 41(4), 212–218.

Krathwohl, D. R., Bloom, B. S., Masica, B. B., & Association of College and University Examiners. (1964). Taxonomy of educational objectives: The classification of educational goals. Handbook 2, Affective domain.

Kratus, J. (1995). A developmental approach to teaching improvisation. International Journal of Music Education, 26, 27–38.

Kraus, E. (1990). Zoltan Kodaly's legacy to music education. In Carder, P. (Ed.). The eclectic curriculum in American music education. Reston, VA: Music Educators National Conference.

Kristeller, P. O. (1951). The modern system of the arts: A study in the history of aesthetics. Journal of the History of Ideas, 12, pp. 496–527, 13, pp. 17–46.

Kronman, A. (2007). Education's end: Why our colleges and universities have given up on the meaning of life. New Haven, CT: Yale University Press.

Kusek, D., Leonhard, G. (2005). The future of music: Manifesto for the digital music revolution. Boston, MA: Berklee Press.

Kvet, E. J., & Williamson, J. E. (Eds.) (1998). Strategies for teaching high school band. Reston, VA: Music Educators National Conference.

Labuta, J. A. (1974). Guide to accountability in music instruction. Paramus, NJ: Parker Pub. Co.

Lackó, Miklós (1987). The intellectual environment of Bartók and Kodály, with special regard to the period between the two World Wars. In Rankí, György (Eds.). Bartók and Kodály Revisited. Budapest, Hungary: Académiai Kiadó.

Lamb, R. (1996). Discords: Feminist pedagogy in music education. Theory into Practice, 35(2), 124–131.

Lamb, R., Dolloff, L. A., & Howe, S. W. (2002). Feminism, feminist research, and gender research in music education: A selective review. In R. Colwell & C. Richardson (Eds.). The new handbook of research on music teaching and learning (pp. 648–674). Toronto, Canada: Oxford University Press.

Landers, Ray (1980). The talent education school of Shinichi Suzuki: An analysis. Smithtown, New York: Exposition Press.

Langer, S. (1957). Philosophy in a new key. Cambridge: Harvard University Press.

Lather, P. (1992). Critical frames in educational research: Feminist and post-structural perspectives. Theory into Practice, 31(1), 87–99.

Lather, P. (2006). Paradigm proliferation as a good thing to think with: Teaching research in education as a wild profusion. International Journal of Qualitative Studies in Education, 19(1), 35–57.

Lave, J. & Wenger, E. (1991). Situated learning: Legitimate peripheral participation. New York: Cambridge University Press.

Lazerson, M. (Ed.) (1987). A nation at risk. American Education in the Twentieth Century: A Documentary History. New York: Teachers College Press.

Lecanuet, J. P. (1996). Prenatal auditory experience. In I. Delige & J. Sloboda (Eds.). Musical beginnings: Origins and development of musical competence (pp. 3–34). New York: Oxford University Press.

Lee, C. D. & Smagorinsky, P. (2000). *Vygotskian perspectives*. New York: Cambridge University Press.

Lee, Ling-Yu. (2002). *Music as a means for fostering young children's knowledge of dual cultures*. Unpublished doctoral dissertation. New York: Teachers College, Columbia University.

Legette, R. M. (2003). Multicultural music education: Attitudes, values, and practices of public school music teachers [Electronic Version]. *Journal of Music Teacher Education (Online)*, *13*, 51–59. Retrieved March 15, 2007.

Lehman, P. R. (1999). National assessment of arts education a first look. *Music Educators Journal*, *85*(4) 34–37.

Leonhard, C., & House, R. W. (1959). *Foundations and principles of music education*. New York: McGraw-Hill.

Lessig, L. (2004). *Free culture: How big media uses technology and the law to lock down culture and control creativity*. New York: Penguin Press.

Leung, J. (2006). The conceptualization of faculty-student performing ensembles. *American Music Teacher, April/May*, 24–25.

Levitin, D. J. (2006). *This is your brain on music: The science of a human obsession*. New York: Penguin.

Levitin, D. J. (2008). *The World in Six Songs*. New York: Dutton.

Levin, T. Y. & von der Linn, M. (1994). Elements of a radio theory: Adorno and the Princeton Radio Research Project. *The Musical Quarterly*, *78*(2) 316–324.

Lewin, K. (1946). Behavior and development as a function of the total situation. In Carmichael, L. (Ed.), *Manual of child psychology*. (pp. 791–844). Hoboken, NJ: John Wiley.

Liao, M.-Y., & Davidson, J. W. (2007). The use of gesture techniques in children's singing. *International Journal for Music Education*, *25*(1), 82–96.

Lieberman, A. & Miller, L. (2004). *Teacher leadership*. San Francisco: Jossey-Bass.

Liess, A. (1966). *Carl Orff*. (translated Adelherd & Parkin) New York: St Martin Press.

Littleton, D. (1991). *Influence of play settings on preschool children's music and play behaviors*. Unpublished doctoral dissertation, University of Texas at Austin.

Littleton, D. (1998). Music learning and child's play. *General Music Today*, *12*(1), 8–15.

Long, N. H. (1972). Performance and music discrimination: A study in correlations. *Music Educators Journal*, *58*(7) (Mar., 1972), 50–51.

Lortie, D. (1975). *Schoolteacher: A sociological study*. Chicago: University of Chicago Press.

Lowther, D. L., Jones, M. G., & Plants, R. T. (2000). Preparing tomorrow's teachers to use Web-based education. In Beverly Abbey (Ed.), *Instructional and cognitive impacts of web-based education* (pp. 129–146). Hershey, PA: IDEA group publishing.

Malloch, S. & Trevarthen, C. (Eds.) (2008). *Communicative musicality:*, Oxford, UK: Oxford University Press.

Marina, G. & Breeze, N. (2007). The sub-culture of music and ICT in the classroom, *Technology, Pedagogy and Education* *16*(1), 41–56.

Mark, M. L. (1982). "The evolution of music education philosophy from utilitarian to aesthetic." *Journal of Research in Music Education*, *30*(1), 20.

Mark, M. L. (2002). *Music education: Source readings from ancient Greece to today*. New York: Routledge.

Mark, M. L., & Gary, C. L. (1992). *A history of American music education*. New York; Toronto; Schirmer Books; Maxwell Macmillan Canada; Maxwell Macmillan International.

Marsh, K. (2008). *Musical playground: Global traditions and change in children's songs and games.* New York: Oxford University Press.

Martin, J. R. (1976). What should we do with a hidden curriculum when we find one? *Curriculum Inquiry, 6*(2), 135–151.

Mason, L. (1834). *Manual for the Boston Academy of Music for instruction in the elements of vocal music on the system of Pestalozzi.* Boston: Boston Academy of Music.

MayDay Group (n.d.) *Action for Change in Music Education.* Retrieved November 23, 2008, from http://www.maydaygroup.org/index.php

McCall, R. (1995). On definitions and measures of mastery motivation. In R. H. MacTurk and G. A. Morgan (Eds.). *Mastery motivation: origins, conceptualizations, and applications.* Ch. 12 (pp. 273–292). Norwood, NJ: Ablex.

McCarthy, M. (1999). Gendered discourse and the construction of identity: Toward a liberated pedagogy in music education. *Journal of Aesthetic Education, 33*(4), 109–125.

McCarthy, M. (2002). Social and cultural contexts. In Colwell, R. & Richardson, C. (Eds.). *The new handbook of research on music teaching and learning,* pp. 563–566. New York: Oxford University Press.

McCarthy, M., & Goble, J. S. (2002). Music education philosophy: Changing times. *Music Educators Journal, 89*(1), 19–27.

McCarthy, M. & Goble, S. J. (2005). The praxial philosophy in historical perspective. In D. J. Elliott, (Ed.). *Praxial music education: Reflections and dialogues.* New York: Oxford University Press.

McCullough-Brabson, E. (1995, January). Teaching in the Elderhostel program. *Music Educators Journal, 81,* 41–44.

McCutchan, A. (1999). *The muse that sings: Composers speak about the creative process.* New York: Oxford University Press.

McLaren, P. (1989). *Life in schools: An introduction to critical pedagogy in the foundations of education.* White Plains, NY: Longman Publishing.

McLaren, P. (2003). Critical pedagogy: A look at the major concepts. In Darder, A Baltodano, M., Torres, R. (Eds). *The critical pedagogy reader.* New York, NY: RoutledgeFalmer.

McMahon, T. (1999). Is reflective practice synonymous with action research? *Educational Action Research, 7*(1), 163–169.

McNeill Carely, I. (Ed.) (1997). *Orff re-echoes: Selections from the Orff Echo and the supplements.* American Orff-Schulwerk Association.

McPherson, G. E. (1997). Cognitive strategies and skill acquisition in musical performance. *Bulletin of the Council for Research in Music Education, 133,* pp. 64–71.

Merriam, A. P. (1964). *The anthropology of music.* [Evanston, Ill.]: Northwestern University Press.

Merriam, S. (1998). Qualitative research and case study applications in education. San Francisco: Jossey-Bass.

MENC (1986). *The school music program: Descriptions and standards.* Reston, VA: Music Educators National Conference.

MENC (1987). *Music teacher education: Partnership and process.* Reston, VA: Author.

MENC (1994). Opportunity-to learn standards for music instruction: Grades preK-12. Reston, VA: MENC: The National Association for Music Education.

MENC (2002). *Music education in the law—and what to do about it.* Unpublished manuscript, Reston, VA.

MENC: The National Association for Music Education. (1996). *Aiming for excellence: The impact of the Standards Movement on music education.* Reston, VA: MENC: The National Association for Music Education.

MENC: The National Association for Music Education. (2003). *Inclusivity in music education: position statement.* Retrieved February 12, 2005 from http://www.menc.org/connect/surveys/position/inclusivitystatement.html

MENC: The National Association for Music Education. (2003). *MENC Contest Guidelines.* Retrieved October 9, 2007 at http://www.menc.org/guides/nsync/contest.htm

Miksza, P. (2006). Relationships among impulsiveness, locus of control, sex, and music practice. *Journal of Research in Music Education, 54*(4), 308–323.

Milgram, R. N. (1990). Creativity: An idea whose time has come and gone? In R. S. A. Mark A. Runco (Ed.), *Theories of creativity* (pp. 215–233). Newbury Park, CA: Sage.

Mills, M., Martino, W. & Lingard, B. (2007). Getting boys' education 'right': The Australian Government's Parliamentary Inquiry Report as an exemplary instance of recuperative masculinity politics, *British Journal of Sociology of Education, 28*(1), 5–21.

Molinar-Szakacs, I. & Overy, K. (2006). Music and mirror neurons: From motion to "e"motion. *Social Cognitive and Affective Neuroscience, 1*, 235–241.

Monson, I. (1996). *Saying something: Jazz improvisation and interaction.* Chicago: University of Chicago Press.

Moog, H. (1976). *The musical experiences of the preschool child.* London: Schott Music.

Moore, D. G., Burland, K., & Davidson, J. W. (2003). The social context of musical success: A developmental account. *British Journal of Psychology, 94*, 529–549.

Moorhead, G. & Pond, D. (1978). *Music of young children.* (Reprinted from the 1941–1951 editions.) Santa Barbara, CA: Pillsbury Foundation for the Advancement of Music Education.

Morton, C. (Spring 2001). Boom diddy boom boom: Critical multiculturalism and music education. *Philosophy of Music Education Review, 9*(1), 32–41.

Mueller, R.. (2002). Perspectives from the sociology of music. In Colwell, R. & Richardson, C. (Eds.). *The New Handbook of Research on Music Teaching and Learning,* (pp. 584–604). New York: Oxford University Press.

Music Educators Journal (March 2005). Special focus: Reconceptualizing curriculum, *91*(4).

National Center for Education Statistics (1999). National assessment of educational progress (NAEP), 1997 Arts assessment. Washington, DC.: National Center for Education Statistics.

Nayler, J. M. & Keddie, A. (2007). Focusing the gaze: Teacher interrogation of practice, *International Journal of Inclusive Education 11*(2), 199–214.

New York State School Music Association. (2006). *NYSSMA manual, a resource of solo & ensemble music suitable for contests and evaluatio festivals, Edition XXVIII.* New York: NYSSMA.

North, C. E. (2007). What do you mean by 'anti-oppressive education'? Student interpretations of a high school leadership program, *International Journal of Qualitative Studies in Education 20*(1), 2007, 73–97.

Norton, A., Winner, E., Cronin, K., Overy, K., Lee, D. J., & Schlaug, G. (2005). Are there pre-existing neural, cognitive, or motoric markers for musical ability? *Brain and Cognition, 59*(2), 124–134.

Nussbaum, M. (1997) *Cultivating Humanity*. Cambridge, MA: Harvard University Press.

Oppenheimer, T. (2003). *The flickering mind: The false promise of technology in the classroom and how learning can be saved*. New York: Random House.

Osterlind, S. J. (1998). Constructing test items: Multiple-choice, constructed-response, performance and other formats (Evaluation in education and human services). Norwell, MA: Kluwer Academic Publishers.

Ostwald, P. F. (1985). *Schumann: Music and madness*. London: Orion.

O'Toole, P. (2005a). I sing in a choir but I have "no voice." *Visions of Research in Music Education, 6*(1). Retrieved February 20, 2006 from www.rider.edu/~vrme/

Paige, R. (2004). Elementary and secondary education: Key policy letters signed by the Education Secretary or Deputy Secretary. Retrieved July 2, 2007, from http://www.ed.gov/policy/elsec/guid/secletter/040701.html

Palinscar, A. S. & Brown, A. (1984). Reciprocal teaching of comprehension- fostering and comprehension-monitoring activities. *Cognition and Instruction, I*(2), 117–175. New Jersey: Erlbaum Associates, Inc.

Panksepp, J. (1995). The emotional sources of "chills" induced by music. *Mucic Perception, 13*(2), 171–207.

Papousek, M. (1996). Intuitive parenting: A hidden source of musical stimulation in infancy. In I. Delige & J. A. Sloboda (Eds.). *Musical beginnings: Origins and development of musical competence* (pp. 88–112). New York: Oxford University Press.

Patel, A. D. (2008). *Music, language, and the brain*. Nw York: Oxford.

Patton, M. Q. (2002). *Qualitative research and evaluation methods* (3rd ed). Thousand Oaks, CA: Sage Publications.

Pegley, K. (2008). *Coming to you wherever you are: MuchMusic, MTV & youth identities*. Middletown, CT: Wesleyan.

Pestalozzi, J. H. (1894). *How Gertrude teaches her children*. (translated by Lucy, E. Holland and Frances C. Turner). (ed. Ebenezer Cooke.) New York: Godron Press.

Phenix, P. H. (1964). *Realms of meaning; a philosophy of the curriculum for general education*. New York: McGraw-Hill.

Phillips, K. H. (2008). *Exploring research in music education and music therapy*. New York: Oxford University Press.

Piaget, J. (1962). *Play, dreams, and imitation in childhood*. New York: Norton.

Pinar, W. (Sep., 1978). Notes on the Curriculum Field 1978. *Educational Researcher, 7*(8), 5–12.

Pinar, W. (Summer, 1980). Reply to my critics. *Curriculum Inquiry, 10*(2), 199–205.

Pinar, W. (2000). (ed). *Curriculum Studies: The Reconceptionalization Troy*, New York: Educator's International Press, Inc.

Pink, D. (2005). *The whole new mind: Why right brainers will rule the future*. New York: Riverhead.

Pinker, S. (1999). *How the mind works*. London: Penguin.

Pitts, L. B. (1943). Mobilizing for the new day. *Music Educators Journal, 30*(1), 21–22.

Plato. (2000). Apology. In *The trial and death of Socrates*, (G. M. A. Grube, Trans.). Indianapolis: Hackett Publishing Company. Original publishing date unknown.

Podsen, I. J., & Denmark, V. M. (2000). *Coaching and mentoring first-year and student teachers*. Larchmont, NY: Eye on Education.

Pogonowski, L. (Jul., 2001). A personal retrospective on the MMCP. *Music Educators Journal, 88*(1), pp. 24–27 & 52.

Poland, B. & Wakefield, S. (2005). Family, friend or foe? Critical reflections on the relevance and role of social capital in health promotion and community development. *Social Science and Medicine. 60*(12), 2819–2832.

Pond, D. (1979). *The roots and the creative emergence in a free environment of the young child's native musicality.* Paper presented at the MENC Eastern Division Conference, Atlantic City.

Popkewitz, T. (Autumn, 1980). Global education as a slogan system. *Curriculum Inquiry, 10*(3), 303–316.

Pruitt, K. (1990). Coping with life on a pedestal. In F. R. Wilson and F. L. Roehmann. (Eds.). *Music and child development.* (pp. 309–324) St. Louis, MO: Music-Magna Baton.

Radziszewska, B. & Rogoff, B. (1988). Influence of adult and peer collaborators on children's planning skills. *Developmental Psychology, 24*(6), 840–848.

Rauscher, F. H., & Shaw, G. L. (1998). Key components of the "Mozart Effect." *Perceptual and Motor Skills, 86,* 835–841.

Reese, S. (1995). Music learning in your school computer lab. *Music Educators Journal, 85*(3), 31–36.

Reese, S., McCord K., & Walls, K. (Eds) (2001). *Strategies for teaching: Technology.* Reston, VA: MENC Publications.

Regelski, T. (December 2004). Social theory, and music and music education as praxis. *Action, Criticism & Theory for Music Education, 3*(3), 3–53.

Regelski, T. (2005). Music and music education—Theory and praxis for "Making a difference", *Educational Philosophy and Theory, 37*(1), 7–27.

Regelski, T. (January, 2005). Critical theory as a foundation for critical thinking in music education. *Visions of Research in Music Education, 6,* 1–25.

Regelski, T. A. (1998). The Aristotelian bases of praxis for music and music education as praxis. *Philosophy of Music Education Review, 6*(1), 22–59.

Regelski, T. A, (2005). Curriculum: implications of aesthetic versus praxial philosophies. In D. Elliott (Ed.). *Praxial music education: Reflections and dialogues* (pp. 52–78). New York: Oxford University Press.

Reimer, B. (1970). *A philosophy of music education.* Englewood Cliffs, NJ: Prentice-Hall.

Reimer, B. (1989). *A philosophy of music education* (2nd ed.). Upper Saddle River, NJ: Prentice Hall.

Reimer, B. (2003). *A philosophy of music education: Advancing the vision* (5th ed.). Upper Saddle River, NJ: Prentice Hall.

Reninger, R. (2000). Music education in a digital world. *Teaching Music, 7*(9), 25–31.

Richardson, L. (2000). Evaluating ethnography. *Qualitative Inquiry, 6*(2), 253–255.

Robbins, J., Burbank, M K., & Dunkle, H. (2007). Teacher research: Tales from the field. *Journal of Music Teacher Education, 17*(1), 42–55.

Roberts, B. A. (1994, Winter). The challenge of over-rapport. *Bulletin of the Council for Research in Music Education, 123,* 90–96.

Robertson, R. (1992). *Globalization: Social theory and global culture.* London: Sage.

Robertson, R. (1994). Globalisation or Glocalisation? *Journal of International Communication 1*(1): 33–52.

Robertson, R. (1995). Glocalization: Time-space and homogeneity–heterogeneity. In M. Featherstone, S. Lash, & R. Robertson (Eds.). *Global modernities* (pp. 25–44). London: Sage.

Robertson, R. & White, K. E. (2005). Globalization: Sociology and cross-disciplinarity. In C. Calhoun, C. Rojek and B. S. Turner (Eds.). *The Sage handbook of sociology* (pp. 345–366). London: Sage.

Robinson, M. (2003). The teacher shortage versus alternative routes to certification. In C. M. Conway (Ed.). *Great beginnings for music teachers* (pp. 139–150). Reston, VA: MENC.

Rogoff, B. (1990). *Apprenticeship in thinking: Cognitive development in social context.* New York: Oxford University Press.

Rogoff, B. (1991). Guidance and participation in spatial planning. In L. B. Resnick, J. M. Levine, & S. B. Teasley (Eds.). *Perspectives on socially shared cognition* (pp. 349–364). Washington. DC: American Psychological Association.

Rogoff, B. (1994). Developing understanding of the idea of communities of learners. *Mind, Culture and Activity, 1,* 209–229.

Rogoff, B. (2003). *The cultural nature of human development.* New York: Oxford University Press.

Rosabal-Coto, G. (2006). On [gay] self-awareness in a music foundations course: A Latin-American experience. *Gender, education, muisc, and society journa.* Retrieved June 23, 2009, from http://www.queensu.ca/music/links/gems/past/No.%204/RosabalCotoArticle.html

Rosenthal, R., Wilson, M., Evans, M. & Greenwalt, L. (1988). Effects of different practice conditions on advanced instrumentalists' performance accuracy. *Journal of Research in Music Education, 36*(4), 250–257.

Ross, J. (1994, November/December). National Standards for arts education: The emperor's new clothes. *Arts Education Policy Review, 96*(2), 26–30.

Rousseau. J. (1956). (William Boyd, trans.). *The Emille of Jean Jacques Rousseau selections.* New York: Teachers College Press.

Rudolph, T. E. (2004). *Teaching music with technology* (2nd ed.). Chicago: GIA Publications.

Rudolph, T. E., Richmond, F., Mash, D., Webster, P., Bauer, W. I., & Walls, K. (2005). *Technology strategies for music education* (2nd ed.). Wyncote, PA: TI:ME Publications.

Rutkowski, J. & Miller, M. S. (2003). The effectiveness of frequency of instruction and individual/small group singing activities on first graders' use of singing voice and developmental music aptitude. *Contributions to Music Education, 30*(1), 23–38.

Sargeant, D. (1969). Experimental investigation of absolute pitch. *Journal of Research in Music Education, 17*(1), 135–143.

Savage, J. (2007). Reconstructing music education through ICT. *Research in Education 78,* 65–77.

Sawyer, R. K. (2003). *Group creativity: Music, theatre, collaboration.* New Jersey: Lawrence Erlbaum Associates.

Saxon, W. (1998, August 9). Obituary Max Kaplan, 87, a musician and scholar in art of leisure. *The New York Times.*

Schaefer, Z. (2000). *Arts best practice: Inquiry Project—Full Report.* Retrieved November 23, 2008 from http://www.mmea.org/PDFs/BestPractices/inquiryproject.pdf

Schiller, N. (2000). A short history of black feminist scholars. *The Journal of Blacks in Higher Education.* New York: Oct 31, 2000., 29 p. 119

Schlaug, G., Jancke, L., Huang, Y., & Steinmetz, H. (1995). In vivo evidence of structural brain asymmetry in musicians. *Science, 267,* pp. 699–701.

Schlessinger, A. (1991). *The disuniting of America.* New York: Whittle.

Schmeck, H. M. (1957). Nation is warned to stress science. *The New York Times.* Retrieved June 20, 2006, from http://www.nytimes.com/learning/general/specials/sputnik/sput-15.html.

Schmidt, P. (2007). Democracy and dissensus: Constructing conflict in music education. *Action, Criticism & Theory for Music Education, 7*(1), 10–20.

Schneider, C. (2005). Measuring student achievement in the future based on lessons from the past: The NAEP arts assessment. *Music Educators Journal, 92*(2), 56–61.

Schoenberg, A. (1950). *Style and idea.* New York: Philosophical Library Inc.

Schon, D. (1983). *The reflective practitioner.* New York: Basic Books.

Schon, D. (1987). *Educating the reflective practitioner: Toward a new design for teaching and learning in the professions.* San Francisco: Jossey-Bass.

Schutz, A. (1967). *The phenomenology of the social world* (G. Walsh & F. Lenhert, Trans.). Chicago: Northwestern University Press.

Schwab, J. (Nov., 1969). The practical: A language for curriculum. *The School Review, 78,*(1), 1–23.

Schwadron, A. A. (1967). Music in Soviet education. *Music Educators Journal, 53*(8), 86–93.

Schwartz, H. (1996). The changing nature of teacher education. In J. Sikula, T. J. Buttery, & E. Guyton (Eds.). *Handbook of research on teacher education* (2nd. Ed. Pp. 2–13). New York: Macmillan.

Seago, A. (2004). The "Kraftwerk-Effek": Transatlantic circulation, global networks and contemporary pop music. *Atlantic Studies,1*(1), 85–106.

Seashore, C. E. (1919). Manual of instructions and interpretations for measures of musical talent. New York: Columbia Gramophone Co.

Seidman, I. (1991). *Interviewing as qualitative research.* New York: Teachers College Press.

Seidman, I. (2006). *Interviewing as qualitative research* (3rd. ed.). New York: Teachers College Press.

Serafine, M. L. (1988). *Music as cognition: The development of thought in sound.* New York: Columbia University Press.

Shaddy, J. J. (2003). *Mentoring and musicians: How mentors and proteges in a conservatory of music experience and make meaning of their mentoring relationships.* Unpublished doctoral dissertation, Teachers College, Columbia University.

Shahjahan, R. A. (2008). In the belly of paradox: Teaching equity in an [in]equitable space as a graduate Teaching Assistant (TA) *Teaching International Journal of Progressive Education, 4*(1), 24–48.

Shepard, L. A. (2000). The role of assessment in a learning culture. Educational Researcher, 29 (7) 4–14.

Shih, Hu. (1963). The right to doubt in ancient Chinese thought. *Philosophy East and West: A Journal of Oriental and Comparative Thought, XII*(4), 295–298.

Shonkoff, J. P. & Phillips, D. A. (Eds.) (2000). *From neurons to neighborhoods: The science of early childhood development.* Washington, DC: National Academy Press.

Sidsel, K. & Sture, B. (2008). Exploring the music festival as a music educational project. *International Journal of Music Education, 26*(4), 363–373.

Siegel, D. J. (1999). *The developing mind: Toward a neurobiology of interpersona experience.* New York: Guilford Press.

Silvey, P. (2005). Learning to perform Benjamin Britten's "Rejoice in the Lamb": The perspectives of three high school choral singers. *Journal of Research in Music Education, 53*(2), 102–19.

Simpson, B. J. (1966). The classification of educational objectives: Psychomotor domain. *Illinois Journal of Home Economics, 10*(4), 110–144.

Sims, W. L. (2001). Characteristics of preschool children's individual music listening during free choice time. *Bulletin of the Council for Research in Music Education no. 149*, 53–63.

Sims, W. L. (2005). Effects of free versus directed listening on duration of individual music listening by prekindergarten children. *Journal of Research in Music Education, 53*(1), 78–86.

Slavin, R. S. (2002). Evidence-based education policies: Transforming educational practice and research. *Educational Researcher, 31*(7), 15–21.

Sloboda, J. A. & Davidson, J. W. (1996). The young performing musician. In I. Deliège & J. Sloboda (Eds.). *Musical beginnings: Origins and development of musical competence* (pp. 171–187). Oxford, UK: Oxford University Press.

Small, C. (1998). *Musicking: The meaning of performing and listening.* Hanover, MD: Wesleyan University.

Sosniak, L. A. (1985). Learning to be a concert pianist. In B. S. Bloom (Ed.), *Developing talent in young people* (pp. 19–67). New York: Ballentine Books.

Sparshott, F. (1987). Aesthetics of music: Limits and grounds. In P. Alperson, (Ed.). *What is Music?* (pp. 33–98). New York: Haven Press.

St. John, P. (2003). *Building on children's strengths: Do you hear what I hear?* Poster presented at The Music Educators National Conference, Eastern Division Biennial In-Service Conference, Providence, RI.

St. John, P. A. (2004). *A community of learners: An investigation of the relationship between flow experience and the role of scaffolding in a Kindermusik classroom.* Unpublished Doctoral Dissertation, New York: Teachers College, Columbia University.

St. John, P. A. (2005). Developing community, defining context, discovering content: Young children's negotiation of skill and challenge. *Early Childhood Connections, 11*(1), 41–47.

St. John, P. A. (2006a). Finding and making meaning: Young children as musical collaborators. *Psychology of Music, 34*(2), 238–261.

St. John, P. A. (2006b). *"Let's dance!"—Inviting musical discovery through relationship.* Paper presentation at the International Society of Music E ducation/Early Childhood Commission biennial meeting, Taipei, Taiwan and Poster presentation at the International Society of Music Education biennial meeting, Kuala Lumpur, Malaysia.

Stake, R. (1995). *The art of case study research.* Thousand Oaks, CA: Sage.

Stalhammar, B. (2003). Music teaching and young people's own musical experience. *Music Education Research, 5*(1), 61–69.

Standley, J. M. (1998). The effect of music and multimodal stimulation on response of premature infants in neonatal intensive care. *Pediatric Nursing, 26*(6), 532–538.

Standley, J. M. (2002). Music therapy in the NICU: Promoting the growth and development of premature infants. *Journal of Zero to Three, 25*(1), 23–30.

Stavrou, N. E. (2006). Reflecting on the curriculum: The case of the Cyprus music curriculum for primary education. Arts Education Policy Review, *107*(4), 31–38.

Stem, M. (1992). *Calculating visions: Kennedy, Johnson, and Civil Rights.* New Brunswick, NJ: Rutgers University Press.

Stern, D. J. (2000). Putting time back into our consideration of infant experience: A microdiachronic view. *Infant Mental Health Journal, 21*(1–2), 21–28.

Stevens, H. M. (2001). *A teacher/action research study of student reflective thinking in the choral music rehearsal.* Ph.D. dissertation, The University of Texas at Austin, United States—Texas. Retrieved June 26, 2008, from Dissertations & Theses: Full Text database. (Publication No. AAT 3008454).

Stevenson, D. (2007). The impact of the national standards for music education on the perception and pedagogy of the discipline: A philosophical inquiry. (Doctoral dissertation, Boston University, 2007). *Dissertation Abstracts*, AAT 3240641.

Stone, C. A. (1993). What is missing in the metaphor of scaffolding? In E. Forman, N. Minick, & C. A. Stone (Eds.). *Contexts for learning: Sociocultural dynamics in children's development* (pp. 169–183). New York: Oxford University Press.

Storr, A. (1992). *Music and the mind.* New York: Ransom House.

Straub, D. (Oct., 1992). MENC Connections. *Music Educators Journal, 79*(2), 4–5.

Stravinsky, I. (2003). *Poetics of Music.* (Arthur Knodel & Ingolf Dahl, Trans.). Cambridge, MA: Harvard University Press.

Stravinsky, I. (1942). *Poetics of Music.* Cambridge, MA: Harvard University Press.

Strong, E. K., Jr., Campbell, D. P., Harmon, L. W., Hansen, J. I. C., Borgen, F. H., & Hammer, A. L. (1994). Strong interest inventory. Stanford: Stanford University Press.

Strouse, L. (Nov. 2003). Planning for success: The first year and beyond. *Music Educators Journal, 90*(2), 28–33.

Subedi, B. & Daza, S. L. (2008). The possibilities of postcolonial praxis in education. Race *Ethnicity and Education, 11* (1), 1–10.

Suzuki, S. (1983). *Nurtured by love: The classic approach to talent education.* Miami, FL: Warner Bros. Publications Inc.

Swanwick, K. (1999). *Teaching music musically.* London: Routledge.

Swanwick, K., & Tillman, J. B. (1986). The sequence of musical development: A study of children's composition. *British Journal of Music Education, 3*, 305–339.

Tagore, R. (1926/1997). A poet's school. In K. Dutta & A. Robinson (Eds.). *Rabindranath Tagore: An anthology* (pp. 248–261). London: Macmillan.

Tanner, D & Tanner, L. (Jun., 1979). Emancipation from research: The reconceptualist prescription. *Educational Researcher, 8*(6), 8–12.

Tanner, D., Tanner, N. (Eds.) (1980). *Curriculum development: Theory into practice.* New York: Macmillan.

Tarnowski, S. M. (1994). *Musical play of preschoolers and the effects of teacher-child interaction style on those behaviors.* Paper presented at the ISME Early Childhood Music Seminar, Vital connections: Young children, adults, and music, Columbia, Missouri, USA.

Taylor, I. A. (1959). The nature of the creative process. In P. Smith (Ed.), *Creativity* (pp. 51–82). New York: Hastings House.

Texas Education Agency (1978). Achievement in reading and mathematics 6th grade. Austin, TX: Author.

Thomas, R. (Feb.-Mar. 1964). Learning through composing. *Music Educators Journal, 50*(4), 106&108.

Thomas, R. (Dec., 1991). Music fluency: MMCP and today's curriculum. *Music Educators Journal, 78*,(4), 26–29.

Thorndike, R. M. (2004). Measurement and evaluation in psychology and education (7th ed. p. 608). (2005). New York: Macmillan.

Thorndike, R. M. (2005). *Measurement and evaluation in psychology and education.* Upper Saddle River, NJ: Pearson Merrill Prentice Hall.

Tierney, R. J., Carter, M. A., & Desai, L. E. (1991). *Portfolio assessment in the reading-writing classroom*. Norwood, MA: Christopher-Gordon.

Tolbert, E. (2001). Music and meaning: An evolutionary story. *Psychology of Music, 29*, 84–94.

Tolstoy, L. (1960). *What is Art?* (Aylmer Maude, Trans.). Indianapolis, IN: Bobbs- Merrill Company.

Torrance, E. P. (1983). The importance of falling in love with "something". *Creative Child and Adult Quarterly, 8*, 72–78.

Torrance, E. P. (1984a). Sounds and images productions of elementary school pupils as predictors of the creative achievements of young adults. *Creative Child and Adult Quarterly, 7*, 8–14.

Torrance, E. P. (1984b). *Torrance Tests of Creative Thinking: Streamlined (revised) manual, Figural A and B*. Bensenville, IL: Scholastic Testing Services.

Torrance, E. P. (1988). The nature of creativity as manifest in its testing. In R. J. Sternberg (Ed.), *The nature of creativity* (pp. 43–75). New York: Cambridge University Press.

Torrance, E. P & Ball, O. E. (1984). *Torrance Tests of Creative Thinking: Streamlined (revised) manual, Figural A and B*. Bensenville, IL: Scholastic Testing Services.

Trehub, S. E. (2001). Musical predispositions in infancy. In R. J. Zatorre & I. Peretz (Eds.). *The biological foundations of music* (pp. 1–16). New York: New York Academy of Sciences.

Trehub, S. E. (2002). Mothers are musical mentors. *Journal of Zero to Three, 25*(1), 19–22.

Trehub, S. E., & Schellenberg, E. G. (1995). Music: Its relevance to infants. *Annals of Child Development, 11*, 1–24.

Trehub, S. E., Unyk, A. M., & Trainor, L. J. (1993). Maternal singing in cross- cultural perspective. *Infant Behavior & Development, 16*(3), 285–295.

Trevarthen, C. (1999). Musicality and the intrinsic motive pulse: Evidence from psychobiology and human communication. *Musicae Scientiae (Special Issue: Rhythm, Musical Narrative, and Origins of Human Communication)*, 155–211.

Trevarthen, C. (2002). Origins of musical identity: Evidence from infancy for musical social awareness. In R. MacDonald, D. Hargreaves, & D. Miell (Eds.). *Musical identities* (pp. 21–38). New York: Oxford University Press.

Trillingham, C. C. (1959). Creative arts in American education. *Music Educators Journal, 46*(2), 19–32.

Trybendis, J. (2007). Unpublished manuscript.

Turner, R., & Ioannides, A. (2009). Brain, music and musicality: Inferences from neuroimaging. In S. Malloch, and Trevarthen, C. (Eds.). *Communicative Musicality* (pp. 147–181). New York: Oxford University Press.

Tyler, R. (Dec., 1948). Educability and the Schools. *The Elementary School Journal, 49*(4), 200–212.

Tyler, R. W. (1949). *Basic principles of curriculum and instruction* Chicago: University of Chicago Press.

U. S. Congress. (2001). *No Child Left Behind Act of 2001*. Washington, DC: Author.

U. S. Department of Education. (1965). *Elementary and secondary education act. Title I – Improving the academic achievement of the disadvantaged, statement of purpose*. Retrieved June 28, 2006. from http://www.ed.gov/policy/elsec/.

U. S. Department of Education. (1991). *America 2000: An education strategy*. Washington, DC: [Dept. of Education]: Supt. of Docs., U.S. Government Printing Office.

U. S. Department of Labor-Women's Bureau. (1999). *Women's Bureau.* Washington, DC: U.S. Department of Labor-Women's Bureau. Document Number).

U. S. Department of Education. (1995). *Goals 2000: Educate America Act (Contract No. RR93002002).* Washington, DC: U.S. Government Printing Office.

U. S. Department of Education. (2001). *No Child Left Behind Act of 2001.* Retrieved July 12, 2007, from http://www.ed.gov/policy/elsec/leg/esea02/index.html.

LII/Legal Information Institute (1992). *Brown v. the Board of Education of Topeka, 347.* Retrieved March 10, 2005 from http://www.law.cornell.edu/supct/html/historics/USSC_CR_0347_0483_ZS.html

United States. National Commission on Excellence in Education. (1983). *A nation at risk : the imperative for educational reform : a report to the nation and the Secretary of Education, United States Department of Education.* Washington, DC: The Commission on Excellence in Education.

Valerio, W., Reynolds, A., Bolton, B., Taggart, C., Gordon, E. (1998). *Music play.* Chicago: GIA Publications.

Vallance, E. (Summer, 1980). A deadpan look at humor in curriculum discourse. *Curriculum Inquiry, 10*(2), 179–189.

Vaugeois, L. (2007). Social justice and music education: Claiming the space of music education as a site of postcolonial contestation. *Action, Criticism, and Theory for Music Education* 6/4: 163–200. Retrieved November 24, 2008, from http://act.maydaygroup.org/articles/Vaugeois6_4.pdf

Vaughn, K. & Winner, E. (2000). SAT scores of students who study the arts: what we can and cannot conclude about the association. *The Journal of Aesthetic Education, 34*(3–4), 77–89.

Verrastro, R., & Leglar, M. (1992). Music teacher education. In R. Colwell (Ed.). *Handbook of research on music teaching and learning* (pp. 676–696). New York: Schirmer Books.

Volk, T. M. (1994). Folk musics and increasing diversity in American music education: 1900–1916. *Journal of Research in Music Education, 42*(4), 285–305.

Volk, T. (1998). *Music, education, and multiculturalism.* New York: Oxford University Press.

von Glasersfeld, E. (1995). *Radical constructivism: A way of knowing and learning.* London: Falmer.

Vygotsky, L. (1978). *Mind in society: The development of higher psychological processes.* (M. Cole, V. John-Steiner, S. Scribner & E. Souberman, Eds.) Cambridge, MA: Harvard University Press.

Walden, J. & Veblen, K. (2008). *The medium is the message: Cybespace, community and music learning.* Paper presentation at the International Society of Music Education biennial conference, Bologna, Italy.

Walker, D. (1984). *Promise, potential, and pragmatism: Computers in high school.* Institute for Research in Educational Finance and Governance Policy Notes, *16*(5), 3–4.

Walker, R. (1984). Innovation in the music classroom: II. The Manhattanville Curriculum Project. *Psychology of Music, 12*(1), 25–33.

Wallas, G. (1926). *The art of thought.* London: J. Cape.

Wartofsky, M. (1984). The child's construction of the world and the world's construction of the child. In F. S. Kessel & A. W. Siegel (Eds.). *The child and other cultural inventions.* New York: Praeger.

Watkins, J. G., & Farnum, S. E. (1954). *The Watkins-Farnum performance scale for all band instruments.* Winona, MN: Hal Leonard Music.

Watson, S. (Ed.) (2005). *Technology guide for music educators*. Belmont, CA: Thomson Higher Education.

Weber, E. (2007). Globalization, "glocal" development,and teachers'work: A research agenda. *Review of Educational Research, 77*(3), 279–309.

Weber, M. (1959/1958). *The Rational and Social Foundations of Music*. Carbondale: Southern Illinois University Press.

Webster, P. R. (1990). Creativity as creative thinking. *Music Educators Journal, 76*(9), 22–29.

Weiler, K. (1991). Freire and a feminist pedagogy of difference. *Harvard Educational Review, 61*(4), 449–474.

Whitmore, L. E. (1996). *Applications of electronic keyboards in middle school general music*. Unpublished doctoral dissertation, New York: Teachers College, Columbia University.

Whiteley, S. & Rycenga, J. (Eds.) (2006). *Queering the popular pitch*. New York: Routledge.

Wiersma, W., Jurs, S. G. (2005). *Research methods in education* (8th ed.). Boston: Pierson.

Wiggins, G. P. (1989). A true test: Toward more authentic and equitable assessment. *Phi Delta Kappan, 70,* 703–713.

Wiggins, G. P. (1998). *Educative assessment: Designing assessments to inform and improve student performance*. San Francisco, CA: Jossey-Bass.

Williams, B. (1998). The internet: We're wired, now what? In Zimmerman, I. K., & Hayes, M. F. (Eds.). *Beyond technology... learning with the wired curriculum*. Wellesley, MA: Massachusetts Association for Supervision and Curriculum Development.

Williams, D. B., Webster, P. R. (2006). *Experiencing music technology* (3rd ed.). Belmont, CA: Thomson Higher Education.

Wilson, B. (1996). *Models of music therapy interventions in school settings: From institutions to inclusion*. Silver Spring, MD: National Association for Music Therapy.

Wing, L., Barrett, J. R. (Eds.) (2002). Music teacher education. In R. Colwell & C. P. Richardson (Eds.). *The new handbook of research on music teaching and learning* (pp. 757–904). New York: Oxford University Press.

Winner, E. & Hetland, L. (2000). The arts in education: evaluating the evidence for a causal link. *The Journal of Aesthetic Education, 34*(3/4), 3–10.

Wolf, D. (1987/1988). Opening up assessment [ARTS PROPEL Project in Pittsburgh, Pa.]. *Educational Leadership, 45,* 24–29.

Wolf, D. P., & Pistone, N. (1991). *Taking full measure: Rethinking assessment through the arts*. New York: College Board Publications.

Wood, D. J., Bruner, J., & Ross, G. (1976). The role of tutoring in problem solving. *Journal of Child Psychology and Psychiatry, 17,* 89–100.

Woodford, P. (2005). *Democracy and music education: Liberalism, ethics, and the politics of practice*. Bloomington, IN: Indiana University Press.

Woods, P. (1985). Conversations with teachers: Some aspects of life history method. *British Educational Research Journal, 11*(1), 13–26.

Woody, R. H., Burns, K. J. (2001). Predicting music appreciation with past emotional responses to music. *Journal of Research in Music Education, 49*(1), 57–70.

Wright, H. K. (2006). Qualitative researchers on paradigm proliferation in educational research: A question-and-answer session as multi-voiced text, *International Journal of Qualitative Studies in Education 19*(1), 77–95.

Wright, H. K. & Maton, K. (2004). Cultural studies and education: From Birmingham origin to glocal presence. *Review of Education, Pedagogy, and Cultural Studies, 26*(2), 73–89.

Young, P. (1964). *Zoltan Kodaly: A Hungarian musician.* London: Ernest Benn Limited.

Young, S. (1999). Just making a noise? Reconceptualizing the music-making of three- and four-year-olds in a nursery context. *Early Childhood Connections, 5*(1) 14–22.

Young, S. (2003). Music with the under fours. London: RoutledgeFalmer.

Zajonc, R. B. (1965). Social facilitation. *Science, 149,* 269–274.

Zajonc, R. B. (1980). Feeling and thinking: Preferences need no inferences. *American Psychologist, 35,* 151–175.

Zajonc, R. B. (1984). On the primacy of affect. *American Psychologist, 39,* 117–123.

Zajonc, R. B. & Markus, H. (1984). Affect and cognition: The hard interface. In C. E. Izard, J. Kagan, & R. Zajonc (Eds.). *Emotion, cognition, and behavior* (pp. 73–102). New York: Cambridge University Press.

Zdzinski, S. F & Barnes, G. V. (2002). Development and validation of a string performance rating scale. *Journal of Research in Music Education, 50,* 245–255.

Zimmerman, B. (2002). Achieving academic excellence: A self-regulatory perspective. In M. Ferrari (Ed.), *The pursuit of excellence through education* (pp. 85–110). New Jersey: Lawrence Erlbaum Associates.

Zimmerman, I. K., & Hayes, M. F. (1998). *Beyond technology...learning with the wired curriculum.* Wellesley, MA: Massachusetts Association for Supervision and Curriculum Development.

Zimmerman, M. P. (1964). The responses of children to musical tasks embodying Piaget's principle of conservation. *Journal of Research in Music Education, 12*(4), 251–268.

Zimmerman, M. P. (1967). Conservation laws applied to the development of music intelligence. *Journal of Research in Music Education, 15*(3), 215–223.

Zimmerman, M. P. & Sechrest, L. (1968). Conservation-type responses of children to musical stimuli. *Bulletin of the Council for Research in Music Education, 13,* 19–36. http://www.newhorizonsmusic.org/nhima/biographies.html#iris

Zuar, Brian Edward (2006). The New York State music assessment: History, development, and analysis of the data generated by the 2002 field test. Ed.D. dissertation, Teachers College, Columbia University, United States—New York. Retrieved June 26, 2008, from Dissertations & Theses: Full Text database. (Publication No. AAT 3225209).

INDEX

Accountability, 8–10, 89, 155
Action research, 299–300
Adolescence, 64, 114, 119, 124, 131, 133, 135, 138, 279
Adorno, Theodore, 27–28, 34, 159, 220
Aesthetics, 5, 43–44, 47, 49, 51–53, 55–56, 279
Affective measures, 176–177
Antiracist, 32–33
Apprenticeship, 90, 97–98, 104, 106, 263
Aptitude, 73, 80, 109, 117, 126, 174
Armstrong, Victoria, 35
Assessment:
    alternative approaches to, 176, 178
    formative, 169, 181
    informal, 167–168, 170
    portfolio, 184–185, 266, 299
    summative, 169, 176
    traditional, 175–179
Assistive technology, 244, 247
Audiation, 117, 188, 210–211
Australia, Australian, 31–32

Band(s), 9, 11, 15, 17, 31, 35, 43, 45, 50, 59, 104, 109, 125, 128–130, 133, 140, 144, 157, 179, 185–189, 200, 217–218, 217, 231, 233, 253–254, 277, 289, 306, 314–315
    all-girl, 230
    garage, 34, 93–95, 97, 107–108, 111, 124, 138, 157
    marching, 62, 93, 111, 138, 170, 217–218
    military, 3
Bandura, Albert, 95–96, 111
Beginning music teachers, 264–266, 268–274, 315
Behaviorism, 77–78
Bernstein, Leonard, 63, 230

Blog, 248, 256
Bloom's taxonomy, 81–84
Bobbitt, Franklin, 148–152, 154, 159, 164–165, 175, 212
Bradley, Deborah, 26, 32, 158
Brain function and music, 64–69, 80, 91, 128, 133, 141
Bronfenbrenner, Urie, 92, 124–125, 142
Bruner, Jerome, 79–80, 89–90, 99–100, 152–153, 175

CAI (Computer-Aided Instruction), 236, 239, 242, 243–244, 246–248
Canada, Canadian, 25, 32, 36, 202, 230
Case study, 31, 293–294
Causal-comparative (ex post facto), 282–283, 288
Choir (and choral), 11, 14, 36, 39, 45, 50, 71, 87, 88, 93, 94, 104, 107, 125, 131, 133, 138–139, 140, 149, 151, 159, 162, 179, 185, 188, 193, 204, 207, 210–211, 216, 222, 227, 230, 235, 250, 277, 280, 293, 308, 314, 315
Cobb, Edith, 63, 137
Cognitive stage theory, 118–122
    cognitive tests, 176
Collaboration, 7, 19, 37, 95, 99, 101–103, 108, 110–112, 123, 260, 265, 274, 289, 299–300, 303–308, 310, 314, 318
Communities of practice, 90, 314
Community of learners, 87–110, 318
Competitions, 161, 219
Composition, 27, 45, 47, 72, 77, 88–89, 96–97, 104, 109–110, 122, 135, 153, 183–184, 196, 202–204, 237, 242, 246–252, 255–256, 263, 284, 289, 293, 299
Conceptual frameworks, 278, 298
Conservation studies, 121–122

Printed in the USA/Agawam, MA
August 15, 2017

657069.037